THE INTERNATIONAL LEGAL PERSONALITY OF THE INDIVIDUAL

The International Legal Personality of the Individual

ASTRID KJELDGAARD-PEDERSEN

OXFORD
UNIVERSITY PRESS

OXFORD
UNIVERSITY PRESS

Great Clarendon Street, Oxford, OX2 6DP,
United Kingdom

Oxford University Press is a department of the University of Oxford. It furthers the University's objective of excellence in research, scholarship, and education by publishing worldwide. Oxford is a registered trade mark of Oxford University Press in the UK and in certain other countries

First Edition published in 2018

Published in the United States of America by Oxford University Press
198 Madison Avenue, New York, NY 10016, United States of America

British Library Cataloguing in Publication Data
Data available

Library of Congress Control Number: 2018934172

ISBN 978–0–19–882037–6

Acknowledgements

This book has been in the making for almost ten years. I owe much gratitude to my family and all of my friends and colleagues in Aarhus, Oslo, and Copenhagen, who in various ways have assisted me along the way.

I am grateful to the Department of Law, Aarhus University, for granting me a PhD fellowship, and in particular to Professor Jens Vedsted-Hansen for taking on the role as my supervisor. Moreover, I am deeply indebted to my PhD examiners, Professor Tine Sommer, Professor André Nollkaemper, and Attorney-at-Law Ole Spiermann, as well as to the anonymous reviewers of my book proposal. All of their insightful comments have significantly improved the manuscript.

I also owe thanks to Max Sørensens Mindefond for generously supporting my research stay at the University in Oslo, and to the Danish Council for Independent Research for funding the first two years of my postdoctoral research. The manuscript was finalized under the auspices of iCourts—the Danish National Research Foundation's Centre of Excellence for International Courts (Grant No. DNRF105).

I dedicate this work to my two favourite individuals, who both have personality in abundance—my daughters Gertrud and Thyra.

Contents

Table of Cases xi
Table of Treaties xix
Table of Other Materials xxv
List of Abbreviations xxix

1. Introduction 1
1.1 Setting the Scene: The Mainstream Approach to International Legal Personality 1
1.2 The Argument 5
1.3 Preliminary Caveats, Definitions, and Assumptions 6
1.3.1 Individuals 7
1.3.2 International law and domestic law 7
1.3.3 Primary rules and secondary rules 9
1.4 Guide to the Reader 10

2. International Legal Personality as a Theoretical Construct 14
2.1 International Legal Personality before the Twentieth Century 16
2.2 'States Are the Only International Legal Persons' 17
2.2.1 'States may confer derivative international legal personality on non-State entities, but there is a presumption against it' 20
2.3 'The International Legal Personality of Any Entity Depends Solely on the Content of an International Norm Addressing It' 23
2.4 'The Individual Human Being Is the Ultimate International Legal Person' 30
2.5 'There Are No International Legal Persons—Only Participants in the International Legal Order' 37
2.6 Conclusion: International Legal Personality as a Theoretical Construct 43

3. The Personality of Individuals in Positive International Law—General Issues 47
3.1 The Application of Treaties to Individuals 48
3.1.1 The Vienna Convention on the Law of Treaties 48
3.1.2 The PCIJ and the ICJ 49
3.1.2.1 1920: Drafting the Statute of the Permanent Court of International Justice 49
3.1.2.2 PCIJ and ICJ practice on individual rights and obligations under treaties 51
3.1.2.2.1 PCIJ 1928: *Jurisdiction of the Courts of Danzig* 52
3.1.2.2.2 ICJ 2001: *LaGrand* 56
3.1.2.2.3 ICJ 2004: *Wall* 57
3.1.2.2.4 ICJ 2010: *Kosovo* 58

3.2 The Application of Customary International Law to Individuals 60
3.2.1 The High Court of International Justice proposed to the Advisory Committee of Jurists 60
3.3 The Doctrine of Diplomatic Protection 62
3.3.1 A legal fiction: Whose rights are being asserted? 63
3.3.1.1 Classification of claims: The ICJ's 2004 Judgment in *Avena* 66
3.3.2 Diplomatic protection and the international legal personality of individuals 68
3.3.2.1 The exhaustion of local remedies rule 68
3.3.2.2 The future of diplomatic protection 69
3.4 Treaty Interpretation: Individual Rights or Obligations? 70
3.4.1 Individual rights vs human rights 71
3.4.2 The VCLT rules on treaty interpretation 72
3.4.3 Examples of treaty interpretation: individual rights or obligations? 73
3.4.3.1 Individual rights 74
3.4.3.2 Individual obligations 75
3.4.3.3 Other non-State entities 76
3.5 Conclusion: The Personality of Individuals in Positive International Law—General Issues 76

4. The Legal Personality of Individuals in International Claims 79
4.1 International Claims before the First World War 80
4.1.1 Early international claims practice 80
4.1.1.1 The International Prize Court 81
4.1.1.2 The Central American Court of Justice 83
4.2 International Claims in the Interwar Period 85
4.2.1 Arbitration of distinct claims 86
4.2.2 Post-First World War tribunals and commissions 87
4.2.2.1 Mixed Arbitral Tribunals established by the Peace Treaties 87
4.2.2.2 The US Mixed Claims Commissions 88
4.2.2.3 Upper Silesia Arbitral Tribunal and Mixed Commission 89
4.2.3 The Mexican Revolution Commissions 91
4.3 International Claims after the Second World War 94
4.3.1 Post-Second World War tribunals and commissions 94
4.3.1.1 Germany 94
4.3.1.2 Italy and Japan 95
4.3.2 Iran–United States Claims Tribunal 96
4.3.3 Three recent examples of international claims commissions 99
4.3.3.1 The United Nations Compensation Commission 99
4.3.3.2 Commission for Real Property Claims of Displaced Persons and Refugees 100
4.3.3.3 Eritrea–Ethiopia Claims Commission 101
4.4 Conclusion: The Legal Personality of Individuals in International Claims 102

5. **The Legal Personality of Individuals in International Humanitarian Law** 104
5.1 The Law of International Armed Conflict before the Second World War 105
5.1.1 The Law of The Hague 105
5.1.1.1 The Martens Clause 108
5.1.2 The Law of Geneva 109
5.2 The Law of International Armed Conflict after the Second World War 110
5.2.1 The Geneva Conventions of 1949 110
5.2.2 Additional Protocol I of 1977 114
5.3 The Law of Non-International Armed Conflict before the Second World War 115
5.3.1 Recognition of belligerency 116
5.4 The Law of Non-International Armed Conflict after the Second World War 120
5.4.1 Common Article 3 of the Geneva Conventions 120
5.4.2 Additional Protocol II of 1977 124
5.4.3 The bindingness of the law of non-international armed conflict on armed opposition groups 125
5.4.3.1 The bindingness of customary international law 126
5.4.3.2 The bindingness of treaties on third parties 127
5.4.3.3 The bindingness of treaties by control over a particular territory 129
5.4.3.4 The principle of legislative jurisdiction 130
5.5 Customary International Humanitarian Law 131
5.6 Conclusion: The Legal Personality of Individuals in International Humanitarian Law 132

6. **The Legal Personality of Individuals in International Criminal Law** 135
6.1 International Criminal Law before the Second World War 136
6.1.1 Precedents of international criminal law 136
6.1.2 The interwar years: Prosecutions under the Versailles Treaty 136
6.2 International Criminal Law after the Second World War 138
6.2.1 The IMT 140
6.2.2 The ILC's formulation of the Nürnberg Principles 141
6.2.3 The ICTY and the ICTR 145
6.2.3.1 The International Criminal Tribunal for the former Yugoslavia 145
6.2.3.2 The International Criminal Tribunal for Rwanda 147
6.2.4 The ICC 149
6.2.5 Does individual responsibility for international crimes arise a priori or a posteriori? 151
6.3 What Defines an International Criminal Court? 153
6.3.1 The legal nature of the London Agreement and the IMT Charter 153
6.3.2 The definition of an international criminal court in post-Second World War scholarship 156

6.3.3 The SCSL 160
6.3.4 The ECCC 162
6.4 Conclusion: The Legal Personality of Individuals in International Criminal Law 164

7. The Legal Personality of Individuals in International Human Rights Law 167
7.1 International Human Rights Law before the Second World War 167
7.1.1 The abolition of slavery 168
7.1.2 Minorities protection 169
7.2 International Human Rights Law after the Second World War: The Example of the ECHR 172
7.2.1 The procedural status of individuals before the ECtHR 173
7.2.2 Special rules of interpretation for human rights treaties? 179
7.2.2.1 The ECHR drafting process 179
7.2.2.2 The practice of the Court 180
7.2.3 The ECHR in the international legal system 186
7.3 Conclusion: The Legal Personality of Individuals in International Human Rights Law 190

8. The Legal Personality of Individuals in International Economic Law 194
8.1 State Contracts 196
8.1.1 The nature of State contracts 196
8.1.2 The law applicable to State contracts 198
8.2 International Investment Law 202
8.2.1 The International Centre for Settlement of Investment Disputes 203
8.2.2 Primary rules of international investment law 205
8.2.2.1 Countermeasures as a circumstance precluding wrongfulness 210
8.2.3 Secondary rules of international investment law 212
8.2.3.1 The power of investors to waive international arbitration 215
8.3 European Union Law 219
8.3.1 The right of individuals to petition the CJEU 219
8.3.2 A new legal order? 221
8.4 Conclusion: The Legal Personality of Individuals in International Economic Law 227

9. Conclusion 230

Bibliography 237
Index 263

Table of Cases

INTERNATIONAL COURTS

Caribbean Court of Justice

Myrie v. Barbados and Jamaica, CCJ Application No. OA 002 of 2012, Judgment, 4 October 2013 226–7
Tomlinson v. Belize and Tomlinson v. Trinidad and Tobago, CCJ Applications No. OA 1 and OA 2 of 2013, Judgment, 10 June 2016 227
Trinidad Cement Ltd. v. Caribbean Community, CCJ Application No. AR 3 of 2008, Judgment, 5 February 2009 226
Trinidad Cement Ltd. v. Guyana, CCJ Application No. AR 1 of 2008, Judgment, 15 January 2009. 226

Central American Court of Justice

Dr Pedro Andres Fornos Diaz v. The Government of the Republic of Guatemala, Decision, 6 March 1909 84
09-04-08-1996. 227

Court of Justice of the European Union

Council of the European Union v. Front populaire pour la libération de la saguia-el-hamra et du rio de oro (Front Polisario) [2016] ECLI:EU:C:2016:973. 221
European Commission and Others v. Yassin Abdullah Kadi [2013] ECLI:EU:C:2013:518 225
Front populaire pour la libération de la saguia-el-hamra et du rio de oro (Front Polisario) v. Council of the European Union [2015] ECLI:EU:T:2015:953 221
Inuit Tapiriit Kanatami and Others v. European Parliament and Council of the European Union [2013] ECLI:EU:C:2013:625 220
Opinion 1/09 (Unified Patent Litigation System) [2011] ECLI:EU:C:2011:123. 222
Opinion 2/13 (on EU accession to the ECHR) [2014] ECLI:EU:C:2014:2454 . . . . . 4, 226

European Court of Human Rights

Al-Dulimi and Montana Management Inc. v. Switzerland, Application no. 5809/08, Grand Chamber Judgment, 21 June 2016 189–90
Al-Jedda v. United Kingdom, Application no. 27021/08, Grand Chamber Judgment, 7 July 2011 187–8
Behrami and Behrami v. France, Saramati v. France, Germany and Norway, Application Nos. 71412/01 & 78166/01, Grand Chamber Decision, 2 May 2007 186–7
Bosphorus Hava Yollari Turizm ve Ticaret Anonim Sirketi v. Ireland, Application No. 45036/98, Grand Chamber Judgment, 30 June 2005 186–7
Case relating to Certain Aspects of the Laws on the Use of Languages in Education in Belgium, 23 July 1968, Series A, No. 6, 34. 184
Handyside v. United Kingdom, Application no 5493/ 72, 7 December 1976. 184
Ireland v. United Kingdom, App no 5310/ 71, 18 January 1978 180–2
Loizidou v. Turkey, Application no. 15318/89, Grand Chamber Judgment (preliminary objections), 23 March 1995 186
Nada v. Switzerland, Application no. 10593/08, Grand Chamber Judgment, 12 September 2012. . . . . . 188–9, 192
Wemhoff v. Germany, Application no 2122/64, 27 June 1968. 180–4

European Court of Justice

Commission v. Jégo Quéré [2004] ECLI:EU:C:2004:210 220
Flaminio Costa v. ENEL [1964] ECLI:EU:C:1964:51 222
Les Verts v. European Parliament [1986] ECLI:EU:C:1986:166 222
Marshall v. Southampton and South-West Hampshire Area Health Authority [1986] ECLI:EU:C:1986:84 224
Opinion 1/91 (EEA Agreement I) [1993] ECLI:EU:C:1991:490 222
Paraiki-Patraiki v. Commission [1985] ECLI:EU:C:1985:18 219
Unión de Pequeños Agricultores v. Council [2002] ECLI:EU:C:2002:462 220
Van Gend en Loos v. Nederlandse Administratie der Belastingen [1963] ECLI:EU:C:1963:1 .... 4, 200, 221, 222, 226, 227, 229
Plaumann v. Commission [1963] ECLI:EU:C:1963:17 219
Yassin Abdullah Kadi & Al Barakaat International Foundation v. Council & Commission [2008] ECLI:EU:C:2008:461 .... 4, 187, 189, 190, 224–5

General Court of the European Union

Front populaire pour la libération de la saguia-el-hamra et du rio de oro (Front Polisario) v. Council of the European Union [2015] ECLI:EU:T:2015:953 221
Inuit Tapiriit Kanatami and Others v. European Parliament, Council of the European Union, Kingdom of the Netherlands, European Commission [2011] ECLI:EU:T:2011:419 220
Yassin Abdullah Kadi v. European Commission [2010] ECLI:EU:T:2010:418 224

Inter-American Court of Human Rights

International Responsibility for the Promulgation and Enforcement of Laws in Violation of the Convention (Arts. 1 and 2 of the American Convention on Human Rights), Advisory Opinion, OC-14/94, 9 December 1994, Inter-Am. Ct. H.R. (Ser. A) No. 14 (1994) 13
Right to Information on Consular Assistance in the Framework of the Guarantees of the Due Process of Law, Advisory Opinion, OC-16/99, 1 October 1999, Inter-Am. Ct. H.R. (Ser A) No. 16 (1999) 56, 72

International Court of Justice

Accordance with International Law of the Unilateral Declaration of Independence in Respect of Kosovo (Advisory Opinion) [2010] ICJ Rep 403 .... 58–9, 75, 230
Ahmadou Sadio Diallo (Republic of Guinea v. Democratic Republic of the Congo)
(Preliminary Objections) (Judgment) [2007] ICJ Rep 582 .... 63, 64, 65
(Merits) (Judgment) [2010] ICJ Rep 639 64
(Compensation) (Judgment) [2012] ICJ Rep 324 35
Anglo-Iranian Oil Co. (United Kingdom v. Iran) (Jurisdiction) (Judgment) [1952] ICJ Rep 93 196
Armed Activities on the Territory of the Congo (Democratic Republic of the Congo v. Uganda), (Judgment) [2005] ICJ Rep 168 65
Arrest Warrant of 11 April 2000 (Democratic Republic of the Congo v. Belgium) (Judgment) [2002] ICJ Rep 3 .... 64, 161
Avena and Other Mexican Nationals (Mexico v. United States of America) (Judgment) [2004] ICJ Rep 12 .... 64, 65, 66–7
Barcelona Traction, Light, and Power Company, Limited (Belgium v. Spain)
(Preliminary Objections)(Judgment) [1964] ICJ Rep 6 93
(Second Phase) (Judgment) [1970] ICJ Rep 3 .... 64, 65
Case Concerning Elettronica Sicula SpA (ELSI) (United States of America v. Italy) (Judgment) [1989] ICJ Rep 15 64
Case Concerning Kasikili/Sedudu Island (Botswana/Namibia) (Judgment) [1999] ICJ Rep 1045 185
Certain Norwegian Loans (France v. Norway) (Judgment) [1957] ICJ Rep 9 201–2

Interhandel (Switzerland v. United States of America) (Judgment) [1959] ICJ Rep 6 . . . . 64, 68
Judgments of the Administrative Tribunal of the ILO upon complaints made against the UNESCO (Advisory Opinion) [1956] ICJ Rep 77 23
Jurisdictional Immunities of the State (Germany v. Italy; Greece intervening) (Judgment) [2012] ICJ Rep 99 . . . . 35, 108
LaGrand (Germany v. United States of America) (Judgment) [2001] ICJ Rep 466. . . . . 23, 56–7, 64, 66–7, 72, 74–5, 77, 78, 113, 114, 230
Legal Consequences of the Construction of a Wall in the Occupied Palestinian Territory (Advisory Opinion) [2004] ICJ Rep 136. . . . . 57–8, 230
Legal Consequences for States of the Continued Presence of South Africa in Namibia (South West Africa) notwithstanding Security Council Resolution 276 (1970) (Advisory Opinion) [1971] ICJ Rep 53. 59
Legality of the Threat or Use of Nuclear Weapons (Advisory Opinion) [1996] ICJ Rep 226. 109
Military and Paramilitary Activities in and against Nicaragua (Nicaragua v. United States of America) (Judgment) [1986] ICJ Rep 14 109
Nottebohm Case (Liechtenstein v. Guatemala) (Second Phase) (Judgment) [1955] ICJ Rep (1955) 4. 64
Oil Platforms (Islamic Republic of Iran v. United States of America) (Judgment) [2003] ICJ Rep 161 64
Reparations for Injuries Suffered in the Service of the United Nations (Advisory Opinion) [1949] ICJ Rep 174 . . . . 2, 20, 22, 23, 74, 76, 78, 197
United States Diplomatic and Consular Staff in Tehran (United States of America v. Iran) (Judgment) [1980] ICJ Rep 3 64
Vienna Convention on Consular Relations (Paraguay v. United States of America)
(Provisional Measures) (Order of 9 April 1998) [1998] ICJ Rep 248 . . . . 56, 57
(Order of 10 November 1998) [1998] ICJ Rep 426. . . . . 56, 64

International Criminal Court

Prosecutor v. Thomas Lubanga Dyilo, ICC-01/04-01/06, Pre-Trial Chamber I, Decision on Confirmation of Charges, 29 January 2007 150

Permanent Court of Arbitration

The North Atlantic Coast Fisheries Case (Great Britain v. United States of America) (Award), 7 September 1910, *Reports of International Arbitral Awards*, vol. XI, 167–226. 85
Norwegian Shipowners' Claims (Norway v. United States of America) (Award), 13 October 1923, *Reports of International Arbitral Awards*, vol. I, 309–44 86

Permanent Court of International Justice

Case Concerning the Payment in Gold of Brazilian Federal Loans contracted in France (Judgment) [1929] PCIJ Ser. A, No. 21. . . . . 199, 201
Case Concerning the Payment of Various Serbian Loans Issued in France (Judgment) [1929] PCIJ Ser. A, No. 20. . . . . 56, 64, 196, 198–9, 201, 227, 232
Case of the SS Lotus (Judgment) [1927] PCIJ Ser. A, No. 10. 17–18
Denunciation of Treaty of November 2nd, 1865 between China and Belgium (Order) [1927] PCIJ Ser. A, No. 8. 51
Jurisdiction of the Courts of Danzig (Advisory Opinion) [1928] PCIJ Ser. B, No. 15 . . . . .52–5, 72, 74–5, 77, 90, 91, 98, 131, 199, 230
Jurisdiction of the European Commission of the Danube between Galatz and Braila (Advisory Opinion) [1927] PCIJ Ser. B, No. 14 . . . . 2, 52
Mavrommatis Palestine Consessions (Preliminary Objections) (Judgment) [1924] PCIJ Ser. A, No. 2 . . . . 51, 56, 64, 65
Panevezys-Saldutiskis Railway (Judgment) [1939] PCIJ Ser. A/B, No. 76 64
Phosphates in Morocco (Preliminary Objections) (Judgment) [1938] PCIJ Ser. A/B, No. 74. . . .68–9

Questions Concerning the Acquisition of Polish Nationality (Advisory Opinion) [1923] PCIJ Ser. B, No. 7 . . . . . 51, 74, 170
Questions Relating to Settlers of German Origin in Poland (Advisory Opinion) [1923] PCIJ Ser. B, No. 6 . . . . . 51, 170
Rights of Minorities in Upper Silesia (Judgment) [1928] PCIJ Ser. A, No. 15 56

ARBITRAL TRIBUNALS AND COMMISSIONS OF THE INTERWAR PERIOD

Great Britain–Mexico Claims Commission

Mexican Union Railway (Ltd.), February 1930, *Reports of International Arbitral Awards*, vol. IV, 115–29 . . . . . 92, 93

Mixed Arbitral Tribunals Established by the Peace Treaties

The Sopron–Köszeg Local Railway Company, 18 June 1929, *Reports of International Arbitral Awards*, vol. II, 361 (English translation: *American Journal of International Law*, vol. 24 (1930), 164–74) 86

Upper Silesia Arbitral Tribunal

Steiner and Gross v. Polish State, 30 March 1928, *Annual Digest of Public International Law Cases*, vol. 4 (1927–8) 291–2 90–1

US–Austria/Hungary Mixed Claims Commission

Administrative Decision No. I, 25 May 1927, *Reports of International Arbitral Awards*, vol. VII, 203–12 89

US–Germany Mixed Claims Commission

Administrative Decision No. II, 1 November 1923, *Reports of International Arbitral Awards*, vol. VII, 23–32 89
Administrative Decision No. V, 31 October 1924, *Reports of International Arbitral Awards*, vol. VII, 119–55 89
Edward A. Hilson, 22 April 1925, *Reports of International Arbitral Awards*, vol. VII, 176–84 89
Mary Barchard Williams, 11 March 1925, *Reports of International Arbitral Awards*, vol. VII, 170–6 89
Opinion in the Lusitania Cases, 1 November 1923, *Reports of International Arbitral Awards*, vol. VII, 32–44 74

US–Mexico General Claims Commission

Dickson Car Wheel Company, July 1931, *Reports of International Arbitral Awards*, vol. IV, 669–91 . . . . . 93–4, 103
International Fisheries Company, July 1931, *Reports of International Arbitral Awards*, vol. IV, 691–746 93
Jennie L. Corrie, 4 April 1927, *Reports of International Arbitral Awards*, vol. IV, 149 94
Melczer Mining Company, 30 April 1929, *Reports of International Arbitral Awards*, vol. IV, 481–6 92
North American Dredging Company of Texas, 31 March 1926, *Reports of International Arbitral Awards*, vol. IV, 26–35 . . . . . 93, 94
William A. Parker, 31 March 1926, *Reports of International Arbitral Awards*, vol. IV, 35–41 94

SPECIFIC CLAIMS ARBITRAL AWARDS OF THE INTERWAR PERIOD

France–Great Britain (Affaire Chevreau), 9 June 1931, *Reports of International Arbitral Awards*, vol. II, 1117–43 86
Great Britain–Costa Rica (Tinoco Case), 18 October 1923, *Reports of International Arbitral Awards*, vol. I, 375–99 86

Great Britain–Ethiopia (Attaque de la caravane du Maharao de Cutch), 7 October 1927, *Reports of International Arbitral Awards*, vol. II, 824–7 86
Sweden–US (the 'Kronprins Gustaf Adolf'), 18 July 1932, *Reports of International Arbitral Awards*, vol. II, 1244–1305 86
US–Guatemala (Shufeldt Claim), 24 July 1930, *Reports of International Arbitral Awards*, vol. II, 1083–102 86
US–Peru (Landreau Claim), 26 October 1922, *Reports of International Arbitral Awards*, vol. 1, 352–67 86

ARBITRAL TRIBUNALS AND COMMISSIONS AFTER THE SECOND WORLD WAR

Anglo-Japanese Property Commission

United Kingdom in re Hong Kong & Shanghai Banking Corporation v. Japan, 21 November 1960, *International Law Reports*, vol. 29, 383–9 96

Eritrea–Ethiopia Claims Commission

Eritrea's Damages, Final Award, *Reports of International Arbitral Awards*, vol. XXVI (2009) 505–630 102
Ethiopia's Damages, Final Award, *Reports of International Arbitral Awards*, vol. XXVI (2009) 631–770 102

Iran–United States Claims Tribunal

Amoco International Finance Corp. v. Government of the Islamic Republic of Iran, 14 July 1987, *Iran–USCTR*, vol. 15, 189–309 . . . . . 98, 103
Esphahanian v. Bank Tejarat, 29 March 1983, *Iran–USCTR*, vol. 2, 157 98
Islamic Republic of Iran v United States (Cases A15(IV) & A24), 28 December 1998, *Iran–USCTR*, vol. 34, 105–81 98
Islamic Republic of Iran v. United States (Case No. A18) (Dual Nationality), 6 April 1984, *Iran–USCTR*, vol. 5, 251–337 97
Islamic Republic of Iran v. United States (Case No. A21), 4 May 1987, *Iran–USCTR*, vol. 14, 324–36 98
Leonard & Mavis Daley and Islamic Republic of Iran, Concurring/Dissenting Opinion of Assadollah Noori, 3 June 1988, *Iran–USCTR*, vol. 18, 244–74 98
Lord Corporation v. Iran Helicopter Support and Renewal Company, 29 January 1988, *Iran–USCTR*, vol. 18, 377–90 98

Mixed Commission for the Agreement on External Debts of Germany

Community of Heirs of the Late Fritz Cahn v. Federal Republic of Germany and Pensionsverein, 12 November 1964, *International Law Reports*, vol. 35, 253–61 95
Doninelli v. Ebeling, 28 October 1965, *International Law Reports*, vol. 35, 261–78 95

United Nations Claims Commission

Decision No. 1: Criteria for Expedited Processing of Urgent Claims, 2 August 1991, UN Doc. S/AC.26/1991/1 100
Decision No. 10: Provisional Rules for Claims Procedure, 26 June 1992, UN Doc. S/AC.26/1992/10 100
Decision No. 18: Distribution of Payments and Transparency, 24 March 1994, UN Doc. S/AC.26/Dec.18 100

COMMERCIAL ARBITRAL TRIBUNALS

Administration of Posts and Telegraphs of Czechoslovakia v. Radio Corporation of America, 1 April 1932, *American Journal of International Law*, vol. 30 (1936) 523 199

Petroleum Development Ltd. v. Sheikh of Abu Dhabi, September 1951, *International Law Reports*, vol. 18, 144–61 199
Revere Copper & Brass, Inc. v. Overseas Private Investment Corporation, Award, 24 August 1978, *International Law Reports*, vol. 56 (1980) 261–330 197
Sandline International Inc. v. Papua New Guinea, Interim Award, 9 October 1998, *International Law Reports*, vol. 117 (2000) 552–65 . . . . . 198, 227
Sapphire International Petroleums Ltd v. National Iranian Oil Company, Award, 15 March 1963, *International Law Reports*, vol. 35 (1967) 136–92 198
Saudi Arabia v. Arabian American Oil Company, Award, 23 August 1958, *International Law Reports*, vol. 27 (1963) 117–233 . . . . . 180, 200
Texaco Overseas Petroleum Company and California Asiatic Oil Company v. The Government of the Libyan Arab Republic, Award on the Merits, Sole Arbitrator Dupuy, 19 January 1977, *International Law Reports*, vol. 53 (1979) 422–512 . . . . . 196–7, 228

International Centre for Settlement of Investment Disputes

AGIP SpA v. The Government of the People's Republic of the Congo, Award, 30 November 1979, *ICSID Reports*, vol. 1 (1993) 306–29. . . . . 198, 199
Aguas del Tunari v. Bolivia, Decision on the Respondent's Objection to Jurisdiction, 21 October 2005, available at http://www.iisd.org/pdf/2005/AdT_Decision-en.pdf 217, 218
Archer Daniels Midland Company and Tate & Lyle Ingredients Americas, Inc. v. United Mexican States, Award, 21 November 2007, available at www.icsid.worldbank.org 210–1
Azurix Corp. v. Argentina, Decision on Jurisdiction, 8 December 2003, 43 *International Legal Materials* (2004) 262 217
CAA and Vivendi Universal (CGE) v. Argentina, Decision on Annulment, 3 July 2002, 6 *ICSID Reports* (2004) 340. . . . . 217, 218
Cargill, Incorporated v. United Mexican States, 18 September 2009, ICSID No. ARB(AF)/05/2. 211–2
CMS Gas Transmission Company v. Argentina, Decision of the Tribunal on Objections to Jurisdiction, 17 July 2003, 42 *International Legal Materials* (2003) 788 215
Corn Products International, Inc. v. United Mexican States, Decision on Responsibility, 15 January 2008, available at www.icsid.worldbank.org. 211, 212
Lanco International Inc. v. Argentina, Preliminary Decision, 8 December 1998, 5 *ICSID Reports* (2002) 367 216
Loewen Group, Inc. and Raymond L. Loewen v. United States of America, Award, 26 June 2003, 7 *ICSID Reports* (2005) 421 . . . . . 213–4, 228
S. D. Myers, Inv. v. the Government of Canada, Award (Merits), 13 November 2000, 8 *ICSID Reports* (2005) 18 207
SGS Société Générale de Surveillance SA v. Philippines, Decision on Objections to Jurisdiction, 29 January 2004, 8 *ICSID Reports* (2005) 515. . . . . 206, 216
TSA Spectrum de Argentina SA v. Argentina, Award, 19 December 2008, available at http://italaw.com/sites/default/files/case-documents/ita0874.pdf 216, 217
Urbaser et al. v. The Argentine Republic, Award, 8 December 2016, available at https://www.italaw.com/sites/default/files/case-documents/italaw8136_1.pdf. 193, 209
Waste Management, Inc. v. United Mexican States, Award, 30 April 2004, 43 *International Legal Materials* (2004) 967 214

AD HOC CRIMINAL TRIBUNALS

Extraordinary Chambers in the Courts of Cambodia

Case No. 001/18-07-2007-ECCC-OCIJ (PTC01), Decision on Appeal against Provisional Detention Order of Kaing Guek Eav alias 'Duch', 3 December 2007. 163

Case No. 002/19-09-2007-ECCC-OCIJ, Ieng Sary's Supplementary Observations on the Application of the Theory of Joint Criminal Enterprise at the ECCC, 24 November 2008 . . . 163
Case No. 002/19-09-2007-ECCC-OCIJ, Order on the Application at the ECCC of the Form of Liability Known as Joint Criminal Enterprise, 8 December 2009 . . . 163
Case No. 002/19-09-2007-ECCC/OCIJ (PTC38), Public Decision on the Appeals Against the Co-Investigative Judges Order on Joint Criminal Enterprise, 20 May 2010 . . . 163–4
Case No. 002/19-09-2007-ECCC/OCIJ(PTC 75), Ieng Sary's appeal against the closing order, 25 October 2010 . . . 164
Case No. 002/19-09-2007-ECCC/TC, Decision on the Applicability of Joint Criminal Enterprise, 12 September 2011 . . . 163–4
Case No. 002/19-09-2007-ECCC/TC, Case 002/01 Judgment, 7 August 2014 . . . 163
Case No. 002/19-09-2007-ECCC/SC, Appeal Judgment, 23 November 2016 . . . 164

International Military Tribunal at Nuremberg

Judgment, 1 October 1946, *American Journal of International Law* (1947) vol. 41, 172–333 . . . 74, 75–6, 78, 105, 140–1, 144, 146, 148, 152–4

International Criminal Tribunal for the Former Yugoslavia

Prosecutor v. Blaskić, Case No. IT-95-14-A Appeals Chamber, Judgment on the Request of the Republic of Croatia for Review of the Decision of Trial Chamber II of 18 July 1997, 29 October 1997 Case No. IT-95-14 . . . 146–7
Prosecutor v. Delalić et al., Trial Chamber, Judgment, 16 November 1998, Case No. IT-96-21-T . . . 146
Prosecutor v. Furunžija, Trial Chamber, Judgment, 10 December 1998, Case No. IT-95-17/1 . . . 146
Prosecutor v. Kordić and Čerkez, Appeals Chamber, Judgment, 17 December 2004, Case No. IT-95-14-T/2-A . . . 146
Prosecutor v. Limaj et al., Trial Chamber, Judgment, 30 November 2005, Case No. IT-03-66-T . . . 121
Prosecutor v. Tadić, Trial Chamber, Decision on the Defence Motion on Jurisdiction, Case No. IT-94-1, 10 August 1995 . . . 145–6
Prosecutor v. Tadić, Appeals Chamber, Decision on the Defence Motion for Interlocutory Appeal on Jurisdiction, Case No. IT-94-1-AR72, 2 October 1995 . . . 121, 145–6

International Criminal Tribunal for Rwanda

Prosecutor v. Akayesu, Case No. ICTR-96-4-T, Trial Chamber, Judgment, 2 September 1998 . . . 148
Prosecutor v. Kanyabashi, Case No. ICTR-96-15-T, Trial Chamber, Decision on the Defence Motion on Jurisdiction, 18 June 1997 . . . 147–8

Nuremberg Military Tribunals

United States of America v. Alfried Krupp et al. ('Krupp'), Judgment, 31 July 1948, Trials of War Criminals Before the Nuernberg Military Tribunals (Washington, DC: US Government Printing Office 1949–53) vol. IX, 1327–452 . . . 109

Special Court for Sierra Leone

Prosecutor v. Charles Ghankay Taylor, Case No. SCSL-2003-01-I, Appeals Chamber, Decision on Immunity from Jurisdiction, 31 May 2004 . . . 5, 160–2
Prosecutor v. Morris Kallon & Brima Bazzy Kamara, SCSL-2004-15-AR72(E), Appeals Chamber, Decision on Challenge to Jurisdiction: Lomé Accord Amnesty, 13 March 2004 . . . 127
Prosecutor v. Sam Hinga Norman, SCSL-2004-14-Ar72(E), Appeals Chamber, Decision on Preliminary Motion Based on Lack of Jurisdiction (Child Recruitment), 31 May 2004 . . . 4, 126

NATIONAL COURTS

Denmark

Supreme Court of Denmark, *Ajos*, Case 15/2014, Judgment, 6 December 2016, U.2017.824H 225

Germany

Federal Constitutional Court of Germany, Decision, 28 June 2004, 2 BvR 1379/01 108
'German War Trials: Judgment in Case of Commander Karl Neumann', *American Journal of International Law*, vol. 16, (1922), 704–8 138
'German War Trials: Judgment in the Case of Karl Heynen', *American Journal of International Law*, vol. 16 (1922), 674–84 138
'Kunduz incident', Regional Court of Bonn, Decision, 11 December 2013, Case No. 1 O 460/11 108
'Varvarin case', Federal Constitutional Court of Germany, Decision, 13 August 2013, 2 BvR 2660/06 108

Greece

Prefecture of Voiotia v. Federal Republic of Germany, Hellenic Supreme Court, Case No. 11/2000, Judgment, 4 May 2004, *International Law Reports*, vol. 129, 513 107–8

Japan

Case No. 1218–1994, Tokyo District Court, 30 November 1998, reprinted in *Japanese Annual of International Law*, vol. 42, 143 107

Norway

Public Prosecutor v. Klinge, Supreme Court of Norway, Judgment of 27 February 1946, *Norsk Retstidende* (1946) 198 109

United Kingdom

Republic of Ecuador v. Occidental Exploration and Production Company (No. 1), Court of Appeal, 9 September 2005, *International Law Reports* (2010), vol. 138, 92 209

United States

Medellin v. Texas, US Supreme Court, 25 March 2008, 552 U.S. 491 225
The Prize Cases, US Supreme Court, 67 U.S. (2 Black) (1862) 635 117
The Santissima Trinidad, US Supreme Court, 1822, 20 US 283 117

Table of Treaties

Additional Protocol to the Convention Relative to the Creation of an International Prize Court, 19 September 1910 82
Additional Protocol I to the Geneva Conventions of 12 August 1949, and relating to the Protection of Victims of International Armed Conflicts, 8 June 1977 (Additional Protocol I) 104, 114
Article 1 . . . . 121, 114
Article 10 114
Article 11 115
Article 43 115
Article 44 115
Article 45 115
Article 51 114
Article 75 . . . . 115, 132
Article 80 114
Additional Protocol II to the Geneva Conventions of 12 August 1949, and relating to the Protection of Victims of Non-International Armed Conflicts, 8 June 1977 (Additional Protocol II) 104, 124–31
Agreement Establishing the World Trade Organization, 15 April 1994 (Marrakesh Agreement) 195
Agreement of German External Debts (or the London Debt Agreement), 27 February 1953 95
Agreement between the Government of the Federal Democratic Republic of Ethiopia and the Government of the State of Eritrea, 12 December 2000 101
Agreement on International Humane Trapping Standards between the European Community, Canada and the Russian Federation, 25 December 1997 70
Agreement for the Promotion and Protection of Investments between the members of the Association of Southeast Asian Nations, 15 December 1987 207
Agreement for the Prosecution and Punishment of the Major War Criminals of the European Axis, 8 August 1945 (London Agreement) 139, 153–5, 165
Agreement between the United Nations and the Government of Sierra Leone on the Establishment of a Special Court for Sierra Leone, 15 January 2002 (SCSL Agreement) 160
Agreement between the United Nations and the Royal Government of Cambodia concerning the Prosecution under Cambodian Law of Crimes Committed during the Period of Democratic Kampuchea, 6 June 2003 162
Andean Subregional Integration Agreement, 26 May 1969 (Cartagena Agreement). 227
Austro-German Treaty Concerning the Settlement of Property Relations, 15 June 1957 95
Charter of the International Military Tribunal, 8 August 1945 (IMT Charter). 139–42, 150, 153–4, 162, 165
Article 3 140
Charter of the United Nations (UN Charter), 26 June 1945. . . .2, 22, 33, 145, 147, 159–60, 162
Article 1(3). 172
Article 51 57
Article 103 . . . . 186–90, 192, 224
Colombia–Spain (Convention of Truxillo), 26 November 1820 116
Convention respecting the Bank for International Settlements, 20 January 1930 94
Convention on Cluster Munitions, 30 May 2008 107
Convention concerning the Employment of Women before and after Childbirth, 28 November 1919. 169
Convention for the Establishment of a Central American Court of Justice, 20 December 1907. . . . . 81, 83
Convention concerning Forced or Compulsory Labour, 28 June 1930 169

Convention Instituting the Definitive Statute of the Danube, 23 July 1921 . . . 51
Convention on the Prevention and Punishment of the Crime of Genocide, 9 December 1948 (Genocide Convention) . . . 145
Article VI . . . 149
Convention on the Prohibition of the Development, Production, Stockpiling and Use of Chemical Weapons and on their Destruction, 3 September 1992. . . . 106
Convention on the Prohibition of the Use, Stockpiling, Production and Transfer or Anti-Personnel Mines and on their Destruction, 18 September 1997 . . . 107
Convention on Relations between the Three Powers and the Federal Republic of Germany, 26 May 1952
Article 9 . . . 95
Convention Relative to the Creation of an International Prize Court, 18 October 1907. . . . 81–2, 93
Article 3 . . . 82
Article 4 . . . 81, 93
Article 5 . . . 81
Article 7 . . . 81
Convention on the Settlement of Investment Disputes between States and Nationals of Other States, 18 March 1965 (ICSID Convention)
Article 25(1). . . . 203
Article 42(1). . . . 227
Convention on the Settlement of Matters Arising Out of the War and the Occupation, 26 May 1952 . . . 94
Article 6 of Chapter III . . . 95
Article 3 of Chapter V. . . . 94
Article 7 of Chapter V. . . . 95
Convention concerning to the Status of Refugees Coming from Germany, 10 February 1938 . . . 169
Convention of 8 September 1923 (US–Mexico General Claims Commission) . . . 91
Convention of 10 September 1923 (US–Mexico Special Claims Commission) . . . 91
Article I . . . 91
Article IV . . . 92
Article IX . . . 92
Convention of 25 September 1923 (France-Mexico Claims Commission). . . 91
Convention of 16 March 1925 (Germany–Mexico Claims Commission) . . . 91
Convention of 25 November 1925 (Spain–Mexico Claims Commission) . . . 91
Convention of 19 November 1926 (Great Britain–Mexico Claims Commission) . . . 91
Convention of 13 January 1927 (Italy–Mexico Claims Commission) . . . 91
Covenant of the League of Nations, 28 April 1919
Article 14 . . . 50
Article 22 . . . 169
Declaration on the Launching of Projectiles and Explosives from Balloons, 29 July 1899 (1899 Hague Declaration I) . . . 106
Declaration concerning the Laws of Naval War, 26 February 1909 . . . 83
Declaration Renouncing the Use, in Time of War, of Explosive Projectiles Under 400 Grammes Weight, 29 November/11 December 1868 (St Petersburg Declaration). . . . 105
Declaration Respecting Maritime Law, 16 April 1856 (Declaration of Paris) . . . 105
Declaration on the Use of Bullets Which Expand or Flatten Easily in the Human Body, 29 July 1899 (1899 Hague Declaration III) . . . 106
Declaration on the Use of Projectiles the Object of Which is the Diffusion of Asphyxiating or Deleterious Gases, 29 July 1899 (1899 Hague Declaration II) . . . 106
Energy Charter Treaty, 17 December 1994 (ECT) . . . 205, 209
Article 13(1). . . . 207
Article 13(2). . . . 206
Article 26(1). . . . 213
Article 26(2). . . . 213, 216
European Convention for the Protection of Human Rights and Fundamental Freedoms, 4 November 1950 (ECHR) . . . 4, 13, 167, 172–93, 226, 233–4
Article 5 . . . 184
Article 6 . . . 189

Article 8 188
Article 13 188–9
General Framework Agreement for Peace in Bosnia and Herzegovina, 14 December 1995 (Dayton Peace Agreement) 100
General Treaty of Peace and Amity, 20 December 1907
Article I 83
Article II. 83
Article VI 84
Article XVII 84
General Treaty on the Renunciation of War, 27 August 1928 140
Geneva Convention for the Amelioration of the Condition of the Wounded in Armies in the Field, 22 August 1864
Article 6 109
Article 8 109
Geneva Convention for the Amelioration of the Condition of the Wounded and Sick in Armed Forces in the Field, 6 July 1906 109
Geneva Convention for the Amelioration of the Condition of the Wounded and Sick in Armies in the Field, 27 July 1929 109–11
Article 2 111
Article 21 110
Article 23 110
Geneva Convention for the Amelioration of the Condition of the Wounded and Sick in Armed Forces in the Field, 12 August 1949 (Geneva Convention I). 104, 111
Article 3 . . . . . 116, 120–34, 231
Article 6 111
Article 7 111
Article 12 110
Geneva Convention for the Amelioration of the Condition of Wounded, Sick and Shipwrecked Members of Armed Forces at Sea, 12 August 1949 (Geneva Convention II) 104
Article 3 . . . . . 116, 120–34, 231
Article 6 111
Article 7 111
Article 12 110
Geneva Convention Relative to the Protection of Civilian Persons in Time of War, 12 August 1949 (Geneva Convention IV) 104
Article 3 . . . . . 116, 120–34, 231
Article 7 111
Article 8 111–12
Article 27 . . . . . 110, 114
Geneva Convention Relative to the Treatment of Prisoners of War, 27 July 1929. 109
Article 42 110
Article 62 110
Article 64 110
Article 105 110
Article 106 110
Geneva Convention Relative to the Treatment of Prisoners of War, 12 August 1949 (Geneva Convention III) 104
Article 3 . . . . . 116, 120–34, 231
Article 6 111–12
Article 7 111–12
Article 13 110
Article 78 110
Geneva Convention Relating to Upper Silesia, 15 May 1922. . . . . 56, 87, 89–90, 103, 171, 190–1
Article 5 89
Article 58 89
Geneva Protocol for the Prohibition of the Use in War of Asphyxiating, Poisonous or Other Gases, and of Bacteriological Methods of Warfare, 17 June 1925 106
Hague Convention (I) on Pacific Settlement of International Disputes, 29 July 1899 (1899 Hague Convention I) 105
Hague Convention (II) on Laws and Customs of War on Land, 29 July 1899 (1899 Hague Convention II). 106, 108
Hague Convention (III) on Adaptation to Maritime Warfare of Principles of Geneva Convention of 1864, 29 July 1899 (1899 Hague Convention III) 109
Hague Convention (IV) on Laws and Customs of War on Land, 18 October 1907 (1907 Hague Convention IV), including Annex to the Convention: Regulations Respecting the Laws and Customs of War on Land (Hague Regulations) 106
Preamble 108–9
Article 3 106–7

Article 46 of the Hague Regulations 106, 108
Hague Convention (IV) on Prohibiting Launching of Projectiles and Explosives from Balloons, 29 July 1899 (1899 Hague Convention IV) 106
Hague Convention (V) respecting the Rights and Duties of Neutral Powers and Persons in Case of War on Land, 18 October 1907 106
International Covenant on Civil and Political Rights, 16 December 1966 (ICCPR) 35, 172
Article 8 168
Article 14 164
Article 15 163–4
Article 16(2) 35
International Covenant on Economic, Social and Cultural Rights, 16 December 1966 172
Mexico–US, 11 April 1839 80
North American Free Trade Agreement, 17 December 1992 (NAFTA) 205, 207–8, 210–12, 213, 216–17, 228
Article 1105 207
Article 1116 213
Article 1117 213
Article 1120 . . . . 213, 216
Revised Treaty of Chaguaramas, 5 July 2001 (RTC) 226
Slave Trade and Importation into Africa of Firearms, Ammunition, and Spirituous Liquors, 2 July 1890 (General Act of Brussels) 168
Slavery, Servitude, Forced Labour and Similar Institutions and Practices Convention, 25 September 1926 168
Spain–US, 27 October 1795 80
Statute of the International Court of Justice, 26 June 1945 (ICJ Statute) 49, 179
Article 34 49
Article 38 . . . . 31, 35, 179–80
Statute of the International Criminal Court, 17 July 1998 (ICC Statute) 149–51, 162
Article 5 149
Article 6 149
Article 7 149
Article 12 150
Article 13 150
Article 21 149
Article 22 149
Article 24 149
Article 25 149
Article 27 162
Statute of the International Criminal Tribunal for the former Yugoslavia, 25 May 1993 (ICTY Statute) 145
Article 1 145
Article 2 145
Article 3 145
Article 4 145
Article 5 145
Article 7 145
Article 29 146–7
Statute of the International Criminal Tribunal for Rwanda, 8 November 1994 (ICTR Statute)
Article 1 147
Article 2 147
Article 3 147
Article 4 147–8
Article 6 148
Statute of the Permanent Court of International Justice, 13 December 1920 (PCIJ Statute) 49–51
Article 34 49
Treaty Establishing the European Economic Community, 25 March 1957 (EEC Treaty) 222
Article 12 223
Article 173(4) 219–21
Treaty Establishing Friendly Relations between the United States and Hungary, 29 August 1921 87
Treaty of Friendship, Commerce and Navigation between China and Belgium, 2 November 1865 51
Treaty on the Functioning of the European Union, latest consolidated version, 26 October 2012 (TFEU)
Article 263(4) 219–21
Article 267 219
Article 340 219
Treaty of Lausanne (Allied Powers–Turkey), 24 July 1923 . . . . 87, 169
Treaty of Lisbon amending the Treaty on European Union and the Treaty establishing the European Community, 13 December 2007 (Lisbon Treaty) 220

Treaty of Neuilly (Treaty of Peace between the Allied and Associated Powers and Bulgaria), 27 November 1919 . . . . 87, 169
Treaty of Peace with Italy (or Paris Peace Treaty with Italy), 10 February 1947 . . . 95
Treaty of Peace with Japan (or the San Francisco Peace Treaty), 12 June 1952 96
Treaty of Peace between the United States and Austria, 24 August 1921 87
Treaty of Peace between the United States, the British Empire, France, Italy, Japan and Poland (Polish Minorities Treaty), 28 June 1919 . . . . 51, 87, 169–71
Article 2(2) 170
Article 12 170
Treaty of Peace between the United States and Germany, 25 August 1921 . . 87
Treaty of St Germain-en-Laye (Treaty of Peace between the Allied and Associated Powers and Austria), 10 September 1919 . . . . 86–7, 169
Treaty of Trianon (Treaty of Peace between the Allied and Associated Powers and Hungary), 4 June 1920 . . . . 86, 87, 169
Treaty of Versailles (Treaty of Peace between the Allied and Associated Powers and Germany), 28 June 1919
Article 93 169
Article 227 137–8
Article 228 . . . . 26, 138, 140–1
Article 229 138
Article 230 138
Article 297 87
Article 304 87
United Nations Convention against Torture and Other Cruel, Inhuman or Degrading Treatment or Punishment, 10 December 1984 145
Universal Declaration of Human Rights (UDHR), 10 December 1948 . . . . 35, 172
US–Austria and Hungary (Agreement for the Determination of the Amounts to be paid by Austria and by Hungary (. . .)), 26 November 1924 88
US–Germany (Agreement supplementary to Treaty of 25 August 1921), 10 August 1922 88
US–Great Britain, 19 November 1794 (Jay Treaty) 80
Vienna Convention on Consular Relations, including Optional Protocol concerning the Compulsory Settlement of Disputes, 24 April 1963 (VCCR)
Article 36(1) 56, 66, 75, 114
Vienna Convention on the Law of Treaties, 23 May 1969 (VCLT)
Article 3 127–8
Articles 31–33 . . . . 72–8, 113, 125, 131, 133, 183–5, 208, 215, 231, 234
Articles 34–36 128

Table of Other Materials

ADVISORY COMMITTEE OF JURISTS

Procès-verbaux of the Proceedings of the Committee (16 June–24 July 1920, with Annexes) (The Hague: van Langenheusen Brothers) 49–51, 60–2

COUNCIL OF EUROPE

Collected Edition of the Travaux Préparatoires of the Convention (1975–85) vols I–VII, (Dordrecht: Martinus Nijhoff) . . . 173–80

Short- and Medium-Term Programme of the Council of Europe in the General Field of Human Rights, (Recommendation 683), CM(74)180, Appendix IV, Opinion of the Commission, 19 July 1974. 177

Short- and Medium-Term Programme of the Council of Europe in the General Field of Human Rights (Recommendation 683), CM(74)180, Appendix IV, Opinion of the Court, Appendix IV, 4 September 1974 177–8

INTERNATIONAL CENTRE FOR SETTLEMENT OF INVESTMENT DISPUTES

Convention on the Settlement of Investment Disputes between States and Nationals of Other States, vol. I: Analysis of Documents Concerning the Origin and the Formulation of the Convention (Washington, DC: ICSID, 1970), and vol. II: Documents Concerning the Origin and the Formulation of the Convention (Washington, DC: ICSID, 1968). 202–5

INTERNATIONAL COMMITTEE OF THE RED CROSS

Commentary on the First Geneva Convention (2nd edn, 2016) (available at https://ihl-databases.icrc.org/ihl/full/GCI-commentary, accessed 7 April 2018) . . 112

Commentary on the Second Geneva Convention (2nd edn, 2017) (available at https://ihl-databases.icrc.org/ihl/full/GCII-commentary, accessed 7 April 2018). 112

Draft Revised or New Conventions for the Protection of War Victims (1948) (Geneva: International Committee of the Red Cross) 111

Final Record of the Diplomatic Conference of Geneva of 1949 (1950–1) (Bern: Federal Political Dept) 111, 114, 121–2

Official Records of the Diplomatic Conference on the Reaffirmation and Development of International Humanitarian Law Applicable in Armed Conflicts (1978) (Bern: Federal Political Dept) 115, 124

Report on the Work of the Conference of Government Experts for the Study of the Conventions for the Protection of War Victims (1947) (Geneva: International Committee of the Red Cross) 111, 120

Report on the Work of the Preliminary Conference of National Red Cross Societies for the study of the Conventions and of various Problems relative to the Red Cross (1947) (Geneva: International Committee for the Red Cross) 111, 120

INTERNATIONAL LAW ASSOCIATION

Final Report on the Impact of International Human Rights Law on General International Law, Rio De Janeiro Conference, 2008 71
Reports of the International Law Association's Committee on Non-State Actors (2005–2016). 7

INTERNATIONAL LAW COMMISSION

Diplomatic Protection

Comments and Observations Received from Governments, 58th Session, 2006, UN Doc. A/CN.4/561/Add.2, ... 65
Diplomatic Protection—Titles and texts of the draft articles adopted by the Drafting Committee on first reading, text adopted by the ILC on first reading at its 56th session, 24 May 2004, UN Doc. A/CN.4/L/647 65
Draft Articles on Diplomatic Protection (ADP), as adopted by the ILC, 58th session, 30 May 2006, including commentaries (Diplomatic Protection Commentaries), Official Records of the General Assembly, 61st session, Supplement No. 10, UN Doc. A/61/10, chapter IV 63
Article 1 65–6
Article 19 70
First Report on Diplomatic Protection, Special Rapporteur Mr John Dugard, 7 March 2000, UN Doc. A/CN.4/506. . . . . 38, 64, 70
Preliminary Report on Diplomatic Protection, Special Rapporteur Mohamed Bennouna, 4 February 1998, UN Doc. A/CN.4/484 . . . . . 63, 69
Second Report on Diplomatic Protection, Special Rapporteur Mr. John Dugard, 28 February 2001, UN Doc. A/CN.4/514 . . . . 10, 66–9
Seventh report on diplomatic Protection, Special Rapporteur Mr John Dugard, 7 March 2006, UN Doc. A/CN.4/567 . . . . 63, 69–70

Formulations of the Nürnberg Principles, the Draft Code of Offences against the Peace and Security of Mankind, and the International Criminal Court

Formulation of Nürnberg Principles, Report by Special Rapporteur Mr J. Spiropoulos, 12 April 1950, *Yearbook of the International Law Commission* (1950) vol. II, 181–95. . . . . 140, 142–3
Formulation of Nürnberg Principles (as adopted by the ILC), *Yearbook of the International Law Commission* (1950) vol. II, 374–8 141
Report of the Commission to the General Assembly on the work of its forty-sixth session, *Yearbook of the International Law Commission* (1994) vol. II, 20–73 149
Report of the Commission to the General Assembly on the work of its forty-eighth session, *Yearbook of the International Law Commission* (1996) vol. II, 30–50 145
Report of the International Law Commission covering its second session, 44th–49th meetings, 12–19 June 1950, *Yearbook of the International Law Commission* (1950) vol. I, 28–64 143
Summary Records of the First Session, 17th meeting, 9 May 1949, *Yearbook of the International Law Commission* (1949) vol. I, 129–34. . . . 141
Summary Records of the First Session, 25th–29th meetings, 23–27 May 1949, *Yearbook of the International Law Commission* (1949) vol. I, 183–214. . . . . 136, 142
Second report by M. J. Spiropoulos, Special Rapporteur, 12 April 1951, *Yearbook of the International Law Commission* (1951) vol. II, 43–57. 142–3

Fragmentation of International Law

Fragmentation of International Law: Difficulties Arising from the Diversification and Expansion of International Law, Report of the Study Group of the International Law Commission, Finalized by Martti Koskenniemi (Fragmentation

Report), 13 April 2006, UN Doc. A/CN.4/L.682 . . . . 185, 222

Identification of Customary International Law

Draft report of the ILC on the work of its 68th session, Chapter V: Identification of customary international law, Special Rapporteur Ki Gab Park, 20 June 2016, UN Doc. A/CN.4/L.883/Add.1 7

Responsibility of International Organizations

Seventh Report on Responsibility of International Organizations, Special Rapporteur Giorgio Gaja, 27 March 2009, UN Doc. A/CN.4/610. 187

State Responsibility

Fourth report on State Responsibility by Mr F. V. Garcìa-Amador, Special Rapporteur, *Yearbook of the International Law Commission* (1959) vol. II, 1–35 197

Draft Articles on Responsibility of States for Internationally Wrongful Acts (ARSIWA), *Yearbook of the International Law Commission* (2001) vol. II, 26–143 . . . . 9, 63
- Article 22 210
- Article 33 . . . . 57, 72
- Article 44 63
- Article 49 210

MODEL BILATERAL INVESTMENT TREATIES

Austria Model BIT, 2008 206
China Model BIT, 1997 . . . . 206–7, 213
France Model BIT, 2006. . . . . 207, 213
Germany Model BIT, 2008. . . . . 213, 216
The Netherlands Model BIT, 2004 207
Turkey Model BIT, 2009 . . . . 207, 213
UK Model BIT, 2005 . . . . 207, 212
US Model BIT, 2012 207

UNITED NATIONS

General Assembly Resolutions

Resolution 95 (I) (1946). 141
Resolution 177 (II) (1947) 141, 144
Resolution 260B (III) (1948) 145

Security Council Resolutions

Resolution 687 (1991) 99, 101
Resolution 692 (1991) 99
Resolution 827 (1993) 145
Resolution 955 (1994) 148
Resolution 1244 (1999) 58
Resolution 1267 (1999) 188
Resolution 1315 (2000) 160
Resolution 1333 (2000) 188
Resolution 1368 (2001) 57–8
Resolution 1373 (2001) 57–8
Resolution 1390 (2000) 188
Resolution 1483 (2003) 189
Resolution 1546 (2004) 187

MISCELLANEOUS

The American Law Institute, Restatement of the Law Third: The Foreign Relations Law of the United States (1987) vol. 2, 261 194

Central American Peace Conference at Washington (September, November, and December 1907): *Minutes, Supplementary Documents, and Treaties signed on 20 December 1907* (Washington, DC: Government Printing Office) 84

'Commission on the Responsibility of the Authors of the War and on Enforcement of Penalties' (1920), *American Journal of International Law*, vol. 14, 95–154 137

'Harvard Research Draft on Piracy' (1932), *American Journal of International Law*, vol. 16, Supplement, 739–885 136

History of the United Nations War Crimes Commission and the Development of the Laws of War (1948), compiled by the United Nations War Crimes Commission (London: His Majesty's Stationery Office) 138

Law on the Establishment of the Extraordinary Chambers in the Courts of Cambodia for the Prosecution of Crimes Committed During the Period of Democratic Kampuchea, with inclusion of amendments as promulgated on 27 October 2004 (NS/RKM/1004/006). . . 162

Report of the Preparatory Committee on the Establishment of an International Criminal Court, Addendum 1, UN Doc. A/CONF.183/2/Add.1, 14 April 1998. 149–50

Report of Robert H. Jackson, United States Representative to the International Conference on Military Trials (1949) (Washington, DC: Department of State, Publication 3080) 139

List of Abbreviations

AD	*Annual Digest of Public International Law Cases*
ADP	Articles on Diplomatic Protection
AJIL	*American Journal of International Law*
ARSIWA	Articles on Responsibility of States for Internationally Wrongful Acts
BIT	bilateral investment treaty
BYBIL	*British Yearbook of International Law*
CACJ	Central American Court of Justice
CARICOM	Caribbean Community
CCJ	Caribbean Court of Justice
CJEU	Court of Justice of the European Union
CJICL	*Cambridge Journal of International and Comparative Law*
Cornell ILJ	*Cornell International Law Journal*
CTS	Consolidated Treaty Series
ECCC	Extraordinary Chambers in the Courts of Cambodia
ECHR	European Convention on Human Rights
ECJ	European Court of Justice
ECT	Energy Charter Treaty
ECtHR	European Court of Human Rights
EECC	Eritrea–Ethiopia Claims Commission
EJIL	*European Journal of International Law*
HILJ	*Harvard International Law Journal*
IACHR	Inter-American Convention on Human Rights
IACtHR	Inter-American Court of Human Rights
ICC	International Criminal Court
ICCPR	International Covenant on Civil and Political Rights
ICJ	International Court of Justice
ICLQ	*International & Comparative Law Quarterly*
ICRC	International Committee of the Red Cross
ICSID	International Centre for Settlement of Investment Disputes
ICTR	International Criminal Tribunal for Rwanda
ICTY	International Criminal Tribunal for the former Yugoslavia
ILC	International Law Commission
ILO	International Labor Organization
ILR	*International Law Reports*
IMT	International Military Tribunal
IMTFE	International Military Tribunal for the Far East
IUSCT	Iran–United States Claims Tribunal
JCE	joint criminal enterprise
JHIL	*Journal of the History of International Law*
JICJ	*Journal of International Criminal Justice*
LJIL	*Leiden Journal of International Law*
LNOJ	*League of Nations Official Journal*
LNTS	League of Nations Treaty Series

LPICT	*Law and Practice of International Courts and Tribunals*
NAFTA	North American Free Trade Agreement
NMTs	Nuremberg Military Tribunals
PCIJ	Permanent Court of International Justice
Recueil des Cours	*Recueil des cours de l'Académie de droit international de La Haye*
RIAA	*Reports of International Arbitral Awards*
RTC	Revised Treaty of Chaguaramas
SCSL	Special Court for Sierra Leone
SICA	Central American Integration System
TFEU	Treaty on the Functioning of the European Union
TWC	*Trials of War Criminals before the Nuernberg Military Tribunals*
UDHR	Universal Declaration of Human Rights
UNCC	United Nations Compensation Commission
UNCITRAL Rules	Arbitration Rules of the United Nations Commission on International Trade Law
UNTS	United Nations Treaty Series
UNWCC	United Nations War Crimes Commission
US	United States Reports
VCCR	Vienna Convention on Consular Relations
VCLT	Vienna Convention on the Law of Treaties
WTO	World Trade Organization
YILC	*Yearbook of the International Law Commission*
ZaöRV	*Zeitschrift für ausländisches öffentliches Recht und Völkerrecht*

1

Introduction

The concept of 'personality' has been a pressing topic since the infancy of international legal thinking. Traditionally, it serves the purpose of drawing a distinction between those entities that are relevant to the international legal system and those that are not. Few scholars have seriously disputed the international legal personality of States. But the general consensus does not seem to go much beyond that. The academic debate on the conditions for acquiring international legal personality, and the consequences following from this label, is ongoing. This book contributes to the debate by scrutinizing the historical and actual relationship between the concept of international legal personality as a theoretical construct and the position of individuals as a matter of positive international law. More specifically, the book tests the four main theoretical conceptions of international legal personality against historical and existing international legal norms that regulate the conduct of individuals. With the presumption that findings concerning the ultimate subject[1]—the individual—by implication apply to other non-State entities,[2] the overarching aim is to assess how the concept of international legal personality has functioned historically and still functions in the current legal reality. The present introductory chapter will provide the background for the study. First, Section 1.1 sets the scene by describing the dominant academic position on the international legal personality of individuals. Section 1.2 then spells out the main argument of the book. Section 1.3 explains the key definitions and assumptions underlying the study and clarifies a number of preliminary caveats. Finally, Section 1.4 outlines the structure of the subsequent chapters.

1.1 Setting the Scene: The Mainstream Approach to International Legal Personality

The concept of international legal personality was a particularly contentious issue in international legal theory in the first half of the twentieth century. Several schools of thought developed during this period with radically diverging views on the role of the individual in the international legal system. At the time, however, relatively few

[1] The terms 'international legal personality' and 'subjectivity in international law' are regarded as synonymous throughout this book.

[2] See further Section 1.3.1.

The International Legal Personality of the Individual. Astrid Kjeldgaard-Pedersen. © Astrid Kjeldgaard-Pedersen 2018. Published 2018 by Oxford University Press

treaty provisions and customary norms regulated the conduct of individuals directly. By comparison, academic interest in international legal personality as a theoretical construct declined after the Second World War, while the number of positive international legal norms governing individuals grew exponentially. Since 1945, issues ranging from investment protection to criminal liability that used to fall within the exclusive domain of national law have widely become subject to international regulation.

A standard contemporary textbook includes a chapter entitled 'International Legal Personality' or 'Subjects of International Law'. This chapter is typically limited to an account of the traditional definition of international law as 'the law governing the relationship between States' and subsequent developments towards further involvement of individuals, particularly the rise of international human rights law and international criminal law during the second half of the twentieth century.[3] But the concept of international legal personality as a theoretical construct is not usually discussed at length. Many textbooks limit themselves to referring to the International Court of Justice's (hereafter ICJ) *Reparations for Injuries* Advisory Opinion of 1949 as the end-all of the academic debate on this issue.[4] Having stated that international legal personality '... is no doubt a doctrinal expression, which has sometimes given rise to controversy',[5] the Court famously found:

> The subjects of law in any legal system are not necessarily identical in their nature or in the extent of their rights, and their nature depends upon the needs of the community. Throughout its history, the development of international law has been influenced by the requirements of international life, and the progressive increase in the collective activities of States has already given rise to instances of action upon the international plane by certain entities which are not States. This development culminated in the establishment in June 1945 of an international organization whose purposes and principles are specified in the Charter of the United Nations. But to achieve these ends the attribution of international personality is indispensable.[6]

The ICJ deemed it necessary to assess the overall question of whether the parties to the UN Charter had intended to endow the UN with international legal personality before pronouncing on the capacity of the organization to bring an international

[3] See for example Antonio Cassese, *International Law* (2nd edn, OUP, 2005) 71–2; Malcolm Shaw, *International Law* (7th edn, CUP, 2014) 188ff; Martin Dixon, *Textbook on International Law* (7th edn, OUP, 2013) 115ff; Frédéric Mégret, 'International Law as Law' in James Crawford and Martti Koskenniemi (eds), *The Cambridge Companion to International Law* (CUP, 2012) 65–6.

[4] *Reparations for Injuries Suffered in the Service of the United Nations* (Advisory Opinion) [1949] ICJ Rep 174 (hereafter *Reparations for Injuries*). The ICJ had been asked by the General Assembly to give an Advisory Opinion on whether the UN could bring an international claim concerning injury suffered by the organization itself or by its agents while performing their duties. In 1927, the Permanent Court of International Justice (hereafter PCIJ) had already insinuated, in *Jurisdiction of the European Commission of the Danube between Galatz and Braila* (Advisory Opinion) [1927] PCIJ Ser. B, No. 14, 64, that international organizations may possess international legal personality: 'As the European Commission is not a State, but an international institution with a special purpose, it only has the functions bestowed upon it by the Definitive Statute with a view to the fulfilment of that purpose, but it has power to exercise these functions to their full extent, in so far as the Statute does not impose restrictions upon it.' See further Ole Spiermann, 'Twentieth Century Internationalism in Law' 18 *EJIL* (2007) 785, 795–6.

[5] *Reparations for Injuries* (n 4) 178. [6] Ibid.

claim. As explained further below, this line of reasoning follows the modified 'States-only' conception of international legal personality.[7] With the apparent support of the ICJ, most twenty-first-century textbooks on international law thus convey the following narrative to students: The developments in positive international law correspond to the change in the 'States-only' conception from the orthodox version, which by definition excluded all non-State entities, to the modified version accepting that even individuals may be granted derivative or secondary international legal personality.[8]

The present study shows, however, that this account of the evolution of the role of the individual in the international legal system is flawed. Contrary to conventional wisdom, international law did not apply to States alone until the Second World War, only to transform during the second half of the twentieth century so as to include individuals as its subjects. Rather, positive law developments since the eighteenth century consistently corroborate Hans Kelsen's 'a posteriori' conception according to which the international legal personality of an entity—be it a State, an armed opposition group, or an individual—is solely contingent upon interpretation of international norms. In other words, the answer to the question of individual rights and obligations under international law is, and always has been, strictly empirical. The major change since the Second World War lies not in the formation of new international legal persons, but rather in the substantive issues governed by international law. In the words of James Crawford: 'Our system is one which international lawyers of four generations ago would have had no particular difficulty in recognising or working with, once they had got over its bulk.'[9]

The attentive reader is perhaps already wondering why it matters to present-day international lawyers that theory and practice pertaining to the international legal personality of individuals were not quite in accord with one another throughout history. Given that the modified 'States-only' conception, which is currently the prevalent theoretical position, accepts that individuals may be granted direct rights, duties, and capacities, there would seem to be no imminent real-world problem. This book demonstrates, however, that it does in fact matter.

First of all, the modified 'States-only' conception promotes an unwarranted bias against the international legal personality of individuals. Treaty provisions are interpreted under the assumption that the parties did not intend to govern individuals directly. Moreover, when this assumption is rebutted because the evidence that an international norm does indeed regulate the conduct of individuals is deemed to be sufficiently convincing, the norm in question is interpreted restrictively. As a result, individuals are sometimes granted a lesser material status in international law than positive norms merit.[10]

[7] See Section 2.2.1. [8] See Section 2.2.

[9] James Crawford, *International Law as an Open System* (Cameron May, 2002b) 17. See also Gerhard Hafner, 'The Emancipation of the Individual from the State under International Law' 358 *Recueil des Cours* (2011) 262, 437.

[10] See further Section 6.3.2, Section 7.2.2, Section 8.2.2.1, and Section 8.3.2.

Secondly, the book will show that the orthodox 'States-only' conception continues to influence how contemporary scholars, as well as judges of international courts, distinguish between international and national legal norms. When the orthodox 'States-only' conception dominated international legal scholarship, norms were categorized as international or national simply by reference to their addressees: international norms were directed at States, while norms governing all other kinds of entities by definition could not form part of the international legal system, irrespective of the nature of their source. Although the orthodox 'States-only' conception has long since been discarded in favour of the modified version, the idea that a legal norm may be categorized as international or national according to the kind of entity it regulates still thrives. The most obvious example is perhaps the (then) European Court of Justice's (hereafter ECJ) seminal 1962 *Van Gend en Loos* Judgment. The Court concluded that '... the Community constitutes a new legal order of international law ...', because the subjects of Community law '... comprise not only Member States but also their nationals'.[11] Hence, the characterization of Community law as 'a new legal order' unambiguously rests on the assumption that international law—in contrast to Community law—cannot apply directly to individuals. Since 1962, the ECJ and its successor, the Court of Justice of the European Union (hereafter CJEU), have consistently repeated this line of reasoning to affirm the separateness of EU law from the international legal system. The CJEU's 2014 *Opinion 2/13 (on EU accession to the ECHR)*[12] is a recent case in point. As we saw in the ECJ's famous 2008 *Kadi I* Judgment,[13] the idea of EU law as a new legal order on its own has important consequences for the relationship between EU law and conflicting norms of international law, including measures imposed by the UN Security Council.[14]

EU law is not the only discipline, however, where the orthodox 'States-only' conception of international legal personality continues to influence the application of international legal norms. In the field of international humanitarian law, for example, it is frequently inferred that insurgents are not directly bound by common Article 3 of the Geneva Conventions and Additional Protocol II, because treaties cannot by definition govern non-State entities. This rationale was explicitly invoked by the Appeals Chamber of the Special Court for Sierra Leone (hereafter SCSL) in its 2004 Decision on Jurisdiction in the *Norman* case. The Appeals Chamber noted that the law of non-international armed conflict only applies to armed opposition groups to the extent that the provisions in question are reflective of customary international law.[15] This of course complicates any attempt to hold members of armed

[11] *Van Gend en Loos v. Nederlandse Administratie der Belastingen* [1963] ECLI:EU:C:1963:1 (hereafter *Van Gend en Loos*), 12.

[12] *Opinion 2/13 (on EU accession to the ECHR)* [2014] ECLI:EU:C:2014:2454 (hereafter *Opinion 2/13 (on EU accession to the ECHR)*).

[13] *Yassin Abdullah Kadi & Al Barakaat International Foundation v. Council & Commission* [2008] ECLI:EU:C:2008:461 (hereafter *Kadi I*).

[14] See Section 8.3.2.

[15] *Prosecutor v. Sam Hinga Norman*, SCSL-2004-14-Ar72(E), Appeals Chamber, Decision on Preliminary Motion Based on Lack of Jurisdiction (Child Recruitment), 31 May 2004, para. 22 (hereafter *Norman Decision*). See further Section 5.4.3.1.

opposition groups responsible for violations of international humanitarian law, as it must not only be proven that they have breached a relevant treaty norm but also that this norm is a part of customary international law.

In the field of international criminal law, it is a widespread notion that the categorization of criminal courts revolves around 'the involvement of the international community'. Surely, it would seem straightforward to define criminal courts according to the legal nature of the source of their authority. A court would then be international if it is established by a treaty, and national if it is set up under the domestic law of a particular State. However, reluctance to accept the direct application of international law to individuals led post-Second World War scholarship to define 'an international court' as 'a court instituted by one or a group of nations with the approval of the international community'. This definition is recurrent in academic writings as well as in recent rulings issued by for example the SCSL, the Extraordinary Chambers in the Courts of Cambodia (hereafter ECCC), and the International Criminal Court (hereafter ICC). The SCSL's 2004 Judgment in the *Taylor* case[16] and the ECCC's 2011 decision in *Case 002*[17] illustrate that emphasizing 'the approval of the international community' rather than the nature of the court's constituent document has significant ramifications for the application of the customary rules on immunities as well as the extent to which defendants may invoke domestic constitutional rights in the proceedings.[18]

These examples show how present-day international lawyers continue to allow a line of reasoning, which was merely a scholarly invention of the nineteenth century, to influence the interpretation and application of international law. It is high time to bring international legal theory into alignment with positive international law.

1.2 The Argument

This book argues, first and foremost, that positive international law does not corroborate the common narrative that the international legal system was transformed during the second half of the twentieth century so as to include individuals as its subjects. The orthodox positivist notion that international law exclusively regulates the relationship between States, while domestic law governs the conduct of individuals, was never more than a theoretical position. Rather, the evolution of positive international legal norms since the eighteenth century supports Hans Kelsen's idea that the international legal personality of any entity depends exclusively on the content of international norms. Against this background, the book claims that we must abandon the currently dominant modified 'States-only' conception of international legal personality, which in practice unfolds as a presumption against direct

[16] *Prosecutor v. Charles Ghankay Taylor*, SCSL-2003-01-I, Appeals Chamber, Decision on Immunity from Jurisdiction, 31 May 2004 (hereafter *Charles Taylor Decision on Immunity*).

[17] Case No. 002/19-09-2007-ECCC/OCIJ (PTC75), Public Decision on Ieng Sary's Appeal Against the Closing Order, 11 April 2011.

[18] See further Section 6.3.

individual rights or obligations in international law. Moreover, it is long overdue that international lawyers stopped relying on the notion that norms of international law may be separated from national legal norms on the basis of their respective addressees. Only the orthodox 'States-only' conception of international legal personality, which has long been discarded in international legal theory, draws this link between the notion of personality and the question of whether a norm is international or national in kind.

Importantly, the argument put forward in this book is based on the assumption that adopting Kelsen's 'a posteriori' conception of international legal personality does not imply an endorsement of his heavily criticized postulate of necessary unity between international law and national law. Indeed, there are no impediments to supporting the 'a posteriori' conception of international legal personality while at the same time endorsing a dualistic construction of the relationship between international law and national law. This combination has two main consequences. One is that the international legal personality of any entity is solely a matter of presumption-free interpretation of international norms. Whether individuals have rights and obligations under international law is thus entirely an empirical question. The other is that the entities governed by a particular norm tell us nothing about the legal system to which that norm belongs. Instead, the distinction between international law and national law revolves exclusively around the nature of the source of each particular norm.

1.3 Preliminary Caveats, Definitions, and Assumptions

As outlined above, this book's purpose is to expose the epistemic bias against the international legal personality of individuals, seemingly prolific among contemporary international lawyers, and thereby to provide guidance to the practitioners, such as judges and legal advisers, who face the task of solving concrete legal problems. Before embarking on the substantial inquiry, however, it is important to spell out what is *not* the aim of the book. For example, it should be emphasized at the outset that the book is not meant to be a *de lege ferenda* exercise. The purpose is not to promote a particular normative agenda. Neither is it to conduct a sociological study of the influence of international legal scholars on practitioners or vice versa. The ambition is simply to show that scholars, including those who pledge allegiance to positivism, have failed to provide a satisfactory account of the position of the individual as a matter of positive international law, and that this misconstruction influences the way in which international law is currently interpreted and applied in practice.

An integral part of the book's argument is that the categorization of a norm as either international or national turns exclusively on the nature of its source. It is an important caveat, however, that this is not an inquiry into law-ascertainment, that is the distinction between law and non-law. The book does not attempt to contribute to the continuous debate on how we identify the sources of international law, except to say that the concept of international legal personality is of no value in that regard.

A related topical issue in the current academic debate, which the book does not address either, is whether individuals have gone 'from law-takers to law-makers'.[19] The extent to which individuals take part in contemporary international lawmaking processes is not directly relevant to the present study.[20] The book therefore only addresses the argument that international legal personality is conditional upon State-like features, including international lawmaking capacities.[21]

1.3.1 Individuals

Judged by its title, this book concentrates exclusively on the international legal personality of 'individuals'. But its purpose is not to define the legal personality of human beings vis-à-vis other actors on the international stage. Rather, the primary aim is to use the example of the individual as the ultimate non-State actor to examine the relationship between the theoretical concept of international legal personality and positive norms of international law. The rationale is that if an argument concerning international legal personality holds true for individuals, it applies by implication to all other non-State entities, including, for example, groups of individuals, private companies, and intergovernmental and non-governmental organizations. Limiting the object of the study to individuals is thus a mere matter of expediency, and other entities are included in the analysis where pertinent.[22]

1.3.2 International law and domestic law

This book does not address the question of how to solve concrete conflicts between norms originating from different legal systems. It only purports to examine whether the concept of international legal personality is useful in the determination of the

[19] The expression originates from Math Noortmann and Cedric Ryngaert (eds), *Non-State Actor Dynamics in International Law—From Law-Takers to Law-Makers* (Ashgate, 2010).

[20] On the role of non-state actors in formation of customary international law, see the Draft report of the ILC on the work of its 68th session, Special Rapporteur Ki Gab Park, *Chapter V: Identification of customary international law* (available at http://undocs.org/A/CN.4/L.883/Add.1, 20 June 2016, 10ff, accessed 21 January 2018), the reports of the International Law Association's Committee on Non-State Actors (2005–2016) (available at http://www.ila-hq.org/index.php/committees, accessed 21 January 2018), and Iain Scobbie and Sufyan Droubi (eds), *Non-State Actors and the Formation of Customary International Law* (Manchester University Press, forthcoming 2018). See also Jean d'Aspremont, 'International Law-Making by Non-State Actors: Changing the Model or Putting the Phenomenon into Perspective?' in Math Noortmann and Cedric Ryngaert (eds), *Non-State Actor Dynamics in International Law—From Law-Takers to Law-Makers* (Ashgate, 2010) 171; Jean d'Aspremont, 'Subjects and actors in international lawmaking: The paradigmatic divides in the cognition of international norm-generating processes' in Catherine Brölmann and Yannick Radi (eds), *Research Handbook on the Theory and Practice of International Lawmaking* (Edward Elgar, 2016) 32; and Sandesh Sivakumaran, 'Who Makes International Law? The Case of the Law of Armed Conflict' (available at SSRN: https://ssrn.com/abstract=3084238, accessed 21 January 2018).

[21] See further Section 2.5. The contention that it would improve the legitimacy of international law if individuals were to participate more extensively in international lawmaking processes is briefly mentioned in Section 2.4.

[22] In Chapter 4 on international claims and Chapter 8 on international economic law, for example, corporations are equated with individual human beings. Another key example is the role of armed opposition groups in international humanitarian law, discussed in detail in Chapter 5.

legal system to which a particular norm belongs. Nonetheless, some introductory remarks on the relationship between international law and domestic law are necessary.

Contemporary textbooks generally include a chapter on the relationship between international law and national law, presenting the dichotomy between 'monism' and 'dualism' in international legal theory. It is a common notion that 'monism is dead, and dualism has been replaced by pluralism.'[23] However, like the standard approach to the concept of international legal personality,[24] most textbooks claim that this debate is primarily of academic value and consequently of little use for the understanding of practice.[25]

The subsequent chapters will provide several examples of how the scholarly debate on the concept of international legal personality has consistently been intertwined with the debate on monism versus dualism/pluralism. The aim of the present section is merely to explicate that the 'dualistic' approach, which is recognized by most twenty-first-century scholars as the better reflection of positive law,[26] rests on the following two assumptions: first, international law and national law are separate legal systems; second, the rules of any national legal system decide the impact of international law in national law and vice versa.

The term 'monist' is frequently used about a State which automatically incorporates international legal norms into its domestic legal system, whereas a 'dualist' State requires international law to be 'translated' into national law before it can be applied by national courts.[27] This terminology is unfortunate, because it conflates the overall relationship between the international legal system and the national legal system(s) with the concrete approach to the incorporation of international law into domestic law within a particular State.

Many misunderstandings about the position of the individual in the international legal system seem to originate from a confusion of the status of a norm in international law with its effect in national law. Alexander Orakhelashvili, for example, claims that treaties can be directly applicable to individuals *only* if the constitutional legislation of the State in question gives primacy of international law over national law.[28] In this way, Orakhelashvili fails to acknowledge that from the perspective of

[23] See, for example, Armin von Bogdandy, 'Pluralism, direct effect, and the ultimate say: On the relationship between international and domestic constitutional law', 6 *International Journal of Constitutional Law* (2008) 397, 397–8. See also Alexander Somek, 'Monism: A Tale of the Undead' in Matej Avbelj and Jan Komárek (eds), *Constitutional Pluralism in the European Union and Beyond* (Bloomsbury, 2012) 343. See, however, Jochen von Bernstorff, *The Public International Law Theory of Hans Kelsen* (CUP, 2010) 266.

[24] See further Section 1.1.

[25] See, for example, Peter Malanczuk, *Akehurst's Modern Introduction to International Law* (7th edn, Routledge, 1997), 63–4, Dixon (n 3) 91–4; James Crawford, *Brownlie's Principles of Public International Law* (8th edn, OUP, 2012) 48–50; and Jan Klabbers, *International Law* (CUP, 2013) 296.

[26] See, for example, Giorgio Gaja, 'Dualism—a Review', and Janne Nijman and André Nollkaemper, 'Beyond the Divide', in Janne Nijman and André Nollkaemper (eds), *New Perspectives on the Divide Between National and International Law* (OUP, 2007) 52, 52–3; 341. See also James Crawford, 'Chance, Order, Change: The Course of International Law', 365 *Recueil des Cours* (2013) 9, 170.

[27] See, for example, Klabbers (n 25) 295.

[28] Alexander Orakhelashvili, 'The Position of the Individual in International Law', 31 *California Western International Law Journal* (2001) 241, 266. See similarly Kaarlo Tuori, 'Transnational law—On

international law, the validity of treaty provisions is not contingent upon the effect they are given in a particular national legal system. A State may very well incur international responsibility if it does not implement a treaty in domestic law. However, from the national viewpoint, national law decides the effect to be given to that treaty. In other words: whereas international law determines the content of an international legal rule and the consequences of ignoring it, national law decides the effect that the rule is given in the domestic setting. As will become apparent in the following chapters, disregard for this fundamental distinction continues to muddle the academic debate on the position of the individual in the international legal system.[29]

1.3.3 Primary rules and secondary rules

It is commonplace to distinguish between primary and secondary rules in international law. As this distinction is central in the examination of several issues under scrutiny in this book,[30] it calls for a brief presentation up front.

Roberto Ago is celebrated for having introduced the distinction in 1962 in connection with the International Law Commission's (hereafter ILC) work on the law of State responsibility.[31] By Ago's definition, primary rules are '… the rules of international law which, in one sector of inter-State relations or another, impose particular obligations on States'. Secondary rules, which cover the field of responsibility, '… are concerned with determining the consequences of failure to fulfil obligations established by the primary rules.'[32] In the early 1960s, however, it was hardly an innovation to divide rules of international law into a primary and a secondary category. Charles de Visscher, for example, had contended in 1925 that it is fundamental to distinguish between 'les règles *primaires* ou *normatives*' and 'les règles *secondaires, constructives* ou *techniques*'.[33] In *A Textbook of International Law* from 1947, Alf Ross argued that international law comprises 'central primary norms of intercourse', which must be 'supplemented by secondary rules relating to breaches of law and responsibility.'[34] Even though HLA Hart's *The Concept of*

legal hybrids and perspectivism' in Miguel Maduro, Kaarlo Tuori, and Suvi Sankari (eds), *Transnational Law—Rethinking European Law and Legal Thinking* (CUP, 2014) 11, 22: 'The municipal legal order has lost its monopoly over determining legal relations involving private individuals. Even in states whose constitutional choice with regard to international law has been the dualistic model, transnational norms may be directly effective, regardless of a transformative act of the national legislator.'

[29] See, for example, Sections 5.4.1 and 8.3.2. The idea that the dichotomy of international law and domestic law is insufficient to encompass all law and the consequent development of 'transnational law' as a separate field of study is discussed in Section 2.6.

[30] See in particular Section 3.3 on diplomatic protection and Section 8.2 on international investment law.

[31] The ILC's project on State responsibility began in 1956 and became one of the Commission's most controversial and longest-running studies. In 2001, the Draft Articles on Responsibility of States for Internationally Wrongful Acts (hereafter ARSIWA) were adopted at ILC's 53rd session. The report, which also contains the ILC's commentary on the draft articles, appears in II *YILC* (2001) 26–143.

[32] II *YILC* (1970) 179.

[33] Charles de Visscher, 'La Codification du droit international', 6 *Recueil des Cours* (1925) 325, 341 (emphasis in original).

[34] Alf Ross, *A Textbook of International Law* (Longmans, Green and Co., 1947) 75–8. For a schematic representation of Ross's 'system of international law', see 76; the law of State responsibility is consistently

Law, which was first published in 1961, is frequently cited as the theoretical basis for the distinction between primary and secondary rules of international law,[35] it is more likely that Ago was inspired by civil law writers such as Ross.[36] Regardless of its theoretical origin, however, the distinction remains controversial and should be applied with caution.[37] Throughout this book, the distinction between primary and secondary rules is therefore used strictly as an analytical tool, and only to the extent that it serves to promote the understanding of the issues at hand. The term 'primary rules' refers to rules governing substantive rights and obligations, whereas the term 'secondary rules' will be used (more broadly than the ILC definition) in reference to all the 'meta-rules' that regulate the normative context of the operation of primary rules. Besides rules of responsibility, 'secondary rules' thus also include rules of interpretation and rules of change.[38]

1.4 Guide to the Reader

The book is structured as follows. Chapter 2 discusses the concept of international legal personality as a theoretical construct, and is, first and foremost, intended to lay the theoretical foundation for the study in Chapters 3–8 of the position of individuals as a matter of positive international law. It is not the ambition to conduct a detailed study of the intellectual history based on the wealth of existing literature on the fundamental notion of personality in international law. The idea is merely to identify four main schools of thought pertaining to the concepts of 'law' and

referred to as 'secondary rules', see 241, 254, and 271. See also Ole Spiermann, 'A National Lawyer Takes Stock: Professor Ross' Textbook and Other Forays into International Law', 14 *EJIL* (2003a) 675, 697–9.

[35] According to Hart, a primary rule governs conduct. Human beings are required under primary rules 'to do or abstain from certain actions, whether they wish to or not.' Secondary rules, however, are in Hart's words 'parasitic' upon primary rules, for they allow for the creation, alteration, or extinction of primary rules. HLA Hart, *The Concept of Law*, (2nd edn, OUP, 1994) 81.

[36] Ago was presumably less preoccupied with the jurisprudential underpinnings of the distinction. His aim was primarily to remove the substantial rules regarding the treatment of aliens from the ILC's study on state responsibility. See *Second Report on Diplomatic Protection*, Special Rapporteur John Dugard, UN Doc. A/CN.4/514 (2001) para. 9 and Spiermann (n 34) 697.

[37] As illustrated in Section 3.3, certain international legal rules are extremely hard to classify as being in one category or the other, even with the ILC's limited definition of secondary rules as merely operational rules of state responsibility. See further Jean Combacau and Denis Alland, 'Primary and Secondary Rules in the Law of State Responsibility: Categorizing International Obligations', 16 *Netherlands Yearbook of International Law* (1985) 81. The article attempts to divide primary obligations into categories corresponding to particular types of responsibility. The intrinsic difficulties in such an endeavour are clearly evidenced. See also André Nollkaemper and Dov Jacobs, 'Shared Responsibility in International Law: A Conceptual Framework', 34 *Michigan Journal of International Law* (2013) 359, 408ff, and Jean d'Aspremont, 'The Idea of "Rules" in the Sources of International Law', 84 *BYBIL* (2013) 103, 107.

[38] For similar use of the term see Annemarieke Vermeer-Künzli, 'As If: The Legal Fiction in Diplomatic Protection', 18 *EJIL* (2007a) 37, 50; Thomas M. Franck, *The Power of Legitimacy Among Nations* (OUP, 1990) 184; and André Nollkaemper, *The Power of Secondary Rules of International Law to Connect the International and National Legal Orders* (30 November 2009) Amsterdam Center for International Law Working Paper (available at http://ssrn.com/abstract=1515771, accessed 21 January 2018) 4.

'Statehood', which lead to four different views on the conditions for acquiring international legal personality and the competences ensuing from this status. The four conceptions of international legal personality will be described on the basis of the work of one or more of their most prominent advocates. The examination primarily concentrates on the role attributed by the selected scholars to individuals in the international legal system. Furthermore, particular attention is devoted to these scholars' perceptions of the relationship between international law and national law, and the weight they give to the notion of personality in the determination of the legal order to which a particular norm belongs. A number of the scholars whose writings are discussed in Chapter 2 have played a significant role as, for example, arbitrators, judges, participants in treaty drafting committees, or members of the ILC. The account of these authors' respective conceptions of international legal personality will thus inform the analysis of their statements as practitioners.

Chapter 3 begins the study of the role of individuals as a matter of positive international law with an examination of a number of issues of general relevance. First, it discusses the concept of individual rights and obligations under treaties, as well as customary international law, by scrutinizing, in particular, relevant Judgments and Advisory Opinions of the ICJ and its predecessor the PCIJ. Second, Chapter 3 illustrates that the customary rules on diplomatic protection have given rise to a great deal of confusion as to the international legal personality of individuals. Hence, a thorough examination of the relationship between the concept of individual rights under international law and the doctrine of diplomatic protection is necessary as a prelude to the inquiry into the special fields of international law in Chapters 4–8. Third, Chapter 3 provides some preliminary remarks on treaty interpretation, especially the question of how to determine whether a provision contains direct individual rights or obligations, or merely governs the relationship between the contracting States.

Chapters 4–8 deal in turn with special disciplines in international law, which characteristically involve the interests of individuals. Each chapter will study legal documents, including treaties and secondary legislation, *travaux préparatoires*, and case law in order to assess the evolution and the present-day position of the individual in these particular areas. The analysis will focus on the influence of the various conceptions of international legal personality on the formation of positive norms governing the interests of individuals as well as on the subsequent interpretation and application of such norms, including the determination of whether they are international or national in kind.

Chapter 4 discusses international claims, that is, claims arising out of injury inflicted upon an individual by a foreign State in violation of international law. Such claims may be enforced either through diplomatic protection[39] or by granting the injured individual himself the right to bring a case against the foreign State before an international dispute-settlement body. The common idea is that claims of individuals against foreign States were solely asserted through diplomatic protection before

[39] See further Section 3.3.

the Second World War, whereas the right of individuals to petition international courts independently is a post-1945 phenomenon. By studying international claims practice in three historical periods (before the First World War, the inter-war period, and after the Second World War), Chapter 4 tests this account against positive international law, and inquires whether the concept of international legal personality played a role in the contracting States' choice of one method of dispute resolution over the other.

The study of international humanitarian law in Chapter 5 is divided into the law of international armed conflict and the law of non-international armed conflict. Rather than conferring direct rights on individuals, the norms governing international armed conflicts mostly consist of inter-State obligations. The first part of the chapter assesses the extent to which the law of international armed conflict engages individuals directly and the impact of the different conceptions of international legal personality on the formation and application of the relevant treaty norms. The study includes both provisions that do regulate the conduct of individuals directly, and provisions where such direct regulation was discussed but ultimately discarded in favour of an inter-State model.

The (long) historical development of the law of non-international armed conflict, which by nature involves at least one non-State actor, is particularly interesting for present purposes. The second part of Chapter 5 begins by outlining the original response of legal scholars to the practical demand of States for international regulation of civil war—the development of the doctrine of 'recognition of belligerency' between the late eighteenth century and the Second World War. Subsequently, the chapter examines the role of the concept of international legal personality in the post-Second World War formation of treaty norms governing non-international armed conflicts. Chapter 5 ends with a discussion of how the various conceptions of international legal personality are reflected in the diverging jurisprudential explanations for the bindingness of international law on armed opposition groups, which are put forward in the current academic debate.

No one seriously disputes that the individual is a subject of international criminal law. But it is much less certain whether international crimes a priori entail individual responsibility, which would be in line with the 'individualistic' conception of international legal personality,[40] or whether the responsibility arises a posteriori consistent with the Kelsenian approach.[41] Following a brief account of some historical antecedents, Chapter 6 provides a detailed examination of the pivotal post-Second World War trials, and the subsequent development of individual responsibility for international crimes by the International Criminal Tribunal for the former Yugoslavia (hereafter ICTY), the International Criminal Tribunal for Rwanda (hereafter ICTR), and the ICC. Moreover, the chapter shows that the common practice of categorizing criminal courts as either international, internationalized, or domestic according to the 'involvement of the international community' ultimately rests on the orthodox 'States-only' conception of international legal personality.

40 See Section 2.4.

41 See Section 2.3.

Together with international criminal law, international human rights law is frequently presented as the principal evidence that the structure of the international legal system changed in the course of the second half of the twentieth century so as to include individuals as its subjects.[42] Against this background, one might presume international human rights law to be a field where the theory on international legal personality has played a particularly central role for the development of positive norms. Chapter 7 examines whether such an assumption finds support in practice. Following a summary presentation of some key events in the history of international human rights law before the Second World War, the analysis concentrates on one prominent example, namely the European Convention on Human Rights (hereafter ECHR). The chapter deals with three core issues. First, it describes the evolution of the procedural status of individuals before the European Court of Human Rights (hereafter ECtHR). Second, it studies the Court's practice concerning the interpretation of the ECHR, including the margin of appreciation doctrine. Third and finally, Chapter 7 analyses the practice of the ECtHR as regards the place of the Convention in the international legal system.

Under the umbrella of international economic law, Chapter 8 examines the relationship between the concept of international legal personality and positive international norms pertaining to, first, 'State contracts', that is, contracts to which at least one party is a State and at least one other party is an individual. Second, the chapter studies the field of international investment law, which (unlike, for instance, international trade law) is characterized by a considerable degree of involvement of the individual investor. Third and last, some pertinent aspects of EU law in relation to the international legal personality of individuals will be discussed. Considering EU law in this chapter may be unexpected, since it is not commonly regarded as a part of international (economic) law, but rather as 'a new legal order' of its own. However, the point is precisely to challenge the popular conception of EU law as separate from the international legal system, and to illustrate that this notion rests, at least in part, on the orthodox 'States-only' conception of international legal personality.

Chapter 9 summarizes and synthesizes the preceding chapters' findings on the position of the individual as a matter of international *lex lata* as well as the role of the concept of international legal personality in that context. On this basis, the chapter concludes the book by questioning the overall value of the concept of personality in international law.

[42] In a 1994 Advisory Opinion, for example, the Inter-American Court of Human Rights (hereafter IACtHR) stated as follows: 'International law may grant rights to individuals and, conversely, may also determine that certain acts or omissions on their part could make them criminally liable under that law. In some cases, that responsibility is enforceable by international tribunals. In that sense, international law has evolved from the classical doctrine, under which international law concerned itself exclusively with states.' IACtHR, Advisory Opinion OC-14/94, 9 December 1994, para. 52.

2

International Legal Personality as a Theoretical Construct

Throughout the history of the discipline of international law, scholars have discussed what it means to possess international legal personality. The aim of the present chapter is not to provide a comprehensive account of this debate, which is inherently linked to the continuous academic dispute over basic concepts such as 'law' and 'Statehood'. The ambition is merely to lay the theoretical foundation for the study in Chapters 3–8 of the position of individuals as a matter of positive international law. To this end, the subsequent sections will identify and explain four main conceptions of international legal personality through examples of the work of one or more of their most prominent proponents. With particular emphasis on the role attributed to individuals, the examination will focus on the selected scholars' respective criteria for acquiring personality in international law, as well as their views on the consequences following from this label. In addition, each of the following sections addresses the way in which advocates of the various conceptions perceive the relationship between the international legal order and the national legal order(s), and the role of the notion of personality in that context. The four conceptions of international legal personality, which will be presented chronologically in order of their first appearance, may be summed up in the following statements:

1. The 'States-only' conception: 'States are the only international legal persons' (Section 2.2), including the modified version that 'States may confer derivative international legal personality on non-State entities, but there is a presumption against it' (Section 2.2.1).
2. The 'a posteriori' conception: 'The international legal personality of any entity depends solely on the content of an international norm addressing it' (Section 2.3).
3. The 'individualistic' conception: 'There is a presumption *for* the international legal personality of individuals' (Section 2.4).
4. The 'participant' conception: 'There are no international legal persons—only participants in the international legal order' (Section 2.5).

A core objective of this book is to ascertain the role of the individual according to international *lex lata*. Primary attention will therefore be given to the 'States-only', the 'a posteriori', and the 'individualistic' conceptions of international legal personality, which all adopt a rules-based approach and thus, albeit to varying degrees, pledge fidelity to the law 'as it is' as opposed to 'as it should be'. While positivism seems to be the mainstream school of thought among international lawyers,[1] it is, needless to say, a very broad school encompassing significantly diverging views on core themes in international legal theory, including the fundamental concept of personality.

The 'States-only' and the 'a posteriori' conceptions both claim to be strictly positivist, leaving no room for normativity, but nevertheless ascribe profoundly different roles to the individual in the international legal system. Judged by a survey of international law textbooks, the 'States-only' conception is presently predominant in the modified version,[2] which is also invoked in practice on a regular basis, as exemplified in Chapters 3–8. Nevertheless, the orthodox 'States-only' conception is still very much alive in the academic debate as well as in the rulings of international judicial bodies. The 'a posteriori' conception, on the other hand, has few outspoken advocates, but is ultimately endorsed by the present author as the better reflection of historical and existing positive norms of international law.

Although the 'individualistic' conception upholds the distinction between *lex lata* and *lex ferenda*, it also promotes a particular normative agenda. Arguably, there are a number of manifestations of the 'individualistic' conception in practice, particularly in the field of international criminal law.[3] Furthermore, the 'individualistic' conception of international legal personality is an integral part of the popular argument that the international legal system is undergoing a process of constitutionalization. Some international legal constitutionalists, however, build their reasoning on the orthodox 'States-only' conception of international legal personality and thereby, paradoxically, endorse the very theoretical position that the 'individualistic' conception originally set out to criticize.[4]

The 'participant' conception of international legal personality draws on the perception of law as authoritative decision-making process rather than a set of rules. While there are occasional manifestations of the 'participant' conception in practice, it has thus far mainly been of academic interest. It is therefore attributed comparatively less weight than the three positivist conceptions. Instead, a significant part of Section 2.5 is devoted to illustrating how the notion of 'participant' impacts on the contemporary scholarly debate on the role of the individual as a matter of positive international law.

This chapter ends, in Section 2.6, with a reflection on the interrelationship between the four conceptions of international legal personality. It also considers why the 'States-only' conception has consistently held a dominant position among international lawyers.

[1] See, for example, Mónica García-Salmones Rovira, *The Project of Positivism in International Law* (OUP, 2013) 1, and Richard Collins, 'Classical legal positivism in international law revisited', in Jörg Kammerhofer and Jean d'Aspremont (eds), *International Legal Positivism in a Post-Modern World* (CUP, 2014) 23.

[2] See further Section 1.1.

[3] See further Chapter 6.

[4] See Section 2.4.

Very few of the positive norms of international law discussed in this book predate the twentieth century. Apart from the following introductory remarks on the historical origin of the concept of international legal personality, the book will therefore concentrate on post-1900 scholarship.

2.1 International Legal Personality before the Twentieth Century

Although the expression 'international law' is commonly attributed to Jeremy Bentham's *An Introduction to the Principles of Morals and Legislation* of 1789,[5] it was Emmerich de Vattel who first construed the field as 'the law between States' in *Le Droit des Gens ou Principes de la Loi Naturelle* published in 1758: 'The Law of Nations is the science of the rights, which exist between Nations or States, and of the obligations corresponding to these rights.'[6]

Earlier international legal scholarship, including that of Francisco de Vitoria, Alberico Gentili, and Hugo Grotius, had conceived of the law of nations as a combination of natural and man-made rules applicable to rulers of nations and individuals alike.[7] Notably, it was the German philosopher Gottfried Wilhelm Leibniz who in this 'pre-Vattel' era coined the term 'international legal person' ('*persona jure gentium*') in 1693.[8]

Vattel was heavily influenced by Thomas Hobbes, Samuel Pufendorf, and Christian Wolff.[9] Their work had developed contractual theories of the State as a separate person, but Vattel was the first to regard the State as a distinct unit with a will of its own—independent of its constituencies and its ruler.[10] In Vattel's thinking, international law applied only to the separate entity of the State. States were creators of international law, but they were bound by certain natural law principles. During the nineteenth century, Vattel's perception of international law as inter-State law remained largely unchallenged. Instead, the scholarly debate in this period centred on the legal status and creation of international law, in particular the influence

[5] Jeremy Bentham, *An Introduction to the Principles of Morals and Legislation* (The Clarendon Press, 1879), Chapter XVII, § 2, no. XXV, 326.

[6] Emmerich de Vattel, *Le Droit des Gens ou Principes de la Loi Naturelle* (Carnegie, 1916), *Préliminaires* § 3, 1 (translation by Alfred P. Rubin, *Ethics and Authority in International Law* (CUP, 1997) 46).

[7] See further David Kennedy, 'Primitive Legal Scholarship', 27 *HILJ* (1986) 1, 8.

[8] See Gottfried Wilhelm Leibniz, *Codex juris gentium diplomaticus* (Hannover, 1693) in the translation of Patrick Riley (ed.), *Leibniz: Political Writings* (2nd edn, CUP, 1988) 170, and Jan Hendrik Willem Verzijl, *International Law in Historical Perspective, Vol. II: International Persons* (A. W. Sijthoff, 1969) 2. Leibniz's introduction of the concept of international legal personality was aimed at legitimizing the participation of the free German Princes on the international arena, while at the same time establishing their responsibility to abide by the law of nations. For a detailed, contextual analysis of Leibniz's theory, see Janne E. Nijman, *The Concept of International Legal Personality—An Inquiry into the History and Theory of International Law* (TMC Asser Press, 2004) 29–84.

[9] See further Emmanuelle Jouannet, *Emer de Vattel et l'Émergence doctrinale du Droit International Classique* (Editions A. Pedone, 1998), 265–318.

[10] Vattel (n 6), *Préliminaires* § 2, 1.

of natural law.[11] The positivist school, which came to dominate over the course of the nineteenth century, informed the first perception of international legal personality to be discussed.

2.2 'States Are the Only International Legal Persons'

The 'States-only' conception of international legal personality is mainly associated with Heinrich Triepel, Dionisio Anzilotti, and Lassa Oppenheim. These orthodox positivist scholars perceived the State as the culmination of an evolution of social institutions. Rather than a legal status, Statehood is a historical fact existing independently of legal norms. In the original form of the 'States-only' conception of international legal personality, legal persons in international law are such entities that have acquired Statehood. According to Heinrich Triepel: 'If there is an international law, it can only apply between the coordinated States themselves.'[12] Six years later, Dionisio Anzilotti opined unequivocally that 'it is impossible that there will be other subjects of international rights and duties than States',[13] while section 63 of the first edition of Lassa Oppenheim's *International Law* reads:

> The conception of International Persons is derived from the conception of the Law of Nations. As this law is the body of rules which the civilised States consider legally binding in their intercourse, every State which belongs to the civilised States, and is, therefore, a member of the family of Nations, is an International Person. Sovereign States exclusively are International Persons—i.e. subjects of international law.[14]

Advocates of the 'States-only' conception find the applicability of international law to be contingent upon consent, which only States are eligible to give. In other words, international law originates exclusively from the will of States and only States may be bound by it.[15] The following famous statement of the PCIJ in the *Lotus* Judgment is commonly interpreted as an endorsement of this radical form of 'consensualism' or 'voluntarism':[16] 'International Law governs relations between

[11] Roland Portmann, *Legal Personality in International Law* (CUP, 2010) 31 and 38–41, and Nijman (n 8) 84. See, however, Marek St Korowicz, 'The Problem of the International Legal Personality of Individuals' 50 *AJIL* (1956) 533, 534.

[12] Heinrich Triepel, *Völkerrecht und Landesrecht* (JCB Mohr (Paul Siebeck), 1899) 20 (author's translation). See also Heinrich Triepel, 'Les Rapport entre le Droit Interne et le Droit International', 1 *Recueil des Cours* (1923) 77, 81.

[13] Dionisio Anzilotti, *Il diritto internazionale nei giudizi interni* (N Zanichelli, 1905) 44 (author's translation).

[14] Lassa Oppenheim, *International Law: A Treatise—Peace* (Longmans, Green and Co., 1905) 99. See also the more elaborate restatement in Lassa Oppenheim, *International Law: A Treatise* (3rd edn, Longmans, Green and Co., 1920) 17–18.

[15] See, for example, Triepel, *Völkerrecht und Landesrecht* (n 12) 95ff, and Dionisio Anzilotti, *Teoria generale della responsabilità dello Stato nel diritto intemazionale* (F. Lumachi, 1902) 37–8.

[16] See further Jörg Kammerhofer and Jean d'Aspremont, 'Introduction: The Future of International Legal Positivism', in Jörg Kammerhofer and Jean d'Aspremont, *International Legal Positivism in a Post-Modern World* (CUP, 2014) 4–5. For criticism see, for example, Jörg Kammerhofer, 'Gaps, the Nuclear

independent States. Rules of law binding upon States therefore emanate from their own free will'.[17]

In the orthodox 'States-only' conception of international legal personality, international law can neither benefit nor restrain an individual without the interposition of national law. Except as constitutive elements of their home State, individuals are not perceived as directly relevant to international law.[18] Relations between individuals and between States and individuals are by definition regulated through national law, whereas international law exclusively governs the relationship between States. In consequence, international legal rules relating to individuals are always to be perceived as obligations of States to confer rights or obligations on individuals in their respective national legal systems.[19]

Given this a priori reduction of the subjects of international law to entities qualifying for Statehood,[20] the orthodox 'States-only' conception inherently promotes a clear-cut separation between norms of international law and norms of national law. In the famous words of Triepel: 'International law and national law are not only different parts of law, but different legal orders .... They are two circles that at most touch each other but never overlap.'[21]

In *Diritto internazionale nei giudizi interni* published in 1905, Anzilotti explicated the two interrelated criteria that separate international legal norms from norms belonging to national legal systems:

> First of all ... international law stems from the collective will of several States, while rules of municipal law are always the expression of the will of a State .... Secondly, the relations which are respectively governed are different: norms of international law govern relations between coordinated and autonomous entities ... while norms of municipal law govern relations within a society which is legally organized and therefore they implicitly contain an idea of supremacy and subordination ....[22]

In sum, the legal system to which a norm belongs is determined not only on the basis of its foundation, that is, the collective will of several States, but also its addressees.[23]

Interestingly, as of the 1923 version of his *Corso di diritto internazionale*, Anzilotti accepted Hans Kelsen's theory of the *Grundnorm*.[24] But in contrast to Kelsen,[25] Anzilotti asserted that the international legal system has its own *Grundnorm*, namely

Weapons Advisory Opinion and the Structure of International Legal Argument between Theory and Practice', 80 *BYBIL* (2010a) 333–60.

[17] *Case of the SS Lotus* (Judgment) [1927] PCIJ Ser. A, No. 10, 18.

[18] Triepel, *Völkerrecht und Landesrecht* (n 12) 20–1. See also Oppenheim (1905, n 14) § 290, 344.

[19] See also George Manner, 'The Object Theory of the Individual in International Law', 46 *AJIL* (1952) 428.

[20] As discussed in Section 2.6, this idea is in fact more naturalist than positivist.

[21] Triepel, *Völkerrecht und Landesrecht* (n 12) 111 (author's translation).

[22] Anzilotti (n 13), 41–2 (translation by Giorgio Gaja, 'Positivism and Dualism in Dionisio Anzilotti', 3 *EJIL* (1992) 123, 134–5).

[23] Dionisio Anzilotti, 'Trattati generali di diritto internazionale pubblico', 1 *Rivista di Diritto Internazionale* (1906) 33 and 166. See also Gaja (n 22) 134–5.

[24] Anzilotti referred to Hans Kelsen, *Das Problem der Souveränität und die Theorie des Völkerrechts* (Verlag von JCB Mohr, 1920a).

[25] See further Section 2.3.

the principle of *pacta sunt servanda*, and on that basis he maintained a separation between international and domestic law:

Since they emanate from autonomous basic norms, international law and domestic law are separate legal orders.... The basic norm, according to which States should behave as they have agreed to do with other States, represents the criterion that determines which norms are part of the international legal system and that formally distinguishes them from norms pertaining to the various municipal laws, although even the latter may in many ways concern the relations between States.[26]

While it was never uncontested, the original 'States-only' conception of international law seemingly persisted into the twentieth century.[27] In the light of the difficulty in accommodating phenomena like international organizations,[28] a modified version gradually appeared in the interwar period.[29]

Since the Second World War, only a few scholars have upheld the orthodox notion that only States may be subjects of international law. One example is Alf Ross, a leading advocate of Scandinavian legal realism, who argued in 1947 that '[i]nternational law will exist as long as its subjects are the self-governing states and not individuals.'[30] In 1964, Rolando Quadri likewise referred to the State as 'the only category of subjects of international law that exists at the moment and that will exist as long as the human community is of an international character'.[31] In order to accommodate post-Second World War reality within the orthodox 'States-only' framework, such scholars have designated legal norms directed at non-State entities as various genera of national law. A curious example is Ross's characterization of the European Commission of the Danube as 'the organ of a special "River State".'[32] In a recent attempt to adapt 'Triepel's and Anzilotti's kind of dualism' to present-day circumstances, Gaetano Arangio-Ruiz has advocated that we replace the traditional dichotomy between international and national law with a broader dichotomy between international law and 'interindividual' law:

[26] Dionisio Anzilotti, *Corso di diritto internazionale* (3rd edn, Atheneum, 1928) 49–50 (translation by Gaja (n 22) 136–7). See also ibid, 135 and 138.

[27] See further Portmann (n 11) 42.

[28] In the 4th edition of *Oppenheim's International Law*, published in 1928, Arnold McNair argued that the League of Nations itself was an international person *sui generis*, but 'apart from the League of Nations, sovereign States exclusively are International Persons'. McNair found the idea of individual rights and duties under international law to be 'untenable as a general position.' Arnold McNair (ed.), *Oppenheim's International Law* (4th edn, Longmans, Green and Co., 1928) 133 and 520. Accordingly, he construed the rights and duties of the Council, the Assembly, and the Secretariat as 'neither international nor municipal rights and duties, but only rights and duties within the organisation set up by the Covenant' (ibid, 521).

[29] See Section 2.2.1.

[30] Alf Ross, *A Textbook of International Law* (Longmans, Green and Co., 1947) 54.

[31] Rolando Quadri, 'Cours Général de Droit International Public', 113 *Recueil des Cours* (1964-III) 245, 433 (author's translation). See also Prosper Weil, 'Cours Générale du Droit International Public: Le Droit International en Quête de son Identité', 237 *Recueil des Cours* (1992-VI) 9, 122, and Prosper Weil, 'Towards a Relative Normativity in International Law?', 77 *AJIL* (1983) 413.

[32] Ross (n 30) 30. See also Ole Spiermann, 'A National Lawyer Takes Stock: Professor Ross' Textbook and Other Forays into International Law', 14 *EJIL* (2003) 675, 693.

One must distinguish, precisely, international law, on the one hand, and any *species* of interindividual law, on the other hand. The latter *genus* would include both the several national legal systems, on the one hand, and the several internal legal systems of international bodies, on the other hand . . . .[33]

However, outspoken proponents of the orthodox 'States-only' conception of international legal personality remain the exception in post-Second World War scholarship. The predominant trend in international legal theory, which is discussed in the following section, has been to modify the definitional exclusion of non-State entities from the sphere of international law into a presumption against the international legal personality of such entities. On a general level, the vast majority of contemporary international lawyers endorse the view that non-State entities, including individuals, possess at least some degree of international legal personality. Nevertheless, as demonstrated in Chapters 3–8, the orthodox 'States-only' conception of international legal personality seems to be so entrenched in the thinking of many scholars and judges of international courts that, perhaps inadvertently, they continue to rely on it when faced with concrete treaty provisions directed at individuals or groups of individuals. For example, the common practice of categorizing criminal courts according to 'the involvement of the international community',[34] the widespread notion that armed opposition groups are not directly bound by common Article 3 of the Geneva Conventions and Additional Protocol II,[35] and the general perception that EU law is 'a new legal order'[36] all share the underlying assumption that States are the only subjects of international law. In this way, the orthodox 'States-only' conception of international legal personality not only continues to influence the way in which international legal norms are interpreted and applied, but also how we distinguish them from domestic legal norms.

2.2.1 'States may confer derivative international legal personality on non-State entities, but there is a presumption against it'

Especially after the ICJ's *Reparations for Injuries* Opinion in 1949, the idea came to dominate that States may grant derivative international legal personality to non-State entities. But the modified 'States-only' conception, which accepts that States may designate other entities as international legal persons, already emerged during the interwar period with the work of, in particular, Karl Strupp, Arrigo Cavaglieri, and Georg Schwarzenberger. While upholding the basic propositions that the State is a social phenomenon and that international law originates from the will of States,[37]

[33] Gaetano Arangio-Ruiz, 'International Law and Interindividual Law', in Janne Nijman and André Nollkaemper (eds), *New Perspectives on the Divide Between National and International Law* (OUP, 2007) 44. See also Gaetano Arangio-Ruiz, 'Le Domaine Réservé. L'Organisation Internationale et le Rapport entre Droit International et Droit Interne', 225 *Recueil des Cours* 9 (1990-VI) 9, 448ff, and Gaetano Arangio-Ruiz, 'L'État dans le sens du Droit des Gens et la Notion du Droit international', 26 *Österreichische Zeitschrift für öffentliches Recht* (1975–6) 3, 403–5.

[34] See further Section 6.3. [35] See further Section 5.4.3.

[36] See further Section 8.3.2.

[37] See, for example, Arrigo Cavaglieri, 'Régles Genérales du Droit de la Paix', 26 *Recueil des Cours* (1929-I) 310, 321, with reference to Anzilotti.

the factual development on the international stage was perceived to necessitate the inclusion of non-State actors into the international legal system: 'But as [international] law, which primarily regulates relations between States, sometimes attributes rights and obligations to entities of a different nature, we cannot but extend the status of subject of international law to these entities.'[38] Thus adding a sociological element to the orthodox 'States-only' conception, non-State entities, including individuals, were designated as derivative or secondary international legal persons.

> An entity has international personality if it has rights and duties under international law .... The original subjects of international law are sovereign States .... Nonetheless, it is a mistake to deduce from this state of affairs that sovereign States alone are eligible to be subjects of international law. This is a matter within the discretion of each of the existing subjects of international law .... Nevertheless, the sovereign State is the typical subject of international law. Any international person of a different type is, if not an oddity, an exception which has, until now, confirmed the general rule.[39]

Just as existing States could recognize new States as international legal persons, they could also recognize the international legal personality of non-State entities.[40] But whereas new States would be endowed with the full range of attributes, the international legal personality of non-State entities would be strictly limited to the content of the act of recognition in question.[41]

Specifically pertaining to the recognition of individuals as international legal persons, Schwarzenberger asserted as follows in the fifth edition of *A Manual of International Law*:

> The rules governing recognition are so elastic that there is no limit to the objects, which, by recognition, may be transformed into subjects of international law. Thus, the international personality of individuals is not a question of principle, but simply one of fact: is there enough evidence to substantiate the claim that the individual, the basis of national and international life, is more than an object in existing international law?[42]

It is a key component in the modified 'States-only' conception of international legal personality that the factual development in international law does not in itself create new international legal persons. Instead, the evolution of the international legal system has only opened up the possibility for States to extend international legal

[38] Arrigo Cavaglieri, 'I soggetti del diritto internazionale', 20 *Rivista di diritto internazionale* (1925) 18, 174 (author's translation). See also Karl Strupp, *Grundzüge des positiven Völkerrechts* (5th edn, Ludwig Röhrscheid Verlag, 1932) 33.

[39] Georg Schwarzenberger, *A Manual of International Law* (2nd edn, Stevens & Sons, 1950a), 24–6. See similarly Cavaglieri (n 37) 318ff, and Karl Strupp, 'Régles Genérales du Droit de la Paix', 47 *Recueil des Cours* (1934-I) 259, 463ff.

[40] See Karl Strupp, *Das völkerrechtliche Delikt* (Verlag von W. Kohlhammer, 1920) 22.

[41] Cavaglieri (n 37)177, and Schwarzenberger (n 39) 34.

[42] Georg Schwarzenberger, *A Manual of International Law* (5th edn, Friedrick A. Praeger, 1967) 80. See likewise Georg Schwarzenberger, *A Manual of International Law* (6th edn, Professional Book Ltd, 1976) 64. Notably, Schwarzenberger invoked a strong presumption against the international legal personality of individuals in his categorization of the International Military Tribunal (IMT) as a 'joint municipal tribunal'. See further Section 6.3.1. See also Georg Schwarzenberger, 'The Problem of an International Criminal Law' 3 *Current Legal Problems* (1950b) 263, 275ff.

personality to non-State entities if they see fit. In the interpretation of concrete international norms, it is to be presumed that States did not intend to do so: 'Although treaties may speak of the rights of individuals as if they were derived from the treaties themselves, this, as a rule, is not normally the position. Such treaties, rather than creating the rights, impose the duty upon the contracting states to establish them in their national laws.'[43]

Unless there is patent evidence to the contrary, international law governs the relationship between States, while the conditions of individuals are governed by municipal law:

> As the relevance of non-state entities to international law is so far exceptional, the definition of this relevance must be founded on more rigorous and restrictive criteria. The position of these entities in the international legal order must be clearly established and must be constrained to the exact limits of the constitutive act. Any doubt must be resolved by returning the entity to the normal sphere of its activities: the domestic legal order.[44]

The modified 'States-only' conception thus maintained the dualist approach to the relationship between international and national law, and explicitly rejected the monist theories developed by Kelsen among others.[45] Strupp stated:

> Against 'monism' in one form or another speaks first and foremost the diversity of addressees (in international law, subjects of international law, in domestic law respectively the nationals and the residents on the territory) as well as the fact that a domestic legal norm's violation of international law does not affect its validity on the domestic level.[46]

But whereas the orthodox 'States-only' conception automatically categorizes treaty norms governing individuals directly as various genera of national law, the modified version unfolds as a two-sided principle of interpretation: First of all, there is a presumption that international legal norms do not entail direct individual rights or obligations. Second, if it is clearly established that an international legal norm does indeed govern individuals directly, such a norm is to be interpreted restrictively. Judged by the fact that international law textbooks continue to rely on the ICJ's Advisory Opinion in *Reparations for Injuries* as the principal authority on international legal personality, the modified 'States-only' conception appears to remain prevalent among contemporary international legal scholars.[47] In *Reparations for Injuries*, the ICJ determined the international legal personality of the UN, before pronouncing on the ability of the organization to bring an international claim. Thus, the Court's examination of the UN Charter was apparently not aimed at identifying the extent of the rights, duties, and capacities of the UN in order to determine the

[43] Robert Jennings and Arthur Watts (eds), *Oppenheim's International Law* (9th edn, Longman, 1992) 847.

[44] Cavaglieri (n 37) 182–3 (author's translation). See also Strupp (n 39) 466.

[45] See Section 2.3.

[46] Strupp (n 38) 27–8 (author's translation). See also Cavaglieri (n 37) 319, Strupp (n 39) 404ff, and Schwarzenberger (n 39) 19–20.

[47] See further Section 1.1. See also Portmann (n 11) 80, and Robert McCorquodale, 'An Inclusive International Legal System', 17 *LJIL* (2004) 477, 480. See, however, Anne Peters, *Beyond Human Rights—The Legal Status of the Individual in International Law* (CUP, 2016) 414–15.

ramifications of its personality in international law.[48] Rather, the ICJ's approach was the other way around: It first examined whether the States parties had intended to grant the UN international legal personality, and then went on to pronounce on the capacity of the organization to bring an international claim.

A variation of the modified 'States-only' conception of international legal personality attaches crucial importance to the actual existence of an international forum, in which relevant claims may be enforced directly by, for example, individuals.[49] This line of thought, however, was definitively rejected by the ICJ in *LaGrand*.[50]

2.3 'The International Legal Personality of Any Entity Depends Solely on the Content of an International Norm Addressing It'

The 'a posteriori' conception of international legal personality originates from Hans Kelsen's Pure Theory of Law,[51] which was heavily influenced by the quest for scientific knowledge dominating intellectual life in *fin-de-siècle* Vienna.[52] Kelsen's work on international law pursued two main purposes; one theoretical and one political. Apart from developing a strictly legal, that is, non-political, methodology for the discipline of international law, he wanted to advance the political project of a more peaceful world order through the development of an institutionalized and legalized community of States.[53] Both his theoretical and his political projects entailed the subjectivity of individuals in international law.[54] Through scientific critique of inter

[48] *Reparations for Injuries Suffered in the Service of the United Nations* (Advisory Opinion) [1949] ICJ Rep 174, 179. See further Portmann (n 11) 99–105. See also Manuel Rama-Montaldo, 'International Legal Personality and Implied Powers of International Organizations', 44 *BYBIL* (1970) 111, 129. There are, however, diverging opinions on how the ICJ's approach to the concept of international legal personality should be construed. See further Dapo Akande, 'International Organizations', in Malcolm D. Evans (ed.), *International Law* (4th edn, OUP, 2014) 252–3. See also Gleider I. Hernández, 'Non-state actors from the perspective of the International Court of Justice', in Jean d'Aspremont (ed.), *Participants in the International Legal System: Multiple perspectives on non-state actors in international law* (Routledge, 2011) 140, 142–3.

[49] See, for example, Carl Aage Nørgaard, *The Position of the Individual in International Law* (Munksgaard, 1962) 172. See also Humphrey Waldock, 'General Course on Public International Law', 106 *Recueil des Cours* (1962-II) 206ff, and *Dissenting Opinion of Judge Córdova, Judgments of the Administrative Tribunal of the ILO upon complaints made against the UNESCO* (Advisory Opinion) [1956] ICJ Rep 77, 160.

[50] *LaGrand (Germany v. United States of America)* (Judgment) [2001] ICJ Rep 466 (hereafter *LaGrand*). See further Section 3.1.2.2.2.

[51] Additional proponents include Julio A. Barberis, 'Nouvelles Questions Concernant la Personnalité Juridique Internationale', 179 *Recueil des Cours* (1983-I) 145, 168, D. P. O'Connell, *International Law* (2nd edn, Stevens & Sons, 1970), vol. I, 82–6 and 106–12, and Ian Brownlie, *Principles of Public International Law* (1st edn, Clarendon Press, 1966) 60.

[52] On Kelsen's relationship with the Vienna Circle see, for example, Portmann (n 11), 180ff, and Jörg Kammerhofer, 'Hans Kelsen in Post-Modern International Legal Scholarship', in Jörg Kammerhofer and Jean d'Aspremont (eds), *International Legal Positivism in a Post-Modern World* (CUP, 2014) 83ff.

[53] See, for example, Hans Kelsen, *Peace through Law* (University of North Carolina Press, 1944). See further Jochen von Bernstorff, *The Public International Law Theory of Hans Kelsen* (CUP, 2010) 2.

[54] On the relationship between Kelsen's idea of a non-political science of law and his decidedly political cosmopolitan project, see ibid, 247ff. See also Danilo Zolo, 'Hans Kelsen: International Peace through International Law', 9 *EJIL* (1998) 306.

alia the 'States-only' and the 'individualistic' conceptions of the international legal personality, Kelsen sought to improve the functionality of the law as a means to achieving the political aspirations of a more 'juridified international system'.[55]

Inspired by the natural sciences, Kelsen's theoretical project, the Pure Theory of Law, aimed at freeing jurisprudence from 'all the elements foreign to the specific method of a science whose only purpose is the cognition of the law'.[56] Accordingly, Kelsen advocated an objective and logically verifiable 'science of law', which is 'pure' in the sense that it leaves aside everything that is not strictly 'law': 'It is called a "pure" theory of law, because it only describes the law and attempts to eliminate from the object of this description everything that is not strictly law: Its aim is to free the science of law from alien elements.'[57]

Along with the assertion of a 'scientific' jurisprudence, the Pure Theory's defining feature is the categorical distinction between 'is' ('sein') and 'ought' ('sollen').[58] Sociological 'is'-statements are considered irrelevant to an autonomous science of law which is preoccupied purely with the normative 'ought'.[59] But also non-legal 'ought'-statements based on moral and ethical considerations are to be eliminated from the science of law. Kelsen thus attacked both of the two dominant legal philosophies among his contemporaries[60] by criticizing the orthodox positivist notion that international law emanates from the collective will of States,[61] as well as the idea that international law may be derived from natural law principles.[62]

The Pure Theory perceives all law as a self-referential hierarchical system of positive norms with the hypothetical basic norm, *die Grundnorm*, which Kelsen deemed an 'indispensable assumption', as the ultimate law-making authority:[63] 'The essential characteristic of positivism, as contrasted with natural law theory, may be found precisely in the difficult renunciation of an absolute, material justification, in this self-denying and self-imposed restriction to a merely hypothetical, formal foundation in the basic norm.'[64]

[55] von Bernstorff (n 53) 249.

[56] Hans Kelsen, *General Theory of Law and State* (Harvard University Press, 1945) xiv.

[57] Here cited from Hans Kelsen, *Pure Theory of Law*, translation by Max Knight (The Lawbook Exchange, Ltd, 1970) 1.

[58] Hans Kelsen, 'Was ist die Reine Rechtslehre?' reprinted in Hans Klecatsky et al, *Die Wiener rechtstheoretische Schule. Schriften von Hans Kelsen, Adolf Merkl, Alfred Verdross* (Europa Verlag, 1968, first published 1953), vol. 1, 614. On the history of the philosophical 'is–ought problem', see Portmann (n 11) 184–6.

[59] Hans Kelsen, *Hauptprobleme der Staatsrechtslehre* (2nd edn, Scientia, 1960, first published 1923) 8. See further Georg Henrik von Wright, 'Is and Ought', in Stanley L. Paulson and Bonnie Litschewski Paulson (eds), *Normativity and Norms—Critical Perspectives on Kelsenian Themes* (Clarendon Press, 1998) 365ff. See also von Bernstorff (n 53) 44ff.

[60] On this 'doppelte Frontstellung' see further Horst Dreier, *Rechtslehre, Staatssoziologie und Demokratietheorie bei Hans Kelsen* (2nd edn, Nomos, 1990) 27ff. See also Jörg Kammerhofer, 'Hans Kelsen's place in international legal theory', in Alexander Orakhelashvili (ed.), *Research Handbook on the Theory and History of International Law* (Edward Elgar, 2011) 143, 145.

[61] See, for example, Kelsen (n 24) 182ff. For Kelsen's critique of the concept of state will, see Kelsen (n 59) 162ff.

[62] See, for example, Hans Kelsen, *Die philosophischen Grundlagen der Naturrechtslehre und des Rechtspositivismus* (Pan-Verlag Rolf Heise, 1928a) 37ff, and Kelsen (n 56) 39–95. See further von Bernstorff (n 53) 160ff.

[63] Kelsen (n 56) 395–6. [64] Ibid, 396.

In the legal pyramid, *der Stufenbau der Rechtsordnung*,[65] the creation of law on each level is authorized according to the higher-ranking normative level, with the basic norm at the top.[66] When the law descends through the levels of the pyramid, it becomes gradually more specific. As explained in what follows, Kelsen's theory on the sources of law applies to national law as well as international law.[67] Pertaining specifically to the sources of international law, Kelsen placed customary international law at the hierarchical level immediately below the basic norm and above treaties.[68]

Following the notion that a science of law must leave aside everything that is not strictly 'law', including sociological, historical, and psychological elements, Kelsen challenged 'der traditionelle Dualismus von Staat und Recht'.[69] In his opinion, the orthodox positivist view of the State as a social fact had little to do with legal analysis.[70] From a purely juristic point of view, the State must be defined in strictly normative terms as a legal phenomenon, which in effect is 'die Personifikation der totalen Rechtsordnung'.[71] This 'identity thesis' is a cornerstone in Kelsen's development of a new theoretical framework for international law[72] and a determining factor in his conception of international legal personality.

The Pure Theory builds on the assumption that all law, national as well as international, is regulation of human behaviour.[73] Rights and obligations conferred on States by international law thus imply 'that international law obligates and authorizes those human individuals who are State organs.'[74] The State only exists as organs to which human actions are attributed in the national legal order: 'An "organ of the State" is tantamount to an "organ of the law".'[75] It does not follow, however, that only individuals are international legal persons. When the actions of an individual are attributed to a collective entity such as a State, this entity is the addressee of the relevant international norms and thus endowed with international legal personality:

> When we say that a legal person, a company for example, has subjective duties or rights, this means that obligations or rights exist relating to the conduct of an individual, but that this individual possesses these duties or rights in his/her capacity as a member or an organ of this company. We say that the obligations or rights are those of the company. We attribute [rights] and we impose [obligations], because the individual, who is the true subject of these obligations and rights, possesses them in his capacity of member or organ of the company.[76]

[65] Notably, Kelsen attributed notion of the *Stufenbau* to Adolf Merkl. See Kelsen (n 56) xv, including references to Merkl's work.

[66] Kelsen (n 57) 228ff.

[67] See further Kelsen (n 56) 369–70, and Hans Kelsen, 'Theorie du Droit International Public', 84 *Recueil des Cours* (1953-III) 5, 119ff.

[68] Kelsen (n 57) 222–3.

[69] Ibid, 288ff. See also Kelsen (n 24) 10–12.

[70] Hans Kelsen, *Der soziologische und der juristische Staatsbegriff. Kritische Untersuchung des Verhältnisses von Staat und Recht* (2nd edn, Scientia Verlag, 1928b) 4–11.

[71] Kelsen (n 24) 20. See also Kelsen (n 56) 181ff.

[72] See further von Bernstorff (n 53) 50. See also Hersch Lauterpacht, 'Kelsen's Pure Science of Law', in Elihu Lauterpacht (ed.), *International Law: Being the Collected Papers of Hersch Lauterpacht*, vol. II (CUP, 1975, first published in 1933) 404, 414–19.

[73] Hans Kelsen, 'Theorie Générale du Droit International Public—Problèmes Choisis', 42 *Recueil des Cours* (1932-IV) 119, 142. See also Kelsen (n 56) 3ff and 342.

[74] Kelsen (n 56) 342.

[75] Ibid, 192.

[76] Kelsen, 'Theorie du Droit International Public' (n 67) 67 (author's translation).

The status of any entity in international law, be it a State or a private individual, is thus solely contingent upon the international norms directed at it.[77] If interpretation of an international norm leads to the conclusion that the norm governs an entity, it follows that this entity possesses international legal personality.[78] There are no inherent rights and duties of any international legal persons.[79] Rather, the international legal personality of all entities, including individuals, must be established a posteriori on a case-by-case basis. In 1932, Kelsen stated as follows on the status of individuals as a matter of positive international law: 'In general, international law has states as subjects, that is individuals are subjects in an indirect manner—exceptionally also in a direct manner. It is not contrary to the nature of international law that what is today still an exception may one day become the rule.'[80]

Kelsen did not, in contrast to the orthodox positivists, employ the concept of international legal personality as a means to distinguish between legal orders for the obvious reason that he was a monist. But the question is whether the 'a posteriori' conception is inextricably linked to the Pure Theory's premise of the systemic unity of all law and as such inherently incompatible with the idea that the international legal system is separate from the national legal system(s).[81]

Kelsen invoked the unity of national and international law as an epistemological postulate:[82] The axiomatic unity of a science does not allow for the notion of dualism (or pluralism),[83] and a perception of international law and national law as distinct legal systems would, therefore, be equivalent to denying the legal character of one of them.[84]

Kelsen's critique of orthodox positivism thus addressed not only the duality of regulatory objects, but also the duality of sources from which international law and national law draw their validity:[85] If both international law and national law are to be considered valid, they necessarily share the same basic norm.[86]

[77] In 1920, Kelsen was already arguing that treaties could confer direct international legal rights and obligations on individuals and that there was, therefore, no basis for questioning the validity of Article 228(2) of the Versailles Treaty. Hans Kelsen, 'Der völkerrechtliche Strafanspruch wegen völkerrechtswidriger Kriegshandlungen', *Neue Freie Presse Wien* (1920b), 8 September, 3–4. See further Section 6.1.2. See also von Bernstorff (n 53) 146–8.

[78] To Kelsen, the principal difference between states and individuals is that only states are competent to enter into treaties and create customary law. Kelsen, 'Theorie Générale du Droit International Public—Problèmes Choisis' (n 73), 268ff. See also von Bernstorff (n 53) 147.

[79] See further Kelsen (n 56) 248–52. See also Portmann (n 11) 196.

[80] Kelsen (n 73) 170 (author's translation). See similarly Giorgio Balladore Pallieri, 'Le dottrine de Hans Kelsen e il problema dei rapporti fra diritto interno e diritto internazionale', 27 *Rivista di diritto internazionale* (1935) 24, 74.

[81] See Section 1.3.2.

[82] Kelsen (n 24) 123, and Hans Kelsen, *Principles of International Law* (2nd edn, revised and edited by Robert W. Tucker, Holt, Rinehart and Winston, Inc., 1966) 569. See also Hart's critique of Kelsen's postulate: H. L. A. Hart, 'Kelsen's Doctrine of the Unity of Law', in Stanley L. Paulson and Bonnie L. Paulson (eds), *Normativity and Norms. Critical Perspectives on Kelsenian Themes* (Clarendon Press, 1998, first published 1968) 558, 564ff.

[83] Kelsen (n 57) 329. [84] Kelsen (n 24) 152.

[85] Ibid, 136ff. See also Kelsen, *Principles of International Law* (n 82) 553ff, 571, and 575, and Kelsen (n 56) 363ff. See further J. G. Starke, 'Monism and Dualism in the Theory of International Law', 17 *BYBIL* (1936) 66, 74, and von Bernstorff (n 53) 70–3.

[86] Kelsen (n 57) 328–30. See further von Bernstorff (n 53) 81.

Although the primacy of international law over national law was an essential part of his political project, Kelsen insisted on the *Wahlhypothese*, that is, that it would be theoretically viable to designate both international law and national law as the subordinated legal order.[87] The choice between the two possible monistic constructions of the relationship between international law and national law turns solely upon non-legal, political considerations, and the decision thus lies beyond the sphere of the science of law: 'He who treasures the idea of the sovereignty of his state ... will prefer the primacy of national legal order. He who values the idea of a legal organization of the world, will prefer the primacy of international law.'[88] In this way, Kelsen's ambition of eliminating all subjective considerations from 'the science of law' paradoxically required him to acknowledge that the fundamental question of primacy is inherently subjective.[89] To maintain his claim for objectivity, Kelsen demanded that each legal scholar openly made their choice of whether international law or national law was the primary legal order.[90]

As mentioned, Kelsen favoured a unitary legal system that placed international law above national law. Following his 'primacy thesis' the State legal order was to be perceived as a suborder, delegated by international law. In support of this claim, Kelsen invoked 'the principle of effectiveness', which he understood as a positive norm of customary international law forming the basis for the validity of domestic legal systems:

> This means that a norm of general international law empowers an individual or a group of individuals to establish and apply, on the basis of an efficacious constitution, a normative coercive system, thereby legitimizing this coercive system as the valid legal system for the territorial and temporal sphere of its actual efficacy, and legitimizing the system's community as a state in terms of international law.[91]

Proclaiming systemic unity of all law with the primacy of international law over national law naturally raises the issue of conflicts between international legal norms and national legal norms. While as a matter of principle the early Kelsen denied the possibility of conflicts between norms on different levels of the norm pyramid,[92] he later found:

> Upon closer examination, however, it becomes manifest that what is regarded as conflict between the norms of international law and the norms of national law is not a conflict of

87 Kelsen (n 57) 332ff.

88 Here cited from Kelsen, *The Pure Theory of Law* (n 57) 346. Josef L. Kunz, *Völkerrechtswissenschaft und reine Rechtslehre* (F. Deuticke, 1923) 80–3. The *Wahlhypothese* exposed Kelsen to severe criticism from his disciples. See, for example, Josef L. Kunz, 'La Primauté de droit des gens', VI *Revue de droit international et de législation comparée* (3rd Series, 1925) 556, and Alfred Verdross, *Die Einheit des rechtlichen Weltbildes* (Verlag von J. C. B. Mohr, 1923) 134. See also Starke (n 85) 75–8.

89 See also von Bernstorff (n 53) 246.

90 Kelsen (n 24) 317. See also Hans Kelsen, 'Sovereignty', in Stanley L. Paulson and Bonnie L. Paulson (eds), *Normativity and Norms. Critical Perspectives on Kelsenian Themes* (Clarendon Press, 1998, first published in 1962, reprinted in translation) 535.

91 Kelsen, 'Sovereignty' (n 90) 529. See also, for example, Kelsen (n 56) 351. For critique of Kelsen's argument, which HLA Hart labelled 'his central mistake', see Hart (n 82) 560–3.

92 Kelsen (n 24) 113.

norms at all; that the situation can be described in rules of law which in no way contradict each other.[93]

In other words, the late Kelsen argued—based on the assertion that an unlawful norm remains valid until it has been annulled—that norm conflicts between international law and national law do not challenge the notion of systemic unity.[94] As to the distinction between international law and national law, Kelsen looked exclusively to the source of the norm in question:

> there remains a certain truth in the statement that international law is 'interstate' law, whereas national law is, so to speak, one-state law. But ... this differentiation does not concern the subject matter; it concerns the creation of international and national law. Whereas national law is created by acts of one state alone (or by acts which are not acts of state), international law is usually created by cooperation of two or more states. This holds true of customary international law as well as of conventional international law.[95]

Kelsen's acceptance of the idea that international legal norms are indeed separable from national legal norms given the different nature of their respective sources makes it difficult to appreciate the added value of upholding the notion of necessary unity.[96] Arguably, the only implication of Kelsen's theory of monism is the prevalence of international law over domestic law.

While rights and obligations of individuals directly under international law were a key component in Kelsen's vision of a legalized world order,[97] the 'a posteriori' conception of international legal personality is not a result of his political project. But, importantly, it is also not a part of the theoretical underpinning of the postulated unity between international law and national law. Rather, Kelsen's conception of international legal personality is a consequence of the exclusion of non-legal elements from the objective 'science of law' and the notion that all law by definition governs human behaviour. He only discusses international legal personality pertaining to the possible material content of a norm of international law, and not as a deciding element in the determination of the legal system to which the norm belongs. Indeed, he argues as a part of the *Wahlhypothese* that the content of

[93] Here cited from Kelsen, *Pure Theory of Law* (n 57) 330. See also Hart (n 82) 554.

[94] Kelsen (n 57) 342. See also ibid, 331, and Hans Kelsen, 'Les Rapports de Système entre le Droit Interne et le Droit International Public', 14 *Recueil des Cours* (1926-IV) 227, 314–15, and see further Alfred Rub, *Hans Kelsens Völkerrechtslehre—Versuch einer Würdigung* (Schulthess Polygraphischer Verlag, 1995) 427.

[95] Kelsen, *Principles of International Law* (n 82) 555. See also ibid, 575.

[96] Kelsen himself seems to have changed his mind about this late in his life: 'The realization that a conflict of norms is not a logical contradiction destroys my thesis that the *uniqueness* of the normative valid order for a given sphere is a consequence of the principle of *unity* "whose negative criterion is the impossibility of logical contradictions."' Hans Kelsen, *General Theory of Norms* (translated by Michael Hartney, OUP, 1991) 394. See further Jörg Kammerhofer, 'Kelsen—Which Kelsen? A Reapplication of Kelsen's Pure Theory to International Law', 22 *LJIL* (2009) 225, 241.

[97] See, for example, Hans Kelsen, 'Die Technik des Völkerrechts und die Organisation des Friedens', 14 *Zeitschrift für öffentliches Recht* (1934) 240.

international as well as national norms remains entirely unaffected by the choice of either body of norms as the primary.[98] The 'a posteriori' conception of international legal personality is therefore not inherently incompatible with the dualistic (or pluralistic) approach to the relationship between the international legal system and national legal systems endorsed by most twenty-first-century scholars as the better reflection of positive law.[99]

Few contemporary scholars overtly subscribe to Kelsen's 'a posteriori' conception,[100] even though they effectively endorse the idea that the international legal personality of an entity is solely a question of interpretation.[101] There may be several reasons why Kelsen's conception of international legal personality has not caught on. Possibly most international legal scholars disapprove of his 'obsessive search for scientific method' as Martti Koskenniemi puts it in *The Gentle Civilizer of Nations*: 'Most international lawyers today know of this work and many continue to admire him as legal theorist. The admiration is almost without exception tempered by the rejoinder that, of course, it was just theory and therefore could never be realized in practice.' [102]

Another possibility is that scholars believe Kelsen's 'a posteriori' conception of international legal personality to be inseparably connected to his monistic construction of the relationship between international law and domestic law. For example, Jean d'Aspremont states: 'posivitist accounts of the position in international law are not always uniform. This is well illustrated by Kelsenian approaches which provide a unique understanding at odds with mainstream positivism, for the monism defended by Kelsen allows one to grant non-state actors a clear legal status under international law.[103]

This, however, seems to be a misconstruction of Kelsen's argument since Kelsen does not link the concept of personality to the question of the relationship between international law and domestic law. Indeed, the only conception of international legal personality to make that connection is the orthodox 'States-only' conception.

[98] See, for example, Kelsen, 'Sovereignty' (n 90) 531.

[99] See further Section 1.3.2.

[100] Jörg Kammerhofer is a prominent exception. As regards the role of non-state actors in international law, he finds: 'The Pure Theory of Law can on this issue—as on many others—be seen as the theoretical solution closest to the positive law in force.' See, for example, Jörg Kammerhofer, 'Non-state actors from the perspective of the Pure Theory of Law', in Jean d'Aspremont, *Participants in the International Legal System: Multiple perspectives on non-state actors in international law* (Routledge, 2011) 54, 60.

[101] See, for example, Jean d'Aspremont, 'International Law-Making by Non-State Actors: Changing the Model or Putting the Phenomenon into Perspective?', in Math Noortmann and Cedric Ryngaert (eds), *Non-State Actor Dynamics in International Law—From Law-Takers to Law-Makers* (Ashgate, 2010) 171, 172.

[102] Martti Koskenniemi, *The Gentle Civilizer of Nations—The Rise and Fall of International Law 1870–1960* (CUP, 2001) 249.

[103] d'Aspremont (n 101) 173.

2.4 'The Individual Human Being Is the Ultimate International Legal Person'

Kelsen was far from the only scholar to oppose orthodox positivism and the 'States-only' conception of international legal personality in the early twentieth century. Instead of the State, scholars including Georges Scelle, James Leslie Brierly, and Nicolas Politis placed the individual human being at the centre of the international legal system. Although the approaches to international law and, in particular, to the role ascribed to States varied among these critics of the 'States-only' conception, they shared the proposition that individuals existed as international legal persons a priori, independent of any manifestation of State will.[104] Politis asserted that 'international law is in a period of transition: It is no longer exclusively the law of States, but not yet completely that of human beings.'[105] Taking a step further, Scelle perceived of States as a fiction and discarded them as international legal persons altogether.[106] He famously found: 'Only individuals are the subject of law in international law.'[107]

As exemplified in Chapter 6 on international criminal law and Chapter 7 on international human rights law, Hersch Lauterpacht was probably the most influential international legal scholar in the interwar period and especially in the aftermath of the Second World War. The following outline will take his 'individualistic' conception of international legal personality, which conjoins positivist and natural law thinking, as its point of departure.

Like Kelsen,[108] Lauterpacht explicitly opposed the 'orthodox positivist doctrine' concerning international legal personality:[109]

104 See also Portmann (n 11) 126–7.

105 Nicolas Politis, *Les Nouvelles Tendances du Droit International* (Librairie Hachette, 1927) 91 (author's translation). See also Maurice Bourquin, 'Règles Générales du Droit de la Paix' 35 *Recueil des Cours* (1931-I) 5, 46–7.

106 Accordingly, Scelle spoke strongly against the fiction in diplomatic protection. See Georges Scelle, 'Régles Générales du Droit de la Paix', 46 *Recueil des Cours* (1933-IV) 327, 661. See further Section 3.3.1. See also Section 6.2.2 as to Scelle's participation in the ILC's formulation of the Nuremberg Principles.

107 Georges Scelle, *Précis de Droit des Gens, Principes et Systématique* (Librairie du Recueil Sirey, 1932a), vol. I, 42 (author's translation). See further Georges Scelle, 'Some Reflections on Juridical Personality in International Law', in George A. Lipsky (ed.), *Law and Politics in the World Community* (University of California Press, 1953) 49–58. See also James Leslie Brierly, 'Règles Générales du Droit de la Paix' 58 *Recueil des Cours* (1936-IV) 5, 47–8, and James Leslie Brierly, 'The Basis of Obligation in International Law', in Hersch Lauterpacht and C. H. M. Waldock (eds), *The Basis of Obligation in International Law and Other Papers by the Late James Leslie Brierly* (Clarendon Press, 1958) 51ff. See further Nijman (n 8) 134ff. Kelsen criticized Scelle's individualistic conception of international legal personality for making 'a very similar mistake' to that of orthodox positivists (author's translation). See Hans Kelsen, 'Georges Scelle', in Hans Kelsen, Kurt Ringhofer and Robert Walter (eds), *Auseinandersetzungen zur Reinen Rechtslehre, kritische Bemerkungen zu Georges Scelle und Michel Virally* (Springer, 1987) 95.

108 See further Nijman (n 8) 298–9, Koskenniemi (n 102) 356–7, and Iain G. M. Scobbie, 'The Theorist as Judge: Hersch Lauterpacht's Concept of the International Judicial Function', 8 *EJIL* (1997) 264, 269.

109 Hersch Lauterpacht, 'The Subjects of the Law of Nations', reprinted in Elihu Lauterpacht (ed.), *International Law—Being the Collected Papers of Hersch Lauterpacht*, vol. II (1975, first published in two parts in 1947 and 1948) 487, 489–91, and almost identically Hersch Lauterpacht, *International Law and Human Rights* (Stevens & Sons, 1950) 6–9.

There is no rule of international law which precludes individuals and bodies other than States from acquiring direct rights under customary or conventional international law and, to that extent, becoming subjects of the Law of Nations. The question is largely one of ascertaining what is the intention of States in each particular case.[110]

Lauterpacht also followed Kelsen in his perception of the individual as the 'ultimate unit and end of all law, national or international'. But rather than a legal phenomenon, Lauterpacht regarded the State as a functional entity with the sole purpose of safeguarding the interests of the individuals it is composed of.[111] Moreover, Lauterpacht did not subscribe to Kelsen's idea of a hypothetical *Grundnorm* as the foundation of all law. To the contrary, Lauterpacht criticized Kelsen's dismissal of natural law as a source of law: '[Kelsen] ought to admit—as every positivist lawyer ought to do in justice to himself—that positive law has always incorporated and does incorporate ideas of natural law and justice.'[112]

Lauterpacht believed that the final object of all law is 'the effective recognition and protection of "the dignity and worth of the human person" and the development of the human personality'.[113] Like his idea about the purpose of States, Lauterpacht's conception of international legal personality is thus inherently normative as he claimed that the recognition of the individual as a subject of international law is 'based on the assumption of some fundamental and inalienable rights of man'.[114]

To Lauterpacht, the recognition of a direct relationship between the individual and international law was 'an essential stage in the progression of the international community towards the goal of federal integration', and, notably, so was the construction of international law and domestic law as one unified legal system. Referring to the notion of monism 'established by Kelsen by means of juristic analysis' and developed by Scelle 'on both a sociological and an *a priori* basis',[115] Lauterpacht attempted to 'deduce the monistic view' from the practice of States and judicial bodies.

[110] Lauterpacht, 'The Subjects of the Law of Nations' (n 109) 526.

[111] In contrast to Scelle among others, Lauterpacht did not consider human beings to be the exclusive subjects of international law: 'it must be borne in mind that the State is a corporation, a juristic person, and that reasons of convenience and justice require that, in the normal course of affairs, the collective entity of the State should be the subject of responsibility.' Lauterpacht, 'The Subjects of the Law of Nations' (n 109) 521.

[112] Lauterpacht (n 72) 429. In Lauterpacht's view, the 'general principles of law recognized by civilized nations' referred to in Article 38(1)(c) of the ICJ Statute are to be understood as a manifestation of the inclusion of natural law principles as a source of international law. Hersch Lauterpacht, 'International Law—The General Part' (previously unpublished), printed in Elihu Lauterpacht (ed.), *International Law—Being the Collected Papers of Hersch Lauterpacht*, vol. I (CUP, 1970a) 5, 69. See further Iain Scobbie, 'Legal Theory as a Source of International Law: Institutional Facts and the Identification of International Law', in Samantha Besson and Jean d'Aspremont (eds) *The Oxford Handbook on the Sources of International Law* (OUP, 2017) 493, 506–7.

[113] Lauterpacht, 'International Law—The General Part' (n 112) 149.

[114] Ibid.

[115] Hersch Lauterpacht, 'General Rules of the Law of Peace' (previously unpublished), printed in Elihu Lauterpacht (ed.), *International Law—Being the Collected Papers of Hersch Lauterpacht*, Vol. I (CUP, 1970b) 179, 214. As to Scelle's idea of 'fédéralisme normatif', see Georges Scelle, 'La Doctrine de Duguit et les Fondements du Droit des Gens' 1–2 *Archives de Philosophie du Droit et de Sociologie Juridique* (Librairie du Recueil Sirey, 1932b) 83, 108.

> Just as international law is at present an imperfect law in a stage of transition to true law, so its monistic structure is not absolute and thoroughgoing. It is a monism qualified by dualistic exceptions and contradictions.... It is therefore necessary to admit that, so far as positive law is concerned, monism, while providing a working instrument of scientific knowledge for international law as a whole and while providing an adequate and the only possible basis for its development to true law, often breaks down and yields to reality of a dualistic nature.[116]

In sum, Lauterpacht believed that the development of international law into 'true law' presupposed the recognition of the international legal personality of individuals on the basis of certain inherent rights and duties, and a monistic construction of the relationship between international law and domestic law.[117] As long as these improvements have not been realized, however, Lauterpacht underlined that 'it is important to bear in mind that the assertion of conflicting municipal law over international law is merely a rule of municipal law .... From the point of view of international law it constitutes an illegality and gives rise to State responsibility.'[118] While Lauterpacht was thus a dedicated monist *de lege ferenda*, he acknowledged that positive law at the time supported a dualistic relationship between international law and domestic law.[119]

It is significant that Lauterpacht, like Kelsen, did not tie the matter of subjectivity in international law to the question of the separation of legal orders. This link is only drawn by scholars who endorse the orthodox 'States-only' conception of international legal personality. As exemplified in what follows, however, some present-day advocates of the 'individualistic' conception mistakenly assume that a dualistic construction of the relationship between international law and national law necessarily presupposes the orthodox 'States-only' conception of international legal personality.

In contemporary scholarship, the 'individualistic' conception of international legal personality is apparent in the extensive academic debate on 'the constitutionalization of international law'. Jean d'Aspremont is no doubt right in noting that 'international legal constitutionalism is too rich a stream to be considered a uniform approach to international law'.[120] The ambition here is by no means to provide a detailed account of the abundant scholarship discussing various aspects of this trend in international legal thinking. For example, neither the 'hierarchy of norms' perspective relating to the concepts of *jus cogens* and *erga omnes*[121] nor

[116] Lauterpacht (n 115) 179, 214. See also ibid, 228–30.

[117] See further Lauterpacht, 'International Law—The General Part' (n 112) 9–50.

[118] Lauterpacht (n 115) 230.

[119] Lauterpacht would presumably be disappointed to see that positive law developments have only reinforced dualism since his day. See further Section 1.3.2. See also James Crawford, 'Chance, Order, Change: The Course of International Law', 365 *Recueil des Cours* (2013) 9, 159.

[120] Jean d'Aspremont, *Formalism and the Sources of International Law* (OUP, 2011b) 77. See also Wouter Werner, 'The never-ending closure: constitutionalism and international law', in Nicholas Tsagourias (ed.), *Transnational Constitutionalism* (CUP, 2007) 329.

[121] See, for example, Erika de Wet, 'The International Constitutional Order', 55 *ICLQ* (2006) 51, 57–63, Andreas Paulus, 'The International Legal System as a Constitution', in Jeffrey L. Dunoff and Joel P. Trachtman (eds), *Ruling the World? Constitutionalism, International Law and Global Governance* (CUP, 2009) 69, 88ff, and Werner (n 120) 334–7. Notably, it is a common notion that Alfred Verdross is 'the ancestor of global constitutionalism'. See Jan Klabbers, Anne Peters, and Geir Ulfstein, *The Constitutionalization of International Law* (OUP, 2009) 184. See also d'Aspremont (n 120) 80–1. Verdross was among the first international legal scholars to promote the idea of *jus cogens* norms

the question whether the UN Charter may be said to function as a constitution for the international community[122] are of primary interest for present purposes. Rather, the focus of the subsequent pages is limited to the substantive perspective of international legal constitutionalism pertaining specifically to individual rights and obligations.[123] First, it is discussed how present-day scholars build on Lauterpacht's 'individualistic' conception of international legal personality, in particular the normative elements of his argument, to support their claim that international law is in a process of constitutionalization. Second, it is demonstrated that some scholars advocating constitutionalism base their claims on the assumption that the dualistic approach to the relationship between international law and national law is inherently tied to the orthodox 'States-only' conception.

Anne Peters, currently a leading international legal constitutionalist, explicitly follows Lauterpacht in her perception of the State as a functional entity[124] and individuals as the ultimate subjects of international law. But she discards natural law thinking: 'Today, the re-introduction of the individual should not come as natural law in disguise, but should rely on other considerations, and I deem constitutionalist considerations a useful starting point.' According to Peters, 'the ultimate normative source of international law is—from a constitutionalist perspective—humanity, not sovereignty.'[125]

Peters follows a line of international legal constitutionalists, who have gradually moved away from Lauterpacht's reliance on natural law. Essentially, their claim is

embodying an international constitution. See for example, Alfred Verdross, 'Forbidden Treaties in International Law', 31 *AJIL* (1937) 571. See also Bruno Simma, 'The Contribution of Alfred Verdross to the Theory of International Law', 6 *EJIL* (1995) 33. However, Verdross did not subscribe to the idea of the individual as the ultimate subject of international law. In his view the rules on international legal personality implied a fundamental presumption for States. See Alfred Verdross, *Völkerrecht* (1st edn, Springer, 1937) 66–9. See also Portmann (n 11) 149–51.

[122] See, for example, Bardo Fassbender, *The United Nations Charter as the Constitution of the International Community* (Brill, 2009a), Bardo Fassbender, 'Rediscovering a Forgotten Constitution: Notes on the Place of the UN Charter in the International Legal Order', in Jeffrey L. Dunoff and Joel P. Trachtman (eds), *Ruling the World? Constitutionalism, International Law and Global Governance* (CUP, 2009b), Bruno Simma, 'From bilateralism to community interest in international law', 250 *Recueil des Cours* (1994) 217, 256–84, Michael W. Doyle, 'The UN Charter—A Global Constitution?', in Jeffrey L. Dunoff and Joel P. Trachtman (eds), *Ruling the World? Constitutionalism, International Law and Global Governance* (CUP, 2009), 113–32, Paulus (n 121) 69, 76ff, Erika De Wet, 'The Constitutionalization of Public International Law', in Michel Rosenfeld and András Sajó (eds), *The Oxford Handbook of Comparative Constitutional Law* (OUP, 2012) 1209, 1224ff.

[123] The understanding of the ECHR and EU law in constitutionalist terms is discussed in Section 7.2.3 (the ECHR) and Section 8.3.2 (EU law).

[124] See Klabbers, Peters, and Ulfstein (n 121) 179: 'From a constitutionalist perspective ... states—as international legal subjects—are constituted by international law.' See also ibid, 201, with explicit reference to Lauterpacht's work. See further Thomas Kleinlein, 'Non-state actors from an international constitutionalist perspective: participation matters!', in Jean d'Aspremont (ed.), *Participants in the International Legal System* (Routledge, 2011) 41, 43.

[125] Klabbers, Peters, and Ulfstein (n 121) 155. See also Anne Peters, 'Are we Moving towards Constitutionalization of the World Community?', in Antonio Cassese (ed.), *Realizing Utopia* (OUP, 2012) 118, 120–1.

that positive law developments since the Second World War have progressively realized Lauterpacht's vision, rendering arguments based on natural law superfluous.[126]

In his 1994 General Course at the Hague Academy of International Law, for example, Bruno Simma described the post-Second World War developments in international law as a transition from 'bilateralism' to 'community interest' understood as 'a consensus according to which respect for certain fundamental values is not to be left to the free disposition of States individually or *inter se* but is recognized and sanctioned by international law as a matter of concern to all States.'[127] Simma conceded, however, that the notion of 'international community' primarily fulfils 'an ideological function', and that 'a truly worldwide sense of community might be present only with a few international civil servants or experts or, more importantly, with non-governmental organizations active on a global level.'[128] Similarly, Christian Tomuschat contended in his General Course in 1999 that the international legal system had been transformed through the adoption of core values such as democracy, good governance, and human rights.[129]

According to Thomas Kleinlein, international constitutionalism 'is not so much a public international legal theory of its own, but a particular doctrinal approach within the positivist mainstream of public international legal scholarship.'[130] Nevertheless, while international legal constitutionalism maintains the distinction between 'the law as it is' and 'the law as it should be', it clearly frames the developments in international law according to a particular normative agenda, and an important element of this agenda is to promote the position of the individual.[131] As Wouter Werner puts it: 'international constitutionalism aims to bring about what it describes as existing: a legal order that integrates states, fosters international cooperation, checks the exercise of political power and unifies a global community.'[132]

Peters's argument is explicitly normative insofar as she asserts that the involvement of individuals in international lawmaking must be advanced in a process of democratization of the global legal order.[133] First and foremost, however, she claims *de lege lata* that practice in numerous areas of international law manifests a human right to international legal personality, understood as 'a right to have rights'.[134] Peters

[126] The relationship between the 'individualist' and the 'a posteriori' conceptions of international legal personality in contemporary scholarship is discussed further in Section 2.6.

[127] Bruno Simma, 'From bilateralism to community interest in international law', 250 *Recueil des Cours* (1994) 217, 233.

[128] Ibid, 248. See further Werner (n 120) 332 and 348.

[129] Christian Tomuschat, 'International Law: Ensuring the Survival of Mankind on the Eve of a New Century', 281 *Recueil des Cours* (1999) 9, 70. See also Werner (n 120) 70. See further Armin von Bogdandy, 'Constitutionalism in International Law: Comment on a Proposal from Germany', 47 *HILJ* (2006) 223, and Richard Collins, 'Constitutionalism as Liberal-Juridical Consciousness: Echoes from International Law's Past', 22 *LJIL* (2009) 251.

[130] Kleinlein (n 124) 43. See also Collins (n 129) 265ff.

[131] See also Werner (n 120) 330.

[132] Ibid, 338. See also 342 and 366.

[133] See Klabbers, Peters, and Ulfstein (n 121) 159–61 and 236–341.

[134] On a similar note, Antônio Augusto Cançado Trindade argues that humankind as such is now a subject of international law. A principal element of Trindade's argument is that individuals now hold a *jus cogens* right to access to justice. See further Antônio Augusto Cançado Trindade, 'International Law for Humankind: Towards a New Jus Gentium—Part I' 316 *Recueil des Cours* (2005) 9, 318–33, and Antônio Augusto Cançado Trindade, *The Access of Individuals to International Justice* (OUP,

uses the term 'international individual right', which she states 'is meant to encode the *primary* international legal personality of the individual.'[135] The 'international individual right', she finds, is both a part of customary international law[136] and a general principle of law within the meaning of Article 38(1)(c) of the ICJ Statute:

> The general principles of law within the meaning of Article 38(1)(c) of the ICJ Statute may have the content of natural law, but the elements must necessarily have been juridified (formalized) in order to be considered international law.... [T]his formalization occurred by recognizing the legal personality of the individual in domestic law. The original legal personality of the individual thus appears to be a kind of positivized natural law.[137]

In essence, Peters contends that the concept of 'personality' in international law now functions as a notion of positive law, in the way it is applied in many domestic legal systems. She openly draws inspiration from the development of *subjektives öffentliches Recht* in German domestic law.[138] Peters thereby takes international legal constitutionalism's firm embeddedness in domestic constitutionalist traditions a step further,[139] while explicitly presupposing the existence of multiple legal orders. In fact, neither Peters nor other constitutionalist scholars appear to maintain Lauterpacht's advocacy for monism.[140] Along similar lines, however, Peters

2011) 199ff. Cançado Trindade's argument is palpably manifested in his work as ICJ judge. See, for example, *Jurisdictional Immunities of the State (Germany v. Italy: Greece intervening)* (Judgment) [2012] ICJ Rep 99, *Dissenting Opinion of Judge Cançado Trindade*, and *Ahmadou Sadio Diallo (Republic of Guinea v. Democratic Republic of the Congo)* (Compensation, judgment) [2012] ICJ Rep 324, *Separate Opinion of Judge Cançado Trindade*. See also Rafael Domingo, 'Gaius, Vattel and the New Global Law Paradigm', 22 *EJIL* (2011) 627.

[135] Anne Peters, *Beyond Human Rights—The Legal Status of the Individual in International Law* (CUP, 2016) 526 (emphasis in original).

[136] According to Peters, this right is enshrined in Article 6 of the Universal Declaration of Human Rights and Article 16(2) of the International Covenant on Civil and Political Rights (hereafter ICCPR). See ibid, 431 and 551, and Klabbers, Peters, and Ulfstein (n 121) 158–9. See also Nijman (n 8) 466. Notably, Peters refers to Rosalyn Higgins, *Problem and Process—International Law and How We Use It* (Clarendon Press, 1994) 53–4, who in turn refers to Lauterpacht:

> Lauterpacht spoke of rights enuring to the benefit of an individual under an *international instrument*. My suggestion is that the principle is equally applicable without the intervention of an international instrument, and that individuals *can* be the beneficiaries of international law rights which fall upon states to perform as a matter of general international law.

It seems a rather wide interpretation to infer from this quote that Higgins endorses the notion of a customary right to international legal personality. See Peters (n 135) 419. Rather, Higgins's argument simply appears to be that there are no conceptual impediments to idea of individuals as subjects of customary international law as well as treaties.

[137] Peters (n 135) 430. See also ibid, 434, and Klabbers, Peters, and Ulfstein (n 121) 157. On the 'undeniable kinship' between constitutionalism and natural law theory, see d'Aspremont (n 120) 81. Notably, Jörg Kammerhofer criticizes constitutionalist scholars for promoting 'a modern form of natural law theory, hidden under positivist rhetoric.' Kammerhofer (n 60) 151. See also Jörg Kammerhofer, 'Constitutionalism and the Myth of Practical Reason: Kelsenian Responses to Methodological Problems' 23 *LJIL* (2010b) 723, 724.

[138] Peters (n 135) 553. See also von Bogdandy (n 129).

[139] See further Werner (n 120) 353.

[140] Peters's understanding of the international legal personality of the individual is, she states, 'analytically independent of the correctness of monist, dualist, or pluralist theory.' Peters (n 135) 59. See also Anne Peters, 'Supremacy Lost: International Law Meets Domestic Constitutional Law', 3 *Vienna Journal on International Constitutional Law* (2009) 170, and Anne Peters, 'The Globalization of State

has argued for a 'nonformalist, substance-oriented' approach to the relationship between legal orders:

[C]onflicts between international law and constitutional law should be resolved by balancing in the concrete case, not on the basis of a normative hierarchy of the norms' expression in international law as opposed to domestic law.... [F]undamental rights guarantees should prevail over less important norms (independent of their locus and type of codification). The fundamental idea is that what counts is the substance, not the formal category of conflicting norms.[141]

It is noteworthy that a number of contemporary constitutionalists, including towering figures such as Antonio Cassese, build their reasoning on the orthodox positivist notion that the concept of international legal personality is inextricably linked to the distinction between international law and domestic law. In his textbook on international law, Cassese clearly infers that direct individual rights and obligations under international law are incompatible with a dualistic construction of the relationship between international law and national law: 'the dualistic approach did reflect the legal reality, particularly in the nineteenth and the first half of the twentieth century, although it was unable convincingly to explain some exceptional phenomena, such as the fact that a few international rules directly imposed obligations on individuals.'[142]

By the same token, Erika De Wet implies that dualism presupposes the orthodox 'States-only' conception of international legal personality when she claims that '[t]he classic dualist perspective ... does not accept that international law can reach individuals directly, without having first been incorporated by means of a statute.'[143] Likewise, Christian Walter contends:

A concept of international law which puts less emphasis on the role of international legal personality necessarily reduces the importance of the divide between national and international law.... The concept is certainly incompatible with strict dualist positions, since it implies that international law may directly grant rights to individuals or impose duties upon them.[144]

Constitutions', in Janne Nijman and André Nollkaemper (eds), *New Perspectives on the Divide Between National and International Law* (OUP, 2007) 251, 306.

[141] Anne Peters, 'Let Not Triepel Triumph—How to Make the Best Out of Sentenza No. 238 of the Italian Constitutional Court for a Global Legal Order', EJILTalk! Blogpost, 22 December 2014 (available at https://www.ejiltalk.org/let-not-triepel-triumph-how-to-make-the-best-out-of-sentenza-no-238-of-the-italian-constitutional-court-for-a-global-legal-order-part-i/, accessed 21 January 2018). See also Peters (n 135) 425, 496, and 519.

[142] Antonio Cassese, *International Law* (2nd edn, OUP, 2005) 216. Cassese mentions the rules prohibiting piracy as the obvious example of pre-Second World War international legal obligations imposed directly on individuals. However, as is discussed in Section 6.1.1, piracy was not criminalized in international law. The customary international rules on piracy merely granted all states jurisdiction to try suspected pirates according to their respective domestic criminal codes.

[143] Erika De Wet, 'The Constitutionalization of Public International Law', in Michel Rosenfeld and András Sajó (eds), *The Oxford Handbook of Comparative Constitutional Law* (OUP, 2012) 1209, 1211. The same holds true for Andreas Paulus' argument that 'constitutionalization in the sense of a direct effect of international law on the individual is not fully realized.' Paulus (n 121) 105. See also Andreas L. Paulus, 'The Emergence of the International Community and the Divide between International and Domestic Law', in Janne Nijman and André Nollkaemper (eds), *New Perspectives on the Divide Between National and International Law* (OUP, 2007) 216, 229–34.

[144] Christian Walter, 'International Law in a Process of Constitutionalization', in Janne Nijman and André Nollkaemper (eds), *New Perspectives on the Divide Between National and International Law*

Ironically, constitutionalist scholars like Cassese, De Wet, and Walter end up partly endorsing the very theoretical position they aim to oppose by upholding the link between the concept of international legal personality and the question of the relationship between international law and national law. In essence, they treat the orthodox 'States-only' conception not just as an opposing theoretical position, but indeed a correct account of positive international law. This misconstruction has significant ramifications for the way in which these scholars conceive positive norms of international law that directly govern individuals and other non-State entities. In Chapter 5 on international humanitarian law, for example, it is illustrated how Cassese employs the 'States-only' conception of international legal personality in his argument that Additional Protocol II to the Geneva Conventions is only binding on armed opposition groups upon their assent.

As demonstrated in the following section, however, international constitutionalists are not the only scholars to oppose the orthodox 'States-only' conception of international legal personality as a general position, but nonetheless endorse it by implication.

2.5 'There Are No International Legal Persons—Only Participants in the International Legal Order'

The 'participant' conception of international legal personality originates from the New Haven School of policy-oriented jurisprudence developed primarily by Myres S. McDougal and Harold D. Lasswell.[145] In their definition, international law is not a set of rules, but a process of authoritative decision-making.[146] No legal norms exclude or include any entities from this process a priori. The turning point is simply the de facto power exercised by the entity in question. Thus, a participant in the international legal system is an entity taking part in an authoritative decision-making process of an international nature:

> The *participants* in any decision process include those formally endowed with decision competence, such as executives, legislators and judges, and all those other actors who, though not endowed with formal competence, may nonetheless play important roles in influencing

(OUP, 2007) 191, 204–5. See also 207. See further Kleinlein (n 124) 46–7. Remarkably, one of the few present-day proponents of the orthodox 'States-only' conception of international legal personality, Arangio-Ruiz, makes the inverse claim that '"constitutional" concepts of international law are just different, less abstract, forms of monism.' Arangio-Ruiz, 'International Law and Interindividual Law' (n 33) 16. See further Section 2.2.

[145] See principally Harold D. Lasswell and Myres S. McDougal's two-volume treatise *Jurisprudence for a Free Society: Studies in Law, Science and Policy* (Martinus Nijhoff, 1992). See further Anthony D'Amato, 'Non-state actors from the perspective of the policy oriented school: Power, law, actors and the view from New Haven', in Jean d'Aspremont (ed.), *Participants in the International Legal System: Multiple perspectives on non-state actors in international law* (Routledge, 2011) 64, 66–7.

[146] See further W. Michael Reisman, Siegfried Wiessner, and Andrew R. Willard, 'The New Haven School: A Brief Introduction', 32 *Yale Journal of International Law* (2007) 575.

decision outcomes. In international decision, this means examining, in addition to formal international organizations, state officials, non-governmental organizations, pressure groups, interest groups, gangs, and individuals, who act on behalf of other participants and on their own.[147]

The actual participants in international decision-making processes may be deemed international legal persons, although the notion of international legal personality is largely avoided.[148] Given the 'law as process' approach, a precise legal definition of personhood in international law is naturally less important.[149] As Lung-chu Chen has recently explained: 'The meaningful inquiry concerns not what persons are technically subjects and objects for a body of static rules but who actually participates in the global process of decision making and who performs what functions.'[150]

In the European context, the 'participant' conception of international legal personality is commonly ascribed to the work of Rosalyn Higgins, who famously rejected the positivist subject–object dichotomy in international law by stating that '[w]e have erected an intellectual prison of our own choosing and then declared it to be an unalterable constraint.'[151] Specifically pertaining to individuals, Higgins has argued that:

> the topics of minimum standard of treatment of aliens, requirements as to the conduct of hostilities and human rights, are not simply exceptions conceded by historical chance within a system of rules that operates as between states. Rather, they are simply part and parcel of the fabric of international law, representing claims that are naturally made by individual participants in contradistinction to state-participants.[152]

The New Haven School's focus on processes of authoritative decision-making instead of rules leads to a rejection of the monistic as well as dualistic construction of the relationship between international law and national law: '[A]ll the theories,

[147] Ibid, 578, emphasis in original. See further Jordan J. Paust, 'The Reality of Private Rights, Duties and Participation in the International Legal Process', 25 *Michigan Journal of International Law* (2003–4) 1229.

[148] See further Portmann (n 11) 208.

[149] See also Janne E. Nijman, 'Non-State Actors and the International Rule of Law: Revisiting the "Realist Theory" of International Legal Personality', in Math Noortmann and Cedric Ryngaert (eds), *Non-State Actor Dynamics in International Law* (Ashgate, 2010) 91, 105.

[150] Lung-chu Chen, *An Introduction to Contemporary International Law—A Policy-Oriented Perspective* (3rd edn, OUP, 2015) 94–5.

[151] Higgins (n 136) 49. See also Rosalyn Higgins, 'International Law and the Avoidance, Containment and Resolution of Disputes—General Course on Public International Law', 230 *Recueil des Cours* (1991-V) 9, 80–1. Similarly, but with regard to international organizations, see Finn Seyersted, *Objective International Personality of Intergovernmental Organizations* (Krohns, 1963) 44–5. See also Philip Allott, *Eunomia: New Order for a New World* (OUP, 1990) 372–3, Christoph Schreuer, 'The Waning of the Sovereign State: Towards a New Paradigm for International Law?' 4 *EJIL* (1993) 447, Anne-Marie Slaughter, 'International Law in a World of Liberal States', 6 *EJIL* (1995) 503, and ILC, *First report on diplomatic protection*, Special Rapporteur John Dugard (2000), para. 24 (available at http://legal.un.org/ilc/documentation/english/a_cn4_506.pdf, accessed 21 January 2018).

[152] Rosalyn Higgins, 'Conceptual Thinking About the Individual in International Law', in Richard Falk, Friedrich Kratochwil and Saul H. Mendlovitz (eds), *International Law—A Contemporary Perspective* (Westview Press, 1985) 476, 480.

by their focus upon normative-ambiguous rules and putative interrelations of such rules . . . fail to offer an adequate framework of inquiry even for accurate description of the complex patterns of authority and control, including patterns of inclusive and exclusive decision, which in fact prevail in the world arena . . . .'[153]

Rather than discussing a hierarchy of norm systems, the New Haven School conceives international law and national law as 'interpenetrating power processes'.[154] Harold Koh has developed this line of thought further under the heading 'Transnational Legal Process', which studies 'how public and private actors—nation-states, international organizations, multinational enterprises, non-governmental organizations, and private individuals—interact in a variety of public and private, domestic and international fora.'[155]

For scholars understanding law as primarily a set of rules, it is difficult to engage in a meaningful discussion on a concept such as international legal personality with scholars who understand law as a decision-making process. Accordingly, policy-oriented jurisprudence and positivism are generally seen as mutually exclusive, and the 'participant' conception is hardly ever directly reflected in practice.[156]

Nevertheless, the 'participant' conception is relevant for the present study, because some contemporary scholars draw on the notion of 'participation' in their analysis of the role of the individual as a matter of positive international law. Interestingly, these scholars—like their constitutionalist colleagues mentioned above—end up implicitly invoking the orthodox 'States-only' conception of international legal personality. Two examples of this tendency will be provided in the following: First, the development of the notion of 'transnational law', and second, the idea that international legal personality is conditional upon lawmaking capacities.

A large number of legal scholars presently devote their time to studying 'transnational law'. The origin of this term is commonly attributed to Philip Jessup, who in his 1955 Storrs Lectures at Yale Law School defined 'transnational law' as 'all law which regulates actions or events that transcend national frontiers. Both public and private international law are included, as are other rules which do not wholly fit into such standard categories.'[157] By Jessup's definition, transnational situations

[153] Myres S. McDougal, 'The Impact of International Law upon National Law: A Policy-Oriented Perspective', 4 *South Dakota Law Review* (1959) 25, 31.

[154] Ibid. See further Myres S. McDougal, 'The Comparative Study of Law for Policy Purposes: Value Clarification as an Instrument of Democratic World Order', 61 *Yale Law Journal* (1952) 915. Notably, Higgins focuses on the 'real world' role of national courts in the international legal process rather than the theories of monism and dualism. She finds that international law does not allow domestic law to serve as an excuse for non-compliance with international law, whereas domestic law will not accept international obligations as reasons for non-compliance with domestic law. See Higgins (n 136) 209. Although she does not apply that label, her conclusions are thus effectively in line with the idea of dualism put forward in Section 1.3.2.

[155] Harold Hongju Koh, 'Transnational Legal Process', 75 *Nebraska Law Review* (1996) 181, 183–4. See further Harold Hongju Koh, 'Is There a "New" New Haven School of International Law?', 32 *Yale Journal of International Law* (2007) 559. See also Nijman (n 149) 105–6. The notion of 'transnational law' is discussed further in what follows.

[156] See, however, Section 8.1.

[157] Philip Jessup, *Transnational Law* (Yale University Press, 1956) 2.

involve all kinds of actors, including for example States, corporations, and individuals. Jessup is perceived by some to have anticipated the 'participant' conception of international legal personality.[158] Present-day transnational law scholars, however, study a wide range of different issues, taking both policy-oriented and rules-based approaches.[159] Some apply Jessup's definition encompassing both international law and national law,[160] whereas others perceive transnational law as a distinct body of law in its own right.[161]

There seems to be a widespread understanding among transnational law scholars that international law by definition cannot govern individuals directly. In 1956, Jessup opined: 'Conflicts and law are made by man. So are the theories which pronounce, for example, that international law cannot confer rights or impose duties on an individual, because says Theory, the individual is not a subject but an object of international law.'[162]

But, instead of discarding 'Theory' and insisting, on the basis of positive law,[163] that international law is in fact directly applicable to individuals, Jessup created a new field of study under the heading 'transnational law'.[164] This line of thought corresponds to the common perception of EU law as 'a new legal order'.[165] Indeed, Tuori refers to EU law as 'the most advanced epitome of transnational law',[166] but he also categorizes for example the case law of the ECtHR as 'an instance of transnational lawmaking.'[167] Although he finds that both examples can be examined 'from an international law perspective ... as instances of *fragmentation*', Tuori claims:

[158] See further Portmann (n 11) 209. Notably, however, Jessup himself found his conception of 'transnational law' to be 'similar but not identical with Scelle's monistic theory', for, Jessup explained, 'while I agree with him that states are not the only subjects of international law, I do not go to the other extreme and say with Scelle that individuals are the only subjects.' Jessup (n 157) 2.

[159] The concept of transnational legal process developed by Koh is mentioned above. Kaarlo Tuori, 'Transnational law—On legal hybrids and perspectivism', in Miguel Maduro, Kaarlo Tuori, and Suvi Sankari (eds), *Transnational law—Rethinking European Law and Legal Thinking* (CUP, 2014) 11, which is discussed immediately below, provides a recent example of a rules-based approach to the field.

[160] See, for example, ibid. See further Roger Cotterell, 'What Is Transnational Law?', 37 *Law & Social Inquiry* (2012) 500, 501.

[161] See, for example, Peer Zumbansen, 'Defining the Space of Transnational Law: Legal Theory, Global Governance, and Legal Pluralism', 21 *Transnational Law and Contemporary Problems* (2012–13) 305, 307.

[162] Jessup (n 157) 4.

[163] Notably, Jessup was hesitant to claim in 1948 'that states are not the only subjects of international law'. Philip C. Jessup, *A Modern Law of Nations* (Macmillan, 1948), Chapter 2. See also Philip C. Jessup, 'The Subjects of a Modern Law of Nations', 45 *Michigan Law Review* (1947) 383, 384. By 1956, however, he was 'prepared to say that it is now established'. Jessup (n 157) 2.

[164] The same rationale is often employed to explain the categorization of 'private international law' as a part of domestic law. See, for example, Albert de Lapradelle, 'De la delimitation du Droit International Public et du Droit International Privé', 1 *Nouvelle revue de droit international privé* (1934) 9, 19, Martin Wolff, *Internationales Privatrecht* (Springer, 1933) 4ff, and Roberto Ago, 'Régles générales des conflits des lois', 58 *Recueil des Cours* (1936) 243, 275ff and 301. For analysis of this line of thought, see Ole Spiermann, 'Twentieth Century Internationalism in Law' 18 *EJIL* (2007) 785, 792–4. See also Section 8.1.2.

[165] See further Section 8.3.2.

[166] Tuori (n 159) 26.

[167] Ibid, 19. See further Section 7.2.

whether we conceive of the ongoing process as fragmentation of international law or as the dawn of transnational law, the growing plethora of legal sources, legal orders and even legal systems does not fit within the dichotomy of municipal and international law. The municipal legal order has lost its monopoly over determining legal relations involving private individuals.[168]

In this way Tuori, like Jessup, endorses the orthodox positivist notion that international law by definition cannot apply directly to individuals. Essentially, both Jessup and Tuori—like the examples of international constitutionalist scholars discussed in Section 2.4—treat the orthodox 'States-only' conception of international legal personality as if it were a precise description of positive international law rather than a theoretical position.

The development of the field of 'transnational law' is not the only way in which the notion of 'participant', in conjunction with elements of the 'States-only' conception of international legal personality, has informed the scholarly debate on the role of individuals in international law. Robert McCorquodale has attempted to combine the 'participant' conception with a rules-based understanding of law in an argument revolving around the individual's international law-making capacities. McCorquodale notes that the notion of participation is a valuable framework for exploring the international legal personality of individuals: 'if it can be shown that individuals are exercising and enjoying "in fact" (to use the ICJ's words) certain rights, privileges, powers, or immunities in the international legal system then they can be presumed to be acting as international legal persons.'[169]

In express opposition to Higgins, however, he does not accept the idea of law as process, but maintains that his notion of participation 'is still consistent with the dominant State-based concept of the international legal system, as participation in the system could be viewed as largely dependent on State consent.'[170] McCorquodale argues that the capacity to create international law is a key aspect of international legal personality.[171] By highlighting the role of individuals in the development of the right of peoples to self-determination and the rights of indigenous peoples as well as the current influence of non-governmental organizations on international decision-making, he concludes that individuals do participate in the formation of international law.[172]

[168] Tuori (n 159) 22.

[169] Robert McCorquodale, 'The Individual and the International Legal System', in Malcolm D. Evans (ed.), *International Law* (4th edn, OUP, 2014) 284. See also McCorquodale (n 47).

[170] McCorquodale (n 169) 284.

[171] See further, Robert McCorquodale, 'Sources and the Subjects of International Law: A Plurality of Law-Making Participants', in Samantha Besson and Jean d'Aspremont (eds), *The Oxford Handbook on the Sources of International Law* (OUP, 2017) 749.

[172] McCorquodale (n 169) 299ff. Other contemporary authors take the perception of the individual as a participant in the international legal system even further by asserting not only that the individual is indeed a participant, but that participation of individuals in international lawmaking is a precondition for the legitimacy of international rules governing individuals:

> Demanding direct compliance of non-state actors with international obligations can . . . only be justified if those actors have been represented in the adoption process of the rules giving rise to the obligations, or to put it more succinctly, if they are considered as genuine *subjects* of international law.

McCorquodale's analysis is open to question. Given that he explicitly subscribes to 'a State-based concept of the international legal system' and rejects the idea of law as process, it is difficult to see the pivotal importance of occasional de facto influence of individuals on the decision-making process in international law.[173] It seems unwarranted to distinguish the 'law-making capacities' referred to by McCorquodale from other rights, duties, and capacities conferred upon individuals through international law. But above all, what is problematic in McCorquodale's analysis is the combination of his rules-based approach to international law and the idea that international legal personality is contingent upon the capacity to create international law. Like McCorquodale, Orakhelashvili finds that '[a]n important aspect of international personality is the ability to participate in the norm-creating process in international law.'[174] But in contrast to McCorquodale, this presumption leads Orakhelashvili to conclude that the individual human being does *not* possess international legal personality. Regardless of their diverging conclusions, however, both authors build their arguments on the orthodox 'States-only' conception of international legal personality by insisting that an entity must possess all the same features as States to be regarded as a subject of international law.[175]

McCorquodale and Orakhelashvili are not alone in linking international lawmaking capacities to international legal personality.[176] But it is important to underline the profound difference between their argument that international legal personality is conditional upon international lawmaking capacities and, for example, the normative argument that it would improve the legitimacy of international law if individuals were to participate more extensively in international lawmaking processes.[177]

The development of 'transnational law' and the idea that subjectivity requires the capacity to create international law are interesting examples of how scholars have combined elements from the different conceptions of international legal personality; in casu the 'participant' conception and the orthodox 'States-only' conception. But, more importantly in this context, both examples bear witness to the fact that the orthodox 'States-only' conception continues to impact on the academic debate,

(Emphasis in original.) See Cedric Ryngaert, 'Imposing International Duties on Non-State Actors and the Legitimacy of International Law', in Math Noortmann and Cedric Ryngaert (eds), *Non-State Actor Dynamics in International Law* (Ashgate, 2010) 69, 69–70.

173 See further Section 1.3.

174 Alexander Orakhelashvili, 'The Position of the Individual in International Law', 31 *California Western International Law Journal* (2001) 241, 256.

175 See also Jean d'Aspremont, 'Non-State Actors and the Formation of International Customary Law: Unlearning Some Common Tropes', in Iain Scobbie and Sufyan Droubi (eds), *Non-State Actors and the Formation of Customary International Law* (Manchester University Press, forthcoming).

176 See, for example, Paulus (n 121) 76 and Cançado Trindade, *The Access of Individuals to International Justice* (n 134) 4.

177 As mentioned in Section 2.4, international constitutionalist scholars such as Anne Peters promote the idea of further involvement of individuals in international lawmaking. Peters's argument, however, is distinctly normative and not an integral part of her 'individualistic' conception of international legal personality. The extent to which positive international law confers lawmaking capacities on individuals is briefly discussed in Section 1.3.

even though it has long since been abandoned as the dominant theoretical position in favour of the modified version.[178]

2.6 Conclusion: International Legal Personality as a Theoretical Construct

The preceding cursory examination of international legal scholarship since 1900 has identified four main conceptions of international legal personality and explicated their underlying assumptions concerning the key concepts of 'law' and 'State'. Because the four conceptions are based on conflicting perceptions of such fundamental notions, it is scarcely surprising that they convey profoundly different views on the subjectivity of the individual in international law.

First of all, the 'participant' conception of international legal personality is difficult to compare to the other conceptions, because it regards law as a process of authoritative decision-making rather than a set of rules. While the notion of personality is generally avoided by the New Haven School, any entity, including individuals, effectively taking part in international lawmaking may be regarded as an international legal person. The New Haven School rejects both the monistic and the dualistic construction of the relationship between legal systems, and instead conceives international law and national law as 'interpenetrating power processes'.

Scholars endorsing the 'States-only', the 'a posteriori', or the 'individualistic' conceptions of international legal personality all adopt a rules-based approach to law, but differ in their opinions on the nature and function of the State, which leads to opposing views on the role of individuals in the international legal system. The 'States-only' conception, which in the orthodox version by definition excluded non-State entities from the realm of international law, is now predominant in a modified version. The modified 'States-only' conception acknowledges—but applies a presumption against—the international legal personality of non-State entities, including individuals. In contrast, the 'individualistic' conception regards individuals as the ultimate subjects of international law and consequently applies a presumption *for* the international legal personality of individuals when it comes to norms affecting the fundamental interests of human beings. Finally, the 'a posteriori' conception perceives of international legal personality as solely a matter of interpretation of international legal norms. In other words, there are no presumptions for or against the involvement of individuals, and the answer to the question of individual rights and obligations under international law is strictly empirical.

To some degree, however, the 'individualistic' and the 'a posteriori' conceptions may be said to have converged since the days of Kelsen and Lauterpacht. Concurrently with the development of positive law after 1945, Lauterpacht's reliance on natural law has, arguably, become obsolete. The most important contemporary work endorsing the 'individualistic' conception, Anne Peters's *Beyond*

[178] See Section 2.2.1.

Human Rights published in 2016,[179] accordingly dismisses natural law thinking and contends, on the basis of positive international law, that individuals now possess a right to (primary) international legal personality; in her words an 'international individual right'. On the difference between her conception of international legal personality and Kelsen's, Peters states:

> The determination of who in a given legal order is capable of possessing rights and obligations should be made beforehand, because this will help to answer upcoming questions—on whether a concrete legal text contains rights or obligations or not—easily and more consistently. Besides, only an explicit conceptualization of legal capacity makes it possible to confer new rights on an actor, irrespective of whether those rights are granted by a treaty. The equation (rejected here) of legal personality with the existing set of rights would mean that the status of the legal subject would be trapped in the current state of positive law.[180]

To Peters, international legal personality thus precedes the possession of rights and duties, and is not—as Kelsen claims—constituted by them.[181] The development of a positive international legal norm designating the human being as the primary subject of international law is not, of course, in itself incompatible with Kelsen's 'a posteriori' conception of international legal personality. The fundamental question, however, which seems to separate Peters and Kelsen, is whether such a development would—in principle—be reversible. Indeed, Peters acknowledges that her argument is not solely based on positive international law, but inherently embraces a normative element:

> From the philosophical perspective, the new international legal status of the human being is an expression of normative individualism. The idea here is that politics and law ultimately should be guided and justified by the concerns of the persons affected by them.[182]

In addition to the role they ascribe to the individual in the international legal system, the three positivist conceptions adopt diverging positions on the relationship between the concept of international legal personality on one hand and the distinction between international law and national law on the other. In the orthodox 'States-only' conception, the two issues are necessarily intertwined: As States are the only international legal persons, norms governing other entities cannot by definition be a part of international law. Accordingly, international legal norms are separated from national legal norms by reference to their respective addressees.

The monistic construction of the relationship between international law and national law is a key element of Kelsen's thinking. He did not, however, connect this issue with the concept of international legal personality. Kelsen's 'a posteriori' conception is a result of the idea that all law by definition governs human behaviour in conjunction with the elimination of non-legal elements from the objective 'science of law'. Therefore, it is possible to adopt the 'a posteriori' conception of international legal personality without endorsing Kelsen's postulate of necessary unity between

[179] Peters (n 47). The original German version was published in 2014. *Jenseits der Menschenrechte—Die Rechtsstellung des Individuums im Völkerrecht* (Mohr Siebeck, 2014).

[180] Peters (n 47) 41. [181] Ibid, 58–9. [182] Ibid, 553.

international law and national law. If we combine the 'a posteriori' conception with the dualistic approach to the relationship between legal systems, it follows that a legal norm can only be categorized as international or national by looking at the nature of its source. The addressees of a particular norm, on the other hand, tell us nothing about the legal system to which that norm belongs.

Like Kelsen, Lauterpacht strongly supported the idea of monism. But Lauterpacht explicitly acknowledged that positive law in his time reflected a dualistic relationship between international law and domestic law. Parallel to the 'a posteriori' conception, however, Lauterpacht's 'individualistic' conception does not tie the question of personality in international law to the question of the separation of legal orders. Only the orthodox 'States-only' conception of international legal personality draws this link.

In 1943, Hans Aufricht claimed that '[t]hrough constant repetition, the unqualified designation of the State as the only legal person in international law became seemingly self-evident.'[183] In light of massive increase in the number of positive norms governing individuals, post-Second World War proponents of the orthodox 'States-only' conception of international legal personality naturally faced the challenge of explaining why norms following from traditional sources of international law nevertheless do not form part of the international legal system. To adjust the orthodox framework to the reality of the second half of the twentieth century, the modified 'States-only' conception thus introduced a sociological perspective. Non-State entities, including individuals, were designated as derivative or secondary international legal persons. The ICJ's *Reparations for Injuries* Advisory Opinion of 1949, which seemingly endorses this line of thought, was widely perceived as providing effective clarification of the key elements of the concept of personality. This presumably explains why the overall scholarly interest in the concept of international legal personality decreased in comparison to the interest it had attracted in the first half of the twentieth century. It also explains the dominance of the modified 'States-only' conception in contemporary international law textbooks.

Although few international legal scholars of the twenty-first century deny that today even individuals possess at least a degree of international legal personality, Aufricht's statement continues to hold merit. As illustrated in the preceding sections, the orthodox positivist notion that only States are international legal persons, and the ensuing categorization of legal norms as either international or national according to their addressees, plays a significant role in the current academic debate. Several scholars, who build on the 'individualistic' conception of international legal personality in order to argue that international law is undergoing a process of constitutionalization, inadvertently invoke the orthodox 'States-only' conception by insisting on the link between the concept of personality and the question of the relationship between international law and national law. In effect, these scholars perceive the orthodox 'States-only' conception as a faithful representation of positive

[183] Hans Aufricht, 'Personality in International Law', 37 *The American Political Science Review* (1943) 217.

international law rather than 'just' the theoretical position that the 'individualistic' conception was designed to oppose. To some extent the constitutionalists share this notion with scholars who draw inspiration from the 'participant' conception of international legal personality in their analysis of positive norms of international law. 'Transnational law', for example, was developed as a separate field of study, because international law was deemed incapable of governing individuals directly. Thus, while the mainstream theoretical approach was to modify the 'States-only' conception so as to accommodate individuals and other non-State actors as 'secondary international legal persons', the orthodox idea that international law can be distinguished from national law on the basis of their respective addressees still has a strong hold on the academic debate. As exemplified throughout the following chapters, it also significantly affects the way in which some practitioners, including judges of international courts, interpret and apply particular norms of international law that directly govern individuals and other non-State entities.

The remainder of this book is devoted to examining how the concept of international legal personality has functioned historically and still functions in the current legal reality. First and foremost, the subsequent chapters will assess the position of the individual in positive international law. The study maps out the extent to which treaties and customary law have directly regulated the conduct of individuals since the beginning of the twentieth century. The aim is not only to determine which of the four theoretical conceptions of international legal personality best reflects international *lex lata*, but also to exemplify how they have each been taken into account in treaty-drafting processes as well as in judicial practice.

3

The Personality of Individuals in Positive International Law—General Issues

Before embarking on the study of the position of individuals in specialized international legal fields, it is pertinent to examine a number of issues of general relevance to public international law. This chapter first inquires why the overall issue of the applicability of international law to individuals was not long ago resolved once and for all. Focusing on treaty law, Section 3.1 examines why the ILC ended up abandoning Article 66 of the draft Vienna Convention on the Law of Treaties (hereafter VCLT), which was entitled 'The Application of Treaties to Individuals', and the role of the concept of international legal personality in that context. After briefly considering the reasons for the (lack of) procedural role of individuals before the PCIJ and the ICJ, Section 3.1.2 then studies the few, controversial, rulings issued by both courts pertaining to the direct applicability of treaties to individuals.

With the example of the 1920 Advisory Committee of Jurists' discussion of a proposal for the establishment of a High Court of International Justice to prosecute individuals for certain crimes, Section 3.2 illustrates the role of theoretical arguments concerning international legal personality when it comes to individual obligations under customary international law.

Many misunderstandings about the position of the individual in international law seem to originate from the presumption that an individual right only exists if it comes with independent means of enforcement.[1] Section 3.3 is therefore dedicated to the doctrine of diplomatic protection and its correlation to the notion of direct individual rights under international law.

As an introduction to Chapters 4–8, Section 3.4 will sketch out the considerations that are particularly relevant for the determination of treaty provisions as direct individual rights and obligations. Finally, Section 3.5 sums up the conclusions of this chapter.

[1] As a notable example, Charles Leben implies that Kelsen's conception of international legal personality revolves around the ability to bring claims before an international judicial body. See Charles Leben, *The Advancement of International Law* (Hart, 2010) 187. Following the conclusions of Section 2.3, this would appear to be a misinterpretation of Kelsen.

3.1 The Application of Treaties to Individuals

3.1.1 The Vienna Convention on the Law of Treaties

Even though the VCLT would seem an obvious place to find guidance on the application of treaties to individuals, it is not helpful. Interestingly, the ILC did consider including provisions on the matter in the draft VCLT, but ended up abandoning the idea.

In 1959, Special Rapporteur Gerald Fitzmaurice explicitly tried to 'avoid any theoretical controversy about the position of private individuals and juristic entities under international law, and how far they are directly *subjects* of it' (emphasis in original).[2] His successor, Humphrey Waldock, agreed that it was preferable to steer clear of this debate in international legal scholarship. Nevertheless, referring to a number of international tribunals with competence to hear individual claims, such as the Central American Court of Justice (hereafter CACJ)[3] and the Upper Silesian Arbitral Tribunal,[4] Waldock prepared the following draft article for the ILC to consider:

'Article 66. — Application of treaties to individuals

Where a treaty provides for obligations or rights which are to be performed or enjoyed by individuals, juristic persons, or groups of individuals, such obligations or rights are applicable to the individuals, juristic persons, or groups of individuals in question:

(a) through the contracting States by their national systems of law;
(b) through such international organs and procedures as may be specially provided for in the treaty or in any other treaties or instruments in force.'[5]

In essence, the proposed provision merely confirms that *pacta sunt servanda* applies equally when individuals are involved. Yet, the subsequent discussions in the Commission revealed considerable discord. Although several members found it to be a 'recent trend in the development of international law' that treaties could apply directly to individuals and that the determining factor was the will of the contracting parties,[6] only a few members found it necessary—or even advisable—to include the draft Article 66 in the VCLT. For example, the chairman, Roberto Ago, 'could not subscribe to an article that took a positive view on the international personality of the individual at that stage of development of international law.'[7]

[2] II *YILC* (1959) 78. See further ibid, 49 and 79. Articles 32 and 33 of Fitzmaurice's draft contained provisions regarding treaties involving obligations and benefits for private individuals or juristic entities. See also Section 3.4.2.

[3] See further Section 4.1.1.2.

[4] See further Section 4.2.2.3.

[5] II *YILC* (1964) 45–6. See also I *YILC* (1966), Part II, 170. As to Waldock's own perception of individuals in international law, see Humphrey Waldock, 'General course on public international law', 106 *Recueil des Cours* (1962-II) 192–229.

[6] See for example the statements by Verdross, Castrén, Yasseen, Amado, Paredes, and El-Erian in I *YILC* (1964) 114–18.

[7] Ibid, 117. This position corresponds well to Ago's perception of the exhaustion of local remedies rule in diplomatic protection, cf. Section 3.3.2.1. In contrast, Mr Liu, who was one of the few proponents

The ILC debates concerning Article 66 and the Commission's final decision not to take a stand on the international legal personality of individuals certainly bear witness to the controversial nature of this topic in legal theory at the time.[8] But the fact that the Commission did not feel compelled to include provisions on the application of treaties to individuals in the draft VCLT may also be seen as an indication of practical insignificance.[9] Had the international legal personality of individuals been of crucial importance in practice, one might suspect that provisions regulating this issue would have constituted an indispensable component of any attempt to codify the law of treaties.[10] Instead, the ILC left the application of treaties to individuals to be determined through interpretation of concrete treaty provisions. In that respect, the VCLT in its adopted form corresponds well with the 'a posteriori' conception of international legal personality.

3.1.2 The PCIJ and the ICJ

In any study of a fundamental concept of international law, the rulings of the principal judicial organs of the field, the ICJ, and the PCIJ before it, naturally attract particular attention. Both courts have issued controversial Judgments and Advisory Opinions pertaining to the international legal personality of individuals, and this case law is the subject of Section 3.1.2.2. By way of introduction, Section 3.1.2.1 will look briefly at the background for the procedural role—or rather, lack thereof—of individuals before the PCIJ and the ICJ.

3.1.2.1 1920: Drafting the Statute of the Permanent Court of International Justice[11]

As every student of international law knows, the ICJ, like its predecessor, can only hear cases between States.[12] What is perhaps less commonly known is that the Advisory Committee of Jurists, which drafted the PCIJ Statute in 1920, actually

of including Article 66, found that '[t]he article was compatible with modern trends and its inclusion should be regarded as a progressive step.' Ibid.

[8] At the end of the 742nd meeting, the chairman decided to close the discussion before 'it became increasingly obvious that [the Commission] would have to take a definite position on the doctrinal issue.' Ibid, 119.

[9] In the final draft, it is briefly noted that no provision regarding the application of treaties to individuals was included, because the opinions of the ILC members were divided on the matter. See II *YILC* (1966) 177.

[10] The ILC's discussion of the ability of certain other non-State entities, in particular armed opposition groups, to conclude treaties is examined in Section 5.4.3.2.

[11] Section 3.1.2.1 is based on Astrid Kjeldgaard-Pedersen, 'The Influence of the Concept of International Legal Personality in the Drafting on the Statute of the Permanent Court of International Justice' 16 *JHIL* (2014) 9–25.

[12] Article 34 of the PCIJ Statute reads: 'Only States or Members of the League of Nations can be parties in cases before the Court.' The ICJ Statute contains a parallel provision in Article 34(1): 'Only States may be parties in cases before the Court.'

discussed the possibility of extending the competence of the PCIJ to litigation involving individuals.[13]

Two of the ten members of the Committee argued in favour of allowing individuals to act as parties in cases before the Permanent Court. The most radical proponent was the former Dutch Supreme Court judge, Dr B. C. J. Loder, who in 1922 was to become the first president of the PCIJ: 'He saw no reason for limiting the competence of the Court by stipulating that private individuals must be represented by their Governments in order to have access to the Court.'[14] Loder believed that State sovereignty should no longer be used to prevent private individuals from taking action against States. Law Professor of the Sorbonne, Albert de Lapradelle was more hesitant in his statement that 'it might be considered whether the right to have recourse to the Court should not be given to some extent to private individuals, that is to say, in cases of denial of justice.'[15]

The remaining eight members of the Advisory Committee all agreed on limiting the extent of the PCIJ's jurisdiction to States alone. But, remarkably, only two of them argued that individuals lacked international legal personality. Legal Adviser to the Ministry of Foreign Affairs of Italy, Arturo Ricci-Busatti, opined that 'private individuals are not subjects of international law and it is entirely within the realm of that law that the Court is called upon to act.'[16] Raoul Fernandes, former Brazilian delegate to the Paris Peace Conference, concurred, 'since States alone constituted legal persons in international matters.'[17]

Elihu Root, former US Secretary of State, took a pragmatic approach in stating that 'the less restrictions were imposed on States, the greater would be the chance of success.'[18] He and Lord Walter Phillimore both emphasized the word 'international' in Article 14[19] of the Covenant of the League of Nations.[20] According to Lord Phillimore, 'international cases should always be interstate cases'.[21]

Finally, the president of the Advisory Committee, Baron Descamps, Senator and Belgian Minister of State, found that 'international law governs relations between States as such, and it is the duty of States to protect their nationals.'[22] It was clearly implied that the interests of individuals could be secured, even though the Court's

[13] Advisory Committee of Jurists, *Procès-verbaux of the Proceedings of the Committee* (16 June–24 July 1920, with Annexes) (van Langenheusen Brothers 1920), (available at http://www.icj-cij.org/pcij/serie_D/D_proceedings_of_committee_annexes_16june_24july_1920.pdf, accessed 21 January 2018) 203–17 (hereafter *Procès-verbaux*).

[14] Ibid, 206. [15] Ibid, 205. [16] Ibid, 208. [17] Ibid, 215.

[18] Ibid, 207. At a subsequent meeting, however, Root stated that 'only States are subjects of International Law.' Ibid, 505. See further Section 3.2.1.

[19] Article 14 read:

> The Council shall formulate and submit to the Members of the League for adoption plans for the establishment of a Permanent Court of International Justice. The Court shall be competent to hear and determine any dispute of an international character which the parties thereto submit to it. The Court may also give an advisory opinion upon any dispute or question referred to it by the Council or by the Assembly.

[20] *Procès-verbaux* (n 13) 207 and 208. [21] Ibid, 206.

[22] Ibid, 209. See further Nicolas Politis, 'How the World Court has Functioned', 4 *Foreign Affairs* (1925–1926) 443, 448. See also Section 3.2.1 on Descamps' proposal for the establishment of a High Court of International Justice.

competence was limited to inter-State disputes, since States had the possibility of exercising diplomatic protection on behalf of their nationals.[23]

3.1.2.2 PCIJ and ICJ practice on individual rights and obligations under treaties

During the interwar period, an increasing number of multilateral treaties with unprecedented contents as to the involvement of individuals came into existence. The establishment of the League of Nations, for example, gave rise to a number of treaties and secondary legislation about the rights and obligations of its employees. New borders were drawn between the European States in the wake of the First World War, partly as a result of the idea of self-determination in conjunction with measures to ensure minority protection.[24] Two of the PCIJ's early Advisory Opinions concerning one such measure, the Polish Minorities Treaty,[25] briefly refer to the concept of individual rights under treaties. In *Settlers of German Origin in Poland*, the Court stated that '[t]he main object of the Minorities Treaty is to assure respect for the rights of Minorities and to prevent discrimination against them by any act whatsoever of the Polish State.'[26] Shortly thereafter, the PCIJ held in another Advisory Opinion that Articles 3–6 of the same treaty regarding acquisition of nationality were 'of supreme importance to persons of non-Polish origin who are entitled to avail themselves of the provisions in question in order to become Polish nationals.'[27]

By Order of 8 January 1927 in a case concerning China's denunciation of the Treaty of Friendship, Commerce and Navigation[28] between China and Belgium, the PCIJ indicated the first provisional measures in the Court's history.[29] These measures were all aimed at securing the individual rights of Belgian citizens.

In December 1927, the PCIJ issued an Advisory Opinion about the jurisdiction of the European Commission of the Danube, which was operating under the Convention Instituting the Definitive Statute of the Danube of 23 July 1921. The Commission was 'a unique international organization'[30] given its competence to

[23] The PCIJ confirmed this position in *Mavrommatis Palestine Consessions (Preliminary Objections)* (Judgment) [1924] PCIJ Ser. A, No. 2, 12 (hereafter *Mavrommatis*), which is discussed further in Section 3.3.1. See also Ole Spiermann, '"Who Attempts Too Much Does Nothing Well": The 1920 Advisory Committee of Jurists and the Statute of the Permanent Court of International Justice', 73 *BYBIL* (2002) 187, 208.

[24] See further Section 4.2.

[25] Treaty of Peace between the United States, the British Empire, France, Italy, Japan and Poland, 28 June 1919, 13 *AJIL* Supp. (1919) 423–40 (hereafter Polish Minorities Treaty). See further Section 7.1.2.

[26] *Settlers of German Origin in Poland* (Advisory Opinion) [1923], PCIJ Ser. B, No. 6, 25 (hereafter *Settlers of German Origin in Poland*).

[27] *Acquisition of Polish Nationality* (Advisory Opinion) [1923] PCIJ Ser. B, No. 7, 16 (hereafter *Acquisition of Polish Nationality*).

[28] Treaty of Friendship, Commerce and Navigation between China and Belgium, 2 November 1865, 131 *CTS* 373.

[29] *Denunciation of Treaty of November 2nd, 1865 between China and Belgium* (Order) [1927] PCIJ Ser. A, No. 8, 6–8.

[30] Glen A. Blackburn, 'International Control of the River Danube', 42 *Current History* (1930) 1154. See also Edvard Krehbiel, 'The European Commission of the Danube: An Experiment in International Administration', 33 *Political Science Quarterly* (1918) 38.

exercise power directly over individuals, and scholars at the time had trouble reconciling it with the orthodox 'States-only' conception of international legal personality.[31] The Permanent Court's Opinion hinted that entities besides States might be regarded as subjects of international law:

As the European Commission is not a State, but an international institution with a special purpose, it only has the functions bestowed upon it by the Definitive Statute with a view to the fulfilment of that purpose, but it has power to exercise these functions to their full extent, in so far as the Statute does not impose restrictions upon it.[32]

The high point of the PCIJ's practice regarding the status of individuals in international law, however, was no doubt its landmark Advisory Opinion in *Jurisdiction of the Courts of Danzig* from March 1928. As it has given rise to substantial confusion and is relied on by both proponents and opponents of the possibility of direct individual rights under treaties, it deserves particular scrutiny in the present context.

3.1.2.2.1 PCIJ 1928: *Jurisdiction of the Courts of Danzig*

Poland and the Free City of Danzig[33] were in dispute over pecuniary claims brought by railway employees based on the Danzig–Polish Agreement of 22 October 1921 (the so-called *Beamtenabkommen*), which regulated the conditions for employees of the Polish Railway Administration in Danzig.

Danzig argued that railway officials, who had passed from the service of the Free City into Polish service, were authorized to recover pecuniary claims from the Polish Railway Administration in Danzig civil courts. Such claims could be based exclusively on the *Beamtenabkommen*, since '[t]he contents of the individual provisions of the Agreement clearly show the intention and wish of the contracting Governments to create by agreement direct personal rights and obligations for the officials concerned.'[34]

With reference to the writings of, for example, Verdross,[35] Oppenheim, and Cavaglieri,[36] Poland however held that '[t]he *communis opinio* is that international treaties create rights and obligations only in respect of States and not of individuals.'[37] By signing the *Beamtenabkommen* the contracting States merely undertook to amend their internal legislation in accordance with its provisions. Therefore, Poland

[31] See, for example, Alf Ross, *A Textbook of International Law* (Longmans, Green and Co. 1947) 30, with reference to Rolf Knubben, *Die Subjekte des Völkerrechts* (1928) 415–16. See further Section 2.2. See also Josef L. Kunz, 'Experience and Techniques in International Administration', 31 *Iowa Law Review* (1945) 40, 49ff.

[32] *Jurisdiction of the European Commission of the Danube* (Advisory Opinion) [1927] PCIJ Ser. B, No. 14, 64.

[33] See Kate Parlett, 'The PCIJ's Opinion in *Jurisdiction of the Courts of Danzig*. Individual Rights under Treaties' 10 *JHIL* (2008) 119 for a detailed account of the case, including the historical and legal context of the Free City of Danzig.

[34] Appeal by the Government of the Free City of Danzig, *Jurisdiction of the Courts of Danzig* (Documents Relating to Advisory Opinion No. 15) [1928] PCIJ Ser. C, No. 14-I, 115–23, 118.

[35] See Chapter 2, note 121. [36] See Section 2.2.

[37] Reply of the Polish Government to the Appeal by the Senate of the Free City of Danzig, *Jurisdiction of the Courts of Danzig*, (Documents Relating to Advisory Opinion No. 15) [1928] PCIJ Ser. C, No. 14-I, 124, 134.

argued, '[t]he legal position of these officials is regulated by the internal orders of the Polish Railway Administration and by Polish law, and the engagements into which Poland entered in regard to the terms of these orders only had reference to the Free City itself.'[38]

The Court first considered whether Danzig was justified in allowing the *Beamtenabkommen* to form the basis for pecuniary claims before its courts and (in)famously stated:

> It may be readily admitted that, according to a well established principle of international law, the Beamtenabkommen, being an international agreement, cannot, as such, create direct rights and obligations for private individuals. But it cannot be disputed that the very object of an international agreement, according to the intention of the contracting Parties, may be the adoption by the Parties of some definite rules creating individual rights and obligations and enforceable by the national courts.[39]

In order to determine the intention of the parties in the case before it, the PCIJ then carefully analysed the content of the *Beamtenabkommen*,[40] and arrived, in accordance with Danzig's submissions, at the following conclusion: 'The wording and general tenor of the *Beamtenabkommen* show that its provisions are directly applicable as between the officials and the Administration.'[41]

The Court then went on to consider the extent of Poland's obligation to recognize the jurisdiction exercised by Danzig courts in cases based on the *Beamtenabkommen*. In a somewhat circular analysis, the Court stated that since it had been established that Danzig courts had jurisdiction based on the *Beamtenabkommen*, it should be presumed that application of the agreement as substantive law was in conformity with international law. And, in the opinion of the Court, Poland had not presented any arguments to rebut such a presumption.[42] Furthermore, if Poland were to assert that the *Beamtenabkommen* could not be applied directly by Danzig courts, because it was not duly incorporated into Polish law, the Court would observe that 'Poland could not avail herself of an objection which, according to the construction placed upon the *Beamtenabkommen* by the Court, would amount to relying upon the non-fulfilment of an obligation imposed upon her by an international engagement.'[43]

In sum, the Court concluded: (1) that the *Beamtenabkommen* was to be interpreted as having direct effect; and (2) that Poland was obliged to enforce judgments rendered by Danzig courts in accordance with the *Beamtenabkommen*, even though it had not been incorporated into Polish law.

From an operative viewpoint, it is hard to conceive the outcome of the Court's examination as anything other than endorsement of the subjectivity of individuals, since the Court did in fact attribute direct effect to the *Beamtenabkommen*. But the PCIJ's affirmation that 'an international agreement, cannot, as such, create direct

[38] Ibid, 143.

[39] *Jurisdiction of the Courts of Danzig* (Advisory Opinion) [1928] PCIJ Ser. B, No. 15, 17–18 (hereafter *Jurisdiction of the Courts of Danzig*).

[40] On the particular elements for the Court's analysis, see further Section 3.3.

[41] Ibid, 18.

[42] See further Parlett (n 33) 138ff.

[43] *Jurisdiction of the Courts of Danzig* (n 39) 27.

rights and obligations for private individuals' greatly confuses the analysis. Was it really possible for the Court to maintain this position and at the same time find that the *Beamtenabkommen* could be applied directly before the Danzig courts? The president of the PCIJ and member of the drafting committee, Dionisio Anzilotti, apparently believed so. He read the opinion as follows:

> It does not say that a treaty, as such, may create rights and obligations for individuals, without the need to incorporate the relevant rules into domestic law: It only says that the intention of the contracting parties may be to adopt specific rules creating rights and obligations for individuals that may be applied by national courts. If, in the present case, the Court did not consider it necessary to assess whether the rules in the agreement had effectively been adopted, it is because it found that the party, who was obliged to adopt said rules, could not in any event rely on its own non-performance of this obligation to avoid the duties imposed by the agreement towards the other Contracting Party.[44]

Among others, W. E. Beckett agreed that the Court had not given direct effect to the *Beamtenabkommen* itself, but indeed explicitly applied 'the general principle that international law only creates rights and duties between states'.[45] Anzilotti and Beckett basically concurred with Poland's argument that the parties to the *Beamtenabkommen* merely undertook to amend their internal legislation in accordance with its provisions. However, the deciding factor from their perspective was that Poland was prevented from relying on its own failure to meet obligations following from a treaty it had entered into.

As appealing as this line of reasoning may seem, the fact remains that the Court effectively accepted that a treaty could apply directly to individuals. This result could have easily been avoided through a narrow interpretation of Article 9 of the *Beamtenabkommen*, which read: 'All matters affecting officials and workmen transferred to the Polish service shall be dealt with by the Polish State Railways Administration.'[46] Had the Court wished to do so, it could have conveniently construed Article 9 'in a manner which would make the applicability of the provisions of the *Beamtenabkommen* depend on their incorporation into a Polish Regulation.'[47] But the Court did exactly the opposite.

According to Hersch Lauterpacht, the PCIJ's Opinion 'dealt a resounding blow to the dogma of the impenetrable barrier separating individuals from international law',[48] and 'laid down, in effect, that no considerations of theory can prevent the individual from becoming the subject of international rights if the States so wish.'[49]

[44] Dionisio Anzilotti, *Cours de droit international* (Recueil Sirey, 1929) 407–8 (author's translation).

[45] W. E. Beckett, 'Decisions of the Permanent Court of International Justice on Points of Law and Procedure of General Application', 11 *BYBIL* (1930) 1, 4. See also Arnold McNair, *The Law of Treaties* (Clarendon Press, 1961) 337–9, and Wolfgang Friedmann, *The Changing Structure of International Law* (Stevens & Sons, 1964) 239.

[46] Poland had argued in favour of such an interpretation in Reply of the Polish Government to the Appeal by the Senate of the Free City of Danzig, *Jurisdiction of the Courts of Danzig* (Documents relating to Advisory Opinion No. 15) [1928] PCIJ Ser. C, No. 14-I, 124, 126–7 and 42.

[47] *Jurisdiction of the Courts of Danzig* (n 39) 20.

[48] Hersch Lauterpacht, 'The Subjects of the Law of Nations', reprinted in Elihu Lauterpacht (ed), *International Law—Being the Collected Papers of Hersch Lauterpacht*, Vol. II (1975, first published in two parts in 1947 and 1948) 487, 511.

[49] Ibid, 512.

Lauterpacht dismissed the above declaration by the Court as a 'courtesy due to a doctrine which for a long time enjoyed undisputed ascendancy'.[50] In response to proponents of interpreting the Opinion as compatible with the traditional view of individuals in international law, Lauterpacht said: 'the departure from the established view was effected with such ingenious restraint that some have been led to believe that the decision of the Court amounts to a solemn affirmation of the established doctrine.'[51]

In essence, *Jurisdiction of the Courts of Danzig* epitomized the paradoxical ramifications of the orthodox 'States-only' conception of international legal personality which dominated among international legal scholars at the time: although the Permanent Court explicitly rejected the *theoretical* notion of individuals as subjects of international law, it nevertheless—by applying general principles of treaty interpretation—came to the *practical* conclusion that the *Beamtenabkommen* did indeed have direct effect. Against this background, it is hardly surprising that even today scholarly analyses of the Opinion still have diverging outcomes.[52] The present author is inclined to agree with Lauterpacht that one should emphasize what the Court actually did. Its statement about the inability per se of international agreements to create direct rights and obligations for private individuals may be regarded as lip service to the orthodox 'States-only' conception of international legal personality and its advocates in the drafting committee, including president Anzilotti.

Some authors argue that the PCIJ's opinion implies a presumption against the direct effect of treaties.[53] Even Lauterpacht hesitatingly acknowledged this reading.[54] However, the Court's appraisal of Article 9 illustrates that it did not apply such a presumption against direct effect of the *Beamtenabkommen*.[55] Rather, it approved that general rules of treaty interpretation are equally applicable when it comes to individual rights.[56] Notably, in the following month (April 1928) the PCIJ issued

[50] Ibid.

[51] Hersch Lauterpacht, *The Development of International Law by the Permanent Court of International Justice* (Stevens & Sons, 1934) 52.

[52] See for example Roland Portmann, *Legal Personality in International Law* (CUP, 2010) 68–73, and Parlett (n 33).

[53] In 1950, Brierly observed with reference to *Jurisdiction of the Courts of Danzig* that 'a treaty between States may *expressly* create rights for other persons, whether international persons or lesser entities' (emphasis added); cf. II *YILC* (1950) 228–9. See also, for example, Ian Brownlie, 'The Place of the Individual in International Law', 50 *Virginia Law Review* (1964) 435, 440, Sandesh Sivakumaran, 'Binding Armed Opposition Groups', 55 *ICLQ* (2006) 369, 384, and Parlett (n 33) 144–5.

[54] Hersch Lauterpacht, *The Development of International Law by the International Court* (Stevens & Sons, 1958) 175–6: 'What, as a result of that Opinion, remained of the established doctrine was, perhaps, the presumption against direct acquisition of rights; but it was a presumption which could henceforth be rebutted.'

[55] See Ole Spiermann, *International Legal Argument in the Permanent Court of International Justice—The Rise of the International Judiciary* (CUP, 2005) 272.

[56] See further Section 3.3. See also Ole Spiermann, 'The LaGrand Case and the Individual as a Subject of International Law', 58 *Zeitschrift für Öffentliches Recht* (2003b) 197, 209, James Crawford, 'The ILC's Articles of Responsibility of States for Internationally Wrongful Acts: A Retrospect', 96 *AJIL* (2002a) 874, 887, James Crawford, *International Law as an Open System* (Cameron May, 2002b) 27, and Portmann (n 52) 72–3. See also W. Paul Gormley, *The Procedural Status of the Individual before International and Supranational Tribunals* (Martinus Nijhoff, 1966) 40.

a Judgment about the exercise of the rights of minorities in connection with public schools in Upper Silesia under the Geneva Convention Relating to Upper Silesia of 1922.[57] The Court stated that a person belonging 'to a racial, linguistic or religious minority ... is entitled to claim the advantages arising under the provisions which the Treaty comprises with regard to the protection of minorities'.[58]

Generally speaking, the practice of the Permanent Court hardly paints a clear picture of the international legal personality of individuals. Several of the Court's Judgments and Advisory Opinions, such as *Mavrommatis*[59] and *Serbian Loans*,[60] palpably reflect the orthodox 'States-only' perception of international law. But when faced with circumstances where States had nevertheless attributed rights to individuals in treaties, the PCIJ did not refrain from actually giving them direct effect. Only in 2001 did the ICJ seize the opportunity to unequivocally let theory catch up with practice with regard to the position of individuals in international law.[61]

3.1.2.2.2 ICJ 2001: *LaGrand*

The ICJ's Judgment of 27 June 2001 in *LaGrand*[62] concerned the failure of the US to inform two German nationals, Karl and Walter LaGrand, who were arrested and prosecuted in Arizona, of their rights in accordance with Article 36(1) of the VCCR. The Court applied the general principles of treaty interpretation to the text of the relevant provisions, and found that the US had not only violated its obligations to Germany, but also to the LaGrand brothers directly: 'the Court concludes that Article 36, paragraph 1, creates individual rights, which, by virtue of Article 1 of the Optional Protocol, may be invoked in this Court by the national State of the detained person. These rights were violated in the present case.'[63] This Judgment is renowned for clearly affirming the existence of individual rights under treaties. The Court evidently did not require that the individual must be capable of enforcing his right under Article 36(1) for it to be categorized as an individual right. On

[57] Geneva Convention Relating to Upper Silesia, 22 May 1922. Unofficial English translation reprinted in Julius Stone, *Regional Guarantees of Minority Rights* (Macmillan Co., 1933) Appendix I, 213.

[58] *Rights of Minorities in Upper Silesia (Minority Schools)* (Judgment) [1928] PCIJ Ser. A, No. 15, 32. See further Section 4.2.2.3.

[59] See further Section 3.3. [60] See further Section 8.1.

[61] It should be noted that the PCIJ and the ICJ can hardly be blamed for their silence on the matter during most of the twentieth century. Due to the limitations in their respective Statutes, neither court was overrun by cases where it would be relevant to take a stand on the international legal personality of individuals.

[62] The Court had been presented with a similar case in 1998. Paraguay claimed that the US had violated Article 36(1) of the Vienna Convention on Consular Relations (hereafter VCCR) in connection with the arrest and prosecution of Paraguayan national, Angel Francisco Breard, who was eventually sentenced to death. In spite of the Court's indication of provisional measures of 9 April 1998, Breard was executed on 14 April 1998. Paraguay subsequently requested that the case be struck off the Court's list. See *Case Concerning the Vienna Convention on Consular Relations (Paraguay v. United States of America)*(Order) [1998] ICJ Rep 426 (hereafter *Breard*).

[63] *LaGrand (Germany v. United States of America)* (Judgment) [2001] ICJ Rep 466, para. 77. As regards the Court's analysis, see further Section 3.4.3.1. In 1999, the IACtHR interpreted Article 36(1) of the VCCR in the same way. See *Right to Information on Consular Assistance in the Framework of the Guarantees of the Due Process of Law* (IACtHR Advisory Opinion) OC-16/99, 1 October 1999, paras 80–84. See also paras 89–97.

the contrary, it distinguished between the individual right of the LaGrand brothers under Article 36(1) (the primary rule) and Germany's corresponding right to invoke responsibility before the ICJ in accordance with Article 1 of the Optional Protocol to the Vienna Convention on Consular Relations concerning the Compulsory Settlement of Disputes (the secondary rule).[64] Furthermore, the Court removed all doubt that individual rights are not limited to human rights. It also made clear, albeit implicitly, that diplomatic protection not only applies to economic damages, but can be exercised by States in order to protect all kinds of individual rights under international law.[65]

With reference to the *LaGrand* Judgment, the ILC's Commentary on Article 33(2) of ARSIWA explicitly recognized the possibility that individuals are entitled to invoke responsibility independent of their home State: 'It will be a matter for the particular primary rule to determine whether and to what extent persons or entities other than States are entitled to invoke responsibility on their own account.'[66]

3.1.2.2.3 ICJ 2004: *Wall*

In 2004, the ICJ issued an Advisory Opinion on the *Legal Consequences of the Construction of a Wall in the Occupied Palestinian Territory*,[67] which inter alia touched upon the responsibility of non-State actors under international law.

Israel claimed that the wall was lawful, because Article 51 of the UN Charter—in light of a number of Security Council resolutions adopted in the wake of 11 September 2001[68]—should be read as to encompass the right to respond in self-defence to armed attacks not only by foreign States, but also by terrorist groups whose actions were not attributable to any State.[69]

The ICJ underlined that as a starting point Article 51 applies only when the original armed attack is imputable to a foreign State. Nonetheless, the Court left open the possibility that Article 51 could be invoked in situations where self-defence is exercised against a non-State entity. However, the preconditions for such an expansion of the scope of Article 51 were not present in the situation of the Occupied Palestinian Territory. According to the Court, the circumstances of the case at hand differed from the situation contemplated by Security Council Resolutions 1368

[64] The separate opinion of Vice President Shi and the dissenting opinion of Judge Oda are discussed in Section 3.4.3.1. Notably, neither judge opposed to the idea of individual rights under treaties. They merely disagreed with the majority's interpretation of the concrete treaty provisions.

[65] *LaGrand* (n 63) para. 76. See also Zsuzsanna Deen-Racsmány, 'Diplomatic Protection and the LaGrand Case', 15 *LJIL* (2002) 87, 97.

[66] II *YILC* (2001), Part Two, Chapter IV, 95. See also Crawford, 'The ILC's Articles of Responsibility of States for Internationally Wrongful Acts: A Retrospect' (n 56) 887–8.

[67] *Legal Consequences of the Construction of a Wall in the Occupied Palestinian Territory* (Advisory Opinion) [2004] ICJ Rep 136 (hereafter *Wall*).

[68] See Security Council Resolutions 1368 (2001) and 1373 (2001), which referred to the right to self-defence under Article 51 of the UN Charter, but did not pronounce on the legality of an armed attack against terrorist groups under the particular circumstances. See further Ole Spiermann, *Moderne folkeret* (3rd edn, DJØF Publishing, 2006) 432.

[69] *Wall* (n 67) para. 138.

(2001) and 1373 (2001), because the attacks against Israel came from within territory over which Israel exercised control:

The Court also notes that Israel exercises control in the Occupied Palestinian Territory and that, as Israel itself states, the threat which it regards as justifying the construction of the wall originates within, and not outside, that territory. The situation is thus different from that contemplated by Security Council resolutions 1368 (2001) and 1373 (2001), and therefore Israel could not in any event invoke those resolutions in support of its claim to be exercising a right of self-defence.[70]

Against the background of the *Wall* Opinion, it is not entirely clear whether—and, if so, under what circumstances—a State may claim self-defence under Article 51 in response to an armed attack originating from a non-State entity operating from the territory of a foreign State. For present purposes, however, the important point is that the Court did not deem non-State entities irrelevant to Article 51 based on their lack of international legal personality.[71]

3.1.2.2.4 ICJ 2010: *Kosovo*

In its Advisory Opinion of 22 July 2010 on the *Accordance with International Law of the Unilateral Declaration of Independence in Respect of Kosovo* (hereafter *Kosovo*), the ICJ took note of the Security Council's practice of issuing resolutions governing non-State actors:

The Court recalls in this regard that it has not been uncommon for the Security Council to make demands on actors other than United Nations Member States and intergovernmental organizations. More specifically, a number of Security Council resolutions adopted on the subject of Kosovo prior to Security Council Resolution 1244 (1999) contained demands addressed *eo nomine* to the Kosovo Albanian leadership.[72]

The Court stated further: 'When interpreting Security Council resolutions, the Court must establish, on a case-by-case basis, considering all relevant circumstances, for whom the Security Council intended to create binding legal obligations.'[73] Pertaining to the disputed Resolution 1244 (1999), the ICJ concluded that

[70] Ibid, para. 139. Notably, Judge Higgins found the Court's conclusions on this point to be 'formalism of an unevenhanded sort'. In her view, the deciding factor must necessarily be 'where responsibility lies for the sending of groups and persons who act against Israeli civilians and the cumulative severity of such action.' See further ibid, Separate Opinion of Judge Higgins, 207, para. 34. See also Section 2.5.

[71] For a different reading, see Gleider I. Hernández, 'Non-state actors from the perspective of the International Court of Justice', in Jean d'Aspremont (ed), *Participants in the International Legal System: Multiple perspectives on non-state actors in international law* (Routledge, 2011), 140, 144. Hernández infers that the ICJ dismissed the self-defence argument due to the lack of international legal personality of the Palestinian people. Para. 139 of the Advisory Opinion, however, does not support this interpretation. There would be little reason for the Court to consider whether the situation in the *Wall* case was comparable to that of the Resolutions 1368 (2001) and 1373 (2001) if it had already entirely dismissed the possibility of self-defence against non-State actors.

[72] *Accordance with International Law of the Unilateral Declaration of Independence in Respect of Kosovo* (Advisory Opinion) [2010] ICJ Rep 403, para. 116.

[73] Ibid, para. 117.

it could not be interpreted as to include a prohibition, 'addressed in particular to the authors', against declaring Kosovo's independence.[74]

Given the ICJ's inference that the Security Council resolution in question did not bind the Kosovo Albanian leadership, Marko Divac Öberg argues that 'one cannot conclude that [the ICJ] has found that the Security Council can bind nonstate actors.'[75] This would appear to be an excessively cautious interpretation of the Court's Opinion, since the wording of paragraphs 116 and 117 partially cited above gives little indication that the Court meant to leave open the question of the capacity of the Security Council vis-à-vis non-State actors. Correspondingly, it seems straightforward to read the Opinion as confirmation that international duties, such as those stemming from Security Council resolutions, may be imposed on non-State actors, including individuals.[76]

Jacques Hartmann has interpreted the Opinion as to imply a presumption against obligations of non-State actors, because the Court required that the Security Council should state unambiguously whom they intended to bind in resolutions.[77] There is, however, little suggestion in the ICJ's statements that the demands for clarity do not apply equally to resolutions addressing States and non-State actors. Indeed, the Court specifically reiterated the interpretative approach taken in its Advisory Opinion of 1971 on the *Legal Consequences for States of the Continued Presence of South Africa in Namibia (South West Africa) notwithstanding Security Council Resolution 276 (1970)*, where the relevant Security Council resolution was indisputably addressed to States.[78]

Against this background, it is submitted that the *Kosovo* Opinion is to be read as confirmation that individuals may incur international legal obligations. Moreover, there is a general demand that the Security Council must unambiguously state whom—be it States or non-State actors—it purports to bind in resolutions. The latter conclusion has little to do with the personality of individuals in international law, but rather lays down specific requirements to the lawmaking of the Security Council. The question of how to determine whether other international norms, in particular treaty provisions, include individual rights or obligations will be further explored in Section 3.3.

[74] Ibid, para. 118. The Court had previously concluded that the authors of the declaration of independence did not act in their capacity as the Provisional Institutions of Self-Government of Kosovo but rather 'as persons who acted together in their capacity as representatives of the people of Kosovo outside the framework of the interim administration.' Ibid, para. 105.

[75] Marko Divac Öberg, 'The Legal Effects of United Nations Resolutions in the Kosovo Advisory Opinion', 105 *AJIL* (2011) 81, 86.

[76] See, for example, Anne Peters, *Beyond Human Rights—The Legal Status of the Individual in International Law* (CUP, 2016) 97–9, Jean d'Aspremont, 'Non-state actors form the perspective of legal positivism', in Jean d'Aspremont (ed.), *Participants in the International Legal System: Multiple perspectives on non-state actors in international law* (Routledge, 2011a) 23, 25, and Andreas Th. Müller's book review 'Kate Parlett. The Individual in the International Legal System. Continuity and Change in International Law', 23 *EJIL* (2012) 294, 298–9.

[77] Jacques Hartmann, 'Kosovos uafhængighedserklæring', *Juristen*, no. 6/7 (2010) 176, 180.

[78] See *Kosovo* (n 72) para. 117, referring to *Legal Consequences for States of the Continued Presence of South Africa in Namibia (South West Africa) notwithstanding Security Council Resolution 276 (1970)*, Advisory Opinion [1971] ICJ Rep (1971) 16, para. 114. See further Section 3.4.3.2.

3.2 The Application of Customary International Law to Individuals

The debate on the concept of individual rights and obligations under international law primarily revolves around treaties, which is hardly surprising since customary international law inherently governs the coexistence of States. Historically, the issues regulated through customary international law have only exceptionally involved the direct interests of individuals. But, as will become apparent in Chapters 4–8, there are examples of rights and obligations conferred directly on individuals on the basis of customary international law.[79] To illustrate the role of the concept international legal personality, when it comes to individual obligations under customary international law, the following section examines the discussion in the Advisory Committee of Jurists of a proposal for the establishment of a High Court of International Justice to prosecute individuals for certain crimes.

3.2.1 The High Court of International Justice proposed to the Advisory Committee of Jurists[80]

On 13 July 1920, president Descamps of the Advisory Committee of Jurists submitted to his colleagues a proposal for 'the establishment of a High Court of International Justice for the purpose of trying crimes against the universal law of nations.'[81] In his presentation, Descamps raised a number of key questions to be considered, including the existence of crimes against the law of nations: 'International law recognises the existence of such crimes, and experience unfortunately shows that they are no mere myth in the history of international affairs, especially in war time.'[82]

Descamps was convinced that 'as the nations would, sooner or later, establish the institution he had just proposed, it would be better for the Committee to consider the question now.'[83] The debate that followed is interesting for several reasons. Not only does it demonstrate the role of the concept of international legal personality in the Advisory Committee's discussion of international criminal obligations of individuals, but, when compared to Committee's debate about the procedural role of individuals before the PCIJ,[84] it also highlights certain conceptual inconsistencies among the members.

Only two other members, Altamira (Senator and Professor at the University of Madrid) and de Lapradelle, were in favour of proceeding with Descamps' proposal. In the eyes of de Lapradelle, the purpose of the League of Nations was 'to prevent a repetition of the calamities which gave rise to its creation'. This, he believed, would be unachievable without 'a stable judicial organisation ... which could take action

[79] See, for example, Sections 5.5 and 6.2.3.1.

[80] This section is based on Astrid Kjeldgaard-Pedersen, 'The Influence of the Concept of International Legal Personality in the Drafting on the Statute of the Permanent Court of International Justice' 16 *JHIL* (2014) 9.

[81] *Procès-verbaux* (n 13) 498. [82] Ibid. [83] Ibid, 499.

[84] See further Section 3.1.2.1.

against those guilty of crimes against international justice.'[85] Altamira agreed fully with Descamps and de Lapradelle, but underlined the necessity of explaining 'the organic connection undoubtedly existing between the President's proposal and the work covered by the mandate given to the members'.[86] Indeed, the formality concerning the Committee's competence was reason enough for several members to dismiss Descamps' plan. Adatci, Japanese minister to Belgium, and Loder supported the idea of an international court with jurisdiction over future crimes, but believed that the proposal should be referred to a new conference on international law, since it exceeded the task the Advisory Committee had been called upon to complete.[87] They both underlined the uncertainties as to the international legal rules the court would apply, and thereby implied that international law did not (yet) confer obligations on individuals. Loder strongly emphasized the rule of *nulla poena sine praevia lege poenali* and found that the court proposed by Descamps 'could only be of a political nature', since it would be established 'before defining the law to be applied by it.'[88]

Notably, only the argument put forward by Ricci-Busatti corresponds fully to his statements on the possibility of allowing individuals to petition the PCIJ: 'As to individuals, he did not think that they could commit infractions of International Law, as it was law between States; a legal relationship of this kind between States and individuals was, in his opinion, inadmissible.'[89]

Fernandes, however, who together with Ricci-Busatti had invoked the 'States-only' conception of international legal personality during the Committee's debate on the procedural capacities of individuals before the PCIJ, was not opposed to Descamps' idea out of principle, but found that 'steps should be taken to define the crimes and assess the penalties in order to make the operation of a High Court possible.'[90]

Conversely, Root, who had dismissed the idea of granting individuals access to the PCIJ for pragmatic reasons, as he presumed it would be unacceptable to States, referred to the 'States-only' conception of international legal personality in his rejection of the proposed High Court: 'As only States are subjects of International Law, an individual can only be punished if the act which he has committed is punishable according to the national law which applies to the case . . . .'[91]

Lastly, it may be recalled that Descamps himself stated as follows during the Committee's discussions of the possible access of individuals to the PCIJ: '[I]nternational law governs relations between States as such, and it is the duty

[85] See *Procès-verbaux* (n 13) 500. See also ibid, 508–10. [86] Ibid, 501–2.

[87] Ibid, 502 (Adatci) and ibid, 503–4 (Loder). See also ibid, 504–5 (Fernandes) and ibid, 506–8 (Lord Phillimore). With reference to the limited extent of the Committee's mandate, Hagerup refused to take part in discussions of the material contents of the proposal. See ibid, 499–500.

[88] Ibid, 504. Descamps subsequently responded to this argument that: 'Offences against the universal law of nations are . . . defined with sufficient clearness in International Law: they are offences of such a nature as to affect the common safety of all States, and to entitle all to demand that justice should be done.' Ibid, 512.

[89] Ibid, 503. [90] Ibid, 504. [91] Ibid, 505.

of States to protect their nationals.' Nevertheless, he found the establishment of the High Court to be 'necessary to complete the organisation of international justice.'[92]

The comparison between the members' opinions on these two issues is interesting, because it shows that, with the exception of Ricci-Busatti, none of them consistently inferred the theoretical argument that individuals are not subjects of international law. Rather, it was quite possible for several members to assume one position on the international legal personality of individuals as regards the possibility of individual obligations under international law, and another concerning the right of individuals to petition an international court. In other words, a particular theoretical assumption about the subjects of international law can hardly have been the decisive factor for the various positions taken by the vast majority of the Committee's members on the two questions at hand. Instead, the turning point seems to have been whether they found a particular problem involving the interests of individuals to be of such a nature as to require an international solution. Descamps provides an illustrative example: as to the question of the right of petition to the PCIJ, he found the interests of individuals to be fully covered by 'the duty of States to protect their nationals.' Therefore, there was no problem to be solved by international law. However, Descamps clearly found crimes of a certain character to demand an international response: 'It is by no means impossible in this case, and might be necessary in many others, to reconcile the shortcomings in the operation of national jurisdictions and the adequate working of an international tribunal.'[93]

While Adatci and Loder did not argue that individual obligations under international law were altogether impossible, they denied the existence of international crimes. The disagreement on this point was not based on an analysis of the sources of international law, which the Committee had previously discussed.[94] Rather, Adatci and Loder categorized the question as belonging to the national sphere, whereas Descamps, Altamira, and de Lapradelle found it to call for an international solution.[95]

Against this background, it seems that the members of the Advisory Committee primarily pointed to the argument that individuals have no international legal personality, when they wished to emphasize that a particular issue was suitable for domestic regulation and did not demand an international response. Only Ricci-Busatti inferred that all matters concerning the interests of individuals by definition belonged to domestic law. The other members' respective categorizations of the relevant issues as international or national was based on whether they essentially found them to involve the interests of more than one State.

3.3 The Doctrine of Diplomatic Protection

The customary rules on diplomatic protection govern the situation where State A brings a claim against State B alleging that State B has subjected a national of State

[92] Ibid, 510. [93] Ibid, 513. [94] See Spiermann (n 23) 214–18.
[95] Ibid, 227–30.

A to treatment that amounts to a violation of international law. The underlying idea is that the general rules on State responsibility need supplement, because the interests of individuals are involved.[96]

In 2006, the ILC adopted the Articles on Diplomatic Protection (hereafter ADP),[97] which 'give content to [Article 44 of the articles on Responsibility of States for internationally wrongful acts] by elaborating on the rules relating to the nationality of claims and the exhaustion of local remedies.'[98] The ADP predominantly codify customary international law.[99] Given that the ILC had categorized the ARSIWA as secondary rules,[100] and given that rules on diplomatic protection cover the particular part of the law on State responsibility regarding responsibility for injury to foreign nationals, it is only logical that the ILC has consistently perceived of the ADP as a set of secondary rules.[101] For present purposes, however, what is of principal interest is not the content of these secondary rules, but rather the categorization of the underlying primary right, which is being asserted through diplomatic protection. As a consequence, the following sections will focus specifically on the correlation between the diplomatic protection doctrine and the concept of individual rights under treaties.

3.3.1 A legal fiction: Whose rights are being asserted?

It is commonly claimed that the doctrine of diplomatic protection is based on 'a legal fiction': An injury suffered by a national because of a foreign State's violation of international law is treated *as if it were an injury to his home State*. The State of nationality thereby becomes entitled to raise a claim against the host State.[102] The resort to this fiction, which dates back to Vattel,[103] has consistently been a subject

[96] This notion is reflected in Article 44 of the ARSIWA:

> The responsibility of a State may not be invoked if: (a) The claim is not brought in accordance with any applicable rule relating to the nationality of claims; (b) The claim is one to which the rule of exhaustion of local remedies applies and any available and effective local remedy has not been exhausted.

[97] The draft articles including commentaries appear in *Official Records of the General Assembly*, 61st session, Supplement No. 10, UN Doc. A/61/10, Chapter IV, (hereafter Diplomatic Protection Commentaries).

[98] Ibid, 23.

[99] See, for example, *Ahmadou Sadio Diallo (Republic of Guinea v. Democratic Republic of the Congo), Preliminary Objections* (Judgment) [2007] ICJ Rep 582 (hereafter *Diallo (Preliminary Objections)*) para. 39, Annemarieke Vermeer-Künzli, 'Diallo and the Draft Articles: The Application of the Draft Articles on Diplomatic Protection in the Ahmadou Sadio Diallo Case', 20 *LJIL* (2007b) 941, 943, and Kate Parlett, *The Individual in the International Legal System—Continuity and Change in International Law* (CUP, 2011) 86.

[100] II *YILC* (2001), Part II, 31.

[101] See Diplomatic Protection Commentaries (n 97) 22–6. See also *Preliminary Report on Diplomatic Protection* (1998), Special Rapporteur Mohamed Bennouna, paras 55–65, and *Seventh Report on Diplomatic Protection* (2006), Special Rapporteur John Dugard, para. 3.

[102] See further Annemarieke Vermeer-Künzli, 'As If: The Legal Fiction in Diplomatic Protection', 18 *EJIL* (2007a) 37, and Chittharanjan F. Amerasinghe, *Diplomatic Protection* (OUP, 2008) 6ff. See, however, Spiermann (n 56) 211–12.

[103] Emmerich de Vattel, *Le Droit des Gens ou Principes de la Loi Naturelle* (Carnegie, 1916), Liv. II, chap. VI, § 71, 309. See further Amerasinghe (n 102) 10ff.

of heated debate.[104] Opinions remain divided on whether the right being enforced through diplomatic protection is in fact the home State's own right or the right of the national. The *Mavrommatis* Judgment issued by the PCIJ in 1924, which is probably the most cited authority on diplomatic protection, is traditionally interpreted to imply that an injury to an individual in itself constitutes a direct injury to his State of nationality:[105]

It is an elementary principle of international law that a State is entitled to protect its subjects, when injured by acts contrary to international law committed by another State, from whom they have been unable to obtain satisfaction through the ordinary channels. By taking up the case of one of its subjects and by resorting to diplomatic action or international judicial proceedings on his behalf, a State is in reality asserting its own rights—its right to ensure, in the person of its subjects, respect for the rules of international law.[106]

The first examples of what would later be termed the diplomatic protection doctrine date back to the end of the eighteenth century.[107] Historically, the rules on diplomatic protection were developed in conjunction with substantive rules on treatment of aliens. But, as the ICJ unequivocally confirmed in 2007, it is commonly accepted today that diplomatic protection is not limited to violations of such rules:

Owing to the substantive development of international law over recent decades in respect of the rights it accords to individuals, the scope *ratione materiae* of diplomatic protection, originally limited to alleged violations of the minimum standard of treatment of aliens, has subsequently widened to include, inter alia, internationally guaranteed human rights.[108]

[104] For a thorough analysis of the legal fiction in diplomatic protection, see Vermeer-Künzli (n 102).

[105] See for example ILC, *First Report on Diplomatic Protection*, Special Rapporteur John Dugard (2000) para. 62.

[106] *Mavrommatis* (n 23) 12. This dictum has been repeated by both the PCIJ and the ICJ on several occasions. See *Case Concerning the Payment of Various Serbian Loans Issued in France* (Judgment) [1929] PCIJ Ser. A, No. 20 (hereafter '*Serbian Loans*'), 12, *Panevezys-Saldutiskis Railway* (Judgment) [1939] PCIJ Ser. A/B, No. 76, 16, *Nottebohm Case (Liechtenstein v. Guatemala) (Second Phase)* (Judgment) [1955] ICJ Rep 4, 24. See also *Case Concerning the Barcelona Traction, Light and Power Company, Limited (Second Phase) (Belgium v. Spain)* (Judgment) [1970] ICJ Rep 3 (hereafter *Barcelona Traction (Second Phase)*) para. 78. In *Interhandel (Switzerland v. United States of America)(Preliminary Objections)* (Judgment) [1959] ICJ Rep 6 (hereafter *Interhandel*), 27, the ICJ referred to the applicant state as having 'adopted the cause of its national'. See also the claims of the US in *United States Diplomatic and Consular Staff in Tehran* (Judgment) [1980] ICJ Rep 3, para. 8. In addition to the cases of *Breard* (n 62), *LaGrand* (n 63), and *Avena and Other Mexican Nationals (Mexico v. United States of America)* (Judgment) [2004] ICJ Rep 12 (hereafter *Avena*), proceedings brought before the ICJ under the heading of diplomatic protection also include *Elettronica Sicula SpA (ELSI) (United States of America v. Italy)* (Judgment) [1989] ICJ Rep 15, and *Diallo (Republic of Guinea v. Democratic Republic of the Congo)(Merits)* (Judgment) [2010] ICJ Rep 639. See also *Oil Platforms (Islamic Republic of Iran v. United States of America)* (Judgment) [2003] ICJ Rep 161, *Separate Opinion of Judge Rigaux*, para. 10, and *Arrest Warrant of 11 April 2000 (Democratic Republic of the Congo v. Belgium)* (Judgment) [2002] ICJ Rep 3 (hereafter *Arrest Warrant*).

[107] Even earlier on it was custom to issue letters of reprisal when a foreign state (or its nationals) had caused damage to an individual. This practice can be seen as an antecedent to diplomatic protection as it to some extent turned a conflict between a foreign national and a host state into a dispute between the host state and the home state. See Parlett (n 99) 48.

[108] See *Diallo (Preliminary Objections)* (n 99) para. 39. See also Amerasinghe (n 102) 13 and Spiermann (n 68) 377.

Still, there is no broad consensus as to which international rules are to be asserted through diplomatic protection[109] and which are to be enforced by application of the general rules on State responsibility as set out in the ARSIWA. The question is where the scope *ratione materiae* of diplomatic protection ends, and the general rules on State responsibility begin. Evidently, primary rules to be asserted by way of diplomatic protection involve the *interests* of individuals,[110] but are they confined to rules that can be categorized as individual *rights* under international law? For anyone in search of an answer to this question, it is unfortunate that the ILC deliberately limited its study to 'the rules governing the circumstances in which diplomatic protection may be exercised and the conditions that must be met before it may be exercised',[111] but left 'open the question whether the State exercising diplomatic protection does so in its own right or that of its national—or both.'[112]

The *Mavrommatis* formula was reproduced in Article 1 of the ILC's ADP as adopted on first reading in 2004, which clearly stated that a State exercising diplomatic protection is 'adopting in its own right the cause of its national'.[113] Subsequently, this wording was heavily criticized by both States and ILC members. Italy, for example, found that it reflected a concept that was 'no longer accurate in current international law.'[114] As a result of the criticism, the wording of Article 1 was reconsidered by the drafting committee. The final version adopted on second reading in 2006 provides:

> For the purposes of the present draft articles, diplomatic protection consists of the invocation by a State, through diplomatic action or other means of peaceful settlement, of the responsibility of another State for an injury caused by an internationally wrongful act of that State to a natural or legal person that is a national of the former State with a view to the implementation of such responsibility.[115]

[109] It is, however, generally assumed that the rules of diplomatic protection do not apply to cases concerning violations of obligations *erga omnes*. The requirement of nationality is irrelevant where the obligation is owed to the international community as a whole. See *Barcelona Traction (Second Phase)* (n 106) para. 35. See also Article 48(1)(b) of the *Draft articles on Responsibility of States for Internationally Wrongful Acts* and *Armed Activities on the Territory of the Congo (Democratic Republic of the Congo v. Uganda)* (Judgment) [2005] ICJ Rep 168, *Separate Opinion of Judge Simma*, paras 35–41. Giorgio Gaja seems to assume that all human rights obligations are *erga omnes* in Giorgio Gaja, 'The Position of Individuals in International Law: An ILC Perspective', 21 *EJIL* (2010) 11, 13. That is probably stretching the *erga omnes* category too far in light of *Barcelona Traction* (n 106) para. 91. See further Vermeer-Künzli (n 99) 942 and Phoebe Okowa, 'Issues of Admissibility and the Law on International Responsibility' in Malcolm D. Evans (ed.), *International Law* (4th edn, OUP, 2014) 495ff.

[110] Before the designation of diplomatic protection as a topic for independent study by the ILC, an early version of the ARSIWA included a provision (Article 22) requiring exhaustion of local remedies in cases concerning 'obligations which are designed to protect individuals, natural or juridical persons, and which, at the international level, formulate certain requirements and establish certain guarantees concerning the treatment to be accorded by States, at the internal level, to the persons in question and to their property.' See II *YILC* (1977), Part II, 30. See also Spiermann (n 68) 378.

[111] Diplomatic Protection Commentaries (n 97) 24. [112] Ibid, 26.

[113] ILC, *Diplomatic Protection—Titles and texts of the draft articles adopted by the Drafting Committee on first reading*, 2004, UN Doc. A/CN.4/L/647, 1.

[114] ILC, *Comments and Observations Received from Governments* (2006), UN Doc. A/CN.4/561/Add.2, 2. Italy instead proposed a wording of Article 1 based on an extract from para. 40 of the ICJ's *Avena* judgment from 2004. As will be discussed in detail below, this paragraph is quite problematic, and the Italian proposal therefore hardly commendable.

[115] Ibid, 16. The ICJ stated in *Diallo (Preliminary Objections)* (n 99) para. 39, that Article 1 is a reflection of customary international law.

The Commentaries maintain that Article 1 purposely does not answer the question whether a State exercising diplomatic protection is claiming its own right, the right of its national, or both.[116] It would perhaps be the logical and systematic solution to assume that States enforce their own rights in accordance with the ARSIWA, while the rules of diplomatic protection only apply to violations of rights of individuals under international law. Following this line of thought, Vermeer-Künzli has recently concluded: 'There can be no doubt that the injury that stands at the basis of the exercise of diplomatic protection is an injury of individual rights.'[117]

In the eyes of the present author, however, it would appear more accurate to say that diplomatic protection is a set of secondary rules to be brought into play in situations where the primary rule has the purpose of protecting the *interests* of individuals, even if it is construed as a State right. At present, there is hardly sufficient support for the argument that application of the rules on diplomatic protection is contingent upon States having created an international norm, which provides for individual rights. Rather, the decisive factor seems to be the involvement of individual interests.[118]

The so-called mixed claims, which refer to claims based in part on injury to the State itself (direct injury) and in part on injury to the State's national (indirect injury), add to the confusion. In such cases, it is necessary to distinguish between the direct and the indirect part of the claim. Diplomatic protection only applies to the indirect part, whereas the relevant secondary rules as regards the direct part are the ARSIWA. The categorization of a claim as direct or indirect is often a complicated task,[119] and as the *Avena* case before the ICJ revealed, it is not to be taken lightly.

3.3.1.1 Classification of claims: The ICJ's 2004 Judgment in Avena

In the *Avena* case,[120] Mexico claimed that the US had violated the VCCR in fifty-two cases involving Mexican nationals, who had all been sentenced to death. At first glance, the ICJ's Judgment appears to be a replicate of *LaGrand*. But, whereas *LaGrand* gave answers to several essential questions, *Avena* is less commendable upon closer inspection.[121] First of all, *LaGrand* clearly established the existence of individual rights under international law and, second, it affirmed that such rights can be enforced through diplomatic protection without feigning that the State itself suffered the injury. In *Avena*, however, the Court rejected the exercise of diplomatic

[116] Diplomatic Protection Commentaries (n 97) 26. For a critical analysis see Vermeer-Künzli (n 102), 60.

[117] See ibid, 39.

[118] See further Chapter 4.

[119] See further ILC, *Second Report on Diplomatic Protection*, Special Rapporteur John Dugard (2001) para. 19.

[120] *Avena* (n 106).

[121] For a detailed account of the case, see Annemarieke Künzli, 'Case Concerning Mexican Nationals', 18 *LJIL* (2005) 49.

protection and construed Mexico's claim as a direct claim. The Court first reiterated its findings in *LaGrand*, but then went on to say that the rights of the national and the rights of his home State in Article 36(1) are interdependent in the sense that a violation of the national's rights under Article 36(1)(b) may entail violation of the State's rights under Article 36(1)(a) and (c) and vice versa. On this basis, the Court concluded:

> In these special circumstances of interdependence of the rights of the State and of individual rights, Mexico may, in submitting a claim in its own name, request the Court to rule on the violation of rights conferred on Mexican nationals under Article 36, paragraph 1(b). The duty to exhaust local remedies does not apply to such a request.[122]

In spite of the fact that Mexico's original application was a mixed claim based on both direct and indirect injuries, the Court let the injury to Mexico 'absorb' the injury to its nationals thereby rendering it unnecessary to deal with the matter of exhaustion of local remedies.[123] This approach is problematic, especially because it is poorly reasoned.[124] Although there is no general agreement on how to determine whether a claim is direct or indirect,[125] it is regrettable that the Court refrained from carefully considering the classification of the injury to the Mexican nationals.

Scholars recommend various tests to explain the distinction between direct and indirect claims. The 'preponderance test' entails examination of the different elements of the claim in order to determine if the direct or the indirect claim is 'preponderant'.[126] Similarly, the '*sine qua non* test' implies an evaluation of whether the claim including both direct and indirect injury would have been raised without the injury to the national.[127] Had the Court employed these methods, it would have likely concluded that the violation of Article 36(1)(b) should indeed have been treated separately and called for application of the secondary rules of diplomatic protection.[128]

122 *Avena* (n 106) para. 40.

123 The Court's approach was perhaps motivated by the fact that handling Mexico's claim under the rules of diplomatic protection would have required an evaluation of whether local remedies remained available in the cases of all fifty-two Mexican nationals. It seems that local remedies had in fact only been exhausted in three instances. See further Künzli (n 121) 51 and 53, and Enrico Milano, 'Diplomatic Protection and Human Rights before the International Court of Justice: Re-Fashioning Tradition', 35 *NYIL* (2004) 85, 141.

124 Unsurprisingly, para. 40 was heavily criticized in the separate and dissenting opinions. Judges Vereshchetin, Parra-Aranguren, and Tomka and Judge ad hoc Sepulveda all found that Mexico's claim was an act of diplomatic protection. See ICJ, *Avena* (2004), *Separate Opinion of Judge Vereshchetin*, para. 7, *Separate Opinion of Judge Parra-Aranguren*, para. 28, *Separate Opinion of Judge Tomka*, para. 7, and *Separate Opinion of Judge ad hoc Sepulveda*, para. 22.

125 ILC, *Second Report on Diplomatic Protection*, Special Rapporteur John Dugard (2001) para. 19.

126 Ibid, paras 20ff. See also ICJ, *Avena* (2004), *Separate Opinion of Judge Vereshchetin*, paras 7–11 and *Separate Opinion of Judge Parra-Aranguren*, paras 27–28.

127 With regard to other factors to be considered in connection with the classification of a claim, such as 'the subject of the dispute', 'the nature of the claim', and 'the nature of the remedies', see ILC, *Second Report on Diplomatic Protection*, Special Rapporteur John Dugard (2001) paras 24ff.

128 See Künzli (n 121) 53ff.

3.3.2 Diplomatic protection and the international legal personality of individuals

On the basis of the previous sections, it is submitted that the rules on diplomatic protection are a set of secondary rules, which apply when the interests of individuals are at stake. But they are not limited to violations of individual rights. Consequently, the fact that diplomatic protection has been exercised with regard to a particular international rule tells us very little about whether that rule amounts to an individual right or not.[129] Neither can we rely on the various tests concerning the classification of a claim as direct or indirect. These tests weigh the interests of the individual against the interests of the State with the purpose of determining the appropriate set of secondary rules, but they do not determine whether the violated primary rule is an individual right.

In fact, the main point to be drawn from the preceding analysis is that while the rules on diplomatic protection might demonstrate the frequently limited procedural capacities of individuals in international law, they are not helpful in the characterization of the underlying primary norm. Instead, all rests on the rules on treaty interpretation, when we want to determine whether or not the primary norm entails an individual right. Prior to examining the issue of treaty interpretation in Section 3.4, however, it is pertinent to dwell briefly upon two particular aspects of diplomatic protection, where the discussion on the position of individuals in international law appears to have particular impact. As will be demonstrated in the following, the view a scholar or a judge takes on the international legal personality of individuals is often reflected in his perception of the 'exhaustion of local remedies rule' and/or his ideas about the future of diplomatic protection.

3.3.2.1 The exhaustion of local remedies rule

One of the contentious issues in the academic debate on the diplomatic protection doctrine is whether the rule on exhaustion of local remedies is substantial or procedural in nature.[130] The position one takes on this matter has significant consequences inter alia for the nationality of claims principle.[131] But, more importantly for present purposes, it also says something about one's underlying presumptions about the personality of individuals in international law. Regarding the rule on exhaustion of local remedies as substantial corresponds well to the 'States-only' conception of international legal personality, since it would follow that the internationally wrongful act does not occur at the time of injury to the individual, but only when local remedies have been exhausted.

In *Phosphates in Morocco*, the PCIJ dismissed the contention of the Italian government that exhaustion of local remedies was a material requirement. The Permanent

[129] For a different understanding, see Parlett (n 99) Chapter 2.

[130] In the *Interhandel* case of 1959, the ICJ stated that the requirement of exhaustion of local remedies was 'a well-established rule of customary international law'. See *Interhandel* (n 106) 27.

[131] See further ILC, *Second Report on Diplomatic Protection*, Special Rapporteur John Dugard (2001) paras 33ff.

Court found that the relevant administrative decision by the Mines Department was 'a definitive act which would, by itself, directly involve international responsibility.'[132] The issue was thoroughly debated during the ILC's work on State responsibility,[133] and in 1977, Special Rapporteur Roberto Ago, who had appeared as counsel for Italy in *Phosphates in Morocco*, argued that 'the breach of the international obligation has not been completed before [local] remedies are exhausted'.[134] This view was reflected in Article 22 of the ARSIWA adopted on first reading, but it was later abandoned at the initiative of Special Rapporteur James Crawford.[135] Subsequently, the procedural conception of the exhaustion of local remedies rule was promoted in the ILC's work on diplomatic protection. As Dugard concluded in 2001: 'No decisions of the International Court of Justice gives support for the view that the local remedies rule is substantive in nature. While clear judicial support for the procedural view is not forthcoming either, there are some signs that this approach is preferred.'[136]

3.3.2.2 The future of diplomatic protection

In light of the widespread acceptance among contemporary international lawyers that individuals possess at least some degree of international legal personality, the continued relevance of diplomatic protection has been drawn into question. Some scholars argue that the rules of diplomatic protection are merely evidence that individuals did not originally possess international legal personality. As a natural consequence of the development towards further involvement of individuals in international law, they believe that the doctrine of diplomatic protection has now become obsolete.[137] Others advocate that diplomatic protection continues to serve the purpose of ensuring the rights of individuals under international law, but only where no forum exists for the individual to enforce his rights independently against a foreign State. Orrego Vicuña suggested such a residuary role for diplomatic protection in his 1999 report to the International Law Association Committee on

[132] *Phosphates in Morocco (Preliminary Objections)* (Judgment) [1938] PCIJ Ser. A/B, No. 74, 28. See also Spiermann (n 55) 377–8.

[133] See for example II *YILC* (1977), Part II, 34ff.

[134] Ibid, 35. In Ago's opinion, individuals have no personality in international law. See further Section 3.1.1.

[135] See ILC, *Second Report on State Responsibility*, Special Rapporteur James Crawford (1999) paras 146–147.

[136] ILC, *Second Report on Diplomatic Protection*, Special Rapporteur John Dugard (2001) para. 49. See further paras 63–66. See also Spiermann (n 68) 386.

[137] See with further references ILC, *Preliminary Report on Diplomatic Protection*, Special Rapporteur Mohamed Bennouna (1998) para. 2, Vasileios Pergantis, 'Towards a "Humanization" of Diplomatic Protection', 66 *ZaöRV* (2006) 351, 352, and Vermeer-Kunzli (n 102) 44. Also, it is not uncommonly argued in recent writings that several of the preconditions for exercising diplomatic protection, e.g. continuous nationality, the exhaustion of local remedies, and the assessment of damages, suggest that the claim (in addition to the underlying right) belongs to the individual rather than the State. However, as Dugard pointed out in 2006, such arguments overlook the distinction between primary and secondary rules of international law. See ILC, *Seventh Report on Diplomatic Protection*, Special Rapporteur John Dugard (2006) para. 3.

Diplomatic Protection.[138] Similarly, Phoebe Okowa refers to diplomatic protection as 'a default mechanism for the enforcement of claims where there are no direct avenues provided for by international law.'[139] These observations seem to overstate the development as regards the position of individuals as a matter of positive international law. As has been argued here, the diplomatic protection doctrine does not in itself have anything to do with whether or not individuals possess international legal personality. Regardless of whether individuals are commonly accepted as subjects of international law, they presently have limited capacity to enforce their rights. In addition, diplomatic protection remains a relevant instrument for securing interests of individuals that are not protected by way of an international norm prescribing individual rights. Accordingly, it follows from Article 16 of the ADP that the ability of individuals to enforce their rights independently is not affected by the fact that a State is entitled to exercise diplomatic protection with regard to the same injury.

Nevertheless, certain developments in the rules on diplomatic protection clearly indicate a change in the perception of individuals, and are as such somewhat at odds with the general scheme of diplomatic protection. For example, Article 19(c) of the ADP contains a provision recommending that States transfer any compensation obtained through an exercise of diplomatic protection to the injured individual. According to the commentary, this practice has not yet acquired the status of a customary rule, but the ILC finds it to be among the 'desirable practices, constituting necessary features of diplomatic protection, that add strength to diplomatic protection as a means for the protection of human rights and foreign investment.'[140] While it is not uncommon for States to transfer compensation to the injured individual in practice,[141] obliging them to do so runs counter to the principal idea in the diplomatic protection doctrine that the State holds the secondary right to present claim.[142]

3.4 Treaty Interpretation: Individual Rights or Obligations?

In certain treaties, the contracting States explicate that they do not intend for the provisions to apply directly. For example, Article 17(3) of the 1997 Agreement on International Humane Trapping Standards between the European Community, Canada and the Russian Federation provides: 'This Agreement is not self-executing. Each Party shall implement the commitments and obligations arising from this Agreement in accordance with its internal procedures.'[143] However, such explicit

[138] ILC, *First Report on Diplomatic Protection*, Special Rapporteur John Dugard (2000) para. 69.

[139] Okowa (n 109) 483–4.

[140] Diplomatic Protection Commentaries (n 97) 95.

[141] *Seventh Report on Diplomatic Protection*, Special Rapporteur John Dugard (2006) paras 93–103.

[142] See also Vermeer-Kunzli (n 102) 62. Gaja argues that the ILC should have gone further and stated that reparation should always accrue to the injured individual. See Gaja (n 109) 13.

[143] Agreement on International Humane Trapping Standards between the European Community, Canada and the Russian Federation, 25 December 1997, *Official Journal of the European Communities* L42 (14 February 1998) 43–57. See further André Nollkaemper, *National Courts and the International Rule of Law* (OUP, 2011) 135.

statements are exceptional. In the words of André Nollkaemper 'states will generally not bother to express themselves expressly or implicitly on direct effect.'[144] Frequently, it is far from obvious whether a treaty provision involving the interests of individuals does in fact entail direct rights or obligations, or whether it merely governs the relationship between the contracting parties.

The following section (3.4.1) will examine the definitional relationship between individual rights and human rights, while Section 3.4.2 will account briefly for the general rules on treaty interpretation in the VCLT. Finally, on the basis of examples from of Judgments and Advisory Opinions issues by the PCIJ and the ICJ, Section 3.4.3 will outline the criteria for determining whether or not treaty provisions entail individual rights and obligations.

3.4.1 Individual rights vs human rights

Commentators frequently identify individual rights with human rights. For example, the International Law Association's *Final Report on the Impact of International Human Rights Law on General International Law* of 2008 reads: 'International human rights law, in the sense of the present report, includes not merely human rights law *stricto sensu* but any international norm capable of conferring rights and duties directly on individuals regardless of nationality including under international humanitarian law and international criminal law.'[145]

However, classifying every single individual right as a human right is misleading, even though it is explicitly accepted that not all such rights are derived from classical human rights treaties. In effect, this definition of international human rights law may be seen as a reflection of the 'States-only' perception of international legal personality, because it implies that general international law cannot possibly govern the conditions of individuals directly.[146] Granted, the human rights movement has had tremendous influence on the number and extent of rights accruing to human beings as a matter of positive international law, but it has nothing to do with whether or not States have the competence to enter into international agreements conferring all sorts of rights (and obligations) on individuals. Consequently, it is not necessary to determine whether a provision entails a human right in international law in order to categorize it as an individual right.[147] As James Crawford

[144] Ibid.

[145] ILA, Rio De Janeiro Conference, *Final Report on the Impact of International Human Rights Law on General International Law* (2008) 2. See also Milano (n 123) 87–8.

[146] See also Section 7.2.2.

[147] In the field of international investment law, for example, it is nevertheless common for scholars to discuss the capability of investors as direct right-holders under international investment agreement with reference to human rights. See, for example, Anastasios Gourgourinis, 'Investors' Rights Qua Human Rights? Revisiting the "Direct"/"Derivative" Rights Debate', in Malgosia Fitzmaurice and Panos Merkouris (eds), *The Interpretation and Application of the European Convention of Human Rights: Legal and Practical Implications* (Brill, 2012) 147. See further August Reinisch, 'Investors', in Math Noortmann, August Reinisch, and Cedric Ryngaert (eds), *Non-State Actors in International Law* (Hart, 2015) 253, 260, and Martins Paparinskis, 'Investment Treaty Arbitration and the (New) Law of State Responsibility', 24 *EJIL* (2013) 617. See also Section 8.2.

concludes: '[H]uman rights in international law appear to be a sub-set of individual rights . . .'.[148] The ICJ has endorsed this point of view in the *LaGrand* case. Germany's argument that Article 36(1) gave rise to individual rights was partly based on the premise that the provision had assumed the character of a human right pertaining to foreigners.[149] The Court did not, however, find it relevant to determine whether or not the rights under Article 36(1) can be categorized as human rights.[150] It thereby indicated that there is no definitional correlation between individual rights and human rights.[151] Rather, individual rights are 'a pervasive phenomenon'.[152]

3.4.2 The VCLT rules on treaty interpretation

The essential provisions on treaty interpretation in Articles 31 and 32 of the VCLT are quite vague and imprecise. During the preliminary debates on the subject, the ILC focused on whether treaty interpretation was governed by objective or by subjective criteria, that is, centred on the text per se or the intention of parties.[153] In the end, the pragmatic solution proposed by the fourth Special Rapporteur, Humphrey Waldock, prevailed:

> The formulation ultimately adopted by the ILC thus reflects the idea that, while it is the text of the treaty that must be taken as the authentic expression of the agreement of the parties, the treaty is to be read as a whole and respect paid to its object and purpose, rather than simply taking words that are the subject of controversy and digging out their meaning solely from dictionary, grammar and syntax.[154]

[148] Crawford (n 56) 29. See also Spiermann (n 56) 209–10. In contrast, following her theory of 'the international individual right' discussed in Section 2.4, Peters argues: 'Human rights belong to the layer of international constitutional law. The simple individual rights do not belong to this layer, but rather (figuratively) to the layer of ordinary international law "below" that layer.' Anne Peters, *Beyond Human Rights—The Legal Status of the Individual in International Law* (CUP, 2016) 437.

[149] *LaGrand* (n 63), verbatim record 2000/26, 13 November 2000, 56. The US on the other hand contended that the rights in question were not human rights, cf. ibid, verbatim record 2000/31, 17 November 2000, 29.

[150] *LaGrand* (n 63) para. 78. In an Advisory Opinion of 1999, the IACtHR examined the correlation between Article 36(1) and the human right to a fair trial under the ICCPR, the Charter of the OAS, and the American Declaration of the Rights and Duties of Man. See IACtHR, *Right to Information on Consular Assistance in the Framework of the Guarantees of the Due Process of Law* (Advisory Opinion) OC-16/99, 1 October 1999, paras 110–124. Some commentators find it regrettable that the ICJ refrained from entering into a similar evaluation in the *LaGrand* judgment. See Martin Mennecke and Christian J. Tams, 'LaGrand Case (Germany v. United States of America)' 51 *ICLQ* (2002) 449, 454–55, and Milano (n 123) 126ff.

[151] See also the ILC's commentary on Article 33 of ARSIWA, which in addition to *LaGrand* (n 63) refers to *Jurisdiction of the Courts of Danzig* (n 39), cf. II *YILC* (2001), Part Two, 95, and Crawford, 'The ILC's Articles of Responsibility of States for Internationally Wrongful Acts: A Retrospect' (n 56) 887.

[152] Christian J. Tams, 'Consular Assistance: Rights, Remedies and Responsibility: Comments on the ICJ's Judgment in the *LaGrand* Case' 13 *EJIL* (2002) 1257.

[153] I *YILC* (1964) 275ff.

[154] Richard K. Gardiner, *Treaty Interpretation* (OUP, 2008) 144–5.

The ILC envisioned a holistic approach to the general rule in Article 31, so that the individual elements would be applied together in 'a single combined operation' rather than paragraph by paragraph.[155]

Article 32 explicitly categorizes *travaux préparatoires* as a supplementary means of interpretation.[156] In order not to exclude relevant evidence, the ILC did not provide a definition of the concept.[157] McNair referred to the *travaux préparatoires* as 'an omnibus expression which is used rather loosely to indicate all documents such as memoranda, minutes of conferences, and drafts of the treaty under negotiation'.[158] In the present book, the *travaux préparatoires* to treaties serve two purposes. One is as supplementary means of interpretation according to Article 32 of the VCLT in the identification of *lex lata*.[159] The other is as a primary source of information about the influence of the concept of international legal personality as a theoretical construct on the formation of new positive norms of international law.

Notably, the ILC dismissed the idea that a distinction must be drawn between 'law-making treaties'[160] and other treaties for the purposes of interpretation:[161]

> Some jurists in their exposition of the principles of treaty interpretation distinguish between law-making and other treaties, and it is true that the character of a treaty may affect the question whether the application of a particular principle, maxim or method of interpretation is suitable in a particular case (e.g. the *contra proferentem* principle or the use of *travaux preparatoires*). But for the purpose of formulating the general rules of interpretation the Commission did not consider it necessary to make such a distinction.[162]

Against the background of the decisions of the PCIJ and the ICJ discussed in Section 3.1.2.2, it is submitted that general principles of treaty interpretation apply, when it is to be determined whether a particular provision contains direct rights or obligations for individuals. For present purposes, however, it may be fruitful to explore in some detail what 'normal treaty interpretation' entails with regard to provisions that may or may not include individual rights or obligations.

3.4.3 Examples of treaty interpretation: individual rights or obligations?

In order to identify the particular considerations that are relevant to treaty interpretation when it comes to individual rights and obligations, it is appropriate to

[155] II *YILC* (1966) 219. See also Gardiner (n 154) 8 and 141.

[156] See further Jan Klabbers, 'The Declining Importance of Travaux Préparatoires', 50 *Netherlands International Law Review* (2003) 267–88.

[157] II *YILC* (1964) 205.

[158] McNair (n 45) 411. See also Gardiner (n 154) 24.

[159] Arguably, the preparatory works have a more significant bearing on treaty interpretation in practice than Article 32 implies. See further Stephen M. Schwebel, 'May Preparatory Work Be Used to Correct Rather Than Confirm the Clear Meaning of a Treaty Provision?', in Jerzy Makarczyk, *Theory of International Law at the Threshold of the 21st Century: Essays in Honour of Krzysztof Skubiszewski* (Kluwer Law International, 1996) 541, 546.

[160] See generally Catherine Brölmann, 'Law-Making Treaties: Form and Function in International Law', 74 *NJIL* (2005) 383–404.

[161] The third Special Rapporteur, Sir Gerald Fitzmaurice, had proposed to differentiate between treaties on the basis of their content, cf. e.g. II *YILC* (1957) 31. See further Section 7.2.2.2.

[162] II *YILC* (1966) 219.

take a closer look at some concrete examples from the practice of international courts.[163] The PCIJ's Advisory Opinion in *Jurisdiction of the Courts of Danzig* and the ICJ's Judgment in *LaGrand* naturally come to mind as regards individual rights, whereas the *IMT Judgment* of 1946[164] is of specific interest concerning obligations. Inspiration may also be found in case law pertaining to the international legal personality of other non-State entities such as the ICJ's Advisory Opinion of 1949 in *Reparations for Injuries* regarding international organizations.

3.4.3.1 Individual rights

In 1928 (several decades before the adoption of the VCLT), the PCIJ stated: 'The intention of the Parties, which is to be ascertained from the contents of the Agreement, taking into consideration the manner in which the Agreement has been applied, is decisive.'[165] The Court emphasized the wording and general tenor of the *Beamtenabkommen*, exemplified by a number of Articles. For example, the PCIJ underlined, referring to Article 4, 'the necessity, e.g. in matters of discipline, of amending the provisions of the *Beamtenabkommen* in order to make the provisions of the Polish law binding on the Danzig officials.'[166] The Court then went on to examine Poland's contention that Article 9 was evidence of the parties' intention to leave all regulations concerning the Danzig Railway officials, including regulations based on the *Beamtenabkommen*, to Poland.[167] The PCIJ disagreed with Poland and, with reference to inter alia the general tenor of the Agreement, found the scope of Article 9 to be narrower: 'Article 9 of the *Beamtenabkommen* should not be construed in a manner which would make the applicability of the provisions of the *Beamtenabkommen* depend on their incorporation into a Polish Regulation.'[168] Finally, the PCIJ underlined that both parties had recognized the *Beamtenabkommen* as having entered into force as of 1 December 1921.[169]

In the *LaGrand* case of 2001,[170] the ICJ invoked the principle originating from the PCIJ's Advisory Opinion of 1923 in *Acquisition of Polish Nationality* that '[h]aving before it a clause which leaves little to be desired in the nature of clearness, it is bound to apply this clause as it stands.'[171] The ICJ found the relevant provisions of

[163] The practice of national courts is left out as a mere matter of expediency. Pertaining to domestic case law, however, it is important to reiterate the distinction between the question of whether a concrete treaty provision addresses individuals directly, which is a matter of interpretation according to Articles 31–33 of the VCLT, and the question of whether the provision is enforceable before a particular national court, which is a matter of national law. In the present context, the practice of national courts is only of interest as regards the former question.

[164] International Military Tribunal at Nuremberg (hereafter IMT), *Judgment*, 1 October 1946, reprinted in 41 *AJIL* (1947) 172 (hereafter *IMT Judgment*). See further Section 6.2.1.

[165] *Jurisdiction of the Courts of Danzig* (n 39) 18. See also Section 3.1.2.2.1.

[166] Ibid, 19.

[167] Article 9 had the following wording (translation by the Registry): 'All matters affecting officials and workmen transferred to the Polish service shall be dealt with by the Polish State Railways Administration.'

[168] *Jurisdiction of the Courts of Danzig* (n 39) 20.

[169] Ibid, 21.

[170] See further Section 3.1.2.2.2.

[171] *Acquisition of Polish Nationality* (n 27). See also US–Germany Mixed Claims Commission, *Opinion in the Lusitania Cases*, 1 November 1923, VII *RIAA* 32, 43. See also Emmerich de Vattel, *Le*

the VCCR to be sufficiently clear for two main reasons: (1) Because Article 36(1)(b) ends by stating that '[t]he said authorities shall inform the person concerned without delay of *his rights* under this subparagraph' (emphasis in original); and (2) because under Article 36(1)(c), the sending State's right to provide consular assistance to the detained person may not be exercised 'if he expressly opposes such action.' In the opinion of the majority, '[t]he clarity of these provisions, viewed in their context, admits of no doubt... [t]hat Article 36, paragraph 1, creates individual rights'.[172]

Notably, Vice President Shi found that the rights in question were not independent, but rather derived from the rights of the State of nationality to protect and assist its nationals in accordance with the Convention. In his opinion, the majority of the Court put too much emphasis on 'the purported clarity of the language' of Article 36(1), while the negotiating history of the provision did not indicate that the parties had intended to create individual rights.[173] Judge Oda dissented stating inter alia that any individual rights under the Convention 'are strictly limited to those corresponding to the obligations borne by the States under the Convention'.[174]

In summary, the PCIJ in *Jurisdiction of the Courts of Danzig* emphasized the intentions of the parties as expressed in the wording and general tenor of the *Beamtenabkommen* and their subsequent actions, while the ICJ majority in *LaGrand* found no need to resort to other sources than the text of the VCCR.

3.4.3.2 Individual obligations

In its *Kosovo* Advisory Opinion of 2010, the ICJ explicated that the Security Council must state clearly whom—including both States and non-State actors—it intends to bind through its resolutions. It is arguable that such a demand for clarity applies generally to international norms conferring obligations on, for example, individuals. This argument, however, has little to do with the concept of international legal personality. Rather, like the rationale underlying the customary international rule prohibiting retroactive criminalization, the consideration is that individuals (or other entities for that matter) must be able to foresee whether or not they will incur international responsibility for their actions.

In any event, as will be explained at length in Chapter 6, there is significant international case law which cannot reasonably be said to support an interpretative presumption against individual obligations. The key example is the *IMT Judgment* of 1946, which famously asserts the principle of individual responsibility for international crimes as follows: 'Crimes against international law are committed by men,

Droit des Gens ou Principes de la Loi Naturelle (Carnegie, 1916), Liv. II, chap. XVII, § 263, 461: 'La prémiere Maxime générale sur l'Interprétation est, qu'il n'est pas permis d'interpréter ce qui n'a pas besoin d'interprétation.'

172 *LaGrand* (n 63) 77.

173 See *LaGrand* (n 63), *Separate Opinion of Vice President Shi*, paras 4–15. See also Sir Robert Jennings, 'The LaGrand Case', 1 *LPICT* (2002) 13, 45–7.

174 See *LaGrand* (n 63), *Separate Opinion of Vice President Shi*, para. 27.

not by abstract entities, and only by punishing individuals who commit such crimes can the provisions of international law be enforced.'[175]

Some scholars conclude against the background of the *IMT Judgment* that there is a presumption *for* individual responsibility specifically pertaining to international crimes.[176] This question will be discussed further in Section 6.2.5. More generally, one might speculate whether individual obligations are assumed when this is pivotal to effectively achieving the purpose of the relevant international norm, for example because there would otherwise be no subject to hold accountable.

3.4.3.3 Other non-State entities

In an attempt to determine particular criteria for interpretation of treaties involving the interests of individuals, it seems straightforward to look for inspiration in case law regarding other entities on the international plane; the first and foremost being international organizations. In its Advisory Opinion in the *Reparations for Injuries* case of 1949, the ICJ found:

> In the opinion of the Court, the Organization was intended to exercise and enjoy, and is in fact exercising and enjoying, functions and rights which can only be explained on the basis of the possession of a large measure of international personality and the capacity to operate upon an international plane. It is at present the supreme type of international organization, and it could not carry out the intentions of its founders if it was devoid of international personality. It must be acknowledged that its Members, by entrusting certain functions to it, with the attendant duties and responsibilities, have clothed it with the competence required to enable those functions to be effectively discharged.[177]

In other words, this statement promotes the interpretation that will secure the most effective realization of the purpose of an international organization.[178] If this line of thought is conferred on the case of individuals, it confirms that direct individual rights or obligations should be presumed, where such interpretation would advance the actual fulfilment of the international norm in question.

3.5 Conclusion: The Personality of Individuals in Positive International Law—General Issues

The purpose of the present chapter is to lay the ground for the analysis in Chapters 4–8 by addressing a number of issues relating to the personality of individuals, which are relevant across the board in international law.

[175] *IMT Judgment* (n 164) 221. Subsequently, the tribunal stated: '[T]he very essence of the Charter is that individuals have international duties which transcend the national obligations of obedience imposed by the individual state.'

[176] See, for example, Portmann (n 52) 273.

[177] *Reparations for Injuries Suffered in the Service of the United Nations* (Advisory Opinion) [1949] ICJ Rep 174, 179.

[178] See further Spiermann (n 68) 208.

One might expect to find guidance on the position of the individual in the international legal system in core treaties such as the PCIJ Statute and the VCLT. The drafting processes leading to the adoption of both instruments, however, suggest that the concept of international legal personality is strictly a theoretical notion with limited influence on the formation of positive norms of international law. Although some members of the Advisory Committee of Jurists explicitly favoured the orthodox 'States-only' conception of international legal personality, their assertions determined neither the limited role attributed to individuals under the PCIJ Statute nor the rejection of the proposal for a High Court of International Justice. Rather, the standpoint of the majority of members appears to have been motivated by whether they perceived the relevant issue to involve the interests of more than one State. In the case of the VCLT, the ILC abandoned the idea of including a provision regulating the application of treaties to individuals and deliberately chose not to take a stand on the issue of international legal personality. By leaving the question of the position of individuals in international law to be determined solely by interpretation in accordance with Articles 31–33, however, the VCLT in effect ended up embodying the 'a posteriori' conception of international legal personality.

There were several explicit references to the orthodox 'States-only' conception of international legal personality in the PCIJ's decisions. Nevertheless, the Permanent Court's dictum rejecting of the idea of individuals as subjects of international law in *Jurisdiction of the Courts of Danzig* should not cloud the fact that, from an operative viewpoint, the PCIJ gave effect to the *Beamtenabkommen* on the basis of interpretation of its provisions pursuant to the general principles now codified in Articles 31–33 of the VCLT.

In the *LaGrand* Judgment of 2001, the ICJ unequivocally affirmed that individuals may hold direct rights under treaties, and that individual rights need not be categorized as human rights. Moreover, *LaGrand* made clear that individual rights do not presuppose independent means of enforcement. Still, the latter argument continues to give rise to considerable confusion.[179] Based on a study of inter alia Judgments of the PCIJ and the ICJ and the ILC's work on the ARSIWA and the ADP, Section 3.3 argued that the procedural rules on diplomatic protection apply when the *interests* of individuals are at stake. Consequently, we cannot—as both scholars and practitioners frequently do—rely on the fact that diplomatic protection has been exercised in the evaluation of whether or not a certain treaty provision amounts to an individual *right*.

How, then, do we determine whether a treaty provision confers direct rights or obligations on individuals, or whether it—albeit to the benefit or detriment of individuals—only regulates the relationship between the contracting States? Above all, it is submitted that general principles of treaty interpretation as codified in Articles 31–33 of the VCLT apply. In accordance with the 'a posteriori' conception of international legal personality, there are no limitations by definition on what States can agree to in a treaty, as long as they do not violate *jus cogens* norms. In other

[179] See, for example, Sections 5.2.1 and 8.2.2.

words, treaty interpretation must be carried out without preconceptions about international legal personality.

It follows from the VCLT rules, and the ICJ's Judgment in the *LaGrand* case, that the text of the treaty provision is the predominant factor in the determination of whether it entails an individual right or obligation. However, other elements enter into the equation. As illustrated by, for example, the *IMT Judgment* and the *Reparations for Injuries* Advisory Opinion, it may be contended that there is a presumption for direct individual rights or obligations, where such interpretation advances the effectiveness of the treaty in question. The consideration of avoiding a 'subject vacuum' is an element in such an assessment of effectiveness. Also, as will be seen in the analyses in Chapters 4–8, the manner in which a specific area of international law takes account of individuals often reflects whether the field was traditionally regulated in national or international law. For example, human rights were originally regarded as an internal matter for States, whereas international armed conflict has traditionally been governed at the international level. This may be a part of the explanation why human rights treaties predominantly include individual rights, while international humanitarian law mainly consists of inter-State obligations. There are, however, notable exceptions to this pattern. For example, it will be argued in Chapter 5 that international humanitarian law does indeed include a number of individual rights.

The rest of the book comprises analyses of legal documents such as treaties, secondary legislation based on treaties, *travaux préparatoires*, and case law within five different areas of international law, which are characterized by engaging individuals either as holders of rights and capacities or as bearers of duties. The special fields are organized chronologically according to the date of the major part of the material. Drawing on Chapters 2 and 3, the purpose of Chapters 4–8 is both to describe the historical evolution as well as the present-day role of the individual as a matter of positive law within each of these particular areas, and to examine the influence of the various theoretical conceptions of international legal personality on this development.

4

The Legal Personality of Individuals in International Claims

This chapter concerns claims arising out of injury inflicted upon an individual by a foreign State in violation of international law. The aim of the chapter is to examine how international claims practice has engaged individuals, and how the concept of international legal personality has been taken into account in the formation and application of positive norms in this field.

International claims are asserted either through diplomatic protection[1] or by allowing the individual to present his claim independently against the foreign State in an international forum. As sketched out in what follows, the two types of enforcement of international claims have existed alongside one another at least since 1907 and they will likely continue to do so.[2] Against this background and in light of the available material, this chapter focuses primarily on procedural issues, whereas questions concerning substantive rules are discussed to a lesser extent.[3]

The following account is divided into three historical periods. International claims practice before the First World War is addressed briefly in Section 4.1. The practice of the interwar period is the subject of Section 4.2, and international claims practice after the Second World War is examined in Section 4.3. The inquiry is far from exhaustive since many arbitral tribunals and claims commissions besides the ones examined were established to decide international claims.[4] Section 4.4 concludes the chapter with an assessment of the impact of the concept of international legal personality on international claims practice.

[1] See further Section 3.3.

[2] See Section 3.3.1 regarding 'mixed claims' based in part on injury to the State itself (direct injury) and in part on injury to the State's national (indirect injury).

[3] Investment treaty arbitration is deferred to Section 8.2, which deals with the substantive rights and obligations, as well as the procedural capacity, of individuals in international investment law.

[4] An overview of all public international arbitral tribunals reveals the following spread over time: 1776–1800, 7; 1801–25, 20; 1826–50, 17; 1851–75, 66; 1876–1900, 137; 1901–25, 133; 1926–50, 41; and 1951–70, 20. Some of these tribunals dealt with only a single claim, whereas e.g. the post-First World War tribunals heard claims in the thousands. See David D. Caron, 'The Nature of the Iran–United States Claims Tribunal and the Evolving Structure of International Dispute Resolution', 84 *AJIL* (1990) 104, 151. See further A. M. Stuyt, *Survey of International Arbitration 1794–1970* (A. W. Sijthoff, 1972).

4.1 International Claims before the First World War

4.1.1 Early international claims practice

As mentioned, the first examples of what would later be termed the diplomatic protection doctrine date back to the end of the eighteenth century. In 1794, the Jay Treaty between the United States and Great Britain marked the beginning of 'the modern era of international arbitration', and the dispute settlement method it introduced would become an increasingly popular way for States to assert claims concerning injury to their nationals in the nineteenth and early twentieth centuries.[5] The Jay Treaty included provisions establishing two arbitration commissions tasked with settling inter alia claims of British nationals for confiscated debts and claims of US citizens for the alleged illegal seizure of US vessels by British cruisers.[6] The Treaty did not indicate that individuals had rights under international law. Nor did it grant individuals standing before the arbitration commissions as claims could be presented solely by States upon exhaustion of local remedies.[7] It was, however, expressly provided in the Treaty that compensation was to be paid directly to the injured individual.[8]

During the nineteenth century, diplomatic protection became progressively more common and a substantial number of disputes were settled by arbitration.[9] Generally, the treaties did not refer to individual rights, and only in exceptional cases were individuals allowed to participate in the arbitral proceedings.[10] The State of nationality retained full control over the claim,[11] and awards were for the most part paid to the State rather than its national. The individual thus played a rather limited role in the nineteenth century's vast body of international claims cases.[12] The early years of the twentieth century, however, brought about changes in that regard. In particular, 1907 was a remarkable year in the history of international law, not least because of the creation of two international courts with competence

[5] Chittharanjan F. Amerasinghe, *Diplomatic Protection* (OUP, 2008) 13 and 16. See also David D. Caron, 'War and International Adjudication: Reflections on the 1899 Peace Conference', 94 *AJIL* (2000) 4, 8–9.

[6] US–Great Britain (1794), John Bassett Moore, *History and Digest of the International Arbitrations to Which the United States Has Been a Party* (Washington: Government Printing Office, 1898) vol. I, 271ff.

[7] Articles 6 and 7. See ibid, 275–6.

[8] Ibid, 277. Nevertheless, the British claims ended up being settled in 1802 by a lump sum payment to the British government. Article 6 of the Jay Treaty was annulled, and it remains uncertain if any amount was passed on to the claimants. See Moore (n 6) vol. I, 298. The following year, a commission operating on similar terms was established by a treaty between the US and Spain. See Spain–US (1795), Article XXI, Moore (n 6), vol. II, 999–1000. Subsequent treaties adopted in the nineteenth century provided that payment of awards was to be made to the state of nationality. See Parlett (n 9) 37.

[9] See Kate Parlett, *The Individual in the International Legal System—Continuity and Change in International Law* (CUP, 2011) Appendix I, 124–33.

[10] See for example the discussion on the participation of the individual claimants by the Mexico–US Claims Commission set up under Mexico–US (1839), Moore (n 6) vol. II, 1227ff.

[11] See John Bassett Moore, *A Digest of International Law* (Washington: Government Printing Office, 1906), vol. 6, 616.

[12] See further Parlett (n 9) 50ff.

to entertain individual claims. Neither court was very successful measured by the number of cases they heard. The International Prize Court never came into existence, and during its ten years in operation the Central American Court of Justice (hereafter CACJ) only considered five individual claims, out of which only one was decided on the merits—to the disadvantage of the claimant. Nevertheless, the *travaux préparatoires* of the Convention Relative to the Creation of an International Prize Court as well as the *travaux préparatoires* and practice of the Convention for the Establishment of a Central American Court of Justice shed light on the (lack of) practical ramifications of the theoretical debate on the concept of international legal personality at the turn of the twentieth century.

4.1.1.1 The International Prize Court

The Convention Relative to the Creation of an International Prize Court was adopted on 18 October 1907 as the twelfth of thirteen conventions concluded at the Second Hague Peace Conference.[13] German and British delegates had each submitted propositions for the establishment of an international tribunal to decide on the lawfulness of captures made in maritime warfare.[14] The idea was to create an International Prize Court with competence to hear appeals from national prize courts.[15] The question of applicable law was governed by Article 7 of the Convention, stipulating that the Court was to decide cases on the basis of treaty provisions in force between 'the belligerent captor and a Power which is itself or whose subject or citizen is a party to the proceedings, or, absent such provisions, "rules of international law"'.[16] According to Article 4(2), appeals to the Court could be brought by 'a neutral individual' if his State of nationality did not 'forbid' him to do so or presented the case in his place.[17] Once the proceedings had commenced, no limitations were imposed on the participation of the individual claimant.[18] Article 4(2) in the adopted form was drafted by a subcommission to Commission I,[19] directed by a British, a German,

[13] Convention Relative to the Creation of an International Prize Court, reprinted in 2 *AJIL* Supp. (1908) 174.

[14] See second plenary meeting on 19 June 1907, James Brown Scott, *The Proceedings of the Hague Peace Conferences, The Conference of 1907*, vol. I (OUP, 1920b) 55, and William I. Hull, *The Two Hague Conferences* (Ginn & Company, 1908) 427. The original propositions are reprinted in Scott (n 14) 1051–6 (German) and 1056–8 (British).

[15] At the time, the Court was labelled a breakthrough in dispute settlement and a forerunner for international courts with more extensive jurisdiction. For example, Charles Noble Gregory found: 'No achievement in the whole history of international negotiation can be recalled which gives promise of weightier or more beneficent consequence', Charles Noble Gregory, 'The Proposed International Prize Court and Some of Its Difficulties', 2 *AJIL* (1908) 458, 475. See also Henry B. Brown, 'The Proposed International Prize Court', 2 *AJIL* (1908) 476.

[16] If no generally recognized rule of international law could be established, the Court was to 'give judgment in accordance with the general principles of justice and equity'.

[17] See also Articles 4(3) and 5 of the Convention.

[18] Private persons were, however, required under Article 26 to be represented by a qualified member of the legal profession. On the procedure of the International Prize Court, see Articles 28ff.

[19] The conference was divided into six commissions and a number of subcommissions and committees of examination. See further Hull (n 14) 31ff.

and a French delegate. It was based on answers to a questionnaire, which included the following question:

Shall the Court to be created decide only between the belligerent State to which the captor belongs and the State making claim for its subjects who have suffered loss from the capture, or may the matter be laid before it directly by the private persons claiming to have suffered loss?[20]

While the British delegate, Sir Edward Fry, argued that 'in an international court it is logical that only governments, and not individuals, should be suitors',[21] the German delegate, Dr Kriege, presented a number of reasons why the injured individual rather than his government should come before the court. Among other factors, Kriege emphasized that granting legal standing to individuals would prevent a dispute between two governments, and that individuals would be required to bear their own expenses and therefore would be deterred from bringing ill-founded claims.[22] In addition to the German arguments, with which he concurred, the Norwegian delegate, M. Hagerup, underlined that political considerations would often prevent small nations from presenting an appeal on their citizens' behalf and that 'individual appeal is in line with the progress of international law'.[23] The Cuban delegate, M. Bustamente, suggested the compromise that both governments and individuals could apply to the court, while the US delegate, Mr Choate, proposed the adopted solution, which gave governments the possibility to veto individual claims.[24]

This debate is interesting, because it shows that even though one delegate invoked the 'States-only' conception of international legal personality, and another delegate believed that international law had by 1907 evolved to include individuals as its subjects, neither of their observations was a deciding factor. Rather than conceptual quandaries, the principal concern of most drafters of the Convention Relative to the Creation of an International Prize Court was to find a viable way of securing the peaceful coexistence of States with regard to prize cases.

As mentioned, the Convention never entered into force. There was considerable disagreement among the signatories on the capability of the International Prize Court to annul decisions of domestic courts under Article 3,[25] as well as on the applicable

[20] Scott (n 14) 1058. [21] Hull (n 14) 430–1. [22] Ibid, 431. [23] Ibid.

[24] Ibid. See also Joseph H. Choate, *The Two Hague Conferences* (Princeton University Press, 1913) 70–1. In a university lecture delivered in 1908, another member of the US delegation, James Brown Scott, stated: 'International law does now know individuals; international law deals with sovereign states. Why then should the individual appear as a suitor before an international court?' It is not quite clear whether Scott believed that the right of appeal to the International Prize Court had an impact on the status of the individual in international law or vice versa. At any rate, he went on to identify several reasons, along the lines of Kriege's statement, in favour of the adopted Article 4(2). See James Brown Scott, *The Hague Peace Conferences*, vol. I (Johns Hopkins Press, 1909) 487–8.

[25] The US objection that the possibility of annulment of Supreme Court judgments would be unconstitutional was resolved by Additional Protocol to the Convention Relative to the Creation of an International Prize Court of 19 September 1910. See further George C. Butte, 'The "Protocole Additionnel" To the International Prize Court Convention', 6 *AJIL* (1912) 799. See also 'The London Naval Conference', 3 *AJIL Supplement* (1909) 179, 184, and James Brown Scott, 'The Declaration of London of February 26, 1909', 8 *AJIL* (1914) 274, 276–9.

law according to Article 7.[26] However, the way in which it engaged individuals does not seem to have given rise to particular controversy after the Convention was adopted, and was evidently not the reason that the Court was never realized.

4.1.1.2 The Central American Court of Justice

The Convention for the Establishment of a Central American Court of Justice was signed at the Central American Peace Conference of 1907[27] together with the General Treaty of Peace and Amity and six other conventions between the five participating States: Costa Rica, Guatemala, Honduras, Nicaragua, and El Salvador.

The CACJ was based in Cartago, Costa Rica, and composed of one judge from each of the Member States. During its years in function between 1908 and 1918, it heard a total of ten cases, including five individual claims.[28] Under Article I of the General Treaty of Peace and Amity, the States were bound to 'observe the most complete harmony, and decide every difference or difficulty that may arise amongst them, of whatsoever nature it may be, by means of the Central American Court of Justice'. But, the jurisdiction of the CACJ was not limited to inter-State cases, and in contrast to the International Prize Court, there was explicitly no right for the home State to veto an individual claim. Article II of the Convention for the Establishment of a Central American Court of Justice read:

> This Court shall also take cognizance of the questions which individuals of one Central American country may raise against any of the other contracting Governments, because of the violation of treaties or conventions, and other cases of an international character; no matter whether their own Government supports said claim or not; and provided that the remedies which the laws of the respective country provide against such violation shall have been exhausted or that denial of justice shall have been shown.

This provision did not per se require a special interest in the claim on the part of the individual claimant, for example that he had suffered an injury. Rather it enabled him to raise 'questions ... because of the violation of treaties or conventions, and other cases of an international character'. Therefore, it is not obvious whether Article II implied the existence of individual rights under international law. The available

[26] The UK was opposed to the Court's ability to 'give judgment in accordance with the general principles of justice and equity' in the absence of a 'generally recognized rule'. See Scott (n 25), 280ff. Even though this question was partly settled by the *Declaration Concerning the Laws of Naval War*, which was adopted at the London Naval Conference in 1909, the UK continued to withhold ratification. Since the other signatories did not wish to proceed without the UK, no further steps to establishing of the International Prize Court were taken. See Scott (ibid) 275. The project was not revived after the First World War.

[27] The conference followed numerous failed attempts in the eighteenth century to form a federation of Central American States with a judicial organ for the settlement of disputes. See further Sasha Maldonado Jordison, 'The Central American Court of Justice: Yesterday, Today and Tomorrow?', 25 *Connecticut Journal of International Law* (2009) 183, Manley O. Hudson, 'The Central American Court of Justice', 26 *AJIL* (1932) 759, and James Brown Scott, 'The Central American Peace Conference of 1907' 2 *AJIL* (1908) 121–7.

[28] As mentioned only five cases, of which four were inter-State claims, were decided on the merits. For a summary of each of the ten cases see Hudson (n 27) 768–77.

minutes of the conference sessions do not provide much guidance on the matter, except maybe for clarifying that the question of personality of individuals in international law was not an issue of particular concern to the delegates.[29]

Diaz v. Guatemala[30] of 1909, which was the first of the four individual claims to be declared inadmissible due to lack of jurisdiction, concerned the allegedly false arrest and imprisonment of a Nicaraguan national, Dr Diaz, in Guatemala. The CACJ found that some 'legal injuries . . . shall be classed by their nature in the group of matters which, in spite of the individual character of the injury, the law of nations places under its protection'.[31] Although the Court was somewhat hesitant,[32] it thereby seems to have acknowledged that individuals can have rights directly under international law.

In 1914, the CACJ issued its Judgment in *Alejandro Bermúdez Nuñez v. Costa Rica*,[33] which was the one individual claim that was decided on the merits. The claimant was a Nicaraguan national, who resided in Costa Rica. Upon his return from participating in a rebellion against the Nicaraguan government in September 1912, he was expelled by the Costa Rican authorities. Bermúdez Nuñez argued that Costa Rica had thereby violated his rights under Article VI of the General Treaty of Peace and Amity giving equal rights to residents who were nationals of another contracting party,[34] and under Article XVII, which read: 'Every person, no matter what his nationality, who, within the territory of one of the contracting Parties, shall initiate or foster revolutionary movements against any of the others, shall be immediately brought to the capital of the Republic, where he shall be submitted to trial according to law.'[35]

A majority of three CACJ judges found Bermúdez Nuñez's claims to be unsubstantiated. They emphasized that it was an indisputable prerogative of States to deny

[29] Central American Peace Conference at Washington (September, November, and December 1907): Minutes, Supplementary Documents, and Treaties signed on 20 December 1907, 44, 48, and in particular 58–66. See also William I. Buchanan, *The Central American Peace Conference—Report of Mr William I. Buchanan Representing the United States of America* (Washington: Government Printing Offices, 1908) 18–19.

[30] English translation printed in 3 *AJIL* (1909) 737, 742.

[31] The Court went on to say that 'the fundamental rights and powers of the human individual in civil life are placed under the protection of the principles governing the commonwealth of nations, as international rights of man'. See ibid, 742–3.

[32] In the paragraph immediately preceding the quotation, the CACJ stated that restrictions on the Member States' sovereignty should be interpreted narrowly, 'in a manner most suitable to the nation on which it has been imposed and causing the least detriment to its natural liberty'. In this way, *Diaz v. Guatemala* illustrates that neither individual rights under treaties nor questionable restrictive application of them are post-Second World War phenomena. See further Section 7.2.2.2 on the practice of the ECtHR.

[33] See Carlos José Gutierrez, *La Corte de Justicia Centroamericana* (Editorial Juricentro, 1978) 97–104.

[34] Article VI had the following wording:

> The citizens of one of the contracting Parties, residing in the territory of any of the others, shall enjoy the same civil rights as are enjoyed by nationals, and shall be considered as citizens in the country of their residence if they fulfill the conditions which the respective constituent laws provide.

[35] See Gutierrez (n 33) 97–8.

asylum and expel aliens as long as the State complied with international law.[36] In their opinion, Article 17 of the General Treaty of Peace and Amity did not guarantee individuals any right to asylum, but rather conferred rights on the States Parties to take steps against revolutionary movements. Accordingly, they concluded that Costa Rica had violated neither domestic law nor international law by expelling Bermúdez Nuñez. The minority of two judges, however, filed dissenting opinions stating that Costa Rica had denied the claimant the rights given to Costa Ricans under domestic law and, as a consequence, had violated Article VI of the General Treaty of Peace and Amity.[37]

On the basis of the wording of Article II and the *Bermúdez Nuñez* Judgment, Parlett argues that: 'Individuals were not treated as having substantive rights under international law', but 'possessed only a procedural right for the assessment of a State's conduct in accordance with its international obligations.'[38] This analysis is open to challenge, since it is not evident that the CACJ altogether rejected the idea of substantive individual rights under international law. While the majority judges may have interpreted the relevant provisions quite restrictively, they did not dismiss *Bermúdez Nuñez*'s claim as a matter of principle. Moreover, the minority found that his rights under international law had indeed been violated. The disagreement between the majority and the minority thus pertains to the concrete interpretation of particular provisions of General Treaty of Peace and Amity rather than the question of individuals' subjectivity in international law.

Although the precedential value of both the International Prize Court and the CACJ is ambiguous, they are remarkable contradictions to the popular view that States have only been willing to confer independently enforceable treaty rights on individuals since the Second World War.

Before embarking on the international claims practice of the interwar period, mention should be made of the *North Atlantic Coast Fisheries* case from 1910. Notably, the Permanent Court of Arbitration indicated that application of treaties to individuals was solely a question of interpretation of the particular treaty when it stated: 'But considering that the Treaty does not intend to grant to individual persons or to a class of persons the liberty to take fish . . . .'[39]

4.2 International Claims in the Interwar Period

During the years from 1919 to 1939 a vast number of treaties referred specific claims to arbitration. But the interwar period also marks the high point of international claims tribunals and commissions set up to resolve multiple claims. Following a brief note on examples of arbitral awards concerning distinct claims in Section 4.2.1, Section 4.2.2 focuses on the practice of the post-First World War claims tribunals

[36] Ibid, 98. [37] See ibid, 100–2. See also Hudson (n 27) 773. [38] Parlett (n 9) 65.

[39] Permanent Court of Arbitration, *The North Atlantic Coast Fisheries Case (Great Britain/United States of America)* (Award), Case No. 1909-01, 7 September 1910, IX *RIAA* 167, 192.

and commissions, while Section 4.2.3 deals with the commissions that were established in the aftermath of the 1910–20 Mexican Revolution.[40]

4.2.1 Arbitration of distinct claims

Between 1919 and 1939 numerous treaties referred specific claims to arbitration. Examples include *US–Peru (Landreau Claim)* of 1921. In this case, the award was explicitly to be paid to the 'heirs and assigns' of the injured individual, but otherwise the two governments retained full control of the claim.[41] *Great Britain–Costa Rica (Tinoco Case)* of 1922 is an example with no involvement at all of the injured corporations.[42] In *US–Guatemala (Shufeldt Claim)* of 1930, however, the arbitrator explicitly found the injured individual to hold 'an equitable right of which international law takes cognizance', and '[t]he award was to be paid to the US government ... for the account of P. W. Shufeldt.'[43]

A famous example of a distinct claim is the *Sopron–Köszeg Railway* case. It was referred to arbitration in accordance with Article 304 of the Treaty of Trianon and Article 320 of the Treaty of St Germain, which provided that any enduring disagreements concerning the reorganization of privately held railroads of the former Austro-Hungarian Monarchy was to be submitted to arbitrators appointed by the League of Nations. As a reflection of what the tribunal found to be 'a modern view of international law', the Award reads inter alia: '... the rights which a private company derives from a deed of concession cannot be nullified or affected by the mere fact of a change in the nationality of the territory on which the public service conceded is operated'.[44]

For the most part, disputes concerning single claims in the interwar period were solved through diplomatic protection. Whether or not individuals enjoyed direct rights under the applicable instruments and the extent to which they were involved in the proceedings seem to have been quite capricious. As illustrated in the following section, the same can be said about the post-First World War tribunals and commissions.

[40] The other multiple-claims tribunals and commissions created in the period generally functioned according to the rules of diplomatic protection. See for example *Norwegian Shipowners' Claims (Norway v. USA)*, 13 October 1922, I *RIAA* 307. The award overtly states that 'the Government of the Kingdom of Norway, ... and not the individual claimants, "is the sole claimant before this Tribunal."' See ibid, 314. For an overview of international claims tribunals and commissions from 1919 to 1939, see Parlett (n 9) Appendix III, 162–75.

[41] *US–Peru (Landreau Claim)*, 26 October 1922, I *RIAA* 347, 349 and 353.

[42] *Great Britain–Costa Rica (Tinoco Case)*, 18 October 1923, I *RIAA* 370.

[43] *US–Guatemala (Shufeldt Claim)*, 24 July 1930, II *RIAA* 1079, 1098, and 1102. Other examples of single claims settled by arbitration in that period include: *Great Britain–Ethiopia (Attaque de la caravane du Maharao de Cutch)*, 7 October 1927, II *RIAA* 821, *France–Great Britain* (Affaire Chevreau), 9 Juni 1931, II *RIAA* 1113, and *Sweden–US (The 'Kronprins Gustaf Adolf')*, 18 July 1932, II *RIAA* 1239. See further Parlett (n 9) 71.

[44] *Sopron–Köszeg Railway*, 18 June 1929, II *RIAA* 961, 967. Here cited in translation from 'The Sopron-Koszeg Local Railway Company', 24 *AJIL* (1930) 164, 167.

4.2.2 Post-First World War tribunals and commissions

The Peace Treaties adopted at the end of the First World War provided that mixed arbitral tribunals were to be set up between each of the Allied and Associated Powers and each of the Central Powers.[45] The treaties all prescribed substantive rights of individuals. Article 297(e) of the Versailles Treaty, for example, provided that '[t]he nationals of Allied and Associated Powers shall be entitled to compensation in respect of damage or injury inflicted upon their property, rights or interests'.[46] As will become apparent in the following, however, there were substantial differences between the various commissions and tribunals pertaining to the role of the injured individual. Notably, the US never ratified the Peace Treaties, but instead entered into separate agreements with Germany,[47] Austria, and Hungary.[48] In addition, the particular controversy over the territory of Upper Silesia led to the establishment of an Arbitral Tribunal and a Mixed Commission.[49]

4.2.2.1 Mixed Arbitral Tribunals established by the Peace Treaties

A total of thirty-six mixed arbitral tribunals were set up under the Peace Treaties. The extent of their jurisdiction was substantial as it was outlined in more than fifty of the Peace Treaties' provisions, and consequently a vast number of claims were submitted and decided.[50]

In its decision of 13 December 1923 in *Lederer v. German Government*, the Anglo-German Mixed Arbitral Tribunal explicitly affirmed that individuals held direct rights under the Versailles Treaty:

> It would, of course, have been possible for the framers of the Treaty to have left these matters in the hands of the Governments of the Powers concerned. But they have not done so. The

[45] See Treaty of Versailles (Germany), 28 June 1919, Article 304, Treaty of St Germain-en-Laye (Austria), 10 September 1919, Article 256, Treaty of Neuilly (Bulgaria), 27 November 1919, Article 188, Treaty of Trianon (Hungary), 4 June 1920, Article 239, and Treaty of Lausanne (Turkey), 24 July 1923, Article 92. The tribunals were given competence to handle a variety of claims concerning inter alia contracts and property rights.

[46] See, similarly, Treaty of St Germain-en-Laye (Austria) (n 45), Article 249(e), Treaty of Neuilly (Bulgaria) (n 45), Article 177(e), Treaty of Trianon (Hungary) (n 45), Article 232(e). The Treaty of Lausanne (Turkey) (n 45) does not include such a provision, but it provides for individual rights as regards minorities protection. See further Section 7.1.2.

[47] See Treaty of Peace between the United States and Germany, 25 August 1921.

[48] See Treaty of Peace between the United States and Austria, 24 August 1921, Treaty Establishing Friendly Relations between the United States and Hungary, 29 August 1921.

[49] On 20 October 1921, the Conference of Ambassadors decided in accordance with the opinion of the League of Nations Council of 12 October 1921 that the Polish Minorities Treaty (Treaty of Peace between the United States, the British Empire, France, Italy, Japan and Poland, 28 June 1919, 13 *AJIL* Supp. (1919) 423–40) was to apply to Upper Silesia and prescribed the constitution of two supervisory bodies: an Upper Silesian Mixed Commission and an Arbitral Tribunal. See 2 *LNOJ* (1921) 1220, 1231. Accordingly, Germany and Poland adopted the Geneva Convention Relating to Upper Silesia on 15 May 1922. An unofficial English translation of this convention is reprinted in Julius Stone, *Regional Guarantees of Minority Rights* (Macmillan Co., 1933) Appendix I, 213.

[50] See Karin Oellers-Frahm and Norbert Wühler, *Dispute Settlement in Public International Law* (Springer Verlag, 1984) 695. The French–German Mixed Arbitral Tribunal, for example, decided around 20,000 cases.

right to compensation granted by the Treaty is granted as compensation to the national of an Allied and Associated Power. It is granted to him as a facultative right, that is to say, a right of which he may not make use.[51]

Similarly, the French–German Mixed Arbitral Tribunal held in *Sigwald Charles v. Germany* of 27 August 1926 that Article 297(e)[52] of the Versailles Treaty provided the injured individuals with direct rights, which could be enforced without the interposition of the French government.[53] Indeed, it was characteristic for the post-First World War mixed arbitral tribunals that the injured individual acted as claimant independent of his State of nationality.[54] In cases before the Anglo-German tribunal, for example, government agents were to be present during the proceedings, but their role was merely supervisory.[55] Rule 93 of The Anglo-Austrian Mixed Arbitral Tribunal Rules of Procedure provided that the government agents '*may* conduct cases on behalf of their Nationals' (emphasis added), but it is apparent that the injured individual holds the title to the claim.[56] Over time, however, it seems that the government agents came to perform a semi-administrative screening function in that they determined which claims were eligible to be submitted to the tribunals.[57] Otherwise, the individual claimant was in control of the claim.[58]

4.2.2.2 The US Mixed Claims Commissions

As opposed to the Mixed Arbitral Tribunals just discussed, the role of the individual was quite limited in the proceedings before the Mixed Claims Commissions between the US and Germany[59] on one hand and the US and Austria and Hungary on the other.[60] The US–Germany Commission explicitly underlined that the US rather than the injured individual was the proper claimant: 'Though conducted in

[51] Anglo-German Mixed Arbitral Tribunal, *Lederer v. German Government* (Decision) 13 December 1923, III *Recueil des Décision des Tribunaux Arbitraux Mixtes* (1924) 762, 768.

[52] Article 297(e) read: 'The nationals of Allied and Associated Powers shall be entitled to compensation in respect of damage or injury inflicted upon their property, rights or interests ... in German territory as it existed on August 1, 1914 ....'

[53] French–German Mixed Arbitral Tribunal, *Sigwald Charles v. Germany* (Decision) 27 August 1926, 3 *Annual Digest* (1925–6) 337. See further P. K. Menon, 'The subjects of modern international law', 3 *Hague Yearbook of International Law* (1990) 30, 66.

[54] See, for example, the Anglo-German Mixed Arbitral Tribunal, Rules of Procedure, I *Recueil des décision des Tribunaux Arbitraux Mixtes* (1922) 109–20, and the Japanese–German Mixed Arbitral Tribunal, Rules of Procedure, ibid, 124–7.

[55] See, for example, Rule 14(c), Rule 23, Rule 25, and Rule 39.

[56] The Anglo-Austrian Mixed Arbitral Tribunal, Rules of Procedure, I *Recueil des décision des Tribunaux Arbitraux Mixtes* (1922) 622, 635. See also the Anglo-Bulgarian Mixed Arbitral Tribunal, Rules of Procedure, Article 98, in ibid, 653.

[57] Oellers-Frahm and Wühler (n 50) 696.

[58] Norbert Wühler, 'Mixed Arbitral Tribunals' in Rudolf Bernhardt, *Encyclopedia of Public International Law*, vol. III (Elsevier Science BV, 1997) 433–4.

[59] See United States–Germany (Agreement supplementary to Treaty of 25 August 1921), 10 August 1922.

[60] See United States–Austria and Hungary (Agreement for the Determination of the Amounts to be paid by Austria and by Hungary [...]), 26 November 1924.

behalf of their respective citizens, governments are the real parties in international arbitrations.'[61]

Similarly, the US–Austria/Hungary Mixed Claims Commission held that '[a]ll claims ... shall be presented and controlled by the United States as claimant.' However, awards were paid 'to the Government of the United States on behalf of the claimant'.[62] In *Administrative Decision No. V*, the umpire clarified that the US was under an obligation to distribute the award to the injured national:

> [W]hile the private claimant is in all things bound by the action taken by his Government, still, such a claim is not a national claim, nor the fund collected a national fund, in the sense that its private nature no longer inheres in it but is lost and merged into its national character and becomes the property of the nation.[63]

Also, the US–Austria/Hungary Mixed Claims Commission found that '[w]hile the nation's absolute right to control a private claim espoused by it is necessarily exclusive ... [t]he act of espousal does not vest in the nation the title to the claim.'[64]

4.2.2.3 Upper Silesia Arbitral Tribunal and Mixed Commission

The province of Upper Silesia gave rise to particular difficulty in the aftermath of the First World War, and the territorial questions remained unsettled until 20 October 1921.[65] The Geneva Convention Relating to Upper Silesia[66] adopted by Germany and Poland on 15 May 1922 provided for the Upper Silesia Arbitral Tribunal, which had jurisdiction over specific private disputes concerning inter alia 'suppression or diminution of acquired rights' (Article 5) and questions of nationality and right of residence (Article 58),[67] as well as the Upper Silesia Mixed Commission, which was competent to hear cases on minorities protection issues.[68] A central feature of both

[61] US–Germany Mixed Claims Commission, Administrative Decision No. II, 1 November 1923, VII *RIAA* 23, 26. In the subsequent Administrative Decision No. V of 31 October 1924, the American commissioner found that 'a claim has no international status until it is espoused by the Government'. See VII *RIAA* 119, 126.

[62] See for example US–Germany Mixed Claims Commission, *Mary Barchard Williams*, 11 March 1925, VI *RIAA* 170, 176, and *Edward A. Hilson*, 22 April 1925, VI *RIAA* 176, 184.

[63] US–Germany Mixed Claims Commission, *Administrative Decision No. V*, 31 October 1924, VII *RIAA* 119, 153. In opposition, the American commissioner argued that the US was not accountable to the 'subordinate claimant' for the proceeds of the claim. See ibid, 126.

[64] US–Austria/Hungary Mixed Claims Commission, *Administrative Decision No. I*, 25 May 1927, VI *RIAA* 203, 208.

[65] See further 3 *LNOJ* (1922) 117.

[66] Geneva Convention Relating to Upper Silesia (n 49). For historical background of the convention, see Julius Stone, *Regional Guarantees of Minority Rights* (Macmillan Co., 1933) 1ff. See also Georges Kaeckenbeeck, 'The Character and Work of the Arbitral Tribunal of Upper Silesia', 21 *Transactions of the Grotius Society* (1935) 27–8, and Georges Kaeckenbeeck, *The International Experiment of Upper Silesia* (OUP, 1942) 3ff.

[67] See further Kaeckenbeeck, 'The Character and Work of the Arbitral Tribunal of Upper Silesia' (n 66) 28–9. Notably, Article 58 provided for the possibility of submitting questions of interpretation of the Geneva Convention Concerning Upper Silesia to the Arbitral Tribunal.

[68] Geneva Convention Relating to Upper Silesia (n 49) Articles 560–606. As to the division of labour between the Arbitral Tribunal and the Mixed Commission, see Kaeckenbeeck, *The International Experiment of Upper Silesia* (n 66) 26–30 and 480.

the Arbitral Tribunal and the Mixed Commission[69] was the right of petition and full procedural capacity of individuals.[70]

In the limited accessible material[71] from the drafting process of the Geneva Convention Relating to Upper Silesia of 15 May 1922, there is little suggestion that the question of the international legal personality of individuals played any role in the determination of the capacity of the individual claimant before the dispute settlement bodies pertaining to Upper Silesia.[72] It seems to have been generally agreed that the special situation in Upper Silesia called for unusual responses from international law. Clearly influenced by the 'States-only' conception of international legal personality, however, Georges Kaeckenbeeck, who was president of the Upper Silesia Arbitral Tribunal, argued that the tribunal's decisions could not serve as precedents for general international law:

> This international Tribunal may ... decide cases brought by a Polish citizen against the Polish State or by a German citizen against the German State, as well as cases brought by aliens against one of the two Governments. The protection meant by Art. 4 would have been illusory without this, and would not have answered the purpose proclaimed by the Council of the League of Nations.... The decisions of the Arbitral Tribunal must therefore be read cautiously and only in connection with the relevant provisions of the Geneva Convention. They do not at any rate in this matter apply international law at large.[73]

In March 1928, less than four weeks after the PCIJ's Advisory Opinion in *Jurisdiction of the Courts of Danzig*, the Arbitral Tribunal decided a case brought against Poland by a Polish national (Gross) and a Czechoslovak national (Steiner).[74] Poland contended that the tribunal lacked jurisdiction because of the 'general principle of international law that an individual could not invoke an international authority against his own State'. To the contrary, the Tribunal stated: 'The Convention conferred in unequivocal terms jurisdiction upon the Tribunal irrespective of the nationality of the claimants, and, the terms of the Convention being clear, it was unnecessary

[69] See further Section 7.1.2 on minorities protection within the realm of the League of Nations.

[70] See further the rules of procedure of the Arbitral Tribunal, *Verfahrensordnung des Schiedsgerichts für Oberschlesien* printed in Kaeckenbeeck, *The International Experiment of Upper Silesia* (n 66) Appendix IV, 823–35, and those of the Mixed Commission, *Verfahrensordnung der Gemischten Kommission für Oberschlesien* in ibid, Appendix V, 836–41. See also Georges Kaeckenbeeck, 'Upper Silesia under the League of Nations', 243 *Annals of the American Academy of Political and Social Science* (1946) 129–30, and Kaeckenbeeck, 'The Character and Work of the Arbitral Tribunal of Upper Silesia' (n 66) 12–13.

[71] See further Christian Raitz von Frentz, *A Lesson Forgotten: Minority Protection under the League of Nations: the Case of the German Minority in Poland, 1920–1934* (LIT Verlag, 1999) 117.

[72] See for example Recommendation of the Council of the League Forwarded to the Supreme Council of the Allied Powers on 12 October, 1921, printed in 'The Question of Upper Silesia', 2 *LNOJ* (1921) 1220, 1225, and Decision of the Conference of Ambassadors, reprinted in ibid, 1231.

[73] Kaeckenbeeck, 'The Character and Work of the Arbitral Tribunal of Upper Silesia' (n 66) 87. See further Kaeckenbeeck's decision as president of the Arbitral Tribunal in *Niederstrasser v. Polish State*, 6 June 1931, 6 *ILR* 66, 68, in which he underlines the differences between Article 4 of the Geneva Convention Relating to Upper Silesia and general international law. On the prospect of making the PCIJ accessible to private claimants, see Georges Kaeckenbeeck, 'The Protection of Vested Rights in International Law', 17 *BYBIL* (1936) 1, 18.

[74] See *Steiner and Gross v. Polish State*, 4 *AD* (1927–8) 291–2. See also Kaeckenbeeck, *The International Experiment of Upper Silesia* (n 66) 47–54.

to add to it a limitation which did not appear from its wording.'[75] Although the demand for clarity may be read as to imply a presumption against individual rights under treaties,[76] the decision clearly supports the notion of such rights, and it is frequently cited to that effect.[77]

Overall, the practice of the post-First World War claims commissions and tribunals can hardly be described as consistent. No particular logic seems to have determined whether individuals were granted direct material rights and independent procedural capacity and control of the claim. Moreover, the US Mixed Claims Commissions, which functioned under the rules on diplomatic protection, did not follow the doctrine strictly. The haphazard impression given by the distinct claims practice discussed in Section 4.2.1 is thus confirmed by the international claims tribunals and commissions set up after the First World War.

4.2.3 The Mexican Revolution Commissions

Following the Mexican Revolution of 1910–20, seven international commissions were created to handle the claims of foreigners against Mexico:[78] A General Claims Commission with competence to solve disputes arising after the two states' previous claims settlement on 4 July 1868 was established between the US and Mexico,[79] and six Special Claims Commissions (with jurisdiction over claims stemming from the revolution) were set up between Mexico and the US, France, Germany, Spain, Great Britain, and Italy respectively.[80]

The US–Mexico General Claims Commission and all six Special Claims Commissions had jurisdiction over 'claims by citizens' of each country against the other.[81] But the proceedings were generally to be conducted under the doctrine of

[75] Curiously, Friedmann stated in 1969 that *Steiner and Gross v. Poland*, like *Jurisdiction of the Courts of Danzig*, concerned 'a situation arising out of the territorial re-arrangements following the First World War', in which 'individuals and minorities were given a degree of legal protection going far beyond the general international law—not repeated or continued since.' See Wolfgang Friedmann, 'General Course in Public International Law', 127 *Recueil des Cours* (1969-II) 39, 125–6. In 2001, Orakhelashvili found Friedmann's analysis to be 'just as valid today.' See Alexander Orakhelashvili, 'The Position of the Individual in International Law', 31 *California Western International Law Journal* (2001) 241, 268.

[76] As discussed in Section 3.1.2.2.1, the PCIJ's Advisory Opinion in *Jurisdiction of the Courts of Danzig* cannot from an operative viewpoint be read as to imply such a presumption.

[77] See further Ole Spiermann, *Moderne folkeret* (3rd edn, DJØF Publishing, 2006) 216, and Roland Portmann, *Legal Personality in International Law* (CUP, 2010) 73.

[78] For historical background of the claims, see Louis W. McKernan, 'Special Mexican Claims', 32 *AJIL* (1938) 457–8, and A. H. Feller, *The Mexican Claims Commissions* (Macmillan, 1935), 15ff.

[79] See US–Mexico Convention of 8 September 1923, reprinted in Feller (n 78) 321–30.

[80] See US–Mexico Convention of 10 September 1923, reprinted in ibid, 385–93, France–Mexico Convention of 25 September 1923, reprinted in ibid, 412–20, Germany–Mexico Convention of 16 March 1925, reprinted in ibid, 442–52, Spain–Mexico Convention of 25 November 1925, reprinted in ibid, 521–5, Great Britain–Mexico Convention of 19 November 1926, reprinted in ibid, 467–76, and Italy–Mexico Convention of 13 January 1927, reprinted in ibid, 502–10. In addition, an Administrative Arbitral Tribunal was set up between Mexico and Belgium to handle the relatively small number of Belgian claims. See ibid, 28–29.

[81] See US–Mexico Convention of 8 September 1923, Preamble and Article I, ibid. 321 and 322, and US–Mexico Convention of 10 September 1923, Preamble and Article I, ibid. 385–6. See also Preamble and Article I of the France–Mexico Convention of 25 September 1923, which was the prototype

diplomatic protection, with full control over the claim by the State of nationality. In keeping with the language of the conventions and the rules of procedure of the various commissions, the injured individual had no capacity during the proceedings. For example, Article IV of the US–Mexico Convention of 10 September 1923 read: 'Each Government may nominate and appoint agents and counsel who will be authorized to present to the Commission, orally or in writing, all the arguments deemed expedient in favor of or against the claim.'[82]

In addition, the Commission was not to consider any 'statements, documents or other evidence' presented by anyone other than the governments' agents.[83] Awards attributed by all the commissions were to be paid to the governments.[84] Thus, the involvement of the individual was to be limited to signing of the memorial.[85]

In practice, however, the Mexican Revolution Commissions were quite inconsistent as to the role attributed to the injured individuals, and they did not adhere entirely to the customary rules on diplomatic protection.

The requirement that the injured individual sign the memorial prompted discussions as to whether it was a precondition for the Commissions' jurisdiction that the injured individual agreed to the claim. The US–Mexico General Claims Commission held in *Melczer Mining Company* that States have 'a right to press claims before the Commission on proper proof of nationality', while the injured individual had no power to withdraw a claim that had been espoused.[86] In contrast, the Great Britain–Mexico Claims Commission found:

> The award is claimed *on behalf of* a person or a corporation and, in accordance therewith, the Rules of Procedure prescribe that the Memorial shall be signed by the claimant or his attorney or otherwise clearly show that the alien who suffered the damage agrees to his Government's acting in his behalf.[87]

In *Case of Emilia Marta Viuda de Giovanni Mantellero*,[88] the Italy–Mexico Commission stated that it had no jurisdiction if the injured individual had not consented to the claim. The reasoning of the Great Britain–Mexico Commission and the Italy–Mexico Commission is evidently at odds with the notion that the State has

for the subsequent conventions. See ibid, 412–13, and A. H. Feller, 'The German–Mexican Claims Commission', 27 *AJIL* (1933) 62, 63.

[82] US–Mexico Convention of 10 September 1923, Feller (n 78) 389. The other conventions contain similar provisions. See also Rule III of the Rules of Procedure of the US–Mexico General Commission providing that '[a]ll claims must be filed by the respective Governments through or in the name of the agents thereof.' Ibid, 352–3. See further 88 and 287.

[83] US–Mexico Special Claims Commission, Rules of Procedure, Rule VIII, ibid, 404.

[84] See for example Article IX of the US–Mexico Convention of 10 September 1923, ibid, 392. As to the provisions on restoration of property or rights, see ibid, 36, and Parlett (n 9) 79.

[85] See for example US–Mexico Special Claims Commission, Rules of Procedure, Rule IV, Feller (n 78) 403. See also ibid. 233–4.

[86] US–Mexico General Claims Commission, *Melczer Mining Company (USA) v. United Mexican States*, 30 April 1929, IV *RIAA* 481, 484.

[87] Great Britain–Mexico Claims Commission, *Mexican Union Railway (Ltd) (Great Britain) v. United Mexican States*, February 1930, V *RIAA* 115, 120 (emphasis in original).

[88] Italy–Mexico Commission, *Case of Emilia Marta Viuda de Giovanni Mantellero*, Decision No. 3 (unpublished). See Feller (n 78) 90.

full discretion as to when it wants to exercise diplomatic protection, as long as the conditions under customary international law are met.[89]

The practice of the Mexican Revolution Commissions is perhaps most famous for the decisions on a closely related issue, namely the effect of Calvo clauses. In its typical form, a Calvo clause is a provision in a contract between a State and a foreign national whereby the foreign national waives the protection of his home State in all matters concerning the contract.[90] In *North American Dredging Company*, the US–Mexico General Claims Commission explicitly denied 'that the rules of international public law apply only to nations and that individuals can not under any circumstances have a personal standing under it.'[91] Giving effect to the distinction between primary and secondary rules, the Commission nevertheless found that an alien 'can not deprive the government of his nation of its undoubted right of applying international remedies to violations of international law committed to his damage.'[92] In this way the Commission confirmed the customary rule that the entitlement to employ the secondary rules of diplomatic protection always belongs to the State of nationality, even though the primary rule asserted through diplomatic protection may be an individual right.[93] Somewhat illogically, the Commission nonetheless enforced the Calvo clause in question by construing it as a contractual demand to exhaust local remedies. Although Article V of the US–Mexico Claims Convention explicitly provided for derogation from the customary requirement of exhaustion of local remedies, the Commission dismissed the claim in light of the fact that North American Dredging Company had failed to seek redress through the local Mexican legal system.[94]

In sum, the Mexican Revolution Commissions generally operated according to the diplomatic protection doctrine, but there were notable deviations from the customary rules. Moreover, the position attributed to injured individuals varied significantly depending on which of the Commissions they came before.

The theoretical debate on the role of individuals in international law does not appear to have played a major role in the practice of the Commissions, except for the US–Mexico General Claims Commission's Award in *Dickson Car Wheel Company*, which includes an explicit affirmation of the 'States-only' conception of international legal personality:

[89] The ICJ affirmed this position in *Case Concerning the Barcelona Traction, Light and Power Company, Limited (Preliminary Objections) (Belgium v. Spain)* (Judgment) [1964] ICJ Rep 6, 22ff.

[90] See, for example, Feller (n 78) 185ff.

[91] *North American Dredging Company*, 31 March 1926, 4 *RIAA* 26, para. 6. In evidence of the 'antiquated character of this thesis', the commission referred to Article 4 of the Convention Relative to the Creation of an International Prize Court. See further Section 4.1.1.1.

[92] Ibid, para. 11. See also para. 15 and paras 20ff.

[93] See further Section 3.3.1.

[94] *North American Dredging Company* was followed in subsequent cases. See for example US–Mexico General Claims Commission, *International Fisheries Company*, July 1931, IV *RIAA* 691. See also Great Britain–Mexico Claims Commission, *Mexican Union Railway*, February 1930, V *RIAA* 115. For a critical analysis of this practice see Feller (n 78) 187ff. See also John H. Percival, 'International Arbitral Tribunals and the Mexican Claims Commissions', 19 *Journal of Comparative Legislation and International Law* (1938) 98, 102–3.

The relation of rights and obligations created between two States upon the commission by one of them of an act in violation of international law, arises only among those States subject to the international juridical system. There does not exist, in that system, any relation of responsibility between the transgressing State and the injured individual for the reason that the latter is not subject to international law.[95]

Prior to studying international claims practice in the post-Second World War period, a brief note should be made on the Bank for International Settlements, created in 1930, which represents a curious example of practical ramifications of the 'States-only' perception of international legal personality: Because there was uncertainty as to the concept of an international bank, the Bank for International Settlements was set up as a Swiss entity, while Switzerland undertook not to interfere in its dealings.[96] The international legal personality of the bank was only formally acknowledged in Agreement between the Swiss Federal Council and the Bank for International Settlements to determine the Bank's legal status in Switzerland of 10 February 1987.[97]

4.3 International Claims after the Second World War

4.3.1 Post-Second World War tribunals and commissions

Numerous claims tribunals and commissions were established in the wake of the Second World War. The following section will account for only a few, which are illustrative as to the considerable variations to be found in the role attributed to individuals.

4.3.1.1 Germany

The Convention on the Settlement of Matters Arising Out of the War and the Occupation of 26 May 1952[98] inter alia granted persons, who had been disposed of their property during the war, an individual right to claim restitution.[99] It also

[95] US–Mexico General Claims Commission, *Dickson Car Wheel Company*, July 1931, IV *RIAA* 669, 678. In an earlier decision, the same commission had found that 'the private nature of the claim inheres in it and is not lost or destroyed so as to make it the property of the nation.' See US–Mexico General Claims Commission, *William A. Parker*, 31 March 1926, IV *RIAA* 35, 37. See also *North American Dredging Company*, 4 *RIAA* 26, para. 6, which is cited below, and Commissioner Nielsen's concurring opinion to US–Mexico General Claims Commission, *Jennie L. Corrie*, 4 April 1927, IV *RIAA* 149: 'Rights successfully asserted by the claimant Government under international law in cases of this character inure to the benefit of the nationals of the contracting parties.' Here cited from Feller (n 78) 89.

[96] See Convention respecting the Bank for International Settlements, 20 January 1930, 104 *LNTS* 441.

[97] See further Helmut Coing, 'Bank for International Settlements' in Rudolf Bernhardt (ed), *Encyclopedia of Public International Law*, Vol. 1 (Elsevier Science B.V. 1992) 342–343, and Parlett (n 9) 17.

[98] Convention on the Settlement of Matters Arising Out of the War and the Occupation, 26 May 1952, 332 *UNTS* 219.

[99] Ibid, Article 3 of Chapter V.

provided for the establishment of the Arbitral Commission on Property Rights and Interests in Germany, before which the injured individual had control over the claims and was competent to act as party on equal footing with the respondent State.[100] The same convention set up the Supreme Restitution Court, which was to apply domestic law while settling claims arising from the confiscation of property by the Nazi regime.[101] Notably, questions concerning the extent of the competence of both these bodies fell under the jurisdiction of the Arbitration Tribunal, before which only States could be parties.[102]

In addition to the Arbitral Commission on Property Rights and Interests in Germany, individuals were allowed to call upon the Mixed Commission for the Agreement of German External Debts to solve disputes.[103] It is apparent from the reported cases that the individual enjoyed full capacity in these proceedings.[104] Also, the individual claimant could request an opinion from the Austro-German Arbitral Tribunal, which was competent to decide preliminary questions to ensure a uniform interpretation of the Austro-German Property Treaty.[105]

4.3.1.2 Italy and Japan

Whereas individuals were allowed direct access to the dispute resolution institutions concerning Germany, the Italian and Japanese Conciliation Commissions generally operated according to the doctrine of diplomatic protection. Article 83 of the Treaty of Peace with Italy[106] provided for the establishment of Conciliation Commissions with competence to resolve disputes concerning 'property, rights and interests' of the United Nations and their nationals under inter alia Articles 75 and 78.[107] Commissions were subsequently set up between Italy and the US, the UK, Greece, the Netherlands, and France. Each Conciliation Commission had the power to

[100] Ibid, Article 7 of Chapter V and Annex to the Convention: Charter of the Arbitral Commission on Property Rights and Interests in Germany, Article 6(4) and Article 11(2), but see Article 11(3) authorizing any government agent to act on behalf of nationals and residents of his state. See also Article 25ff of the Arbitral Commission's Rules of Procedure, which are reprinted in *Decisions of the Arbitral Commission on Property Rights and Interests* (Coblenz, published by Direction of the Arbitral Commission by W. Euler, 1958) 192–206. States had the right 'to present in writing and orally arguments and submissions' in cases to which their nationals or residents were parties, cf. ibid, Article 51.

[101] See further ibid, Article 6 of Chapter III, including Annex to Chapter III: Charter of the Supreme Restitution Court.

[102] See Article 9 of the Convention on Relations between the Three Powers and the Federal Republic of Germany, 26 May 1952, 331 *UNTS* 327, and Article 9 (5) of Annex B: Charter of the Arbitration Tribunal.

[103] See Article 31(2)(a) of the Agreement of German External Debts, 27 February 1953, 333 *UNTS* 4, and Article 16 of Annex IV to ibid.

[104] See for example Mixed Commission for the Agreement on External Debts of Germany, *Community of Heirs of the Late Fritz Cahn v. Federal Republic of Germany and Pensionsverein*, 12 November 1964, 35 *ILR* 253, and *Doninelli v. Ebeling*, 28 October 1965, 35 *ILR* 261.

[105] Austro-German Treaty Concerning the Settlement of Property Relations, 15 June 1957, reprinted in extract in Oellers-Frahm and Wühler (n 50) 785–90. See Articles 108ff.

[106] Treaty of Peace with Italy, 10 February 1947, 49 *UNTS* 126. See also Article 78.

[107] Notably, the wording the relevant provisions, including first and foremost Article 78, left it open whether the right to reparation accrued directly to the injured individual.

decide its own rules of procedure, but all the Commissions followed a model, which only allowed States to present claims.[108] In practice, nonetheless, the State agents cooperated extensively with the injured individual.[109]

As in the case of Italy, Property Commissions were established to decide claims against Japan concerning the return of property, rights, or interests of the US, the UK, and the Netherlands and their respective nationals.[110] The Japanese Commission also worked predominantly under the doctrine of diplomatic protection.[111]

Similar to the aftermath of the First World War, the post-Second World War tribunals and commissions thus include examples of both diplomatic protection and individual claims.

During the Cold War it became less common to settle international claims in arbitral tribunals, while there was an increase in lump sum agreements.[112] There are, however, significant exceptions to this trend, which will be discussed in what follows.

4.3.2 Iran–United States Claims Tribunal

In November 1979, fifty-two US nationals were detained at the US Embassy in Tehran and the US responded by freezing all Iranian assets on US territory. The governments of the two States subsequently called upon Algeria to solve the crisis. The Algiers Accords of 19 January 1981 included a General Declaration and a Declaration Concerning the Settlement of Claims.[113] The latter established the Iran–United States Claims Tribunal (hereafter IUSCT) with competence to decide 'claims of nationals of the United States against Iran and claims of nationals of Iran against the United States' concerning for example 'debts, contracts . . . expropriations or other measures affecting property rights.'[114] Article III(3) of the Declaration Concerning the Settlement of Claims reads as follows: 'Claims of nationals of the United States and Iran that are within the scope of this agreement shall be presented

[108] See for example Article 7 of the Rules of Procedure of the Anglo-Italian Conciliation Commission, XIV *RIAA* 6. According to Article 14 '[p]ersons concerned or interested in any disputes before the Conciliation Commission shall only be heard as witnesses.' See also Articles 4 and 7–11 of Rules of procedure of the Italian–United States Conciliation Commission, XIV *RIAA* 79 and Articles 7 and 15(b) of the Réglement de Procédure de la Commission de Conciliation Franco-Italienne, XIII *RIAA* 25. See further Maarten Bos, 'The Franco-Italian Conciliation Commission', 22 *Acta Scandinavica Juris Gentium* (1952) 133, 143ff.

[109] See Oellers-Frahm and Wühler (n 50) 730.

[110] See Articles 15(a) and 22 of Japan–Allied Powers, Treaty of Peace with Japan, 8 September 1951, 136 *UNTS* 45, and Agreement for Settlement of Disputes Arising under Article 15(a) of the Treaty of Peace with Japan, 12 June 1952, 138 *UNTS* 183.

[111] See for example Rules of Procedure of the United States–Japanese Property Commission, XIV *RIAA* 465, Articles 6, 10, and 16, and Rules of Procedure of the Netherlands–Japanese Property Commission, XIV *RIAA* 501, Articles 5 and 9. The inter-State nature of the claims is readily apparent from reported decisions such as Anglo-Japanese Property Commission, *United Kingdom in re Hong Kong & Shanghai Banking Corporation v. Japan*, 21 November 1960, 29 *ILR* 383.

[112] See Richard B. Lillich and Burns H. Weston, 'Lump Sum Agreements: Their Continuing Contribution to the Law of International Claims', 82 *AJIL* (1988) 69ff. See also Caron (n 4) 108.

[113] Both declarations are available at http://www.iusct.net.

[114] Declaration Concerning the Settlement of Claims, 19 January 1981, 20 *ILM* 230, Article II(1).

to the Tribunal either by claimants themselves, or, in the case of claims of less than $250,000, by the Government of such national.'[115]

This provision gave rise to dispute as to whether or not the IUSCT operated under the rules of diplomatic protection. In the *Dual Nationality* case, which was decided in 1984, Iran argued that dual nationals of the US and Iran were barred from bringing claims before the Tribunal under the customary rules on diplomatic protection. Iran based its argument partly on the fact that the Tribunal was set up as 'an International Arbitral Tribunal' pursuant to Article II(1) of the Declaration Concerning the Settlement of Claims, with the primary purpose of settling disputes between the two States. In addition, Iran emphasized that the two States rather than private individuals had the competence to appoint the arbitrators, and that the wording 'claims of nationals' in the above-cited Article III(3) 'does not prejudge the nature of the claims nor the law which should be applied to them.' In conclusion, Iran contended that since the structure, spirit, and terms of the Declarations indicated that the Tribunal is 'truly international', and since individuals are not subjects of international law according to the predominant legal theory, the provisions concerning dispute resolution were to be read as reflecting 'classical requirements of diplomatic protection.'[116]

The US, however, asserted that Iran's argument failed to take into account what the two States had in fact agreed to:

> The Iranian position seems to depend on a combined historical and theoretical analysis of what international tribunals should be. The theory is not derived from the facts of how this Tribunal is constructed. The facts are formed to fit the theory. If the facts don't fit the theory, Iran says that they don't really contradict it, however important the facts are.[117]

In its decision, the Tribunal reiterated that its task was to interpret the relevant provisions of the Algiers Declarations in accordance with Articles 31 and 32 of the VCLT. While it did not agree with the US that the text was so clear as to render further analysis superfluous, it concluded:

> [T]his Tribunal is clearly an international tribunal .... [I]t is the rights of the claimant, not of his nation, that are to be determined by the Tribunal. This should be contrasted with the situation of espousal of claims in international law .... Moreover, the object and purpose of the Algiers Declarations was to resolve a crisis in relations between Iran and the United States, not to extend diplomatic protection in the normal sense.[118]

[115] Pertaining to the question of applicable law, Article V simply states: 'The Tribunal shall decide all cases on the basis of respect for law, applying such choice of law rules and principles of commercial and international law as the Tribunal determines to be applicable, taking into account relevant usages of the trade, contract provisions and changed circumstances.'

[116] IUSCT, *Memorial of the Islamic Republic of Iran in Case A18*, 21 October 1983. Here cited from Caron (n 4) 132. See also IUSCT, *The Islamic Republic of Iran v. United States (Case No. A18) (Dual Nationality)*, 6 April 1984, 5 *Iran–USCTR* 251, 254–6.

[117] 1 *US Transcript of the Case A18 Hearing* 140, 9 November 1983. Here cited from Caron (n 4) 132. See also IUSCT, *Dual Nationality* (1984) 256–9.

[118] Ibid, 261. The Consolidated Tribunal Rules of Procedure (a modified version of the UNCITRAL Arbitration Rules) confirm this view by unequivocally providing that the individual claimant is to be regarded as a party with substantial procedural capacity, although certain prerogatives, such as the appointment of arbitrators, cf. Articles 6–8, are reserved for the two governments. See further

Apparently, the Tribunal did not distinguish between claims exceeding or less than $250,000, although the wording of Article III(3) might be read as to imply that small claims were to be asserted through diplomatic protection.[119]

The *Dual Nationality* case was far from the only occurrence of Iran's contention that claims could only be brought before the Tribunal in accordance with the diplomatic protection doctrine.[120] Nonetheless, as expressed in *Case No. A21*, '[t]ribunal awards uniformly recognize that no espousal of claims by the United States is involved in the cases before it.'[121] *Amoco* of 1989 reads correspondingly:

> [T]he Tribunal holds, as it has held earlier, that its jurisdiction over claims raised is determined exclusively by the provisions in the [Declaration Concerning the Settlement of Claims], and that the [Declaration Concerning the Settlement of Claims] does not condition the Tribunal's jurisdiction on the exhaustion of local remedies as the Respondents contend.[122]

The *Amoco* decision of 1989 is particularly intriguing, because the Tribunal explicitly confirmed that individual rights or obligations under treaties are a matter of treaty interpretation: '[W]hether the Treaty did or did not create rights or duties for private persons, cannot be answered in the abstract, but can be decided only by reference to the terms of the Treaty and the procedures available for its implementation.'[123] In the same paragraph, the tribunal underlined that it is irrelevant to the application of international law by an international tribunal whether national courts would be prevented from giving effect to the provision in question, because it had not been incorporated into national law:

> In an adjudication before an international tribunal such as this, which is expressly authorized ... to apply the rules and principles of international law, it is immaterial whether or not the enforcement of such treaty rights and law by domestic courts would be dependent on the enactment of legislation introducing the provisions of the treaty into the law of the State.[124]

In essence, this paragraph corresponds to the argument made by Anzilotti among others concerning the PCIJ's Advisory Opinion in *Jurisdiction of the Courts of Danzig* of 1928 that Poland was prevented from relying on its own failure to meet obligations under a treaty it had entered into.[125] But the IUSCT's rationale in *Amoco* is more straightforward: the conditions of domestic law are simply not of importance from an international law perspective, because the rights in question arise directly under international law.

Charles N. Brower and Jason D. Brueschke, *The Iran–United States Claims Tribunal* (Martinus Nijhoff, 1998) 15–20.

[119] See IUSCT, *Esphahanian v. Bank Tejarat*, 29 March 1983, 2 *Iran–USCTR* 157. See also IUSCT, *Lord Corporation v. Iran Helicopter Support and Renewal Company*, 29 January 1988, 18 *Iran–USCTR* 377, including *Separate Opinion of Seyed Khalil Khalilian*, 382–90. See also Caron (n 4) 134–5.

[120] See for example *Concurring/Dissenting Opinion of Assadollah Noori, Leonard & Mavis Daley and Islamic Republic of Iran*, 3 June 1988, 18 *Iran–USCTR* 244, 245.

[121] IUSCT, *The Islamic Republic of Iran v. United States, Case No. A21*, 4 May 1987, 14 *Iran–USCTR 324*, 330. See also IUSCT, *The Islamic Republic of Iran v. United States (Cases A15(IV) & A24)*, 28 December 1998, 34 *Iran–USCTR* 105, 148.

[122] IUSCT, *Amoco International Finance Corp. v. Government of the Islamic Republic of Iran*, 14 July 1987, 15 *Iran–USCTR* 189, para. 21.

[123] Ibid, para. 103. [124] Ibid. [125] See Section 3.1.2.2.1.

Certain scholars have raised doubts as to 'the nature of the Iran–United States Claims Tribunal', which quite obviously seem to be based on the 'States-only' conception of international legal personality. For example, David Lloyd Jones asked as follows in the early years of the Tribunal's life:

> Is the Tribunal a private arbitral tribunal created to resolve private law disputes arising under different systems of law and to hear private law claims against Iran and the United States, or is it an international or interstate tribunal charged with the task of ruling on the responsibility of the respondent State under public international law . . .?[126]

Lloyd Jones evidently implies that individuals cannot by definition be the bearers of rights under international law. Although he does acknowledge that individuals have often been allowed direct access to international tribunals, he argues that in such instances 'the claim was the State's claim but, as a matter of convenience or procedure, the injured individual was permitted to put forward the complaint.'[127] The Tribunal does not, however, seem to have taken notice of such academic qualms. In opposition to Lloyd Jones's analysis, the IUSCT has employed its mandate free from conceptual restraints and based its decisions concerning the position of the individual solely on presumption-free interpretation of the relevant sources of law.

4.3.3 Three recent examples of international claims commissions

Contemporary international claims commissions and tribunals continue the trend of their predecessors in the sense that some operate under the diplomatic protection doctrine and some allow for individual claims. In particular three recent claims commissions deserve brief mention.

4.3.3.1 The United Nations Compensation Commission

The United Nations Compensation Commission (hereafter UNCC) was set up by the Security Council[128] in 1991 with jurisdiction over claims for damage suffered as a result of Iraq's invasion and occupation of Kuwait in 1990.[129] It processed the last claim in 2005. Rather than being a court or an arbitral tribunal, before which

126 David Lloyd Jones, 'The Iran–United States Claims Tribunal: Private Rights and State Responsibility', 24 *Virginia Journal of International Law* (1983–4) 259, 261.

127 Ibid, 266. See further 274–76. See, for parallel argumentation in international investment case law, Section 8.2.3.

128 As to the debate on whether the establishment of the UNCC exceeds the range of the Security Council's competence, see for example Bernhard Graefrath, 'Iraqi Reparations and the Security Council', 55 *ZaöRV* (1995) 1, and Lawrence D. Roberts, 'United Nations Security Council Resolution 687 and Its Aftermath: The Implications for Domestic Authority and the Need for Legitimacy', 25 *New York University Journal of International Law and Politics* (1992–3) 593. See also David D. Caron and Brian Morris, 'The UN Compensation Commission: Practical Justice, not Retribution', 13 *EJIL* (2002), 183.

129 See Security Council Resolution 687, 3 April 1991, which provides that Iraq is 'liable under international law' for any direct loss, damage, or injury to 'foreign Governments, nationals and corporations' resulting from Iraq's invasion and occupation of Kuwait. See further Report of the Secretary-General (S/22559), 2 May 1991, and Security Council Resolution 692, 20 May 1991.

the parties appear, it was 'a political organ' with an 'essentially fact-finding function'.[130] While its resolutions of disputed claims were quasi-judicial, its primary purpose, to verify claims and evaluate the size of any losses, was not of a judicial nature.[131] According to the Provisional Rules for Claims Procedure, governments were entitled to submit their own claims as well as the claims of individuals and corporations to the UNCC.[132] However, the injured individual had to consent to the presentation of his claim,[133] and the government in question was obliged to distribute any compensation awarded among the claimants.[134] If a government failed to submit a claim, corporations could under certain circumstances have petitioned the UNCC independently under Article 5(3),[135] and in such cases awards were to 'be paid directly to the corporation or other private legal entity.'[136]

On the whole, it seems that the role of governments before the UNCC is somewhere in between mere representation and diplomatic protection.[137] But evidently, the practice of the UNCC as regards corporations is more at odds with the diplomatic protection doctrine than the practice concerning injury to private persons. The rationale behind the procedural framework was explicitly logistical according to the Report of the Secretary-General (S/22559) of 2 May 1991, in which Secretary-General recommended that it be left to the governments to determine procedures for consolidating claims so that the UNCC would not drown in cases.[138]

4.3.3.2 Commission for Real Property Claims of Displaced Persons and Refugees

The Commission for Real Property Claims of Displaced Persons and Refugees was created as part of the Dayton Peace Agreement of 14 December 1995 between The Republic of Bosnia and Herzegovina, the Republic of Croatia, and the Federal

[130] Report of the Secretary-General (S/22559), 2 May 1991, para. 20.

[131] Ibid, para. 25. See also Carlos Alzamora, 'Reflections on the UN Compensation Commission', 9 *Arbitration International* (1993) 349, 353, and Richard Lillich and Charles Brower, 'Opinion Regarding the Jurisdiction and Powers of the United Nations Compensation Commission', 38 *Virginia Journal of International Law* (1997–8) 25, 27ff.

[132] UNCC Governing Council, *Decision No. 10: Provisional Rules for Claims Procedure*, 26 June 1992. See Article 5(1)(a)–(b).

[133] UNCC Governing Council, Decision No. 1: Criteria for Expedited Processing of Urgent Claims, 2 August 1991, para. 20.

[134] UNCC Governing Council, Decision No. 18: Distribution of Payments and Transparency, 24 March 1994.

[135] Under Provisional Rules for Claims Procedure, 26 June 1992, Article 5(1)(d) international organizations may only submit claims on their own behalf. Notably, the Commission has appointed a person to collaborate with certain international organizations on filing claims on behalf of individuals who were unable to have their claims presented by a government. See ibid, Article 5(2) and UNCC Governing Council, Decision No. 5: Guidelines Relating to Paragraph 19 of the Criteria for Expedited Processing of Urgent Claims, 23 October 1991, para. 5.

[136] Decision No. 7: Criteria for Additional Categories of Claims, 17 March 1992, para. 26.

[137] See further Alzamora (n 131) 354. See also Marco Frigessi di Rattalma and Tullio Treves (eds) *The United Nations Compensation Commission: A Handbook* (Kluwer Law International, 1999) 8–9.

[138] See Report of the Secretary-General (S/22559), 2 May 1991, para. 21. See further Linda A. Taylor, 'The United Nations Claims Commission', in Ferstman et al. (eds), *Reparations for Victims of Genocide, War Crimes and Crimes against Humanity* (Koninklijke Brill, 2009) 202ff.

Republic of Yugoslavia.[139] It functioned from 1996 to 2003. The Commission was mandated to decide 'any claims for real property in Bosnia and Herzegovina, where the property has not voluntarily been sold or otherwise transferred since April 1, 1992, and where the claimant does not now enjoy possession of that property.'[140] Individuals had complete control over the claim and participated fully in the proceedings.[141]

4.3.3.3 Eritrea–Ethiopia Claims Commission

The Eritrea–Ethiopia Claims Commission (hereafter EECC) was established pursuant to Article 5(1) of the Peace Agreement of 12 December 2000, which brought an end to more than two years of armed conflict between Eritrea and Ethiopia:

> The mandate of the Commission is to decide through binding arbitration all claims for loss, damage or injury by one Government against the other, and by nationals (including both natural and juridical persons) of one party against the Government of the other party or entities owned or controlled by the other party that are (a) related to the conflict ... and (b) result from violations of international humanitarian law, including the 1949 Geneva Conventions, or other violations of international law.[142]

It was a novelty that the Commission's competence included determination of State responsibility for violations of international humanitarian law.[143] This element of the EECC's work will be discussed further in Section 5.1.2. As regards the procedural capacity of injured individuals, it followed from Article 5(8) that '[c]laims shall be submitted to the Commission by each of the parties on its own behalf and on behalf of its nationals, including both natural and juridical persons.' With certain exceptions,[144] the EECC thus operated on the basis of the rules on diplomatic protection concerning injuries to individuals.[145] On 17 August 2009, the Commission

[139] See Article VII of Annex 7: Agreement on Refugees and Displaced Persons to Dayton Peace Agreement, 14 December 1995 (available at https://www.state.gov/p/eur/rls/or/dayton/52592.htm, accessed 21 January 2018).

[140] See ibid, Article XI.

[141] See ibid, Article XII. See also Book of Regulations (consolidated version of 8 October 2000), which was adopted by the CPRC pursuant to ibid, Article XV. As to the CPRC's decision-making process, see further Carla Ferstman and Sheri P. Rosenberg, 'Reparations in Dayton's Bosnia and Herzegovina', in Ferstman et al. (eds), *Reparations for Victims of Genocide, War Crimes and Crimes against Humanity* (Koninklijke Brill, 2009) 505ff.

[142] Agreement between the Government of the Federal Democratic Republic of Ethiopia and the Government of the State of Eritrea, 12 December 2000, 2138 *UNTS* 94. Notably, a number of the EECC's awards have been heavily criticized. See, for example, Christine Gray, 'The Eritrea/Ethiopia Claims Commission Oversteps Its Boundaries: A Partial Award?', 17 *EJIL* (2006) 699, and Gro Nystuen and Kjetil Tronvoll, 'The Eritrean–Ethiopian Peace Agreement: Exploring the Limits of Law', 26 *Nordisk Tidsskrift for Menneskerettigheder* (2008) 16, 30–32.

[143] Pertaining to UNCC, for example, it was a priori established under Security Council Resolution 687 (1991) that Iraq was 'liable under international law for any direct loss ... as a result of Iraq's unlawful invasion and occupation of Kuwait.' See further George H. Aldrich, 'The Work of the Eritrea–Ethiopia Claims Commission', 6 *Yearbook of International Humanitarian Law* (2003) 435–6.

[144] See for example Article 5(9): 'In appropriate cases, each party may file claims on behalf of persons of Ethiopian or Eritrean origin who may not be its nationals.'

[145] See EECC, *Rules of Procedure*, October 2001 (available at https://pcacases.com/web/sendAttach/774, accessed 21 January 2018).

issued its Final Awards on damages. In contrast to the UNCC and the IUSCT, the two governments are under no obligation to distribute awards paid to the relevant individuals.[146]

4.4 Conclusion: The Legal Personality of Individuals in International Claims

The above inquiry into the establishment and practice of various international arbitral tribunals and commissions since the end of the eighteenth century hardly traces a progressive development in the role attributed to individuals in the field of international claims. Contrary to common belief, it cannot be contended that claims of individuals against foreign States could only be asserted through diplomatic protection before the Second World War. As the 1907 examples of the International Prize Court and the CACJ show, individual rights under treaties and independent means of enforcement are far from being post-Second World War inventions. Neither is it arguable that diplomatic protection has been replaced entirely by individual claims in contemporary international law. The EECC, set up in 2000, for example, operated on the basis of diplomatic protection. Thus, diplomatic protection and individual claims have coexisted throughout the twentieth century, and there are no indications that this state of affairs is about to change.

In all of the examples mentioned above, pragmatic and political concerns appear to have formed the basis of the adoption of substantive as well as procedural rules, while the theoretical debate about the international legal personality of the individual seems to have had very little say in the decision-making of States. For example, it is scarcely possible to discern particular preferences of particular States in the choice between diplomatic protection and individual claims. Neither common law nor civil law States seem to be inclined towards one specific method of dispute resolution. Furthermore, it is difficult to deduce that a distinct type of injury prompts the use of one set of secondary rules over the other. A large number of injured individuals (i.e. potential claimants), however, might be said to point towards diplomatic protection or lump sum agreements. Correspondingly, the lessons of the costly and time-consuming IUSCT are likely what brought about the mass claims processes before the UNCC.[147] Some might perceive of the increase in lump sum agreements during and after the Cold War and the recent examples of diplomatic protection as a return to the 'States-only' conception of international legal personality. Amending

[146] See EECC, *Final Award, Eritrea's Damages*, XXVI *RIAA* (2009) 505 and EECC, *Final Award, Ethiopia's Damages*, XXVI *RIAA* (2009) 631. See further Michael J. Matheson, 'The Damage Awards of Eritrea–Ethiopia Claims Commission', 9 *The Law and Practice of International Courts and Tribunals* (2010) 1, 14–15.

[147] See for example, Andrea Gattini, 'The UN Compensation Commission: Old Rules, New Procedures on War Reparations', 13 *EJIL* (2002) 161, 166–7.

the procedural rules to fit the practical situation at hand, however, is not a new phenomenon.[148] Before the post-First World War mixed arbitral tribunals, for example, government agents in the end came to screen claims that were originally meant to be presented independently by the injured individuals. Rather, the case law from the various courts, tribunals, and commissions described here predominantly supports the impression of the limited practical importance of the concept of international legal personality. For example, the Permanent Court of Arbitration's decision in *North Atlantic Coast Fisheries* of 1910, the Anglo-German Mixed Arbitral Tribunal's decision in *Lederer v. German Government* of 1923, and the French–German Mixed Arbitral Tribunal's decision in *Sigwald Charles v. Germany* of 1926 all implicitly or explicitly acknowledged the existence of individual rights under treaties without accompanying statements as to the subjectivity of individuals in international law.

In a number of cases, the 'States-only' conception of international legal personality was put forward—for example by the US–Mexico General Claims Commission in the *Dickson Car Wheel Company* Award from 1931 and by Iran before the IUSCT—to reinforce arguments that the rules on diplomatic protection applied. However, in the seminal *Amoco* decision of 1989, the IUSCT appropriately dismissed Iran's arguments. Instead, the Tribunal interpreted the relevant treaty provisions without presumptions relating to the status of the individual in international law.

On the whole, the examination in this chapter illustrates that what is important in international claims is what the relevant States consider to be the best practical and politically feasible solution to a concrete problem. When it has suited the purpose and political will of the States in question, they have adopted treaty provisions granting individuals direct rights and independent means of enforcement. For the most part, the judicial bodies set up to oversee international claims instruments have not hesitated to give effect to such provisions by interpreting them without presumptions as regards the concept of personality in international law. In this way, international claims practice may be said to corroborate the idea of international legal personality as an a posteriori concept.

It is nevertheless worth noting Kaeckenbeeck's contention in his capacity of president of the Upper Silesia Arbitral Tribunal that the tribunal did not 'apply international law at large', when it decided cases brought by individuals against Poland or Germany under the Geneva Convention Relating to Upper Silesia of 1922. As will be explained in Sections 7.2.2.2 and 8.3.2, Kaeckenbeeck's reasoning, which in effect amounts to an endorsement of the 'States-only' conception of international legal personality, is similar to arguments invoked by European judges in order to distinguish the ECHR and EU law from international law in general.

[148] See also Section 7.2.1 on the development of the procedural status of individuals before the ECtHR.

5

The Legal Personality of Individuals in International Humanitarian Law

International humanitarian law is traditionally divided into two branches: 'the law of The Hague', which governs the means and methods of warfare, and 'the law of Geneva' pertaining to the protection of victims of war. Moreover, international and non-international armed conflicts have been treated separately throughout history. The latter distinction is not only consistent with the core of the law of Geneva comprising the four Geneva Conventions of 12 August 1949[1] and the two Additional Protocols of 8 June 1977.[2] For present purposes, it also serves to highlight the fact that regulation of the conduct of both parties to a non-international armed conflict necessarily involves rights and obligations of at least one non-State actor. The law of international armed conflict is examined in Sections 5.1 and 5.2, while the law of non-international armed conflict is the subject of Sections 5.3 and 5.4.[3]

International humanitarian law applicable in both international and non-international armed conflicts may impose obligations on individuals in the form of criminal responsibility. This subject will be dealt with substantially in Chapter 6 on international criminal law.[4] The purpose of the present chapter is to examine how individuals have otherwise been engaged by international humanitarian law and the role of the concept of international legal personality in that context.

[1] The 'Geneva Conventions' currently in force are the Geneva Convention for the Amelioration of the Condition of the Wounded and Sick in Armed Forces in the Field (hereafter Geneva Convention I); the Geneva Convention for the Amelioration of the Condition of Wounded, Sick and Shipwrecked Members of Armed Forces at Sea (hereafter Geneva Convention II); the Geneva Convention Relative to the Treatment of Prisoners of War (hereafter Geneva Convention III); and the Geneva Convention Relative to the Protection of Civilian Persons in Time of War (hereafter Geneva Convention IV).

[2] The 'Additional Protocols' are Protocol I Additional to the Geneva Conventions of 12 August 1949, and relating to the Protection of Victims of International Armed Conflicts (hereafter Additional Protocol I); and Protocol II Additional to the Geneva Conventions of 12 August 1949, and relating to the Protection of Victims of Non-International Armed Conflicts (hereafter Additional Protocol II).

[3] Sections 5.3 and 5.4 are based on Astrid Kjeldgaard-Pedersen, 'A Ghost in the Ivory Tower: Positivism and International Legal Regulation of Armed Opposition Groups', 7 *Journal of International Humanitarian Legal Studies* (2016) 32–62.

[4] As to the grave breaches regime, see Kate Parlett, *The Individual in the International Legal System—Continuity and Change in International Law* (CUP, 2011) 188–9 and 221–2. See also Marko Milanović, 'Is the Rome Statute Binding on Individuals? (And Why We Should Care)', 9 *JICJ* (2011) 25, 42.

Although ideas of restricting the means and methods of warfare and relieving the suffering of victims of war emerged much earlier,[5] the following study will begin with the birth of contemporary international humanitarian law in the middle of the nineteenth century.

5.1 The Law of International Armed Conflict before the Second World War

5.1.1 The Law of The Hague

The Declaration of Paris[6] pertaining to maritime warfare, which was concluded at the end of the Crimean War in 1856, was the first multilateral agreement with the purpose of limiting undesired consequences of armed conflict. Soon thereafter, in 1868, the St Petersburg Declaration[7] was adopted as the first instrument to ban the use of specific weapons. Rather than bringing about individual rights and obligations, both Declarations were limited to inter-State obligations, albeit to the benefit of individuals. For example, the St Petersburg Declaration provided: 'The Contracting Parties engage mutually to renounce, in case of war among themselves, the employment by their military or naval troops of any projectile of a weight below 400 grammes, which is either explosive or charged with fulminating or inflammable substances'.[8]

The norms applicable to international armed conflicts have for the most part been consistent with this approach.[9] In 1899 and 1907 two peace conferences were held in The Hague, resulting in respectively the 1899 Hague Convention, comprising four conventions and three declarations, and the 1907 Hague Convention, consisting of thirteen conventions[10] and two declarations. These rules, which are collectively referred to as 'the law of the Hague' govern numerous aspects of the conduct of warfare on land, at sea, and in the air (by use of balloons). Today, some rules have gone out of date, while others are a part of customary international law.[11] The three

[5] See for example Leslie C. Green, *The Contemporary Law of Armed Conflict* (3rd edn, Manchester University Press, 2008) 26ff, and Hilaire McCoubrey, *International Humanitarian Law* (Ashgate, 1998) 8ff. See also Stephen C. Neff, *War and the Law of Nations—A General History* (CUP, 2005).

[6] Declaration Respecting Maritime Law (hereafter Declaration of Paris), 16 April 1856.

[7] Declaration Renouncing the Use, in Time of War, of Explosive Projectiles Under 400 Grammes Weight (hereafter St Petersburg Declaration), 29 November/11 December 1868.

[8] Dietrich Schindler and Jiří Toman (eds) *Laws of Armed Conflicts: A Collection of Conventions, Resolutions, and Other Documents*, (4th edn, Martinus Nijhoff, 2004) 92.

[9] See also George H. Aldrich, 'Individuals as Subjects of International Humanitarian Law', in Jerzy Makarczyk (ed.), *Theory of International Law at the Threshold of the 21st Century: Essays in Honour of Krzysztof Skubiszewski* (Kluwer, 1996) 851.

[10] As for the twelfth convention on the creation of an International Prize Court, see Section 4.1.1.1. Passing mention should be made of the Brussels Declaration of 27 August 1874, which was never ratified, Schindler and Toman (n 8) 21–8, and the Institute of International Law's *Oxford Manual* of 1880, Schindler and Toman (n 8) 29–40. Both documents were part of the basis for the 1907 Hague Conventions.

[11] With regard to the customary nature of the rules of land warfare, see *IMT Judgment*, reprinted in 41 *AJIL* (1947) 172, 248–9. See also Yoram Dinstein, *The Conduct of Hostilities under the Law of International Armed Conflict* (2nd edn, CUP, 2010) 14–15.

Declarations of 1899[12] were framed like the St Petersburg Declaration in that the contracting parties agreed to prohibit or abstain from the use of particular methods of warfare or weapons.[13] For example, the language of Article 1 of the 1899 Hague Convention II, as slightly amended by the 1907 Hague Convention IV,[14] indicates inter-State obligations in that the contracting powers agreed to 'issue instructions to their armed land forces which shall be in conformity with the Regulations respecting the laws and customs of war on land'. Also, the wording of Article 3 on responsibility and compensation, which was introduced in the 1907 version, suggests that the provisions of the Hague Regulations are inter-State obligations rather than directly applicable to individuals: 'A belligerent party which violates the provisions of the said Regulations shall, if the case demands, be liable to pay compensation. It shall be responsible for all acts committed by persons forming part of its armed forces.'[15]

Another example is Chapter III of the 1907 Hague Convention V Respecting the Rights and Duties of Neutral Powers and Persons in Case of War on Land[16] which governs the conditions of neutral persons without including direct individual rights or obligations. Instead, Article 9 obliges a neutral power to ensure that certain obligations are met by companies or private individuals.[17]

The 'inter-State interpretation' is further substantiated by the language and *travaux préparatoires*[18] of Chapter II of the Hague Regulations laying down standards of treatment of prisoners of war. Likewise, the wording of Article 46 indicates inter-State obligations although it addresses core individual interests: 'Family honour and rights, the lives of persons, and private property, as well as religious convictions and practice, must be respected. Private property cannot be confiscated.'[19] Subsequent international agreements on the conduct of warfare were drafted according to this framework.[20]

[12] 1899 Hague Convention IV is identical to 1899 Hague Declaration I.

[13] See Declaration on the Launching of Projectiles and Explosives from Balloons (hereafter 1899 Hague Declaration I); Declaration on the Use of Projectiles the Object of Which is the Diffusion of Asphyxiating or Deleterious Gases (hereafter 1899 Hague Declaration II); and Declaration on the Use of Bullets Which Expand or Flatten Easily in the Human Body (hereafter 1899 Hague Declaration III), 29 July 1899.

[14] Convention (IV) on Laws and Customs of War on Land (hereafter 1907 Hague Convention IV), 18 October 1907, including Annex to the Convention: Regulations Respecting the Laws and Customs of War on Land (hereafter Hague Regulations). See Schindler and Toman (n 8) 55.

[15] The recent examples of domestic case law pertaining to Article 3 of the 1907 Hague Convention IV are discussed at the end of this section.

[16] 1907 Hague Convention V Respecting the Rights and Duties of Neutral Powers and Persons in Case of War on Land, 18 October 1907. See Schindler and Toman (2004) (n 8) 1399.

[17] See Schindler and Toman (n 8) 1401.

[18] The Hague Regulations' provisions on prisoners of war are based on the Articles 23–34 of the Brussels Declaration of 27 August 1874, cf. above. The discussions of the plenary conference on 5 July 1899 is reprinted in James Brown Scott, *The Proceedings of the Hague Peace Conferences, The Conference of 1899* (OUP, 1920a) 55–8.

[19] See, however, the discussion of recent domestic case law at the end of this section.

[20] See, for example, Geneva Protocol for the Prohibition of the Use in War of Asphyxiating, Poisonous or Other Gases, and of Bacteriological Methods of Warfare, 17 June 1925; Convention on the Prohibition of the Development, Production and Stockpiling of Bacteriological (Biological) and Toxin Weapons and on their Destruction, 10 April 1972; Convention on Prohibitions or Restrictions on the Use of Certain Conventional Weapons Which May be Deemed to be Excessively Injurious or to Have Indiscriminate Effects, 10 October 1980; Convention on the Prohibition of the Development,

It seems straightforward to presume that the structure of the law of The Hague was motivated by the 'States-only' conception of international legal personality.[21] However, the *travaux préparatoires* to the Hague Conventions are silent on this issue.

The discussions regarding the above-cited Article 3 of 1907 Hague Convention IV provide an illustrative example of the (lack of) importance attributed to the notion of international legal personality: Originally, Germany had proposed that compensation be paid to injured individuals, that is, 'neutral persons' and 'persons of the hostile party', rather than States. Article 3 was apparently given its present form for pragmatic reasons. The parties simply wanted to avoid misunderstandings concerning the distinction between the two categories of persons. As for the responsibility for members of armed forces, 'the German delegation thought it well to propose that the Convention should extend to the law of nations, in all cases of infraction of the Regulations, the principle of private law according to which the master is responsible for his subordinates or agents.'[22]

The debate implies that theoretical assumptions about the possible subjects of international law were not on the minds of the members of the second commission of the 1907 conference. Rather, the example of Article 3 of 1907 Hague Convention IV indicates that the parties simply did not find it expedient to confer direct rights and obligations on individuals in this particular instance. Thus, the explanation for the 'States-only' framework of the law of The Hague is hardly to be found in a common belief among the parties that treaties could only govern the relationship between States. Of course, it cannot be ignored that treaties at the turn of the twentieth century predominantly followed an inter-State model. But there is a fundamental difference between saying States could not by definition govern individuals directly, and saying that it was not tradition to do so at the time. As described in Section 4.1.1, two other treaties were concluded in the same year where the parties did find it pertinent to govern individuals directly.

Remarkably, Article 3 of the 1907 Hague Convention IV has been subjected to diverging interpretations in recent rulings by domestic courts. The 'inter-State' reading of Article 3 has been adopted by domestic Japanese courts.[23] In contrast, the Hellenic Supreme Court famously ruled in *Prefecture of Voiotia v. Federal Republic of Germany* that the victims of the 'Distomo massacre' of 1944 could bring direct

Production, Stockpiling and Use of Chemical Weapons and on their Destruction, 3 September 1992; Convention on the Prohibition of the Use, Stockpiling, Production and Transfer or Anti-Personnel Mines and on their Destruction, 18 September 1997; and Convention on Cluster Munitions, 30 May 2008.

[21] See for example Parlett (n 4) 93.

[22] The German proposition was presented to the second commission of the conference on 14 August 1907. See James Brown Scott, *The Proceedings of the Hague Peace Conferences, The Conference of 1907*, Vol. III (OUP, 1921) 25–6. See also ibid, 13–14, 245, and 250.

[23] See, for example, Tokyo District Court, Case No. 1218-1994, 30 November 1998, reprinted in 42 *Japanese Annual of International Law* (1997) 143. See further Masahiro Igarashi, 'Post-War Compensation Cases, Japanese Courts and International Law', 43 *Japanese Annual of International Law* (2000) 45.

claims for compensation against Germany on the basis of Article 3 of 1907 Hague Convention IV and Article 46 of the Hague Regulations.[24]

Adopting yet another interpretation, the Federal Constitutional Court of Germany has implied that while individuals do hold primary rights under international humanitarian law, Article 3 does not provide for secondary individual rights:

> Article 3 of the Hague Convention of 1907 does not justify individual claims for compensation, but only promotes the general principle of international law ... of mutual obligations between the contracting parties. The claim for damages differs in this respect from the primary legal claim that the affected persons have to compliance with the prohibitions of international humanitarian law....[25]

This line of reasoning was repeated by the Federal Constitutional Court of Germany in its 2013 Decision in the *Varvarin* case. It is especially noteworthy in the context of the present study that the Court invoked the modified 'States-only' conception of international legal personality as it inferred that the presumption against the subjectivity of individuals in international law has only been rebutted in the case of human rights:

> Despite the—steadily progressing—developments at the level of human rights protection, which have led to the recognition of a partial international legal subjectivity of individuals and the formation of a right to individual complaints, a comparable development as regards secondary claims cannot be established. Claims for damages regarding a State's breach of its international legal obligations towards foreign nationals are, as a matter of principle, reserved exclusively for the home State.[26]

5.1.1.1 The Martens Clause

The famous 'Martens Clause' was introduced in the preamble of the 1899 Hague Convention II and restated in the 1907 Hague Convention IV.[27] It reads:

[24] *Prefecture of Voiotia v. Federal Republic of Germany*, Case No. 11/2000, Judgment, 4 May 2004 (reprinted in 129 *ILR* 513). This judgment was controversial for a number of reasons. For example, the ICJ has dismissed the notion that State immunity does not apply to violations of *jus cogens* norms. See *Jurisdictional Immunities of the State (Germany v. Italy: Greece intervening)* (Judgment) [2012] ICJ Rep 99, paras 92ff.

[25] Federal Constitutional Court of Germany, 2 BvR 1379/01, Decision, 28 June 2004, para. 38 (author's translation, available in German at http://www.bverfg.de/entscheidungen/rk20040628_2bvr137901, accessed 21 January 2018). See also Anne Peters, *Beyond Human Rights—The Legal Status of the Individual in International Law* (CUP, 2016) 171 and 201.

[26] Federal Constitutional Court of Germany, Case No. 2 BvR 2660/06, Decision, 13 August 2013 (available in German at http://www.bverfg.de/e/rk20130813_2bvr266006.html, accessed 21 January 2018), para. 46 (author's translation). See also ibid, para. 7: '[T]he traditional conception of international law as an intergovernmental law does not understand the individual as an international law subject, but only grants indirect protection through the home state. A significant exception to this is the European Convention on Human Rights ...'. See similarly the decision of the Regional Court of Bonn of 11 December 2013 in the '*Kunduz incident*' case, Case No. 1 O 460/11, paras 43–47 (available in German at https://openjur.de/u/667409.html, accessed 21 January 2018). See Section 3.4.1 as regards the relationship between individual rights and human rights. See further Section 3.3.2 on the relationship between the international legal personality of individuals and diplomatic protection.

[27] Similar clauses have been included in various subsequent conventions, for example the Geneva Conventions and Additional Protocols. See further Helmut Strebel, 'Martens' Clause' in Rudolf Bernhardt (ed.), *Encyclopaedia of Public International Law* (Elsevier Science BV, 1997), Vol. III, 326–7.

Until a more complete code of the laws of war has been issued, the High Contracting Parties deem it expedient to declare that, in cases not included in the Regulations adopted by them, the inhabitants and the belligerents remain under the protection and the rule of the principles of the law of nations, as they result from the usages established among civilized peoples, from the laws of humanity, and the dictates of the public conscience.[28]

Originally, it was meant to provide residual humanitarian rules applicable to the population in occupied territories, in particular armed resistance fighters,[29] but given its rather imprecise wording it is hardly surprising that the Martens Clause has been subjected to diverging interpretations.[30] While it clearly affirms that safeguarding individuals is a key objective of international humanitarian law, it seems far-fetched to infer that the Martens Clause in and of itself provides individual rights under international law.[31]

5.1.2 The Law of Geneva

The first version of the Geneva Convention for the Amelioration of the Condition of the Wounded in Armies in the Field was drawn up in 1864 under the auspices of the newly founded International Committee of the Red Cross (hereafter ICRC). Similar to the rules on warfare adopted in those years, it did not contain individual rights or duties, but merely obliged the States parties to secure a certain standard of treatment. For example, Article 6(1) reads: 'Wounded or sick soldiers shall be entertained and taken care of, to whatever nation they may belong', while Article 8 provides that: 'The details of execution of the present convention shall be regulated by the commanders-in-chief of belligerent armies, according to the instructions of their respective governments, and in conformity with the general principles laid down in this convention.'

In light of the experiences of the First World War, the 1864 Geneva Convention[32] was redrafted and replaced by two conventions signed on 27 July 1929: the Geneva Convention for the Amelioration of the Condition of the Wounded and Sick in Armed Forces in the Field, and the Geneva Convention Relative to the Treatment of Prisoners of War. Like the 1864 and 1906 Conventions, the two 1929 Geneva Conventions predominantly contain inter-State obligations rather than individual

[28] Schindler and Toman (n 8) 61.

[29] Theodor Meron, 'The Martens Clause, Principles of Humanity, and Dictates of Public Conscience', 94 *AJIL* (2000a) 78, 79. For an examination of the *travaux préparatoires* to the 1899 Hague Conference and the intentions of Martens, see Antonio Cassese, 'The Martens Clause: Half a Loaf or Simply Pie in the Sky?', 11 *EJIL* (2000) 187, 193–202.

[30] Cassese (n 29) 188. The Martens Clause has been relied on in numerous cases, international as well as national. Famous examples include Supreme Court of Norway, 'Klinge', *Norsk Retstidende* (1946) 198, 200, NMT, *Krupp*, IX *TWC* (1949–53) 1327, 1341, *Military and Paramilitary Activities in and against Nicaragua (Nicaragua v. United States of America)* (Judgment) [1986] ICJ Rep 14, para. 218, *Legality of the Threat or Use of Nuclear Weapons (Merits)* (Advisory Opinion) [1996] ICJ Rep 226, paras 78, 84, and 87.

[31] See also Parlett (n 4) 93.

[32] By the 1899 Hague Convention III, the principles of the convention from 1864 had been adapted to maritime warfare. It was 'improved and supplemented' by Geneva Convention for the Amelioration of the Condition of the Wounded and Sick in Armed Forces in the Field of 6 July 1906.

rights and duties. In this context, the sporadic mention of 'rights'[33] can scarcely be read as laying down direct individual rights under international law.[34] However, the Geneva Conventions of 1949 appear to have brought about substantial changes in that regard.

5.2 The Law of International Armed Conflict after the Second World War

5.2.1 The Geneva Conventions of 1949

Renegotiations of the 1929 Geneva Conventions in the wake of the horrors of the Second World War led to the adoption of the four Geneva Conventions of 12 August 1949.[35] Whether these conventions include individual rights under international law, or merely confer obligations to protect individuals on States participating in an international armed conflict, is not entirely clear. It is common for all four conventions that a relatively small number of articles are worded as to suggest that individuals hold direct rights under international law. Rather, the language of by far the most substantive provisions points towards obligations of States to secure a certain level of protection of various groups of individuals.

Geneva Conventions I and II lay down rules on the protection of the wounded and sick in armed forces in the field and the wounded, sick, and shipwrecked members of armed forces at sea without referring to 'rights' of such individuals. For example, Article 12 of Geneva Convention I provides: 'Members of the armed forces and other persons mentioned in the following Article, who are wounded or sick, shall be respected and protected in all circumstances. They shall be treated humanely and cared for by the Party to the conflict in whose power they may be'.[36]

Geneva Conventions III and IV do articulate a limited number of 'rights', but it is not obvious whether they accrue directly to the individuals in question, or whether States are merely required to secure these rights in municipal law. Article 78 of Geneva Convention III, for example, provides: 'Prisoners of war shall have the right to make known to the military authorities in whose power they are, their requests regarding the conditions of captivity to which they are subjected.'[37] Moreover,

[33] For example, Article 21 of the Geneva Convention for the Amelioration of the Condition of the Wounded and Sick in Armed Forces in the Field of 1929 provides that medical personnel 'have the right to obtain duplicates' of lost certificates of identity, while Article 23 gives medical units 'the right ... to fly their national flag.' Similarly, Articles 42, 62, and 64 of the Geneva Convention Relative to the Treatment of Prisoners of War of 1929 refer to certain 'rights' of prisoners of war. See further Parlett (n 4) 180–1.

[34] Aldrich (n 9) 851.

[35] See note 1.

[36] See similarly Geneva Convention II, Article 12, Geneva Convention III, Article 13, and Geneva Convention IV, Article 27.

[37] Similarly, Article 101 of Geneva Convention IV confers on internees 'the right to present to the authorities in whose power they are, any petition with regard to the conditions of internment'. See further Articles 72 and 73 on procedural rights of relevant persons accused or convicted of a crime, cf. also Article 5. Likewise, see Articles 105 and 106 of Geneva Convention III pertaining to prisoners' rights in connection with judicial proceedings.

Article 27 of Geneva Convention IV reads as follows: 'Protected persons are entitled, in all circumstances, to respect for their persons, their honour, their family rights, their religious convictions and practices, and their manners and customs.'

While the substantive provisions thus paint a blurred image as regards individual rights under the Geneva Conventions, all four contain a saving clause and a non-renunciation clause, which clearly imply that such rights exist.[38] It follows from the saving clause that '[no] special agreements shall adversely affect the situation of [the protected persons], as defined by the present Convention, nor restrict the *rights* which it confers upon them.'[39] Likewise, all four conventions include a non-renunciation clause providing that the protected persons 'may in no circumstances renounce in part or in entirety the *rights* secured to them by the present Convention'.[40]

The saving clauses were substantially amended,[41] and the non-renunciation clauses were entirely new, in all four 1949 Geneva Conventions. Since both provisions explicitly refer to 'rights' of the protected persons, one might have expected to find some clarification of the nature of these rights in the *travaux préparatoires*. But the available documents are not especially helpful. Generally, there seems to have been very little discussion of the matter, and no unequivocal statements were made.[42] There are, however, some indications that the Conventions should be read as attributing rights directly to individuals. In 1946, for example, a preliminary conference 'unanimously recommended that the rights conferred by the Convention on prisoners of war should have a personal and intangible character, allowing the latter to claim them irrespective of the attitude adopted by their home country.'[43] Furthermore, the remarks to a draft version of May 1948 state that the non-renunciation clause in Geneva Convention III 'confirms the individual rights which the Convention gives to prisoners of war in many of its stipulations.'[44] Finally, the Seventeenth International Red Cross Conference approved of the four draft conventions in August 1948, while noting that: 'these Drafts, in particular the new Convention on the Protection of Civilians, correspond to the fundamental aspirations of the peoples of the world and that they define the essential rules for that protection to which every human being is entitled'.[45]

38 See also Peters (n 25) 196–8.

39 Geneva Convention I, Article 6; Geneva Convention II, Article 6; Geneva Convention III, Article 6; and Geneva Convention IV, Article 7 (emphasis added).

40 Geneva Convention I, Article 7; Geneva Convention II, Article 7; Geneva Convention III, Article 7; and Geneva Convention IV, Article 8 (emphasis added).

41 In the 1929 Geneva Convention I, Article 2(2) read: 'Belligerents shall, however, be free to prescribe, for the benefit of the wounded or sick prisoners, such arrangements as they may think fit beyond the limits of the existing obligations.'

42 See for example Report on the Work of the Conference of Government Experts for the Study of the Conventions for the Protection of War Victims (April 1947) 259, Draft Revised or New Conventions for the Protection of War Victims (May 1948) 7, 35–6, 55, 155–6, and Final Record of the Diplomatic Conference of Geneva of 1949 (1950–1), Vol. II(B) 76.

43 Report on the Work of the Preliminary Conference of National Red Cross Societies for the study of the Conventions and of various Problems relative to the Red Cross, 26 July–3 August 1946 (1947) 71.

44 See Article 7 of the draft Geneva Convention III under the heading 'Acquired rights' in Draft Revised or New Conventions for the Protection of War Victims (May, 1948) 55.

45 Report of the Seventeenth International Red Cross Conference (August, 1948) 93.

Consistently, it follows from the ICRC Commentary on Geneva Convention III that the 1929 Geneva Conventions were not 'clearly conceived, as constituting a body of "rights" to which [the protected persons] were automatically entitled.... It was not... until the Conventions of 1949 (in particular Articles 6 and 7 [the saving and non-renunciation clauses]) that the existence of "rights" conferred on prisoners of war was affirmed.'[46]

The ICRC asserts in all four Commentaries on the Geneva Conventions that the 'rights' mentioned in the saving and non-renunciation clauses include 'the whole body of safeguards which the Convention affords to [the protected persons].'[47] For example, the ICRC's comments to the non-renunciation clause in Article 8 of Geneva Convention IV read:

> Undoubtedly, owing to the still undeveloped character of international law, the safeguards protecting the rights conferred on persons to whom the Convention relates are by no means as complete, effective, or automatic as those of national legislations. Nevertheless, Article 8 is of the greatest assistance to all protected persons. It allows them to claim the protection of the Convention, not as a favour, but as a right, and in case of violation, it enables them to employ any procedure available, however rudimentary, to demand respect for the Convention's terms.[48]

Due to the involvement of the ICRC in the drafting process of the four Geneva Conventions, the Commentaries are not to be taken lightly. Even so, they do not amount to a binding interpretation of the Conventions. Since the wording of the material provisions does not unambiguously indicate direct individual rights, the contrary interpretation that the Conventions merely lay down obligations of States cannot be discarded offhand. Among the proponents of the 'inter-State' reading is Françoise Hampson, who without elaborating on the basis of her analysis draws the following conclusion: 'These rules are not based on any notion of the "right" of the individual civilian not to be attacked, the "right" of the prisoner of war to good treatment or the "right" of the injured to

[46] Jean Pictet (ed.), *Commentary III Geneva Convention Relative to the Treatment of Prisoners of War* (ICRC, 1960a) 91 (hereafter Commentary III). See correspondingly Jean Pictet (ed.), *Commentary I Geneva Convention for the Amelioration of the Condition of the Wounded and Sick in Armed Forces in the Field* (ICRC, 1952) 82 (hereafter Commentary I); Jean Pictet (ed.), *Commentary II Geneva Convention for the Amelioration of the Condition of the Wounded, Sick and Shipwrecked Members of Armed Forces at Sea* (ICRC, 1960b) 58 (hereafter Commentary II); Jean Pictet (ed.), *Commentary IV Geneva Convention Relative to the Protection of Civilian Persons in Time of War* (ICRC, 1958) 77 (hereafter Commentary IV). See also Theodor Meron, 'The Humanization of Humanitarian Law', 94 *AJIL* (2000b) 239, 251–3.

[47] Here cited from Commentary III (n 46) 85. See correspondingly Commentary I (n 46) 74, Commentary II (n 46) 52, and Commentary IV (n 46) 70. See also Aldrich (n 9) 855.

[48] See Commentary IV (n 46) 79, and similarly, Commentary III (n 46) 92, Commentary II (n 46) 59, and Commentary I (n 46) 84. The recent second editions of Commentary I and Commentary II clearly confirm that all four Conventions confer rights on individuals. See further ICRC, *Commentary on the First Geneva Convention* (2nd edn, 2016), paras 1000–1001 (available at https://ihl-databases.icrc.org/ihl/full/GCI-commentary, accessed 7 April 2018), and ICRC, *Commentary on the Second Geneva Convention* (2nd edn, 2017), paras 1038–1039 (available at https://ihl-databases.icrc.org/ihl/full/GCII-commentary, accessed 7 April 2018).

medical care. The Conventions are based rather on the reciprocal obligations of States.'[49]

Concurrently, Parlett finds this reading of the Conventions to be 'consistent with a normative (not to say factual) framework in which individuals have no meaningful capacity to exercise their "rights".'[50] As confirmed by the ICJ in *LaGrand*, however, the existence of individual rights in international law is not contingent upon access to an international forum in which such rights may be enforced. Although it goes without saying that the lack of international enforcement mechanisms greatly impairs the possibility for individuals to assert their rights under international humanitarian law, it does not per se indicate that no such rights exist.[51]

In keeping with the analysis of Section 3.4, the interpretation of both the primary and secondary rules of international humanitarian law must be performed according to the general principles of interpretation reflected in Articles 31–33 of the VCLT—free from presumptions concerning the international legal personality of individuals. There is no basis for implying a presumption against direct individual rights.[52] Neither is there, however, as Paola Gaeta asserts, cause to apply a presumption *for* individual rights by taking into account the evolution of human rights law since the Second World War:

> It would ... be preposterous to affirm that the position of the individual as a holder of rights dissolves when their need to be protected against abuses reaches its peak, ie in situations of armed conflict .... The inescapable conclusion is that the relevant rules ... must be interpreted in light of the development of international law in the field of human rights; hence as rules that ... confer corresponding rights on the civilians themselves, and not on the enemy belligerent party.[53]

[49] Françoise J. Hampson, 'Human rights law and international humanitarian law: two coins or two sides of the same coin?' 1 *Bulletin of Human Rights* (1991) 46, 49. See, similarly, René Provost, *International Human Rights and Humanitarian Law* (CUP, 2002) 22ff.

[50] Parlett (n 4) 187. See further Section 5.1.1 for a discussion of the recent German case law pertaining to the 1907 Hague Convention IV, which seems to promote the idea that the holder of primary rights in international humanitarian law may be the individual, although the right to reparation for breaches remains with the State.

[51] See further Section 3.1.2.2.2. See also with specific regard to international humanitarian law, Aldrich (n 9) 854, referring to Hersch Lauterpacht, *International Law and Human Rights* (Stevens & Sons, 1950) 27 and 34–5.

[52] See further Sections 3.1.2.2.1 and 3.4.3.1.

[53] Paola Gaeta, 'Are Victims of War Crimes Entitled to Compensation?', in Orna Ben-Naftali (ed.), *International Humanitarian Law and International Human Rights Law* (OUP, 2011) 305, 319. Likewise, Cançado Trindade concluded as follows in 2011 by explicit reference to the saving clauses of the 1949 Geneva Conventions:

> The considerable evolution in the last decades ... of International Humanitarian Law has contributed decisively to the evidencing and reassertion of the constant contact of the individual with the international legal order. International Humanitarian Law ... considers protected persons not only as the simple object of the regulation that it establishes, but rather as true subjects of International Law.

See Antônio Augusto Cançado Trindade, *The Access of Individuals to International Justice* (OUP, 2011) 3–4, and see further Section 2.4 as to Cançado Trindade's 'individualistic' conception of international legal personality. See similarly Jan Klabbers, Anne Peters, and Geir Ulfstein, *The Constitutionalization of International Law* (OUP, 2009) 170. See also Peters (n 25) 200–1.

In *LaGrand*, the ICJ had no doubt that Article 36(1) of the VCCR includes individual rights.[54] It is arguable that the ICJ's decision supports the ICRC's reading of the 1949 Geneva Conventions, since there are a number of similarities between, for example, the above-cited Articles 27 and 101 of Geneva Convention IV, and Article 36(1)(b) and (c) of the VCCR. The ultimate purpose of all of these provisions is to secure the coexistence of States by safeguarding individuals, and they all contain a mix of references to 'rights' and obligations of States without explicating whether the mentioned rights accrue directly to the individuals in question. There is, however, one major difference in that Article 36(1)(c) of the VCCR, as was emphasized by the ICJ, allows the national in question to expressly refuse action by his home State, whereas the non-renunciation clauses have exactly the opposite effect. Even so, given the circumstances in which the Geneva Conventions apply, this difference should perhaps not be overstated. The correct interpretation of the Geneva Conventions remains an open question and, due to the lack of international enforcement mechanisms, the prospects of finding a definitive answer are perhaps slim.

Nevertheless, it is noteworthy that the ICRC explicitly believed the formulation of the non-renunciation clauses to be 'influenced by the concomitant trend in doctrine, which also led to the universal proclamation of Human Rights'.[55] The reference to 'doctrine' is dubious. Presumably the ICRC was not referring to a change in the dominant theoretical approach to the concept of international legal personality, but rather meant to say that States had become more willing to attribute treaty-based rights to individuals between 1929 and 1949. Correspondingly, there seems to have been no discussion on the international legal personality of individuals when the 1949 Geneva Conventions were drafted.[56] Indeed, international legal theory generally appears to have played a minor role—with the exception maybe of a proposal of the delegation of the Holy See 'that a reference should be made in the Preamble to the divine origin of all rights which protect human liberty and dignity'.[57]

5.2.2 Additional Protocol I of 1977

On 8 June 1977, Additional Protocol I was adopted to upgrade the rules pertaining to international armed conflict. It largely rendered the distinction between 'the law of The Hague' and 'the law of Geneva' superfluous.[58] The *modus operandi* of the 1949 Geneva Conventions was sustained in the sense that Additional Protocol I primarily lays down obligations of States,[59] but also includes a number of references

[54] See further Section 3.4.3.1.

[55] Commentary I (n 46) 82. See also Commentary IV (n 46) 77.

[56] There was some debate on the legal personality of insurgents. See for example *Final Record of the Diplomatic Conference of Geneva of 1949* (1950–1), Vol. II(B) 47. See further Section 5.4.1.

[57] Ibid, 522.

[58] See for example François Bugnion, 'Droit de Genève et droit de La Haye', 844 *Revue internationale de la Croix-Rouge* (2001) 901, Dinstein (n 11) 16–17, and Gary Solis, *The Law of Armed Conflict* (CUP, 2010) 83.

[59] See for example Articles 1(1), 10(1), 51, and 80(1).

to 'rights'.[60] Again, it is not explicitly indicated in the text of the relevant provisions whether these rights accrue directly to the relevant individuals.[61]

The Commentaries on the ICRC's original proposal for Article 11, entitled 'Protection of persons', read inter alia: 'The protection which the present article confers on the physical or mental well-being of protected persons is regarded as an inalienable right.'[62] Moreover, the *travaux préparatoires* to Article 75 entitled 'Fundamental Guarantees' clearly state that the provision incorporates principles contained in human rights instruments, particularly the ICCPR of 1966. Hence, it is arguable that Article 75 like the ICCPR confers rights directly on individuals.[63] Otherwise, neither the discussions during the drafting process[64] nor the commentary on Article 75[65] provide much guidance as to the nature of the included 'rights'.

On the whole, there is little to suggest that the above analysis of the 1949 Geneva Conventions should not be equally applicable to Additional Protocol I. Accordingly, George H. Aldrich, who acted as Rapporteur for Committee III at the 1974–77 Diplomatic Conference,[66] has concluded as follows:

> While the Protocol largely follows tradition in drafting of its protections in terms of duties of the parties to the conflict or of the occupying power, or by the prohibition of certain acts and the requirement of other acts, the substance of many articles is, in effect, the creation of individual rights.[67]

5.3 The Law of Non-International Armed Conflict before the Second World War

Original Western thinking drew a clear distinction between 'civil strife' and 'true war'. Civil strife was regarded as a strictly domestic matter, while the international laws of war only applied to armed conflicts between States. Gradually, however, States began to call for international responses to a number of questions raised by internal armed conflicts. These developments during the eighteenth and nineteenth centuries, which revolved around the doctrine of 'recognition of belligerency', will be traced in the following Section 5.3.1. Subsequently, Section 5.4 will examine the (predominantly) post-Second World War progression, including the adoption of

60 See for example Article 11(5), Articles 44–45, and Article 75.

61 Examples include Articles 11(5), 43(2), 45, and 75(4).

62 ICRC, *Draft Additional Protocols to the Geneva Conventions of August 12, 1949—Commentary* (1973) 21. See also Yves Sandoz, Christophe Swinarski, and Bruno Zimmerman (eds), *Commentary on the Additional Protocols of 8 June 1977 to the Geneva Conventions of 12 August 1949* (ICRC, 1987) 150, paras 455ff (hereafter Commentary on Additional Protocols).

63 See further EECC, *Civilians Claims, Eritrea's Claims 15, 16, 23 and 27–32*, Partial Award, 17 December 2004, paras 30–31, and EECC, *Civilians Claims, Ethiopia's Claim 5*, Partial Award, 17 December 2004, paras 29 and 75.

64 See, for example, ICRC, *Draft Additional Protocols to the Geneva Conventions of August 12, 1949—Commentary* (1973) 80ff, and *Official Records of the Diplomatic Conference on the Reaffirmation and Development of International Humanitarian Law Applicable in Armed Conflicts* (1978), Vol. XV, 25ff.

65 See Commentary on Additional Protocols (n 62) 863, paras 3000ff.

66 Committee III inter alia drafted Article 75.

67 Aldrich (n 9) 856.

common Article 3 of the four 1949 Geneva Conventions and Additional Protocol II of 1977. Finally, Section 5.6 will account for the ongoing academic debate about the jurisprudential justifications for binding armed opposition groups through international law.

5.3.1 Recognition of belligerency

During the eighteenth century, a number of questions, including the matter of applicability of the law of neutrality to third States, began to arise in connection with internal armed conflicts. It became common to distinguish between 'rebellion' (or 'insurrection') and 'belligerency'. 'Rebellion' referred to an ephemeral uprising against the government of a State, and it was regarded as a matter of exclusively domestic concern.[68] If, on the other hand, the opposition endured, and could be regarded as a regular attempt to assume political power over (a part of) the State in question, it would be recognized as 'belligerency'—to which a number of international legal rules applied.

In 1758, Vattel argued that civil conflicts under certain circumstances were to be governed by the laws of war. In keeping with his 'States-only' definition of international law,[69] however, he did not purport to apply international legal rules to individuals. Rather, when conditions were met, he regarded the parties to the civil conflict as separate States: '[W]hen the nation becomes divided into two completely independent parties, which do not recognize a common superior, the state is dissolved and the war between the two parties falls, in every respect, in the same category as war between two different nations.'[70]

It subsequently remained a conceptual necessity to perceive of armed opposition groups as legally on a par with the government they opposed in order for the laws of war to become applicable.[71] The tool invented to this end was the doctrine of 'recognition of belligerency'.

In the late eighteenth century and the beginning of the nineteenth century, attribution of belligerent rights was in effect the same as recognition of Statehood. The American Revolution of 1775–83 is an early example of an internal uprising treated as inter-State war. The British parliament adopted a statute, which equated the insurgent colonists with armed forces of adversary States[72] and invoked the law of neutrality against third States.[73] Likewise, Spain essentially came to treat its opponents in the Latin American independence conflict during 1814–25 as a State enemy,[74] while third States outspokenly perceived of the Latin American parties as

[68] Anthony Cullen, *The Concept of Non-International Armed Conflict in International Humanitarian Law* (CUP, 2010) 8–10. See also Neff (n 5) 215–58.

[69] See further Section 2.1.

[70] Emmerich de Vattel, *Le Droit des Gens ou Principes de la Loi Naturelle* (Carnegie, 1916), Liv. III, chap. XVIII, § 295, 247 (author's translation).

[71] Neff (n 5) 250ff. Notably, Islamic law seems to have already developed in that direction in the Middle Ages. See also Lindsay Moir, *The Law of Internal Armed Conflict* (CUP, 2002) 3.

[72] 17 Geo. 3 *c*. 9 (1777).

[73] See further Erik Castrén, *Civil War* (Suomalaisen Kirjallisruuden Kirjapaino Oy, 1966) 39–40.

[74] For example, it followed from the Convention of Truxillo between Spain and Colombia of 26 November 1820 that both sides to the conflict were bound by the laws of war. See 71 *CTS* 291.

separate States with regard to the hostilities. In the case of *The Santissima Trinidad* of 1822, for example, the US Supreme Court stated:

> The government of the United States has recognized the existence of a civil war between Spain and her colonies, and has avowed a determination to remain neutral between the parties and to allow to each the rights of asylum and hospitality and intercourse. Each party is, therefore, deemed by us a belligerent nation having, so far as concerns us, the sovereign rights of war, and entitled to be respected in the exercise of those rights.[75]

Towards the middle of the nineteenth century, a practice separating recognition of belligerency from the recognition of Statehood developed. States acknowledged that certain rebellious groups had 'belligerent' rights and duties under international law without recognizing them as independent States. Examples include the British conduct in connection with the Greek rebellion against Turkey of 1821–29. Whereas Turkey refused to recognize the belligerent rights of the Greeks,[76] the UK 'professed an impartial Neutrality' and allowed both parties to the conflict 'the free exercise of belligerent rights, such as the Law of Nations warrants'.[77] But, these measures were not equivalent to the recognition of Greece's Statehood.[78] Similarly, a number of States, including Great Britain and France, recognized the belligerent rights of the Confederacy during the 1861–5 American Civil War, while carefully avoiding any implication that it was a State.[79]

Like recognition of Statehood, recognition of belligerency was inherently a political act. In the early practice, a State's recognition of an insurgent group as belligerent was primarily contingent upon the extent of the conflict and the interests at stake for the State in question.[80] The American Civil War, however, prompted debate on whether recognition of belligerency was entirely up to the third State in question, or whether certain objective criteria should be applied. The principal factors under discussion were the extent and duration of the hostilities, the de facto government of the insurgents, and the population and the territory under their control. On one hand, the UK maintained that the US government could not—as it did[81]—claim belligerent rights for itself vis-à-vis third States without automatically acknowledging the belligerent rights of the Confederacy.[82] On the other hand, the US took the position that belligerent rights depended solely on factual conditions, and that the

75 US Supreme Court, *The Santissima Trinidad*, 20 US (1822) 283, 337.

76 Castrén (n 73) 42.

77 Dispatch of 31 December 1824 from British Foreign Secretary, George Canning, to British attaché at Vienna, Henry Richard Wellesley, reprinted in Herbert Arthur Smith, *Great Britain and the Law of Nations* (Kraus, 1932) 294, 295. See further Neff (n 5) 262, and Parlett (n 4) 199.

78 See further Hersch Lauterpacht, *Recognition in International Law* (CUP, 1947) 178–9.

79 See Neff (n 5) 263.

80 Cullen (n 68) 17.

81 See US Supreme Court, *The Prize Cases*, 67 US (2 Black) (1862) 635, 636: 'To create... belligerent rights as against neutrals, it is not necessary that the party claiming them should be at war with a separate and independent power'. See further Neff (n 5) 259.

82 See Report of 16 September 1863 by the then law officers of the Crown, William Atherton, Roundell Palmer, and Robert Phillimore, reprinted in extract in Arnold McNair, *International Law Opinions*, vol. I (CUP, 1956) 139–40. As for the position of other third states, see Quincy Wright, 'The American Civil War (1861–65)' in Richard A. Falk (ed.), *The International Law of Civil War* (Johns Hopkins Press, 1971) 82–3.

UK's recognition of the belligerency of the Southern rebels was 'unprecedented and precipitate'.[83]

By the end of the nineteenth century, the predominant position in legal scholarship was that a set of objective criteria did exist,[84] but that third States were under no obligation to recognize belligerency, even if they were met.[85] In 1900, l'Institut de Droit International adopted a resolution on civil war, which provided the following criteria for third States' recognition of belligerency in Article VIII:

> Third Powers cannot recognize the character of belligerent in a revolutionary party:
> Section 1. If it has not acquired a distinct territorial existence through the possession of a definite portion of the national territory;
> Section 2. If it has not the elements of a regular government exercising in fact the manifest rights of sovereignty over this portion of the territory;
> Section 3. If the fight is not carried on in its name by organized troops, subject to military discipline and conforming to the law and customs of war.[86]

However, the effects in terms of legal status that followed from recognition of belligerency were not quite clear. In his *Treatise on International Law*, which was first published in 1880, William Edward Hall stated that international legal personality was not a consequence of being recognized as belligerents, but only of Statehood: 'As a belligerent community is not itself a legal person, a society claiming only to be belligerent, and not to have permanently established its independence, can have no rights under [international] law.'[87]

This relatively narrow scope of belligerency seemingly generated a need for a subsidiary classification of armed opposition groups. Towards the end of the nineteenth century, a rebellion, which persisted in spite of attempts to suppress it, but nevertheless did not meet the criteria for belligerency, thus came to be placed in the somewhat ill-defined category of 'insurgency', to which no clear legal effects accrued. According to Hersch Lauterpacht: 'Recognition of insurgency creates a factual relation in the meaning that legal rights and duties as between insurgents and outside States exist only in so far as they are expressly conceded and agreed upon for reasons of convenience, of humanity, or of economic interest.'[88]

[83] See correspondence between Lincoln's minister to the Court of St James's, Charles Francis Adams, and UK foreign secretary, Earl Russell, cited in Henry Wheaton, *Elements of International Law, 1866 edn.* (Clarendon Press, 1936) 31–2. Notably, Article 152 of the famous instructions for the Federal army, the Lieber Code of 1863, explicitly separated the application of the laws of war from recognition of independence.

[84] For example, both the US and the UK refused to recognize the belligerency of the rebels during the 1893–4 Brazilian Naval Revolt. See further Parlett (n 4) 203. See also Cullen (n 68) 17–18.

[85] See Lassa Oppenheim, *International Law, A Treatise—War and Neutrality* (Longmans, Green, and Co., 1906) 86.

[86] Rights and Duties of Foreign Powers as Regards the Established and Recognized Governments in Case of Insurrection, 8 September 1900, James Brown Scott (ed.), *Resolutions of the Institute of International Law* (Carnegie, 1916) 159.

[87] William Edward Hall, *Treatise of International Law* (8th edn, Clarendon Press, 1924) 39.

[88] See Lauterpacht (n 78) 277. Similarly, Richard A. Falk defining 'insurgency' as 'a catch-all designation provided by international law to allow states to determine the quantum of legal relations

Like the recognition of belligerency, the recognition of insurgency served the sole purpose of enabling third States to secure their interests vis-à-vis the de facto government in question. The difference between the two categories was that the former entailed international legal rights and duties, whereas the latter did not.[89]

After the First World War, a movement led by the ICRC began to promote the application of humanitarian norms in internal armed conflict. In 1921, the Tenth International Conference of the ICRC adopted Resolution IV, which was moderately worded as follows:

> The Tenth Conference, informed by the tragic experiences of the Red Cross in the countries affected by civil war, drew the attention of all peoples, of all governments and all political parties, national or otherwise, to the fact that the state of civil war cannot justify the violation of international law, and that this body of law must be safeguarded at all costs.[90]

In the more direct Resolution XIV adopted in 1938, the ICRC invited the application of the humanitarian principles following from the Geneva Conventions of 1929 to civil wars.[91]

Especially since the Spanish Civil War of 1936–9, during which the rebels for political reasons were never recognized as belligerents, although they clearly met all of the legal criteria sketched out above,[92] the practice of recognition of belligerency and insurgency has been in steep decline.[93] The necessity of objective criteria for the application of international humanitarian law in civil wars, which were not contingent upon international politics, became readily apparent. Despite the ICRC's efforts, however, the norms concerning the protection of victims of war applied exclusively in inter-State armed conflicts until 1949, when it was decided to include a common Article 3 in all four Geneva Conventions, so as to extend a minimum of humanitarian standards to non-international armed conflicts. This turn of events is the subject of the following section.

to be established with the insurgents'. See Richard A. Falk, 'Janus Tormented: The International Law of Internal War', in James N. Rosenau (ed.), *International Aspects of Civil Strife* (Princeton University Press, 1964) 199. See also Moir (n 71) 5, and Cullen (n 68) 11.

[89] Falk (n 88) 203. See also Erik Castrén, 'Recognition of Insurgency', 4 *Indian Journal of International Law* (1965) 443, 453.

[90] Anton Schlögel, 'La guerre civile', 52 *IRRC* (1971) 137, 139–40 (author's translation).

[91] See ibid, 141.

[92] See further Ann Van Wynen Thomas and A. J. Thomas, Jr., 'The Civil War in Spain' in Richard A. Falk (ed.), *The International Law of Civil War* (Johns Hopkins Press, 1971) 141ff. See also Parlett (n 4) 206–7.

[93] See for example Roscoe R. Oglesby, 'The Decline of Belligerent Recognition: Desuetude in International Law', in Roscoe R. Oglesby (ed.), *Internal War and the Search for Normative Order* (Martinus Nijhoff, 1971) 100ff, and Cullen (n 68) 22–3. See however Yair M. Lootsteen, 'The Concept of Belligerency in International Law', 166 *Military Law Review* (2000) 109.

5.4 The Law of Non-International Armed Conflict after the Second World War

5.4.1 Common Article 3 of the Geneva Conventions

Apart from the Martens clause, which covered all kinds of armed conflict,[94] no treaty-based regulation of civil strife existed before the adoption of common Article 3 of the 1949 Geneva Conventions setting forth a number of provisions, which 'each Party to [an armed conflict not of an international character occurring in the territory of one of the High Contracting Parties] shall be bound to apply as, as a minimum.'

The drafting history of common Article 3 provides an intriguing case study of the role of the concept of international legal personality in the development of the law of non-international armed conflict. What is of key interest is not so much how the original proposition of the ICRC to extend the Geneva Conventions' provisions in their entirety to internal wars turned into the adopted version of common Article 3.[95] It is rather the debate concerning the jurisprudential foundation for conferring obligations on 'each Party to the conflict'. At the outset, however, a few preliminary remarks concerning the scope of common Article 3 are required.

First of all, it should be underlined that it is not clear whether the non-State party to the conflict is perceived as the insurgent group as such or its individual members. As a matter of principle, the Member States of the Geneva Conventions could very well have decided to impose obligations on the insurgents as a group. Pursuant to the overarching argument of the present book,[96] whether they in fact did so depends exclusively on interpretation of the treaty. The fact that common Article 3 binds 'each Party to a conflict' might be said to refer to the insurgents as a group. The phrase is by no means conclusive, however, and the fact that common Article 3 explicitly has no consequences for 'the legal status of the Parties to the conflict' could be read as supporting the argument that the provision binds each individual member.[97] It is unnecessary to pursue this issue further at this juncture as

[94] See further section 5.1.1.1.

[95] Notably, it was envisioned that the conventions would apply 'unless one of [the adverse Parties] announces expressly its intention to the contrary'. Report on the Work of the Preliminary Conference of National Red Cross Societies for the study of the Conventions and of various Problems relative to the Red Cross, 26 July–3 August 1946 (1947) 14–15. It soon became apparent that such a model would be unacceptable to the member States. See further Report on the Work of the Conference of Government Experts for the Study of the Conventions for the Protection of War Victims, 14–26 April 1947 (1947) 8–9, which proposed to apply 'the principles of the conventions' and only if both parties to the conflict consented. See also David A. Elder, 'The Historical Background of Common Article 3 of The Geneva Convention of 1949', 11 *Case Western Reserve Journal of International Law* (1979) 37, 42ff.

[96] See Section 1.2.

[97] The purpose of this reservation was evidently to sever any link between conferral of obligations on insurgents and recognition of their independence. The provision was included very early on in the drafting process and it was essential for securing sufficient will among the member States to include a provision on internal conflict. See further Report of the Seventeenth International Red Cross Conference (August, 1948) 72, and Report on the Work of the Conference of Government Experts for

it is beyond doubt that common Article 3 addresses non-State actors.[98] The flaws of the argument that common Article 3 must be directed at the insurgents as a group, because its individual members cannot possess international legal personality, will be discussed at the end of this section.

A second remarkable point is that common Article 3 contains no definition of an 'armed conflict not of an international character' and no specific criteria for determining when it applies.[99] The *travaux préparatoires* and the ICRC Commentaries on common Article 3 support the interpretation of the term 'armed conflict not of an international character' as equivalent to 'civil war', which in turn is based on the doctrine of recognition of belligerency.[100] Accordingly, it appears that common Article 3 was originally intended to apply only in situations closely resembling international armed conflict. In 1995, the Appeals Chamber of the ICTY nonetheless concluded as follows: '[W]e find that an armed conflict exists whenever there is a resort to armed force between States or protracted armed violence between governmental authorities and organized armed groups or between such groups within a State.'[101]

The considerable drop of the threshold for the application of common Article 3, which the *Tadić* decision implies, amply illustrates the general expansion of issues perceived as involving the interests of several States during the second half of the twentieth century. The inclusion in 1977 of Article 1(4) in Additional Protocol I, which explicitly categorizes wars of national liberation as international armed conflicts, may be seen as an important step along the way. So is of course the—regressive—clarification of the 'material field of application' following from Article 1 of Additional Protocol II, which will be discussed further in Section 5.4.2.[102] But otherwise, the precise meaning of 'armed conflict not of an international character' has little influence on the subject of the present study. The primary questions to be examined here are related to the theoretical justification for conferring direct international rights and obligations on insurgents, rather than the exact factual circumstances under which the relevant rules come into play.

During the Diplomatic Conference of Geneva in 1949, the question of personality in international law was afforded limited attention. The discussion primarily took place in the Special Committee of the Joint Committee, which had been set up

the Study of the Conventions for the Protection of War Victims, 14–26 April 1947 (1947) 9. See also for example Commentary III (n 46) 43, and Moir (n 71) 65.

[98] See Section 1.3. See further Katharine Fortin, *The Accountability of Armed Groups under Human Rights Law* (OUP, 2017) 194–5.

[99] See further Moir (n 71) 34ff.

[100] See *Final Record of the Diplomatic Conference of Geneva of 1949* (1950–1), Vol. II(B) 121, and Commentary I (n 46) 49–51, and similarly Commentary III (n 46) 35–7, Commentary IV (n 46) 35–6. Pursuant to Commentary II (n 46) 33, however, common Article 3 applies to 'conflicts which are in many respects similar to an international war.' See further Cullen (n 68) 49ff and 60.

[101] *Prosecutor v. Tadić*, IT-94-1, Appeals Chamber, Decision on Defence Motion for Interlocutory Appeal on Jurisdiction, 2 October 1995, para. 70. Subsequently, this test for determining the existence of an armed conflict has been applied consistently by the ICTY. See, for example *Prosecutor v. Limaj et al.*, IT-03-66-T, Trial Chamber, Judgment, 30 November 2005, para. 84. See further Cullen (n 68) 117ff.

[102] For a detailed analysis, see Cullen (n 68) 86ff.

to deal with the many diverging opinions on how the Geneva Conventions might apply to internal conflicts. A number of members of this committee took issue with the fact that the provision that would eventually become common Article 3 (Article 2, paragraph 4 of the draft) presupposed a legal personality on the part of the insurgents, 'which they could not possess.'[103] These members opined that insurgents could not be party to any international agreement, and that no obligations could therefore be imposed on them by the Geneva Conventions.[104] The Greek member, Agathocles, however, disagreed with the latter implication. He argued that 'failure by the insurgents to accede to the Conventions was not an insurmountable obstacle'. To the contrary, insurgents should be considered bound by them for two reasons:

> (a) The Conventions which were being drafted could and should be considered as law making Conventions, i.e., as rules which should be applicable not only on behalf of or against the Contracting Parties, but also in circumstances which were analogous to those governed by the said Conventions;
> (b) Insurgents and even bandits were obviously nationals of some State, and were thereby bound by the obligations undertaken by the latter; since practically all civilized States would sign the Conventions which were being drawn up, it therefore followed that, subject to exceptions, any insurgent or bandit would be a national of a Signatory State, and would *ipso facto* be bound by the Convention. This legal interpretation enabled insurgents to be considered as automatically bound by the Convention—the aim of the rules which were being drawn up ....[105]

While Agathocles' description of 'law making Conventions' is somewhat puzzling,[106] his second reason is more to the point. Essentially, he invokes the idea, which will be discussed further in Section 5.4.3.4, that States have the power to adopt a treaty which confers direct obligations on individuals within their jurisdiction. In the end, however, no conclusions pertaining to the theoretical underpinnings for binding insurgents by common Article 3 were drawn during the Diplomatic Conference.

According to Commentary I, common Article 3 is the result of a change in the framework of the international legal system:

[103] See for example the comments made by the Italian delegate, Maresca. *Final Record of the Diplomatic Conference of Geneva of 1949* (1950–1), Vol. II(B) 47.

[104] See for example the comments made by the British delegate, Craigie, and Australian delegate, Hodgson. Ibid, 94.

[105] Ibid.

[106] Although it is by no means a well-defined concept, the label 'law-making treaty' is commonly attached to treaties that govern individuals directly. See, for example, with reference to the ECHR, Franz Matscher, 'Methods of Interpretation of the Convention', in R. S. J. Macdonald et al. (eds), *The European System for the Protection of Human Rights* (Martinus Nijhoff, 1993) 63, 66, Rudolf Bernhardt, 'Thoughts on the Interpretation of Human Rights Treaties', in Franz Matscher and Herbert Petzold (eds), *Protecting Human Rights: The European Dimension—Studies in Honour of Gerard Wiarda* (Carl Heymanns Verlag, 1988) 65, 70–1. As argued in Section 7.2.2, the notion of 'law-making treaties' is misleading. A straightforward alternative would be to simply acknowledge that a treaty may have whatever content the contracting States see fit, including provisions regulating the interests of individuals (but excluding of course violations of *jus cogens* norms).

The words 'each Party' mark the great progress which the passage of a few years has sufficed to bring about in international law. For until recently it would have been considered impossible in law for an international Convention to bind a non-signatory Party—a Party, moreover, which was not yet in existence and which was not even required to represent a legal entity capable of undertaking international obligations ....[107]

Then, somewhat inconsistently, the Commentary goes on to explain the bindingness of the Convention on insurgents by reference to their State-like features: '[I]f the responsible authority at their head exercises effective sovereignty, it is bound by the very fact that it claims to represent the country, or part of the country.'[108]

Ultimately, Commentary I concludes that the legal basis of common Article 3 has little practical value: 'If an insurgent party applies Article 3, so much the better for the Victims of the conflict. No one will complain. If it does not apply it, it will prove that those who regard its actions as mere acts of anarchy or brigandage are right.'[109]

Whereas the Commentaries on the other Geneva Conventions[110] reiterate these arguments, Commentary II, which was the last of the four to be completed, also includes an additional explanation, namely that common Article 3 is automatically incorporated in the domestic law of many States:

Some doubt has been expressed as to whether insurgents can be legally bound by a Convention which they have not themselves signed. The answer is provided in most national legislations; by the fact of ratification, an international Convention becomes part of law and is therefore binding upon all the individuals of that country.[111]

The confusion between the perspectives of international and national law is readily apparent. Clearly, the bindingness of a treaty from the point of view of international law does not depend on the way in which it is incorporated into domestic law.[112]

A number of scholars argue that common Article 3 does not in fact confer obligations on individuals, but rather attributes an extraordinary kind of international legal personality on the insurgents as a group. Castrén, for example, finds it to be a 'justifiable conclusion ... that the Geneva Convention has conferred on a party rebelling against the lawful Government a restricted status as an international subject within the meaning of this Article.'[113] Similarly, G. I. A. D. Draper contended as follows in 1958: 'When individuals group themselves in a particular way so that they become a party to an internal conflict, then they are given collectively a sufficient legal personality to enable them to be subject to the obligations and hold rights conferred or imposed on them by these Conventions.'[114]

107 Commentary I (n 46) 51.

108 Ibid. This argument will be discussed further in Section 5.4.3.3.

109 Ibid, 52.

110 See Commentary II (n 46) 34, Commentary III (n 46) 37–8, Commentary IV (n 46) 37.

111 Commentary II (n 46) 34.

112 See further Section 1.3.2. See also Antonio Cassese, 'The Status of Rebels under the 1977 Geneva Protocol on Non-International Armed Conflicts', 30 *ICLQ* (1981) 416, 429–30.

113 Castrén (n 73) 87.

114 G. I. A. D. Draper, *The Red Cross Conventions*, (Frederick A. Praeger, 1958) 17.

By 1965, however, Draper had seemingly changed his mind and abandoned the notion of an ad hoc international legal personality for insurgents as a group in favour of the legislative jurisdiction reasoning.[115]

> A possible solution avoiding that complexity and artificiality is to consider that the obligations imposed by the article devolve upon the whole of the population of the State concerned, at any time, so that any person taking part in an internal conflict on either side is exposed to the risk of being in breach of an international obligation if he acts in violation of Article 3.[116]

The debate concerning the jurisprudential justification for conferring rights and duties on armed opposition groups was revived in connection with the adoption of the Additional Protocols in 1977.

5.4.2 Additional Protocol II of 1977

Additional Protocol II was conceived to 'develop and supplement' common Article 3 of the Geneva Conventions. In comparison with common Article 3, which binds 'each Party' to an 'armed conflict not of an international character', Article 1(1) gives Additional Protocol II a much more precise scope. It applies to:

> ... all armed conflicts ... which take place in the territory of a High Contracting Party between its armed forces and dissident armed forces or other organized armed groups which, under responsible command, exercise such control over a part of its territory as to enable them to carry out sustained and concerted military operations and to implement this Protocol.

The *travaux préparatoires* to Additional Protocol II reveal that this considerable change of wording regarding the field of application was the result of discussion of the question whether direct rights and obligations were in fact conferred on insurgents. A number of delegations claimed that Additional Protocol II could not impose obligations directly on insurgents, because they did not possess international legal personality. The Italian delegation, for example, submitted that '[i]n ratifying this instrument, the High Contracting Parties will assume obligations, not towards rebel forces (which are neither subjects of international law nor Parties to Protocol II), but towards the other Contracting Parties, the international community and world opinion.'[117]

Similarly, the Zairian delegation argued that 'dissident armed forces are primarily a group of rebels with no international legal personality. Their only legal status is that granted them under the domestic laws of their national State.'[118]

The delegation of the Soviet Union essentially concurred with these arguments, when it stated that the Protocol would bind Member States as well as 'all citizens

[115] See further Section 5.4.3.4.

[116] G. I. A. D. Draper, 'The Geneva Conventions of 1949', 114 *Recueil des Cours* (1965-I) 60, 96.

[117] Official Records of the Diplomatic Conference on the Reaffirmation and Development of International Humanitarian Law Applicable in Armed Conflicts, 1974–77 (1978), Vol. VII, 122.

[118] Ibid, Vol. VII, 104. See also the Sudanese contention that '[t]he Protocol did not involve any international agreements but simply a concession on the part of States which agreed to apply it to their own nationals.' Ibid, Vol. VII, 201.

within the territory of the state in question', but only through the interposition of national law.[119] Belgium, however, contended that since common Article 3 bound both States and insurgents directly, so did Additional Protocol II: '[T]he entire philosophy of the provisions of common Article 3, whether explicitly reaffirmed or not, is included in the Protocol. It is implicit that the same applies to the basic sovereign principle that the obligations of the Protocol are equally binding on both Parties to the conflict.'[120]

In this way, the *travaux préparatoires* of Additional Protocol II scarcely paint a clear image as to whether the intention of the parties was to bind armed opposition groups directly. However, Italy, Zaire, and the Soviet Union did not explicitly oppose the idea of binding insurgents directly, but rather argued that such a disposition would be impossible as a matter of doctrine. More importantly, interpretation of the provisions of the Protocol according to the general rules of interpretation under Articles 31–33 of the VCLT reasonably leads to the conclusion that Additional Protocol II does indeed confer rights and obligations directly on insurgents. Aside from the fact that it was conceived to 'develop and supplement' common Article 3, which clearly governs insurgents directly, the structure and wording of its provisions indicate that Additional Protocol II is directed at armed opposition groups as well as States.[121]

5.4.3 The bindingness of the law of non-international armed conflict on armed opposition groups

The academic debate on the jurisprudential foundation for binding armed opposition groups by the law of non-international armed conflict is ongoing.[122] The question is not *if* insurgents are bound by this body of international norms, but *how* it is possible to bind them. While theoretical discussion about the diverging conceptions of international legal personality play merely a peripheral role, the 'States-only' conception is apparent as an underlying presumption of some authors. The debate centres on the following justifications for conferring rights and obligations directly on insurgents:

(1) the bindingness of customary international law,
(2) the bindingness of treaties on third parties,
(3) the bindingness of treaties through effective control over a particular territory, and
(4) the principle of legislative jurisdiction.[123]

119 Ibid, Vol. XIV, 314. 120 Ibid, Vol. VII, 76.

121 See also Cassese (n 112) 424–8, Marko Milanović, 'Is the Rome Statute Binding on Individuals? (And Why We Should Care)', 9 *JICJ* (2011) 25, 40, and Parlett (n 4) 216.

122 Recent contributions include Fortin (n 98), Sandesh Sivakumaran, 'Binding Armed Opposition Groups', 55 *ICLQ* (2006) 369, Jann K. Kleffner, 'The Applicability of International Humanitarian Law to Organized Armed Groups', 93 *International Review of the Red Cross* (2011) 443, Daragh Murray, 'How International Humanitarian Law Treaties Bind Non-State Armed Groups', 20 *Journal of Conflict and Security Law* (2015) 101.

123 Notably, some authors rely on several of these arguments in conjunction. See for example D. Schindler, 'The Different Types of Armed Conflicts According to the Geneva Conventions and Protocols', 163 *Recueil des Cours* (1979-II) 117, 151–2.

These four arguments will be discussed in turn in the following sections.

5.4.3.1 *The bindingness of customary international law*

The issue at stake here is not the material extent to which non-international armed conflicts are governed by customary international law.[124] Rather, it is the contention that insurgents are not bound by the rules of common Article 3 and Additional Protocol II as treaties, but because they reflect customary international law.[125] One advocate of this view is Lindsay Moir, who finds that 'most theoretical difficulties can be overcome if the binding force of Article 3 for insurgents is removed from the domestic law sphere and instead applies directly through customary international law.'[126]

This reasoning was invoked by the Appeals Chamber of the Special Court for Sierra Leone in its 2004 Decision on Jurisdiction in the *Norman* case:

> [I]t is well-settled that all parties to an armed conflict, whether states or non-state actors, are bound by international humanitarian law, even though only states may become parties to international treaties. Customary international law represents the common standard of behaviour within the international community, thus even armed groups hostile to a particular government have to abide by these laws.[127]

Concurringly, Yoram Dinstein finds that '[e]ven the most superficial discussion of [the conceptual underpinning for the proposition that armed opposition groups are bound by the law of non-international armed conflict] must draw a distinction between treaty law and customary law.'[128] He goes on to assert that '[an] insurgent group ... is not vested by international law with a legal personality',[129] and that '[denied] legal personality, the groups must be seen for what they are: clusters of individuals.'[130] Dinstein argues that since '[t]here is a clear-cut precedent for conferring—by treaty—collective human rights without the tool of an international legal personality', armed opposition groups may benefit from such rights. In contrast, he finds that there are no precedents for imposing collective obligations on groups by treaty.[131] Moreover, Dinstein submits that since armed opposition

[124] See Section 5.5.

[125] A variation of this argument is that armed opposition groups are bound because common Article 3 and Additional Protocol II reflect general principles. See further Sivakumaran (n 122) 375ff.

[126] Moir (n 71) 56–8.

[127] *Prosecutor v. Sam Hinga Norman*, SCSL-2004-14-Ar72(E), Appeals Chamber, Decision on Preliminary Motion Based on Lack of Jurisdiction (Child Recruitment), 31 May 2004, para. 22. See also *Prosecutor v. Morris Kallon & Brima Bazzy Kamara*, SCSL-2004-15-AR72(E), Appeals Chamber, Decision on Challenge to Jurisdiction: Lomé Accord Amnesty, 13 March 2004, para. 47:

> [F]or the purpose of the present case, ... no one has suggested that insurgents are bound because they have been vested with personality in international law of such a nature as to make it possible for them to be a party to the Geneva Conventions. Rather, a convincing theory is that they are bound as a matter of international customary law to observe the obligations declared by Common Article 3 ....

[128] Yoram Dinstein, *Non-International Armed Conflicts in International Law* (CUP, 2014) 64.

[129] Ibid, 65. [130] Ibid, 66.

[131] Ibid, 68. This part of Dinstein's argument would seem to be at odds with the wording of the very provisions that he is discussing, since interpretation of common Article 3 and Additional Protocol

groups cannot be parties to treaties, they are only bound by customary international law: 'Just as customary international law can bind states regardless of their consent, it is also capable of imposing obligations on all individuals and groups anywhere.'[132]

The 'States-only' conception of international legal personality and its voluntarist foundation are clearly apparent in this justification. But even if we were to accept the premise that international legal personality is reserved exclusively for States, the argument does not adequately explain how customary international law may bind insurgents, while treaties may not. The only possible way of defending a distinction between treaties and customary law in this respect would be to regard insurgents as third parties. The material difference between 'the bindingness of customary international law' justification and 'the bindingness of treaties on third parties' justification thus appears to be that the former denies the ability of armed opposition groups to accede to treaties, whereas the latter accepts it.

5.4.3.2 The bindingness of treaties on third parties

The treaty-making capacity of armed opposition groups was seemingly a controversial issue on the ILC's agenda when the VCLT was drafted. In the 1962 draft, Article 1(a) defined the term treaty as 'an international agreement ... between two or more States or other subjects of international law'. The Commission's commentary explained that:

> The phrase 'other subjects of international law' is designed to provide for treaties concluded by: (a) international organizations, (b) the Holy See, which enters into treaties on the same basis as States, and (c) other international entities, such as *insurgents*, which may in some circumstances enter into treaties. The phrase is not intended to include individuals or corporations created under national law, for they do not possess capacity to enter into treaties nor to enter into agreements governed by public international law.[133]

Article 3(1) of the same draft provided that '[c]apacity to conclude treaties under international law is possessed by States and by other subjects of international law.' The commentary on Article 3(1) explicitly refers to the modified 'States-only' conception of international legal personality as it states that the phrase 'other subjects of international law' is intended inter alia to 'leave room for more special cases such as an insurgent community to which a measure of recognition has been accorded.'[134] In the final version of the VCLT, all references to 'other subjects of international law' in the treaty text were omitted except for a new Article 3, which underlines that the Convention does not apply to 'international agreements concluded between States and other subjects of international law or between such other subjects of international law'. According to the Commentary, these changes

II according to the general principles reflected in Articles 31–33 of the VCLT naturally lead to the conclusion that armed opposition groups do indeed have obligations under international law. See further Section 5.4.3.4.

[132] Ibid, 72. [133] II *YILC* (1962) 162 (emphasis added). [134] Ibid, 164.

were not 'in any way intended to deny that other subjects of international law, such as international organizations and insurgent communities, may conclude treaties.'[135]

In an influential article from 1981, Cassese examined the provisions of Additional Protocol II in light of the provisions on 'treaties and third parties' in Part III, Section 4 of the VCLT. Recalling that the VCLT only applies to agreements between States (cf. Article 1), Cassese declared that 'the customary rules on the matter have a broader scope, in that they govern the effects of treaties on any international subject taking the position of a third party vis-à-vis a treaty.'[136] He asserted that, following Articles 34–36 of the VCLT, a treaty can create obligations or rights for third parties only if the States parties to the treaty intend to confer such rights or obligations on the third party, and if the third party accepts them. Having first concluded, in spite of the ambiguous statements of some delegations in the *travaux préparatoires*, that it was in fact the intention of the parties to confer rights and obligations on armed opposition groups, Cassese argued that such rebellious entities would be bound by Additional Protocol II only upon their assent.[137]

Both the ILC's commentary on Article 3 of the VCLT and Cassese's article rest on the same presumption as the 'bindingness of customary international law' argument, namely that international law by definition cannot govern insurgents directly. They also share this presumption with the claim that insurgents are bound through incorporation of the law of non-international armed conflict into domestic law.[138] However, instead of requiring that the treaty provisions in question be implemented in domestic law in order to apply to insurgents, insurgents are lifted to the legal level of States[139]—an approach which is similar to the theoretical explanations for the recognition of belligerency in the eighteenth and nineteenth centuries.[140]

Christine Chinkin's *Third Parties in International Law* from 1993 to some extent supports this line of reasoning. But in her opinion individuals cannot be said to be third parties to treaties: 'Individuals ... do not have treaty rights vested in them, unless those rights have become basic norms of municipal law, customary international law, or *jus cogens*.'[141] Nevertheless, Chinkin concludes that while 'the juridical basis for holding that Protocol 2 creates legal effects for individuals remains problematic', this 'discrepancy with the rigid treaty rule' was justifiable for humanitarian reasons.[142] In effect, Chinkin thus leaves the question of how insurgents are bound by the law of non-international armed conflict unanswered.

135 II *YILC* (1966) 189. 136 Ibid, 423. 137 Cassese (n 112) 424–30.

138 This argument, which was, for example, put forward in the ICRC Commentary on Geneva Convention II, is discussed—and refuted—in Section 5.4.1.

139 See also Antonio Cassese, *International Law* (OUP, 2005) 71.

140 See further Section 5.3.1.

141 Christine Chinkin, *Third Parties in International Law* (Clarendon Press, 1993) 121–2.

142 Ibid, 133.

5.4.3.3 The bindingness of treaties by control over a particular territory

As mentioned in Section 5.4.1, the ICRC Commentaries on common Article 3 in part explain its bindingness on insurgents by reference to the fact that they exercise 'effective sovereignty' and 'claim to represent' at least a part of the State in question. Other authors, including Liesbeth Zegveld, support this analysis in a slightly different version, which emphasizes the insurgents' de facto authority over a certain part of the territory rather than their explicit claim to be representing it.[143]

Both versions of 'the control argument' may be read as to imply that the international rules on State succession are extended to govern armed opposition groups under certain circumstances at least as regards international humanitarian law. But they each fail to provide a source for such an extension. The norms concerning State succession by definition govern legal aspects of 'the replacement of one State by another in the responsibility for the international relations of territory.'[144] They only come into play upon the actual formation of a new State (or the transfer of territory between existing States) and are thus clearly irrelevant for the question whether treaties bind non-State entities such as armed opposition groups, which may or may not aspire for Statehood.[145] The relevant question is not what binds the armed opposition group in case it eventually acquires Statehood.[146] Rather, what we are concerned with here is how it may be bound by international obligations while it is still 'just' an armed opposition group.

Alternatively, 'the control argument' can be interpreted simply as an elaboration of the notion that an extraordinary kind of international legal personality is attributed to the insurgents as a group.[147] Either way, the argument fails in both variants to provide an explanation for the bindingness of common Article 3 in situations where the armed opposition groups do not meet the threshold level of control.[148]

Notably, there is nothing to prevent the parties to the Geneva Conventions and Additional Protocol II from attaching critical importance to the degree of authority exercised by insurgents. That was indeed what the States did in Article 1(1) of Additional Protocol II. But this fact does nothing to explain the ability of States to govern armed opposition groups in a treaty. The source of the States' competence in that regard must be found elsewhere, and it is frequently explained with reference to the principle of legislative jurisdiction.

[143] Liesbeth Zegveld, *The Accountability of Armed Opposition Groups in International Law* (CUP, 2002) 15ff. See also Richard Baxter, 'Jus in Bello Interno: the Present and Future Law', in John Norton Moore, *Law and Civil War in the Modern World* (The Lawbook Exchange, Ltd, 1974) 518, 527–8.

[144] See Article 2(b) of the Vienna Convention on Succession of States in respect of Treaties (1978), 1146 *UNTS* 3.

[145] See also Sivakumaran (n 122) 380.

[146] On this issue, see the commentary on Article 10 of ARSIWA in ILC, *Report of the International Law Commission on the Work of Its Fifty-Third Session*, A/56/10 (2001).

[147] See further Section 5.4.1.

[148] Zegveld finds that 'the control argument' always applies to Additional Protocol II, since its scope of application presupposes a degree of de facto authority over a particular territory. In contrast, she argues that groups lacking said authority are only bound by common Article 3 to the extent that it has been incorporated into the domestic law of the relevant State. See Zegveld (n 143) 15ff.

5.4.3.4 The principle of legislative jurisdiction

As indicated in the above-cited 1965 quote by Draper,[149] the essence of the principle of legislative jurisdiction is that a State may govern the whole of its population and everyone present on its territory, including factions rebelling against it. Like the Commentaries on common Article 3 of the Geneva Conventions, the ICRC Commentary on the Additional Protocols supports the application of the principle of legislative jurisdiction:

> The question is often raised how the insurgent party can be bound by a treaty to which it is not a High Contracting Party. It may therefore be appropriate to recall here the explanation given in 1949: the commitment made by a State not only applies to the government but also to any established authorities and private individuals within the national territory of that State and certain obligations are therefore imposed upon them. The extent of rights and duties of private individuals is therefore the same as that of the rights and duties of the State. Although this argument has occasionally been questioned in legal literature, the validity of the obligation imposed upon insurgents has never been contested.[150]

But, whereas the Commentaries on common Article 3 provided additional—inconsistent—arguments, which greatly confused the overall image,[151] the Commentary on the Additional Protocols is limited to the quoted paragraph.

Some scholars object that 'the principle of legislative jurisdiction' argument misinterprets the relationship between international and domestic law.[152] Indeed, a number of observers overlook the difference between this argument and the notion that armed opposition groups are bound through incorporation into domestic law.[153] To adequately reject this critique, it must be made clear that invoking the principle of legislative jurisdiction in this context builds on the presumption that non-State entities may possess rights, duties, and capacities directly under international law. Traditionally, 'legislative jurisdiction' has to do with a State's competence to enact national law. The claim that a State has legislative jurisdiction usually means that no international legal norm prevents that State from regulating the conduct of particular entities. However, the fact that no rule of international law precludes the

[149] See note 116 and its accompanying text.

[150] Commentary on Additional Protocols (n 62) 1345, para. 4444 (footnotes omitted).

[151] See Section 5.4.1.

[152] See for example Thomas Fleiner-Gerster and Michael A. Meyer, 'New Developments in Humanitarian Law: A Challenge to the Concept of Sovereignty' 34 *ICLQ* (1985) 267, 272 and 277, Michael Bothe et al., *New Rules for Victims of Armed Conflicts* (Martinus Nijhoff, 1982) 700. A different challenge put forward by Cedric Ryngaert is that the principle of legislative jurisdiction lacks legitimacy, because the armed opposition group has not participated in the formation of the norms that bind them. See further Cedric Ryngaert, 'Non-state actors in international humanitarian law', in Jean d'Aspremont (ed.), *Participants in the International Legal System: Multiple Perspectives on Non-State Actors in International Law* (Routledge, 2011) 284, 285–6. As mentioned in Section 1.3, questions concerning the legitimacy of international norms lie outside the scope of this book.

[153] See, for example, Cassese (n 112) 429, and Moir (n 71) 53–5. See also Andrew Clapham, 'Accountability/Liability for Violations of the Law: Focusing on Non-State Actors', in Andrew Clapham and Paola Gaeta (eds), *The Oxford Handbook of International Law in Armed Conflict* (OUP, 2014) 755, 772. This is the presumably the 'confusion' Sivakumaran refers to in his explanation for abandoning the term of 'legislative jurisdiction' in Sandesh Sivakumaran, *The Law of Non-International Armed Conflict* (OUP, 2012) 241, note 43. See further Kleffner (n 122) 447–8.

State from issuing regulation on a certain issue says nothing about the legal character that this regulation may assume. The principle of legislative jurisdiction thus only provides half of the justification for binding armed opposition groups through international law. The other half is the assumption that international legal personality may be conferred on non-State entities. In other words, an armed opposition group may be bound by the law of non-international armed conflict, because we assume that there are no inherent limits to the kind of entities that may possess international legal personality, *and* because the State in question has jurisdiction under international law to govern the particular insurgents.[154]

Critics protest that there is presumption against direct rights and obligations of non-State actors under international law, and that it is not sufficiently clear that the parties to the Geneva Conventions and Additional Protocol II intended to bind armed opposition groups directly. Relying on the PCIJ's Advisory Opinion in *Jurisdiction of the Courts of Danzig*,[155] Sandesh Sivakumaran invokes such a presumption, but concludes that it is indeed rebutted in the examples of common Article 3 and Additional Protocol II. While the preceding analysis does not provide a clear-cut answer, there are strong indications that the parties to the Geneva Conventions and Additional Protocol II did intend to confer rights and obligations directly on armed opposition groups. Sivakumaran's argument in favour of a rebuttal under the concrete circumstances thus has significant merit. But the question is whether he is right in asserting a presumption against direct individual rights and obligations of non-State entities in the first place. As argued in Section 3.1.2, the Judgments and Advisory Opinions of the ICJ and its predecessor can hardly be said to provide significant support for the idea that there is an inherent presumption against direct individual rights and obligations under international law. On this basis, there would seem to be little reason why such a presumption should be applied in the assessment of the bindingness of the law of non-international armed conflict on armed opposition groups. It follows that common Article 3 and Additional Protocol II should simply be interpreted according to the general principles of interpretation reflected in Articles 31–33 of the VCLT.

5.5 Customary International Humanitarian Law

Based on an extensive study of treaty law and the practice of States and non-State actors pertaining to both international and non-international armed conflict,

[154] See also Section 6.2.4. In her recent book, Katharine Fortin contends that 'the principle of legislative jurisdiction' argument 'is rooted in the view that international humanitarian law is an exception to the principle that an international treaty will only create direct international rights and obligations for individuals in instances where the State is *monist* or the treaty is self-executing.' Fortin (n 98) 187. In contrast, the present book argues that international humanitarian law is not an exception with regard to the international legal personality of individuals. Rather, the 'principle' referred to by Fortin confuses the distinction between the question of which entities an international legal norm governs and that norm's effect in domestic law. See further Section 1.3.2.

[155] See Section 3.1.2.2.1.

Jean-Marie Henckaerts and Louise Doswald-Beck, working under the auspices of the ICRC, presented a number of 'rules' of customary international humanitarian law in 2005.[156] The authors note that the vast majority of provisions of the Hague Regulations, the Geneva Conventions and the Additional Protocols have acquired customary status. The 'rules' are generally articulated as obligations of 'parties to the conflict'. For example, Rule 109 reads: 'Whenever circumstances permit, and particularly after an engagement, each party to the conflict must, without delay, take all possible measures to search for, collect and evacuate the wounded, sick and shipwrecked without adverse distinction.'[157]

In light of the explicit stance on the matter taken in ICRC's Commentaries on the Geneva Conventions,[158] it is somewhat surprising that the authors of the study chose not to include a detailed discussion of the existence of individual rights under customary international humanitarian law.

Chapter 32, entitled 'Fundamental Guarantees',[159] identifies a number of rules applicable to all civilians in the power of the party to a conflict, who are not taking part in the hostilities, including persons *hors de combat.* These rules largely run parallel to international human rights law, and human rights instruments and case law correspondingly form a significant part of the basis for the study. Nevertheless, the rules are not formulated as individual rights, but rather as obligations of the parties to the conflict. For example, Rule 87 reads: 'Civilians and persons *hors de combat* must be treated humanely.' In the introduction to the chapter, the authors explain that '[m]ost of the rules set out in this chapter are couched in traditional humanitarian language, because this best reflects the substance of the corresponding customary rule.'[160] It is seemingly implied that 'traditional humanitarian language' entails obligations of States to provide protection rather than individual rights. The authors are thus reluctant to infer that customary international humanitarian law provides for rights of individuals. The study does, however, include a few references to rights of certain groups of protected persons, without specifying whether they apply directly.[161]

5.6 Conclusion: The Legal Personality of Individuals in International Humanitarian Law

Rather than conferring direct rights on individuals, the law of international armed conflict for the most part consists of inter-State obligations. The rules on means and methods of warfare adopted between the middle of the nineteenth century and the early twentieth century are consistent with this approach. Similarly, the first

[156] Jean-Marie Henckaerts and Louise Doswald-Beck, *Customary International Humanitarian Law* (ICRC, 2005), vol. I (*Rules*) and vol. II (*Practice*).

[157] Another example is Rule 90: 'Torture, cruel or inhuman treatment and outrages upon personal dignity, in particular humiliating and degrading treatment, are prohibited.' See also Rules 87–9.

[158] See further Sections 5.2.1 and 5.4.1.

[159] See also Additional Protocol I, Article 75, discussed in Section 5.2.2.

[160] Henckaerts and Doswald-Beck (n 156) 299.

[161] See for example Rules 106–8.

Geneva Conventions from 1864, 1906, and 1929 did not contain individual rights or duties, but merely obliged the States parties to secure a certain standard of treatment. However, there is little support in the *travaux préparatoires* to suggest that the 'States-only' framework of the pre-Second World War law of international armed conflict was motivated by jurisprudential considerations concerning the concept of international legal personality.

The appropriate interpretation of the four Geneva Conventions adopted in 1949 is less clear when compared to their predecessors. The scholarly literature and domestic case law show considerable disagreement as to whether or not they govern individuals directly. While the language of the predominant part of the substantive provisions is indicative of inter-State obligations to secure a certain level of protection of various groups, all four 1949 Geneva Conventions contain a number of provisions, including a saving clause and a non-renunciation clause, which refer to 'rights' of various protected persons. Arguably, interpretation of these provisions according to the general principles reflected in Articles 31–33 of the VCLT points towards individual rights. But the answer is hardly clear-cut. The same applies to Additional Protocol I and to customary international humanitarian law.

The evolution of the law of non-international armed conflict is particularly interesting for the present study. The (long) historical development of this field not only illustrates that it is the definition of 'an international problem', which has evolved over time, rather than the nature and number of international legal persons. It also provides ample evidence of the continued influence of the orthodox 'States-only' conception on international legal scholars in spite of the formation of clearly contradictory positive norms.

In the course of the eighteenth century, it became apparent that an internal armed conflict often affects the interests of several States. Naturally, this situation was problematic for the 'States-only' conception of international legal personality prevailing among scholars at the time, because an international legal response would necessarily involve governing at least one non-State actor. In the words of Stephen C. Neff, 'state practice took the leading role, with doctrine following demurely in its wake.'[162] When the need to regulate civil strife at the international level first arose, considerable academic efforts were therefore made to place armed opposition groups on a legal par with the government they were fighting. It would have been somewhat simpler to acknowledge that the call for international regulation of internal armed conflicts was altogether incompatible with the idea that international legal personality is reserved for States alone. The development of the doctrine of 'recognition of belligerency' and, subsequently, the processes culminating in the adoption of common Article 3 of the Geneva Conventions and Additional Protocol II clearly suggest that it is the material content of international legal norms that has changed, not the framework of the system as such. In this way, the evolution of the law of non-international armed conflict corroborates the notion that the international legal personality of any entity must be established a posteriori through case-by-case interpretation of

[162] Neff (n 5) 251.

international norms. Nevertheless, the orthodox 'States-only' conception is still very much apparent in the ongoing academic debate on the jurisprudential justifications for binding armed opposition groups through international law. For example, the common arguments that insurgents are only bound by customary international law, or as consenting third parties to treaties, ultimately rest on the idea that States alone possess international legal personality.

It is submitted that the theoretical explanation for the bindingness of the law of non-international armed conflict on armed opposition groups consists of two elements: first, we must assume that there are no inherent limits to the kind of entities that may possess international legal personality; and second, we must establish that the State in question has jurisdiction under international law to govern the particular insurgents. Granted, this argument will presumably have little effect in terms of compliance, which is perhaps the most imminent problem concerning the legal obligations of insurgents. As Kelsen noted, '[t]here is no assurance . . . that . . . [rebel] forces will agree to consider themselves bound by the 'fundamental' obligations laid down in Article 3.'[163] But an armed opposition group is nevertheless formally bound when the State, on whose territory it operates, has ratified a treaty conferring obligations on such a group, or when a customary norm governs it directly. Whether such obligations exist, and, in particular, whether they are conditional upon a certain level of control over territory, is solely a matter of interpretation of relevant norms of international law.

[163] Hans Kelsen, *Principles of International Law* (2nd edn, revised and edited by Robert W. Tucker. Holt, Rinehart, and Winston, Inc., 1966) 127.

6

The Legal Personality of Individuals in International Criminal Law

This chapter addresses two central questions pertaining to the role of the concept of international legal personality in the field of international criminal law.

The first question relates to the nature of individual criminal responsibility under international law. While it is hardly disputable that the individual is a subject of international criminal law, the nature and source of individual responsibility for international crimes is less certain. As will become apparent in Section 6.2, discerning the right interpretation of the available case law is not an uncomplicated endeavour, and there is no obvious answer to whether the responsibility (and thereby the international legal personality) of individuals arises a priori or a posteriori. If international crimes a priori entail individual responsibility, which would be in line with the 'individualistic' conception of international legal personality,[1] it would be unnecessary to establish separately whether a concrete international crime is directed at individuals. It would simply be inherent in the international norm criminalizing the particular behaviour that individuals are bound directly by it. If, conversely, the responsibility of individuals arises a posteriori,[2] it must be examined on a case-by-case basis whether the international norm criminalizing certain acts applies to individuals. For reasons of expediency, Section 6.2 focuses on the case law that has contributed most directly and substantially to the development of international criminal law.[3] Following a brief account for some historical antecedents to international criminal law in Section 6.1, Section 6.2.1 examines the seminal *IMT Judgment*. Section 6.2.2 studies the ILC's formulation of the Nürnberg Principles, while Sections 6.2.3 and 6.2.4 discuss the development of individual responsibility for international crimes by the ad hoc tribunals set up by the Security Council in the 1990s as well as the ICC.

Section 6.3 examines the second central question, namely how the concept of international legal personality—specifically the 'States-only' conception—continues to influence the way in which contemporary scholars and practitioners distinguish between international, internationalized, and domestic criminal courts. There is no generally recognized definitional distinction between the various kinds

[1] See Section 2.4. [2] See Section 2.3.

[3] Domestic cases and case law from 'internationalized' courts will only be mentioned exceptionally. See, however, Section 6.3.

of criminal courts, and the predominant view among international lawyers appears to be that the deciding factor is the degree of 'involvement of the international community'. Section 6.3 traces the emphasis on this inherently elusive criterion to quandaries about the international legal personality of individuals in post-Second World War scholarship and shows that present-day scholars as well as judges continue to rely on it. Subsequently, Sections 6.3.3 and 6.3.4 illustrate by rulings of the SCSL and the ECCC that the practice of focusing on 'the involvement of the international community' rather than the legal nature of a criminal court's founding document has significant ramifications for questions concerning applicable law and the customary rules on immunity. Section 6.4 sums up the conclusions of the chapter.

6.1 International Criminal Law before the Second World War

6.1.1 Precedents of international criminal law

No efforts to establish international criminal institutions bore fruit before the end of the Second World War. But a number of previous practices are traditionally referred to as precedents of conferring criminal liability to individuals in international law. Upon closer scrutiny, however, these events prove to be inherently different from what is now known as international criminal law. For example, domestic courts have tried and convicted individuals for war crimes since the late Middle Ages, but the legal basis for these prosecutions was domestic rather than international law. Similarly, the trial and execution of Sir Peter von Hagenbach in Austria in 1474, which is frequently cited as the first international prosecution, has little precedential value for holding individuals criminally liable under international law, since both the constitution of the 'international panel' and the law it applied remain unclear.[4] Moreover, piracy is commonly referred to as an early international crime, but this characterization seems to confuse primary and secondary rules.[5] Piracy was not criminalized in international law. The customary international rules on piracy merely conceded that all States had jurisdiction to try a suspected pirate in their domestic courts according to their respective domestic law.[6]

6.1.2 The interwar years: Prosecutions under the Versailles Treaty

During the interwar years, two attempts were made to set up international tribunals with jurisdiction to hold individuals criminally liable for violations of international law. One was the proposal for a High Court of International Justice discussed by the Advisory Committee of Jurists.[7] The other, which will be examined in the following,

[4] See further Kate Parlett, *The Individual in the International Legal System—Continuity and Change in International Law* (CUP, 2011) 230–4.

[5] See Section 1.3.3.

[6] See for example 'Harvard Research Draft on Piracy', 16 *AJIL* Supp. (1932) 739, 759–860, and Kriangsak Kittichaisaree, *International Criminal Law* (OUP, 2001) 15. See also the statements of Amado in connection with the ILC's formulation of the Nürnberg Principles, I *YILC* (1949) 186.

[7] See Section 3.2.1.

was included in the Versailles Treaty. Though neither of these tribunals ever came into existence, they are of interest as forerunners of contemporary international criminal law.

In the preliminary phase of the Paris Peace Conference in January 1919, the plenary session created a Commission on the Responsibility of the Authors of the War and on Enforcement of Penalties to study and report on inter alia 'the facts as to breaches of the laws and customs of war committed by the forces of the German Empire and their Allies', 'the degree of responsibility for these offences attaching to particular members of the enemy forces … and other individuals, however highly placed', and 'the constitution and procedure of a tribunal appropriate for the trial of these offences.'[8]

The Commission did not discuss the concept of individual obligations under international law, but the final report clearly implies their existence. The report concluded that '[a]ll persons belonging to enemy countries … who have been guilty of offences against the laws and customs of war or the laws of humanity, are liable to criminal prosecution.'[9] According to the Commission, international law allowed for every belligerent to prosecute individuals within its jurisdiction for violations of the laws and customs of war.[10] For this purpose, the Commission found, each belligerent had the power to set up an appropriate military or civil tribunal.[11] As regards certain groups of suspected perpetrators, including persons of authority, the Commission recommended that an international 'high tribunal' be established, which would apply 'the principles of the law of nations as they result from the usages established among civilized peoples, from the laws of humanity and from the dictates of public conscience.'[12]

Notably, the American members disagreed with findings of the rest of the Commission on several key issues, including 'the unprecedented proposal of creating an international criminal tribunal'.[13] In particular, the American representatives underlined that they knew 'of no international statute or convention making a violation of the laws and customs of war—not to speak of the laws or principles of humanity—an international crime, affixing a punishment to it, and declaring the court which has jurisdiction over the offence.'[14] Rather, the Americans found, the acts in question were violations of municipal law, which should be applied in trials of suspected perpetrators before existing municipal tribunals or commissions.[15]

Pursuant to Article 227 of the Versailles Treaty, Kaiser Wilhelm II was to be prosecuted before an international tribunal with judges from each of the victorious States

[8] 'Commission on the Responsibility of the Authors of the War and on Enforcement of Penalties', 14 *AJIL* (1920) 95.

[9] Ibid, 117. In addition, the Commission expressly dismissed the notion that immunity might accrue to for example Heads of State, since 'the position from an international point of view is quite different' from the municipal setting.

[10] See further ibid, 112–15.

[11] Ibid, 121.

[12] Ibid, 122. See also Section 5.1.1.1 regarding the Martens Clause.

[13] 'Memorandum of Reservations Presented by the Representatives of the United States to the Report of the Commission of Responsibilities', reprinted in 14 *AJIL* (1920) (n 8) 129.

[14] Ibid, 146.

[15] Ibid, 146–7.

of the First World War. The tribunal had the following mandate: 'In its decision the tribunal will be guided by the highest motives of international policy, with a view to vindicating the solemn obligations of international undertakings and the validity of international morality.' It seems implicit that the Kaiser had violated international law, but the source of the legal obligations he allegedly did not comply with is unclear. The tribunal never came into function, because the Netherlands, where Kaiser Wilhelm II had sought asylum, refused to extradite him.

Articles 228–230 of the Versailles Treaty laid down rules concerning all other 'persons accused of having committed acts in violation of the laws and customs of war', who, depending on the circumstances of the case, were to be prosecuted before the domestic military tribunals of one allied State or military tribunals with members from several of the allied States. In the end, however, the allied powers agreed to Germany's proposition that the trials of suspected war criminals be conducted before the Reichsgericht in Leipzig under domestic German law.[16] Out of the approximately 900 accused only thirteen persons were convicted (and these were given mild sentences).[17] Thus, the provisions of the Versailles Treaty prescribing individual criminal responsibility were never given effect.

6.2 International Criminal Law after the Second World War

Several statements in the early stages of the Second World War indicated that the Allied Powers intended to prosecute perpetrators of war crimes.[18] At the Moscow Conference in October 1943 between the US, the UK, the Soviet Union, and China, the Allied Powers agreed that war criminals from Germany, Italy, Japan, and their associates (the Axis Powers) would be prosecuted when the war was over. The Moscow Declaration signed on 30 October 1943 included a 'Statement on Atrocities' by Roosevelt, Churchill, and Stalin, which reads inter alia:

> German officers and men and members of the Nazi party who have been responsible for or have taken a consenting part in the above atrocities, massacres and executions will be sent back to the countries in which their abominable deeds were done in order that they may be judged and punished according to the laws of these liberated countries and of free governments which will be erected therein.[19]

[16] See for example 'German War Trials: Judgment in the Case of Karl Heynen', 16 *AJIL* (1922) 674. In the trial of Commander Karl Neumann, however, the court referred to the German Military Penal Code as well as 'the legal principles of all other civilized states', see 'German War Trials: Judgment in Case of Commander Karl Neumann', 16 *AJIL* (1922) 704, 707.

[17] See further Parlett (n 4) 238–9.

[18] United Nations War Crimes Commission (hereafter UNWCC), *History of the United Nations War Crimes Commission and the Development of the Laws of War* (His Majesty's Stationery Office, 1948) 87ff. The UNWCC (originally the United Nations Commission for the Investigation of War Crimes) was established in October 1943, inter alia to investigate and identify perpetrators of war crimes committed by Nazi Germany. See further M. E. Bathurst, 'The United Nations War Crimes Commission', 39 *AJIL* (1945) 565.

[19] 'Statement on Atrocities' signed by Roosevelt, Churchill, and Stalin, October 1943 (available at http://avalon.law.yale.edu/wwii/moscow.asp, accessed 21 January 2018).

Apparently, the idea was to try all war criminals according to domestic law in domestic courts, except for 'German criminals whose offenses have no particular geographical localization' and were therefore to be 'punished by joint decision of the government of the Allies.'[20] There was some disagreement on how to handle 'the major war criminals'. Initially, the US and the UK favoured a political rather than judicial solution, whereas the Soviet Union seemingly maintained that no death penalty could be imposed without a trial. In a remarkable telegram of 22 October 1944 from Churchill to Roosevelt, Churchill explains that Stalin (whom he refers to as UJ, which is presumably short for 'Uncle Joe') has taken the 'unexpectedly ultra-respectable line' that 'there must be no executions without trial'. Churchill goes on: 'I pointed out the difficulties in International Law but he replied if there were no trials there must be no death sentences'.[21]

At the Yalta Conference in February 1945, Churchill, Roosevelt, and Stalin reiterated their intent to prosecute perpetrators of international crimes from the Axis Powers, and agreed that 'the question of the major war criminals should be the subject of inquiry by the three Foreign Secretaries'.[22] Only in May 1945, when the US presented an American Draft of Definitive Proposal[23] at the San Francisco Conference, was it finally decided (in principle) to set up an international tribunal with competence to prosecute European Axis War Criminals.[24] The Agreement for the Prosecution and Punishment of the Major War Criminals of the European Axis (hereafter London Agreement) with the annexed Charter of the International Military Tribunal (hereafter IMT Charter) of 8 August 1945,[25] which was adopted by the four victorious States (the US, the UK, France, and the Soviet Union), was a revised version of the original American proposal.

Most likely, when Churchill 'pointed out the difficulties in International Law' to Stalin in the autumn of 1944, he was referring to the fundamental question of whether the acts committed by major German war criminals were in fact criminalized under international law at the time. The conceptual issue of international legal obligations of individuals, however, does not seem to have attracted much attention during the drafting process leading to the London Agreement. Rather than the overall notion of individual responsibility under international law, the debate centred on the definition of the particular international crimes and whether they were an innovation or a codification of already existing customary rules.[26]

[20] Ibid.

[21] See United States Department of State, 'Foreign relations of the United States. Conferences at Malta and Yalta', 1945, 400 (available at https://history.state.gov/historicaldocuments/frus1945Malta/pg_400, accessed 21 January 2018).

[22] The Protocol of Proceedings of the conference is available at http://avalon.law.yale.edu/wwii/yalta.asp (accessed 21 January 2018).

[23] Reprinted in *Report of Robert H. Jackson, United States Representative to the International Conference on Military Trials* (US Government Printing Office, 1949) 23–7.

[24] See further ibid, 22, and 'American Memorandum Presented at San Francisco', 30 April 1945, reprinted in ibid, 28–38.

[25] Agreement for the Prosecution and Punishment of the Major War Criminals of the European Axis, 8 August 1945, 82 *UNTS* 279.

[26] Another major obstacle was the reconciliation of the differences between the parties' various systems of criminal procedure. See further *Report of Robert H. Jackson, United States Representative to the*

6.2.1 The IMT

The indictment of twenty-four Nazi leaders and six organizations included four counts based on Article 6 of the IMT Charter, which identified three broad 'crimes coming within the jurisdiction of the Tribunal for which there shall be individual responsibility': crimes against peace, war crimes, and crimes against humanity. Unsurprisingly, the defence objected to the jurisdiction of the Tribunal at the outset of the proceedings, and argued that the IMT Charter violated international law. For example, the attorneys of all defendants jointly held that '[a]s far as crimes against the peace are concerned, the present trial has ... no legal basis in international law but is a procedure based on new penal law'.[27]

In its Judgment delivered on 1 October 1946, however, the Tribunal drew a distinction between challenges to its jurisdiction and arguments based on the principle of *nullum crimen sine lege*: 'Insofar as it may be a plea to the jurisdiction of the Tribunal' the motion was dismissed as conflicting with Article 3 of the IMT Charter.[28] Correspondingly, the Tribunal did not find it 'strictly necessary to consider whether and to what extent aggressive war was a crime before the execution of the London Agreement', so long as the planning or waging of a war of aggression or a war in violation of international treaties was defined as a crime under the Charter. Presumably to avoid subsequent criticism concerning retroactive criminalization, the IMT nevertheless explicated that Article 6(a) did not go beyond existing international law by reference to inter alia provisions included in the Kellogg–Briand Pact of 1928[29] and in the Hague Conventions of 1907.[30] Having thus established that aggression was in fact a pre-existing international crime, the Tribunal turned to the defence's argument that it was impossible to impose international legal obligations on individuals.[31] This submission was rejected by the Tribunal without much ado: That international law imposes duties and liabilities upon individuals as well as upon States has long been recognized.[32] '... Crimes against international law are committed by men, not by abstract entities, and only

International Conference on Military Trials (n 23), viiiff. For a detailed account of the drafting history, see ibid. See also 'Formulation of Nürnberg Principles', Special Rapporteur Mr. J. Spiropoulos, 12 April 1950, II *YILC* (1950) 181ff.

27 *In re Goering et al.* Defense Motion Challenging Jurisdiction of Tribunal, IMT, 20 November 1945 (available at http://avalon.law.yale.edu/imt/suppb_part1_chap_01.asp, accessed 21 January 2018).

28 Article 3 reads: 'Neither the Tribunal, its members nor their alternates can be challenged by the prosecution, or by the Defendants or their Counsel'. In its Judgment, the IMT reiterated: 'The law of the Charter is decisive and binding upon the Tribunal.' *IMT Judgment*, reprinted in 41 *AJIL* (1947) 172, 216.

29 Ibid, 217–18. The General Treaty on the Renunciation of War, adopted by sixty-three states on 27 August 1928, is also known as the Kellogg–Briand Pact or the Pact of Paris (available at http://avalon.law.yale.edu/20th_century/kbpact.asp, accessed 21 January 2018).

30 Ibid, 218–19. See further Section 5.1.

31 Ibid, 220.

32 In addition to Article 228 of the Versailles Treaty, the Tribunal referred to the US Supreme Court's Judgment of 1942 in *Ex Parte Quirin*, 317 US (1942) 1, and found that '[m]any other authorities could be quoted, but enough has been said to show that individuals can be punished for violations of international law.'

by punishing individuals who commit such crimes can the provisions of international law be enforced.'[33]

It is readily apparent that the IMT saw no conceptual impediments to conferring obligations on individuals by way of customary international law or by treaties. But it is less obvious what the IMT perceived as the legal foundation for imposing international criminal responsibility on the defendants. The precedents referred to by the Tribunal are not overwhelmingly convincing as evidence of a customary rule prescribing individual liability for international crimes.[34] Article 228 of the Versailles Treaty was never given effect, and the US cases including *Ex Parte Quirin* were based on domestic rather than international law. Moreover, these examples only concerned individual responsibility for violations of the laws of war and not crimes against humanity or crimes against peace. Against this background one may reasonably ask: Was it the opinion of the IMT that individual responsibility is an inherent consequence of defining an act as an international crime—at least as regards international armed conflicts?[35] Or did the Tribunal simply assume the existence of a customary rule prescribing individual liability without finding it necessary to enter into a detailed discussion of its source? Since similar questions arise from the practice of subsequent courts and tribunals, discussion of this issue will be deferred to Section 6.2.5.

6.2.2 The ILC's formulation of the Nürnberg Principles

Following a request from the UN General Assembly,[36] the ILC began formulating the principles laid down by the IMT Charter and the *IMT Judgment* during its first session in 1949. By reference to the fact that the principles had already been unanimously affirmed by the General Assembly in 1946,[37] the ILC concluded that it was 'not asked to express any appreciation of the principles applied in the Charter and the Tribunal of Nürnberg as principles of international law. It is asked merely to give formulation to those principles without any indication of their authority.'[38] In this way, the Commission conveniently avoided having to take a stand on whether the

[33] *IMT Judgment*, reprinted in 41 *AJIL* (1947), 220–1. See also the British prosecutor, Sir Hartley Shawcross's submissions on 4 December 1945 (available at http://avalon.law.yale.edu/imt/12-04-45.asp, accessed 21 January 2018).

[34] Numerous scholars have objected strongly to the Tribunal's conclusions on this point. See for example Georg Schwarzenberger, 'The Judgment of Nuremberg', 21 *Tulane Law Review* (1947) 329, 344–7, and Hans Kelsen, 'Will the Judgment in the Nuremberg Trial Constitute a Precedent in International Law?', 1 *International Law Quarterly* (1947) 153, 155–7. See also Robert Cryer, 'Nuremberg International Military Tribunal', in Antonio Cassese (ed.), *The Oxford Companion to International Criminal Justice* (OUP, 2009) 442, and Parlett (n 4) 249.

[35] As for non-international armed conflicts, see Section 6.2.3.1.

[36] See General Assembly Resolution 177(II), 21 November 1947, by which the ILC was directed to:

> (a) Formulate the principles of international law recognized in the Charter of the Nürnberg Tribunal and the judgment of the Tribunal, and (b) Prepare a draft code of offences against the peace and security of mankind, indicating clearly the place to be accorded to the principles mentioned in sub-paragraph (a) above.

[37] See General Assembly Resolution 95 (I), 11 December 1946.

[38] See I *YILC* (1949) 129, 133. See also II *YILC* (1950) 374.

principles laid down by the IMT were an innovation or an already existing part of international law.[39]

The divergent opinions among the members of the Commission as to the concept of individual responsibility under international law became readily apparent during the subsequent meetings. Scelle, for example, considered that 'the cardinal principle was that an individual could commit an international crime.' While, in his opinion, this principle was 'a new one in international law',[40] it 'was only the application of a more general principle . . ., namely that the individual was a subject of international law.'[41] Correspondingly, he submitted an alternative draft of paragraph 1, which read: 'The individual is a subject of international law, including international penal law.'[42]

Paragraph 1 of Scelle's proposal was rejected by six votes to four.[43] Among his supporters was Sir Benegal Rau, who emphasized that the IMT had in fact rejected that international law does not provide for the punishment of individuals. Therefore, he found, it 'would appear to support Professor Scelle's view.'[44] Koretsky, however, strongly disagreed with Scelle's proposal. In his opinion, 'the idea that the individual was subject to international law was not generally accepted; there could not therefore be any question of proclaiming it as a principle.'[45] Similarly, Brierly found that the proposed paragraph did not 'in its present form ... properly speaking set forth a principle of international law.'[46] The Special Rapporteur, Spiropoulos, concurred with Brierly and added that the IMT had merely found 'that an individual was responsible under international law, but it could not be said that he was subject to international law.'[47] Notably, Spiropoulos, Brierly, and Yepes all scorned Scelle's approach for being 'too academic'. Scelle, however, did not give up without a fight. A year later, when he was chairing the discussions on Spiropoulos's second draft of the Nürnberg Principles,[48] Scelle suggested that the following sentence be added to Principle I: 'Thus the individual is subject to international law, at least in criminal

[39] Nevertheless, the question of the proper interpretation of the General Assembly's request was, as will be seen, reopened several times during the ILC meetings that followed. The correspondence between crimes within the competence of the IMT and crimes under customary international law was in fact the very first issue raised during the Commission's material discussions of the first draft of the Nürnberg Principles. See I *YILC* (1949) 183, 183–4. See also the discussion in the General Assembly's Sixth Committee of the ILC's final draft as summarized in Draft Code of Offences against the Peace and Security of Mankind, Second report by Special Rapporteur Mr. J. Spiropoulos, II *YILC* (1951) 43, 45–9.

[40] I *YILC* (1949) 183, 188. [41] Ibid, 186.

[42] Ibid, 206. See also Section 2.4 as to Scelle's 'individualistic' conception of international legal personality.

[43] Ibid, 212. [44] Ibid, 211.

[45] Ibid, 210. Furthermore, Koretsky stated that the IMT had not been created on the basis of international law, but rather because the Allied Powers had assumed sovereignty over the German territory. See Section 6.3.1 for discussion of the legal nature of the IMT Charter.

[46] Ibid, 211.

[47] Ibid. See also Amado's statement: 'The responsibility of the individual was recognized in international law. It was impossible to go any further and state that the individual was subject to international law.' Ibid.

[48] 'Formulation of the Nurnberg Principles', Special Rapporteur J. Spiropoulos, 12 April 1950, II *YILC* (1950), 181–95.

law.'[49] Again, his proposal was rejected by a narrow majority (six members voted against, five in favour).[50] Spiropoulos reiterated his argument concerning the limited practical value of the question: 'If an individual could be regarded as subject to international penal law, it was a theoretical and doctrinal question on which there was no likelihood of unanimity in the Commission.'[51] He also emphasized that the commentary on Principle I in his draft reflected the Commission's previous discussions on the matter. The commentary read inter alia: 'The general principle of law underlying Principle I is that international law may impose duties on the individual, without any interpretation of domestic law directly, a conception which in theory is considered as involving the "international personality" of individuals.'[52]

Ultimately, however, the references to 'theory' and 'the "international personality" of individuals' were deleted. In the final version of the commentary on Principle I, the ILC refrained from drawing any explicit conclusions regarding the concept of international legal personality. Instead, the Commission limited its comments on the issue to the following: 'The general rule underlying Principle I is that international law may impose duties on individuals directly without any interposition of internal law. The findings of the Tribunal were very definite on the question whether the rules of international law may apply to individuals.'[53]

As adopted Principle I reads as follows: 'Any person who commits an act which constitutes a crime under international law is responsible therefor and liable to punishment.' Furthermore, Principle II provides: 'The fact that internal law does not impose a penalty for an act which constitutes a crime under international law does not relieve the person who committed the act from responsibility under international law.'[54]

Similar to the ILC's discussions, the debate in the General Assembly's Sixth Committee revealed considerable discord among the delegations as to whether Principles I and II did or did not affect the then prevalent notion that only States are subjects of international law.[55] Fitzmaurice, for example, agreed with the formulation of the Nürnberg Principles, but objected to the idea that they had any influence on the 'States-only' conception of international legal personality. He submitted 'that, in order to punish the individual, there was no need at all to regard him as being subject to international law, and that the desired result could be attained without affecting the classic concept that international law solely governs relations between States ....'[56] Fitzmaurice's argument is difficult to follow: if the interposition of municipal law is redundant, then individual responsibility for the crimes in

[49] I *YILC* (1950) 30, 35. Principle I of the draft read: 'Any person who commits or is an accomplice in the commission of an act which constitutes a crime under international law is responsible therefor and liable to punishment.' II *YILC* (1950) 181, 191.

[50] This time, Brierly supported Scelle's proposal and argued that 'what was needed was a clear and explicit statement of what was in the mind of the Commission.' I *YILC* (1950) 30, 36.

[51] Ibid. [52] II *YILC* (1950) 181, 192. [53] Ibid, 374. [54] Ibid.

[55] Draft Code of Offences against the Peace and Security of Mankind, Second report by Special Rapporteur Mr. J. Spiropoulos, II *YILC* (1951) 43, 45–51.

[56] Ibid, 50. On Fitzmaurice's approach to individuals as international legal persons, see also Sections 3.1.1, 3.4.2, and 7.2.2.2. Fitzmaurice was supported by the Venezuelan delegate, Cabana, and the Argentine delegate, Bunge. See ibid, 50–1.

question must necessarily arise under international law. Accordingly, several other delegates strongly disagreed with his reasoning. Chaumont, for example, stated that '[i]t was impossible to deny that [individuals] were subjects of international law without denying the possibility of the international punishment of offences under international law.'[57] Similarly, Amado, who had participated in the ILC's formulation of the Nürnberg Principles, found that Principle I 'was a crystallization of the efforts made by a great many jurists to weaken the traditional doctrine under which States were the only subjects of international law.'[58] In addition, Spiropoulos, who had resisted explicit conclusions on international legal personality in the ILC's work, spoke forcefully against Fitzmaurice's analysis: 'The [IMT] judgment proclaimed that international law imposed duties and responsibilities on physical persons, which meant that the individual, whose personality is henceforth recognized, came into contact with international law direct and no longer through the intermediary of the State.'[59]

While it should be borne in mind that the ILC deliberately limited its task to formulating the principles invoked by the IMT, Principle I clearly confirms that individual responsibility for certain crimes arises directly under international law. Thus, the disagreement between the members of the ILC merely concerned the theoretical ramifications of the Principle for the wider context of international law.

In essence, the debate during the drafting of the Nürnberg Principles resembles the ILC's discussions on the status of individuals in international law in the 1950s and '60s, when the VCLT was drawn up.[60] Again, the fact that no definitive conclusion was reached by the ILC may be seen as an indication that the issue is of limited consequence in practice. The explicit rejection of Scelle's proposal as 'too academic' supports this analysis. Overall, it appears that the members of the ILC discussed the concept of international legal personality without establishing exactly what the notion implies. None of the members provided a comprehensive definition of what it means to have international legal personality. Rather, they each seem to have taken their preconceived, but largely unarticulated, ideas on the subject as their point of departure.

In the wake of the *IMT Judgment* and the ILC's formulation of the Nürnberg Principles, further steps were taken to progress international criminal law. The efforts to establish an international criminal court will be examined in Section 6.2.4. As regards substantive law, it was envisioned by General Assembly Resolution 177(II) of 21 November 1947 that the ILC in addition to formulating the Nürnberg Principles would prepare a Draft Code of Offences against the Peace and Security of Mankind. Although the ILC has worked on this topic in two stages, first from 1948 to 1954 and again from 1982 to 1996, a Code has yet to be adopted by the General Assembly. Article 1 of the ILC's draft from 1951 clearly reflected Nürnberg Principle I: 'Offences against the peace and security of mankind, as defined in this

[57] Ibid, 51. [58] Ibid, 49. [59] Ibid, 50. [60] See Section 3.1.1.

Code, are crimes under international law, for which the responsible individuals shall be punishable.'[61]

Despite the attempts to advance both procedural and material[62] aspects of international criminal law, several decades would pass before another international court would have occasion to pronounce on the responsibility of individuals for international crimes.

6.2.3 The ICTY and the ICTR

6.2.3.1 The International Criminal Tribunal for the former Yugoslavia

The ICTY was established in 1993 by the UN Security Council acting under Chapter VII of the UN Charter. Pursuant to Article 1 of the Statute of the International Criminal Tribunal for the former Yugoslavia (hereafter ICTY Statute), the Tribunal was competent 'to prosecute persons responsible for serious violations of international humanitarian law committed in the territory of the former Yugoslavia since 1991.'[63] Article 7(1) of the ICTY Statute provides: 'A person who planned, instigated, ordered, committed or otherwise aided and abetted in the planning, preparation or execution of a crime referred to in articles 2 to 5 of the present Statute, shall be individually responsible for the crime.'

In the *Tadić* case, the defence argued 'that the Security Council could not . . . create criminal liability on the part of individuals'.[64] But the Appeals Chamber dismissed all objections to the legality of the establishment of the Tribunal without devoting any attention to the concept of the individual obligations under the ICTY Statute or general international law.[65] Rather, both the Trial Chamber and the Appeals Chamber pronounced on the notion of individual responsibility for international crimes in connection with the defence's challenges to its subject-matter jurisdiction.

[61] II *YILC* (1951) 134–5. In the revised draft adopted in 1996, this provision was reaffirmed in Article 2(1), which reads: 'A crime against the peace and security of mankind entails individual responsibility'. II *YILC* (1996), Part II, 18.

[62] Rather than prescribing individual responsibility directly, it follows from Article V of the Convention on the Prevention and Punishment of the Crime of Genocide, 78 *UNTS* 277, which was adopted as General Assembly Resolution 260B(III) on 9 December 1948, that '[t]he Contracting Parties undertake to enact . . . the necessary legislation . . . to provide effective penalties for persons guilty of genocide.' See similarly Article 4 of the United Nations Convention against Torture and Other Cruel, Inhuman or Degrading Treatment or Punishment, 10 December 1984, 1465 *UNTS* 85. See further Section 6.2.4 on the ICC Statute.

[63] Specifically, the ICTY had jurisdiction to hear cases concerning grave breaches of the Geneva Conventions of 1949 (Article 2), war crimes (Article 3), genocide (Article 4), and crimes against humanity (Article 5). The Tribunal closed down in 2017.

[64] *Prosecutor v. Tadić*, IT-94-1, Trial Chamber, Decision on Defence Motion on Jurisdiction, 10 August 1995, para. 2 (hereafter *Tadić (Jurisdiction)* Trial Chamber).

[65] *Prosecutor v. Tadić*, IT-94-1, Appeals Chamber, Decision on Defence Motion for Interlocutory Appeal on Jurisdiction, 2 October 1995, paras 4–48 (hereafter *Tadić (Jurisdiction)* Appeals Chamber). Unlike the Appeals Chamber, the Trial Chamber did not assume to have the authority to rule on the legality of Resolution 827 (1993). It did, however, present a number of comments to the defence's contentions, including that no 'basis [has] been established for denying to the Security Council the power of indirect imposition of criminal liability upon individuals through the creation of a tribunal having criminal jurisdiction.' *Tadić (Jurisdiction)* Trial Chamber, para. 36.

By reference to the *IMT Judgment*, the Trial Chamber found that '[t]he individual criminal responsibility of the violator need not be explicitly stated in a convention for its provisions to entail individual criminal liability.'[66] The Appeals Chamber also relied exclusively on the *IMT Judgment* as it outlined the following criteria for determining whether particular violations of international law involve individual responsibility.

> ... the clear and unequivocal recognition of the rules of warfare in international law and State practice indicating an intention to criminalize the prohibition, including statements by government officials and international organizations, as well as punishment of violations by national courts and military tribunals .... Where these conditions are met, individuals must be held criminally responsible ....[67]

When judging the circumstances of the *Tadić* case against these criteria, the Appeals Chamber had no doubt that the disputed acts entailed individual criminal responsibility, 'regardless of whether they are committed in internal or international armed conflicts.'[68] Since there was scarcely any case law to support this conclusion with regard to internal armed conflict,[69] the decision may be read as to imply that individual liability follows automatically from the categorization of an act as an international crime. Subsequent ICTY practice may also be said to support this notion, which will be discussed further in Section 6.4. See, for example, the Appeals Chamber's Judgment in *Kordić and Čerkez* indicating that individual responsibility may arise from treaty violations even if the treaty in question does not explicitly impose obligations on individuals: 'The maxim of *nullum crimen sine lege* is also satisfied where *a State* is already treaty-bound by a specific convention, and the International Tribunal applies a provision of that convention irrespective of whether it is part of customary international law.'[70]

Aside from the question of individual responsibility for international crimes, the ICTY has also ruled on the competence of the Tribunal to address a *subpoena duces tecum* or *ad testificandum* directly to State officials. In *Blaskić*, the Appeals Chamber found that Article 29 of the ICTY Statute confers on 'States' a duty to cooperate and to provide judicial assistance, and that 'being the addressees of such obligation, [States] have some choice or leeway in identifying the persons responsible for, and the method of, its fulfilment.'[71] Clearly, the Appeals Chamber did not thereby imply that international law cannot as a matter of principle address individuals directly.[72] It only found that Article 29 is addressed to States as such rather than individual

[66] Ibid, para. 70. [67] *Tadić (Jurisdiction)* Appeals Chamber (n 65) , para. 128.

[68] Ibid, para. 129. See also *Tadić (Jurisdiction)* Trial Chamber (n 64) para. 74, *Prosecutor v. Delalić*, IT-96-21-T, Trial Chamber, Judgment, 16 November 1998, para. 307, and *Prosecutor v. Furundžija*, IT-95-17/1-T, Trial Chamber, Judgment, 10 December 1998, paras 140 and 169.

[69] See, for example, Bruno Simma and Andreas Paulus, 'The Responsibility of Individuals for Human Rights Abuses in Internal Conflicts: A Positivist View', 93 *AJIL* (1999) 302, 312–13.

[70] *Prosecutor v. Kordić and Čerkez*, IT-95-14/2-A, Appeals Chamber, Judgment, 17 December 2004, para. 44 (emphasis added).

[71] *Prosecutor v. Blaskić*, IT-95-14, Appeals Chamber, Judgment on the Request of the Republic of Croatia for Review of the Decision of Trial Chamber II of 18 July 1997, 29 October 1997, para. 43 (hereafter *Blaskić*). See also ibid, para. 41.

[72] See also Giorgio Gaja, 'Dualism—a Review', and Andreas L. Paulus, 'The Emergence of the International Community and the Divide between International and Domestic Law', in Janne Nijman

State representatives, and that it is for each State to determine how its obligations are to be fulfilled—and by whom. In this respect, the Judgment is a fine illustration of the point that international legal personality is simply a matter of interpretation of international legal norms. It is somewhat confusing, however, that the Appeals Chamber did not leave its discussion of the matter with a determination of the addressees of Article 29, but instead went on to discuss the customary rules on the functional immunity of State representatives.[73] Procedural questions concerning State representatives' immunity may arise when enforcement of a substantive international legal obligation of a State representative is sought before a foreign domestic court or an international court. But the issue of functional immunity is irrelevant when there is no substantive obligation of the State representative in the first place. Given that, in this particular case, Article 29 does not confer obligations on specific State representatives, it therefore makes little sense to discuss whether they might invoke immunity before the ICTY.

6.2.3.2 *The International Criminal Tribunal for Rwanda*

Akin to the ICTY, the ICTR was established by the UN Security Council acting under Chapter VII of the UN Charter in 1994. According to Article 1 of the Statute of the International Criminal Tribunal for Rwanda (hereafter ICTR Statute), the ICTR was competent to 'prosecute persons responsible for serious violations of international humanitarian law committed in the territory of Rwanda and Rwandan citizens responsible for such violations committed in the territory of neighbouring States between 1 January 1994 and 31 December 1994'.[74]

Similar to the arguments presented in *Tadić* before the ICTY, the defence in the *Kanyabashi* case asserted that the ICTR had no jurisdiction, because the Security Council lacked authority over individuals.[75] But rather than simply relying on the Appeals Chamber's decision in *Tadić*, the Trial Chamber stated as follows:

> The Trial Chamber recalls that the question of direct individual responsibility under international law is and has been a controversial issue within and between various legal systems for several decades and that the Nüremberg trials in particular have been interpreted differently in respect of the position of the individual as a subject under international law. By establishing [the ICTY and the ICTR], however, the Security Council explicitly extended international legal obligations and criminal responsibilities directly to individuals for violations of international humanitarian law. In doing so, the Security Council provided an important innovation of international law, but there is nothing in the Defence Counsel's motion to suggest that this extension of the applicability of international law against individuals was not

and André Nollkaemper (eds), *New Perspectives on the Divide Between National and International Law* (OUP, 2007) 52, 55; 216, 230.

[73] *Blaskić* (n 71) paras 41–42.

[74] The crimes within the ICTR's jurisdiction were genocide (Article 2), crimes against humanity (Article 3), and violations of Article 3 common to the Geneva Conventions and of Additional Protocol II (Article 4). The ICTR closed down in 2015.

[75] *Prosecutor v. Kanyabashi*, ICTR-96-15-T, Trial Chamber, Decision on the Defence Motion on Jurisdiction, 18 June 1997, para. 33.

justified or called for by the circumstances, notably the seriousness, the magnitude and the gravity of the crimes committed during the conflict.[76]

By labelling the Security Council's extension of criminal liability to individuals in the ICTY and ICTR Statutes an 'innovation in international law', the Trial Chamber seems to dismiss the precedential value of the *IMT Judgment* altogether. It has been noted that the Trial Chamber was 'presumably referring to the recognition of individual criminal responsibility for violations of international humanitarian law applicable in internal armed conflict.'[77] But the reference to the uncertainty surrounding the *IMT Judgment* suggests that the Trial Chamber did not under any circumstances find individuals to be the bearers of international criminal responsibility under customary international law. In this way the *Kanyabashi* decision runs counter to preceding practice. The defence decided not to appeal the Trial Chamber's decision. As it is likely that the common Appeals Chamber of the ICTY and the ICTR, given the opportunity, would have been guided by its previous decision in *Tadić*, the value of the ICTR's decision in *Kanyabashi* should perhaps not be overstated.[78]

With reference to Article 4, the UN Secretary-General opined as follows in a report to the Security Council on the ICTR Statute: '[T]he Security Council has … included within the subject-matter jurisdiction of the Rwanda Tribunal international instruments regardless of whether they were considered part of customary international law or whether they have customarily entailed the individual criminal responsibility of the perpetrator of the crime.'[79] Predictably, the existence of customary rules ascribing criminal liability to individuals in internal armed conflicts was also brought into question in the practice of the ICTR. In the *Akayesu* case, the Trial Chamber ostensibly implied that individual criminal liability must be established separately, even when it has already been determined that an international crime has been committed: 'Even if Article 6 of the Statute provides for individual criminal responsibility as pertains to Articles 2, 3, and 4 of the Statute, it must also be shown that an individual committing serious violations of these customary norms incurs, as a matter of custom, individual criminal responsibility thereby.'[80]

Nonetheless, the Trial Chamber went on to rely on the Appeals Chamber's findings in *Tadić* in order to conclude that 'the violation of these norms entails, as a matter of customary international law, individual responsibility for the perpetrator.' While the ICTR thus required a customary rule prescribing individual responsibility for the crimes at hand, it referred exclusively to an ICTY precedent which, as discussed in Section 6.2.3.1, barely documented the existence of such a rule.

[76] Ibid, para. 35.

[77] Virginia Morris, 'Prosecutor v. Kanyabashi, Decision on Jurisdiction. Case No. ICTR-96-15-T', 92 *AJIL* (1998) 66, 69.

[78] See also L. J. van den Herik, *The Contribution of the Rwanda Tribunal to the Development of International Law* (Martinus Nijhoff, 2005) 71–2, and Parlett (n 4) 265–6.

[79] Report of the Secretary-General Pursuant to Paragraph 5 of Security Council Resolution 955 (1994), UN Doc. S/1995/134, 13 February 1995.

[80] *Prosecutor v. Akayesu*, ICTR-96-4, Trial Chamber, Judgment, 2 September 1998, para. 611.

6.2.4 The ICC

The idea of an international criminal court was spawned long before the ICC Statute was adopted in Rome on 17 July 1998. Besides the discussions in the Advisory Committee of Jurists in 1920 on the possibility of establishing a High Court of International Justice,[81] forecasts include Article VI of the Genocide Convention of 9 December 1948. The ILC's work on this topic culminated in 1994 with a Draft Statute for an International Criminal Court,[82] which did not restate any principles of individual responsibility for international crimes.[83] Provisions to this effect were subsequently included by the Preparatory Committee on the Establishment of an International Criminal Court, which had been called upon by the General Assembly to prepare the final draft text for submission to a diplomatic conference.[84] Article 25 of the ICC Statute reads inter alia:

1. The Court shall have jurisdiction over natural persons pursuant to this Statute.
2. A person who commits a crime within the jurisdiction of the Court shall be individually responsible and liable for punishment in accordance with this Statute . . . .

Seemingly, these two provisions were not meant to have independent content, but were included as a mere statement of the obvious and confirmation of the principle of individual criminal responsibility as recognized by the IMT with regard to international armed conflict, and subsequently by the ICTY concerning internal armed conflict.[85]

It is not clear whether crimes included under the ICC Statute constitute material obligations,[86] which are directly binding on individuals, or if they merely provide for the jurisdiction of the ICC under certain circumstances, in which case the criminal responsibility for the acts in question must arise under other sources, primarily customary international law. The ICC Statute itself does not provide an unequivocal answer.[87] Its *travaux préparatoires* are not particularly

[81] See Section 3.2.1. [82] II *YILC* (1994) 20–73.

[83] There do not seem to have been much discussion on the concept. The ILC merely referred briefly to the *IMT Judgment*. See ibid, 23.

[84] Report of the Preparatory Committee on the Establishment of an International Criminal Court, Addendum 1, UN Doc. A/CONF.183/2/Add.1, 14 April 1998, 48–9.

[85] The controversy in connection with the formulation of Article 25 primarily revolved around the possibility of including legal persons within the jurisdiction of the Court. A proposal to that effect was ultimately rejected. See further Kai Ambos, 'Article 25', in Otto Triffterer and Kai Ambos (eds), *Commentary on the Rome Statute of the International Criminal Court* (3rd edn, Verlag C. H. Beck, 2016) 983–6. See also M. Cherif Bassiouni, *The Legislative History of the International Criminal Court* (Transnational Publishers, Inc., 2005), vol. 2, 191–5, and Albin Eser, 'Individual Criminal Responsibility', in Antonio Cassese, Paola Gaeta, and John R. W. D. Jones (eds), *The Rome Statute of the International Criminal Court: A Commentary* (OUP, 2002) 770.

[86] The crimes included under the ICC Statute are genocide (Articles 5(a) and 6), crimes against humanity (Articles 5(b) and 7), war crimes (Articles 5(c) and 8), and aggression (Article 5(d) and 8*bis*).

[87] Article 5 lists the crimes within the 'jurisdiction of the Court' indicating that the definitions of crimes in Articles 6–8 are not to be read as substantive provisions criminalizing particular conduct. In contrast, Article 21(1)(a) pertaining to 'applicable law' clearly states that the ICC shall apply the ICC Statute first and foremost, which is barely logical if the punishable crimes only arise from other sources. In addition, Articles 22(1), 24, and the above-cited 25 explicitly talk about criminal responsibility of individuals 'under' or 'in accordance with' the Statute. For a detailed analysis see Marko Milanović, 'Is the Rome Statute Binding on Individuals? (And Why We Should Care)', 9 *JICJ* (2011) 25, 30–2.

helpful,[88] and scholarly writings also point in opposite directions. For example, Claus Kreß has argued that Articles 6–8 articulate 'crimes so that they exist directly under this international treaty',[89] whereas Cassese found that 'the Statute, far from constituting an "international criminal code", only lays down the rules that must guide the Court when it exercises its jurisdiction over the crimes it is called upon to adjudicate.'[90] While the categorization of Articles 6–8 as either substantive or jurisdictional has little practical importance in cases where the ICC has jurisdiction at the time when the crime in question is committed, it is relevant in situations where the Court's jurisdiction is established *ex post facto* by acceptance of a non-Member State under Article 12(3),[91] or referral by the Security Council under Article 13(b).[92] The Pre-Trial Chamber's Decision on Confirmation of Charges of 29 January 2007 in the *Lubanga* case reads inter alia:

> [T]here is no infringement of the principle of legality if the Chamber exercises its power to decide whether Thomas Lubanga Dyilo ought to be committed for trial on the basis of written (*lex scripta*) pre-existing norms approved by the States Parties to the Rome Statute (*lex praevia*), defining prohibited conduct and setting out the related sentence (*lex certa*), which cannot be interpreted by analogy *in malam partem* (*lex stricta*).[93]

While this paragraph may be interpreted as supporting the substantive reading, it is far from conclusive. Nevertheless assuming, for the sake of the argument, that Articles 6–8 are indeed substantive provisions, the following question arises: Would it violate the principle of *nullum crimen sine lege*[94] to convict an accused, who was beyond the jurisdiction of the ICC at the time of the relevant act, of a crime under the ICC Statute which was not also a crime under customary international law?[95] As argued in Section 6.3.1, the Allied Powers had the competence to adopt the London Agreement and the IMT Charter due to the unconditional surrender of Germany. However, even if we make the controversial assumption that a group of States may

[88] Report of the Preparatory Committee on the Establishment of an International Criminal Court, Addendum 1, 14 April 1998, 11ff and 48ff.

[89] Claus Kreß, 'International Criminal Law' (2009) in *Max Planck Encyclopaedia of International Law* (available at http://www.mpepil.com, accessed 21 January 2018). See also Gerhard Werle, *Principles of International Criminal Law* (Asser Press, 2005) 49, Milanović (n 87) 32, and Anne Peters, *Beyond Human Rights—The Legal Status of the Individual in International Law* (CUP, 2016) 143.

[90] Antonio Cassese, *International Criminal Law* (2nd edn, OUP, 2008) 14.

[91] For example, the ICC Statute entered into force for the State of Palestine on 1 April 2015, subsequent to a declaration by the Government of the State of Palestine under Article 12(3) accepting the ICC jurisdiction since 13 June 2014.

[92] For example, the Security Council has referred the situation in Darfur, Sudan, since 1 July 2002 to the ICC's prosecutor by Resolution 1593 of 31 March 2005.

[93] *The Prosecutor v. Thomas Lubanga Dyilo*, ICC-01/04-01/06, Pre-Trial Chamber I, Decision on Confirmation of Charges, 29 January 2007, para. 303.

[94] The *nullum crimen sine lege* principle is presumed to imply that the source of law criminalizing certain conduct must not only be in force, but must be applicable to the particular perpetrator at the time of the act.

[95] The difference between the ICC and, for example, the IMT is of course that criminal sanctions would in all circumstances have been applied retroactively under the IMT Charter had the IMT not presumed that the acts of the German war criminals were also criminalized in customary international law. The ICC Statute, however, only applies to acts committed subsequent to its entry into force on 1 July 2002.

also regulate the conduct of citizens of third States in a treaty outside situations of *debellatio*, it is not evident that the parties to the ICC Statute in fact intended to do so.[96] Further analysis of these issues is excessive in this context. The important point for present purposes is that the answers have little to do with the concept of international legal personality. Instead, they depend solely on interpretation of the relevant norms of international law, which in this case would be the ICC Statute and the customary rules on the legislative jurisdiction of States.[97]

6.2.5 Does individual responsibility for international crimes arise a priori or a posteriori?

It appears to be the predominant view in contemporary international legal scholarship that individuals are international legal persons (at least) as regards international criminal law.[98] But there is some disagreement as to when and how individual responsibility for international crimes arises. Is the responsibility of individuals an inherent part of categorizing an act as an international crime (i.e. individuals are a priori legal persons in international criminal law)? Or must the liability of individuals be established on a case-by-case basis (i.e. individuals are a posteriori international legal persons)?

In other words, the question is whether the practice of international criminal law may best be explained according to the 'individualistic'[99] or the 'a posteriori'[100] conception of international legal personality.

Bruno Simma and Andreas Paulus have argued in favour of perceiving of individuals as 'only' a posteriori international legal persons even in international criminal law. With reference to the *Tadić* case, they state that they 'know of no case in which a national, let alone an international, tribunal prior to the ICTY's establishment has exercised jurisdiction over war crimes in internal conflicts irrespective of the nationality of the victim and the perpetrator.'[101] Nevertheless, they do not subscribe to the idea that individual responsibility is an inherent consequence of any act defined as international crime:

> In the creation of custom, there is always an element of innovation. On the basis of a modern positivism—hence also taking into account the practice of international institutions and accepting as *opinio juris* the legal views expressed by states in international organizations—one

[96] See Milanović (n 87) 34–5 and 47–52.

[97] See also Section 5.4.3.4.

[98] Notably, there are scholars who maintain that the rules of individual criminal responsibility do not bear witness to the international legal personality of individuals. Orakhelashvili, for example, finds that individual criminal responsibility under international law is to be considered a part of State responsibility, because perpetrators of international crimes can only be brought before an international tribunal when it is established that no national legal order is able and willing to conduct the trial. This leads Orakhelashvili to conclude that international criminal responsibility is of a subsidiary character and 'thus interwoven with the objective consequences of violation of State obligations rather than being some inherent capacity of the individual under international law.' See Alexander Orakhelashvili, 'The Position of the Individual in International Law', 31 *California Western International Law Journal* (2001) 241, 275. It seems clear that Orakhelashvili's argument fails to distinguish between primary and secondary rules of international law (see Section 1.3.3), and his analysis is therefore hardly acceptable.

[99] See Section 2.4.

[100] See Section 2.3.

[101] Simma and Paulus (n 69) 312.

can defend the ICTY jurisprudence and the Rwanda Statute on the basis of a combination of developing customary law and existing general principles. We therefore consider the introduction of individual criminal responsibility for war crimes as an example of lawmaking in accordance with the traditional methods of law formation by treaty, custom and general principles.[102]

Also requiring a distinct legal basis for imposing individual criminal responsibility, Dapo Akande finds:

The transformation of the rule establishing violations of international humanitarian law by states into one which imposes individual criminal responsibility on individuals takes place under customary international law. Thus, although reference is made to treaties creating rules of international criminal law, those provisions are not applied qua treaty but rather as the context for a rule of customary law which has developed on top of the treaty rule and which criminalizes the same conduct.[103]

In contrast, Portmann reads the *IMT Judgment* as a manifestation of 'individualistic' conception of international legal personality.[104] In Portmann's opinion, the conclusions of the IMT formulated by the ILC in Nürnberg Principle I have subsequently been followed, in the sense that 'in international criminal law, there is a presumption of the individual being an international person'.[105] He argues that 'there is no need to separately establish whether international crimes bind individual human beings: they automatically do so on the basis of legal principle without a statutory provision or customary practice necessarily indicating so.'[106] Peters agrees with Portmann that no case-by-case establishment of individual responsibility for international crimes is necessary, but she explicitly dismisses 'natural law' as the basis for such an argument. Instead, she finds that 'the legal principle recognizing the international legal personality of an actor must be attributable to one of the recognized sources of international law.'[107] Along similar lines, Robert Kolb asserts that since '[t]here was no review of any pre-existing international custom for the single offences', the *IMT Judgment* (as confirmed by the ILC's Nürnberg Principles and subsequent practice) should be read as to imply that 'customary law itself... dispenses with a case-by-case analysis into State practice in the context of a prosecution for a single offence.'[108]

What separates Portmann, Peters, and Kolb from Simma, Paulus, and Akande seems to be their respective approaches to the relevant international criminal case law within the overarching question of the sources international law, in particular customary international law. Presuming that the development of customary law

[102] Ibid, 313.

[103] See Dapo Akande, 'Sources of International Criminal Law', in Antonio Cassese et al. (eds), *Oxford Companion to International Criminal Justice* (OUP, 2009) 41, 48.

[104] Roland Portmann, *Legal Personality in International Law* (CUP, 2010) 158.

[105] Ibid, 162. See also William Schabas, 'Interpreting the Statutes of the Ad Hoc Tribunals', in L. C. Vohrah et al. (eds), *Man's Inhumanity to Man: Essays on International Law in Honour of Antonio Cassese* (Kluwer, 2003) 847, 887.

[106] Portmann (n 104) 273.

[107] Peters (n 89) 413.

[108] Robert Kolb, 'The Jurisprudence of the Yugoslav and Rwandan Criminal Tribunals on Their Jurisdiction and on International Crimes' 71 *BYBIL* (2001) 265.

inherently involves 'an element of innovation', Simma and Paulus argue that the practice of international criminal courts and tribunals is not necessarily at odds with the idea that international legal personality arises a posteriori and must be determined on a case-by-case basis. In contrast, Portmann and Peters dismiss the idea that the *IMT Judgment* and subsequent judgments of international criminal courts, such as *Tadić*, were in and of themselves instances of creation of customary international law. They believe that the basis for imposing individual criminal responsibility in those cases must be found elsewhere. According to Portmann, the basis is the fact that the individuals in question are 'human beings and as such under an obligation to respect fundamental international norms.'[109] Alternatively, Peters advocates 'that moral philosophical considerations have led to a "juridified" natural law of the legal personality of the individual'.[110]

6.3 What Defines an International Criminal Court?

The legal basis for attributing individual criminal liability is not the only issue in the field of international criminal law which brings the concept of international legal personality to the fore. As illustrated in the following, questions concerning the personality of individuals in international law also appear in the context of the—lack of—definitional distinction between the various kinds of criminal courts. Section 6.3.1 examines the IMT's statements—as well as the scholarly debate they gave rise to—about the legal nature of the London Agreement and the IMT Charter. The academic discussions about the IMT not only illustrate the confusion generated by the divergence between the then dominant 'States-only' conception of international legal personality and the role of individuals as a matter of positive international (criminal) law. As shown in Sections 6.3.2, 6.3.3, and 6.3.4, arguments put forward by scholars in the wake of the *IMT Judgment* still influence the way in which both scholars and judges distinguish between 'international', 'internationalized', and 'domestic' criminal courts today.

6.3.1 The legal nature of the London Agreement and the IMT Charter

The IMT made the following statement on the competence of the States parties to the London Agreement:

> The making of the Charter was the exercise of the sovereign legislative power by the countries to which the German Reich unconditionally surrendered; and the undoubted right of these countries to legislate for the occupied territories has been recognized by the civilized world. The Charter is not an arbitrary exercise of power on the part of the victorious Nations, but in the view of the Tribunals, as will be shown, it is the expression of international law existing at the time of its creation; and to that extent is itself a contribution to international law.

[109] Portmann (n 104) 273.

[110] Peters (n 89) 434 and 125. On Peters' conception of the international legal personality, see further Sections 2.4 and 2.6.

The Signatory Powers created this Tribunal, defined the law it was to administer, and made regulations for the proper conduct of the Trial. In doing so, they have done together what any one of them might have done singly; for it is not to be doubted that any nation has the right to set up special courts to administer law.[111]

This paragraph prompted a heated debate among scholars at the time. Schwarzenberger, for example, contended that the IMT was to be classified as 'a joint municipal tribunal': 'the Nuremberg Tribunal is international more in form than in substance. It is more akin to a joint tribunal under municipal law than to an international tribunal in the normal sense of the word.'[112]

Given that Germany had surrendered unconditionally and had transferred legislative authority to the four victorious States,[113] a tribunal to try the major German war criminals might have been set up by them under municipal law. But it remains a matter of interpretation of the circumstances surrounding the relevant documents whether the four States in fact chose this approach. It seems evident that the signatory States did not perceive of the London Agreement, including the IMT Charter, as municipal legislation exercised on the basis of delegated authority from Germany, but meant for it to have the form of a treaty. Apart from the fact that it explicitly sets up an 'International Military Tribunal', the London Agreement has all the traits of a treaty as regards, for example, the format, wording and signatures, declarations by the parties before and after the signing, and registration with the UN Secretary General.[114] In order to perceive the London Agreement and the IMT Charter as municipal law, one would arguably have to adhere to a conception of international law which by definition leaves all matters concerning individuals to be governed domestically. Correspondingly, Schwarzenberger's categorization of the IMT as a 'joint tribunal under municipal law' appears to be based on his perception of criminal responsibility of individuals as an inherently domestic matter:

Little importance need . . . be attached to the circumstance that the joint sovereigns exercised their jurisdiction as the fountain of law and justice in Germany by an international treaty; for this mode of co-ordinating their sovereign wills is not so much determined by the object of their joint deliberations as by the character of the joint sovereigns as four distinct subjects of international law.[115]

The deciding factor for the categorization of the law governing the IMT in Schwarzenberger's argument is not the fact that the Tribunal was set up by a treaty, which he does not dispute. Instead, he seems to reason that since the object of

[111] *IMT Judgment* (n 28) 216.

[112] Schwarzenberger (n 34) 338. See further ibid, 333–5, and Schwarzenberger, 'The Problem of an International Criminal Law' *Current Legal Problems*, vol. 3 (1950b), 290–1. See also Quincy Wright, 'The Law of the Nuremberg Trial', 41 *AJIL* (1947) 38, 48–51. See further Ilias Bantekas and Susan Nash, *International Criminal Law* (3rd edn, Routledge, 2007) 505–6.

[113] See Berlin Declaration, 5 June 1945 (available at http://avalon.law.yale.edu/wwii/ger01.asp, accessed 21 January 2018).

[114] The fact that it was subsequently ratified by nineteen other States eliminates all doubt that the London Agreement is a treaty.

[115] Schwarzenberger (n 34) 334. See also Georg Schwarzenberger, 'The Fundamental Principles of International Law' 87 *Recueil des Cours* (1955-I) 191, 354–5.

said treaty is to impose criminal responsibility on individuals, it is to be presumed that it belongs to municipal law. In this particular case, Schwarzenberger, who is commonly associated with the modified 'States-only' conception,[116] thus invoked a rather strong presumption against the international legal personality of individuals.

Kelsen appears to have read the IMT's statement that '[t]he making of the Charter was the exercise of the sovereign legislative power'[117] as an affirmation of Schwarzenberger's line of thought. Unsurprisingly, Kelsen found this analysis to be 'problematical'. Instead of pursuing the matter in detail, however, he emphasized the insignificance of the issue from a practical viewpoint: '[I]n relation to the German delinquents the difference between a legislative act of the four occupant powers in their capacity as legitimate successors of the German Government, and a treaty concluded by them and adhered to by other States belonging to the United Nations, is rather formal than substantial.'[118]

Though this observation by Kelsen may be of some merit, it remains open to question whether his reading of the *IMT Judgment* as coherent with Schwarzenberger's reasoning is justified. Kelsen seems to presume that 'sovereign legislative power' is necessarily exercised through domestic law. Conversely, it may be inferred that the Tribunal was not addressing the competence of the signatory States to issue domestic legislation as such, but instead their overall legislative jurisdiction[119] to govern—in the form of a treaty or through domestic law—individuals who were not their own nationals or residents, but belonged to a third State. Following this logic, the Allied Powers could simply choose between exercising their jurisdiction over Germany in a treaty or through domestic law, and it seems that they chose the treaty in the case of the IMT.[120]

Assuming, as argued in this book, that there are no limitations (except for *jus cogens* norms) on the subject matter that may be governed by international law, the choice between issuing domestic law and entering into a treaty is open to all States governing individuals within their jurisdiction—given of course that at least one other State is interested in adopting a treaty on the relevant subject. What is unusual about the post-Second World War circumstances is that the Allied Powers had joint legislative jurisdiction over Germany. Outside situations of *debellatio*, it is less straightforward whether—and, if so, under what circumstances—the legislative jurisdiction of States includes the competence to confer treaty obligations on individuals other than their respective nationals and residents and those present in their respective territories.[121]

116 See Section 2.2.1. 117 The paragraph is cited in full above (n 111).
118 See Kelsen (n 34) 169–70. 119 See also Section 5.4.3.4.
120 For a discussion of the legal nature of the Nuremberg Military Tribunals and the International Military Tribunal for the Far East, see Astrid Kjeldgaard-Pedersen, 'What Defines an International Criminal Court?: A Critical Assessment of "the Involvement of the International Community" as a Deciding Factor' 28 *LJIL* (2015) 113, 122–5.
121 See further Section 6.2.4.

6.3.2 The definition of an international criminal court in post-Second World War scholarship

Given their proliferation over the past twenty years and the great academic interest in the field of international criminal law, it would be reasonable to presume the term 'international criminal court' to be a well-defined concept in contemporary scholarship. However, no generally recognized distinction between an 'international criminal court', an 'internationalized criminal court', and a 'domestic criminal court' appears to exist.[122] In fact, it is common for textbooks and handbooks on international criminal law to completely avoid a discussion of the criteria for categorizing a judicial body as an 'international criminal court'.[123] Instead of explaining what makes a tribunal either 'international', 'internationalized', or 'domestic', textbook authors tend to focus their attention on the pros and cons of prosecuting offenders before the various kinds of tribunals[124] and/or on the particular traits of each of the existing 'internationalized criminal courts'.[125] The distinction between 'international' and 'domestic' courts is implied at best.[126]

Robert Woetzel's *The Nuremberg Trials in International Law* from 1962[127] and *Hybrid and Internationalised Criminal Tribunals* by Sarah Williams in 2012[128] are among the few works attempting to come up with a definition of international and internationalized tribunals respectively—and they both emphasize 'the involvement of the international community' as a crucial element.

In *The Nuremberg Trials in International Law*, Woetzel set out to examine whether the IMT could truly be categorized as an 'international criminal court'. He went

[122] In his 2011 book on the NMTs, Kevin Jon Heller wrote: 'To determine the legal character of the NMTs, we must first identify what distinguishes an international tribunal from a domestic court. Perhaps surprisingly, that issue has been largely ignored by scholars. The primary exception is Robert Woetzel ...'. Kevin Jon Heller, *The Nuremberg Military Tribunals and the Origins of International Criminal Law* (OUP, 2011) 110.

[123] See, for example, William Schabas and Nadia Bernaz (eds), *Routledge Handbook on International Criminal Law* (Routledge, 2011), Antonio Cassese et al. (eds), *The Oxford Companion to International Criminal Justice* (OUP, 2009), Ilias Bantekas and Susan Nash, *International Criminal Law* (3rd edn, Routledge, 2007), and M. Cherif Bassiouni (ed.), *International Criminal Law* (1986), vols. 1–3. A notable exception is Roger O'Keefe, *International Criminal Law* (OUP, 2015) 85–114.

[124] See, for example, Antonio Cassese, 'The Rationale for International Criminal Justice', in Antonio Cassese (ed.), *The Oxford Companion to International Criminal Justice* (OUP, 2009) 123–30, and Florian Jessberger, 'International v. National Prosecution of International Crimes', in Antonio Cassese (ed.), *The Oxford Companion to International Criminal Justice* (OUP, 2009) 208–15.

[125] See, for example, Bantekas and Nash (n 123) 577–84, and Fidelma Donlon, 'Hybrid Tribunals', in William Schabas and Nadia Bernaz (eds), *Routledge Handbook on International Criminal Law* (Routledge, 2011) 85–105.

[126] Notably, Alexander Zahar and Göran Sluiter state in a footnote concerning internationalized criminal courts that 'the source of the court's authority ... is in our view decisive as to the institution's position as part of the international or the national legal order.' Alexander Zahar and Göran Sluiter, *International Criminal Law—A Critical Introduction* (OUP, 2008) 12.

[127] See Robert Woetzel, *The Nuremberg Trials in International Law* (Stevens & Sons, 1962) 49. See also Heller (n 122) 110–11.

[128] Sarah Williams, *Hybrid and Internationalised Criminal Tribunals—Selected Jurisdictional Issues* (Hart, 2012).

through four main theories pertaining to the definition of an international court, which may be summed up as follows:[129]

1. 'A court is international if it applies international law.'
2. 'An international court is a tribunal based on powers of occupation under international law.'
3. 'A tribunal is international if it derives its authority from a treaty or decision of an international council.'
4. 'A court instituted by one or a group of nations is international if it has the approval of the international community.'

Woetzel rejected the first argument for the straightforward reason that national courts also apply international law, whereas he considered the second argument to be unconvincing 'since occupation tribunals are widely considered to be limited in their power by the rules of belligerent occupation'.[130] Against the background of the developments in international criminal law over recent decades, few twenty-first-century legal scholars would be likely to endorse either of the first two arguments.[131] What is more interesting from a contemporary viewpoint is why Woetzel discarded the third argument in favour of the fourth.

Pertaining to the third argument, Woetzel stated that '[i]t would be indisputably international only in so far as the contracting members are affected by it, within their respective spheres of jurisdiction.'[132] He apparently found the label 'international' to imply that the relevant tribunal has jurisdiction over nationals, including State representatives, of third States. Woetzel did not provide any further support for his conclusion 'that a treaty between several states by itself would not be an uncontested basis for an international court.'[133] He only pointed to the somewhat circular argument that the IMT would not have had jurisdiction over German nationals without the approval of the international community.[134] One might speculate that Woetzel preferred to conclude that the IMT was an international tribunal, but had doubts as to the jurisdiction of the Allied Powers over German nationals. Emphasizing 'the approval of the international community' in his definition of an international criminal tribunal allowed him to circumvent the latter issue.[135]

[129] See further Woetzel (n 127) 41ff. [130] Ibid, 42.

[131] See, however, Yaël Ronen, 'Blind in their Own Cause: The Military Courts in the West Bank', 2 *CJICL* (2013b) 738, 740. Ronen claims that the Military Courts in the West Bank are a part of the international legal order because 'they ... draw their authority from the laws of occupation'. Ronen thereby seems to overlook the fundamental difference between setting up a criminal tribunal under international law and setting up a criminal tribunal under domestic law in compliance with international law.

[132] Woetzel (n 127), 43. [133] Ibid.

[134] Ibid, 48–9. Remarkably, Bantekas and Nash imply without further discussion—and without explicit reference to Woetzel—that the recognition of the international community is necessary for a criminal court to be labelled 'international'. In their opinion, however, the IMT did not meet this requirement, since 'although no State objected to its establishment, the Allied powers received only 22 statements of support.' See Bantekas and Nash (n 123) 505–6.

[135] For his account for 'the elements of international sanction', see Woetzel (n 127) 49–55.

Woetzel's subsequent analysis of the position of the individual in international law serves to underline the problems of his definition of an international criminal court and clarifies why he needed to invoke 'the approval of the international community'. According to Woetzel, the direct application of international law to individuals conflicts with the idea that international law and national law are separate legal systems.[136] Thus, in opposition to 'dualist writers who deny that international law applies directly to individuals as well as to states',[137] Woetzel claimed as follows: 'Since . . . international courts can apply international law, this would leave no doubt that before international tribunals at least, international law may be applied directly to individuals, regardless of the provisions of national law.'[138] He thereby conflated the two fundamental questions of (1) the possible entities that international law may govern and (2) the effect of an international norm in domestic law. In the common view, 'dualism' implies that international law and national law are separate legal systems, and that the rules of any national legal system decide the impact of international law in national law and vice versa.[139] But 'dualism' says nothing about the potential content of the material international norm. Whereas the concept of international legal personality is a contentious topic in international law, the direct applicability of international norms in domestic legal systems—regardless of whether they are addressed to individuals—is a matter of domestic law. Woetzel concluded that ' . . . the IMT, an international court, was completely justified in applying international law to the individual defendants.'[140] However, from the point of view of international law, the same could be said about any domestic court. It is a different question altogether whether—under domestic law—a domestic court may impose international legal obligations directly on individuals. In any event, this issue, which may find different answers in different domestic legal systems, cannot be decisive for the definition of an 'international criminal court' under international law.

As argued in the preceding text, it is uncertain whether Woetzel's definition of an 'international criminal court' was in fact in line with the judgments of the post-Second World War tribunals.[141] Nevertheless, 'the involvement of the international community' continues to be attributed significance. Sarah Williams's recent work on *Hybrid and Internationalised Tribunals*, for example, relies heavily on

[136] See ibid, 100:

> [I]t was to be expected that some authors would criticise the Judgment of the Nuremberg Tribunal on the ground that international law applied only to states, while national law applied to individuals. According to their point of view, national law and international law are two spheres which cannot overlap but which exist parallel to each other, even when they are identical in contents.

[137] Ibid, 104. [138] Ibid, 105.

[139] See, for example, Gaja (n 72) 52–3, and Janne Nijman and André Nollkaemper, 'Beyond the Divide', in Janne Nijman and André Nollkaemper (eds), *New Perspectives on the Divide Between National and International Law* (OUP, 2007) 341. See further Section 1.3.2.

[140] See Woetzel (n 127), 108.

[141] It is clear from the academic debate on the nature of these tribunals, however, that he was not the only scholar to view the developments in international criminal law through the lens of the orthodox presumption against the international legal personality of individuals. See Section 6.3.1.

'the involvement of the international community' as a criterion for assessing the legal nature of criminal courts. Based on a survey of existing courts and tribunals commonly referred to as 'internationalized' or 'hybrid', Williams concludes that there is no comprehensive definition of this kind of judicial body.[142] She does, however, identify six 'defining features' of 'internationalized' or 'hybrid' criminal courts, including, for example, the involvement of a party other than the affected State and a mix of international and national elements in their material jurisdiction. Among institutions satisfying those six criteria, Williams notes that there is still a wide range of diversity. She finds: 'Having now conducted this study, it is possible to categorise the various international and national mechanisms for international criminal justice on a sliding scale by looking at the extent and degree of international involvement.'[143]

Essentially, Williams's sliding scale measures the involvement of the UN. Thus, the 'true' international criminal tribunals, for example the ICTY and the ICTR, are set up by the Security Council acting under Chapter VII of the UN Charter. Although not a UN subsidiary, the ICC also fulfils the criteria for being categorized as 'truly international' in light of the number of Member States to the Rome Statute and the possibility of Security Council referrals. Contrary to common terminology, Williams draws a distinction between 'hybrid' and 'internationalized' criminal courts. In the category of 'hybrid courts' Williams places the tribunals such as SCSL and the Special Tribunal for Lebanon because they operate directly on the basis of international law (e.g. an agreement between the UN and the affected state), and because of the 'considerable international involvement in [their] design, establishment and operation'. The category of 'internationalized' tribunals, on the other hand, comprises 'essentially domestic institutions but with significant participation from other states or from international organisations including the United Nations.' The ECCC is an example of an internationalized tribunal.[144] In a fourth category, Williams places tribunals receiving (usually ad hoc) assistance from other States or international organizations, whereas the fifth and final category includes courts set up under domestic law without international assistance.[145]

Williams should perhaps be commended for trying to put flesh on the bone of the inherently elusive 'involvement of the international community' criterion.[146] Nonetheless, it seems reasonable to ask whether it would have been wiser to abandon this criterion altogether. As Williams herself notes, the sliding scale does not help to resolve the legal issues faced by criminal tribunals: 'While such a classification can be a useful first step, of greater importance is a proper analysis of the legal and jurisdictional basis and the constituent instruments of the particular tribunal.'[147] A number of rulings from so-called hybrid and internationalized courts, which will be examined in the following, palpably illustrate this point pertaining to

[142] Williams (n 128) 249. [143] Ibid, 249–50. [144] Ibid, 250.

[145] Ibid, 251.

[146] See also Sarah Nouwen, 'The Special Court for Sierra Leone and the Immunity of Taylor: The Arrest Warrant Case Continued', 18 *LJIL* (2005) 645, 657.

[147] Williams (n 128) 252.

the customary rules on immunities (Section 6.3.3 on the SCSL) and the principle of legality (Section 6.3.4 on the ECCC).

6.3.3 The SCSL

On 14 August 2000 the UN Security Council issued Resolution 1315 requesting the Secretary General to, inter alia, 'negotiate with the government of Sierra Leone to create an independent special court'. The UN and the government of Sierra Leone entered into the Agreement between the United Nations and the Government of Sierra Leone on the Establishment of a Special Court for Sierra Leone (hereafter SCSL Agreement) on 15 January 2002.[148] Article 1 of the SCSL Agreement reads: 'There is hereby established a Special Court for Sierra Leone to prosecute persons who bear the greatest responsibility for serious violations of international humanitarian law and Sierra Leonean law committed in the territory of Sierra Leone since 30 November 1996.'

On 7 March 2003, while he was still head of state of Liberia, the SCSL indicted Charles Taylor. Taylor's defence claimed that he enjoyed immunity *ratione personae* because exceptions to this rule can only 'derive from other rules of international law such as Security Council resolutions under Chapter VII of the ... UN Charter'.[149] To the contrary, the prosecutor submitted:

> Customary international law permits international criminal tribunals to indict acting Heads of State and the Special Court is an international court established under international law.... The lack of Chapter VII powers does not affect the Special Court's jurisdiction over Heads of State. The International Criminal Court ('ICC'), which does not have Chapter VII powers, explicitly denies immunity to Heads of State for international crimes.[150]

The Appeals Chamber dealt with the issue in two steps. It first considered whether the SCSL is an 'international criminal tribunal'. In particular, the Appeals Chamber assessed the implications of the fact that the SCSL—as opposed to the ICTY and ICTR—had not been set up by the Security Council acting under Chapter VII. In the Appeals Chamber's opinion, the crux of the matter was not whether Chapter VII powers had been invoked, but rather whether the SCSL Agreement reflected the will of the international community. The Appeals Chamber stated:

> It is to be observed that in carrying out its duties under its responsibility for the maintenance of international peace and security, the Security Council acts on behalf of the members of the United Nations. The Agreement between the United Nations and Sierra Leone is thus an agreement between all members of the United Nations and Sierra Leone. This fact makes the Agreement an expression of the will of the international community. The Special Court in such circumstances is truly international.[151]

[148] 2178 *UNTS* 138.

[149] *Prosecutor v. Charles Ghankay Taylor*, SCSL-2003-01-I, Appeals Chamber, Decision on Immunity from Jurisdiction, 31 May 2004, para. 6 (hereafter *Charles Taylor Decision on Immunity*).

[150] Ibid, para. 9.

[151] *Charles Taylor Decision on Immunity* (n 149) para. 38. The construction of the SCSL Agreement between the UN and Sierra Leone as an agreement between all members of the UN and Sierra Leone has (rightfully) been widely criticized. See, for example, Frulli, 'The Question of Charles Taylor's Immunity',

It then went on to assess the applicability of the customary rules on immunity. Relying in particular on paragraph 61 of the ICJ's Judgment in the *Arrest Warrant* case (cited and discussed in what follows), the Appeals Chamber found that Heads of State (and other high-ranking State officials) do not enjoy immunity *ratione personae* before international criminal courts. It concluded, inter alia, that 'the principle of state immunity derives from the equality of sovereign states and therefore has no relevance to international criminal tribunals which are not organs of a state but derive their mandate from the international community.'[152] Arguably, this reasoning misrepresents what the ICJ actually said in *Arrest Warrant*. In the last section of the (in)famous paragraph 61 of its Judgment, the Court stated that:

[A]n incumbent or former Minister for Foreign Affairs may be subject to criminal proceedings before certain international criminal courts, where they have jurisdiction. Examples include the International Criminal Tribunal for the former Yugoslavia, and the International Criminal Tribunal for Rwanda, established pursuant to Security Council resolutions under Chapter VII of the United Nations Charter, and the future International Criminal Court created by the 1998 Rome Convention. The latter's Statute expressly provides, in Article 27, paragraph 2, that '[i]mmunities or special procedural rules which may attach to the official capacity of a person, whether under national or international law, shall not bar the Court from exercising its jurisdiction over such a person'.[153]

Along with the Appeals Chamber, a number of scholars, including professors Diane Orentlicher[154] and Philippe Sands,[155] who were appointed by the Chamber as *amici curiae*, have interpreted this section to imply that the label 'international criminal court' always carries with it specific legal ramifications, in particular exceptions to the rules on immunities under customary international law.[156] In other words, these authors find that once it has been established that a criminal tribunal is 'international', exceptions to the customary rules on immunities by definition apply.

It is debatable, however, whether this line of reasoning in fact corresponds to the ICJ's statement in *Arrest Warrant*. By including the words 'certain' and 'where they have jurisdiction' in paragraph 61 and subsequently naming examples of tribunals, which according to their founding documents override the customary rules on immunities under particular circumstances, the ICJ did not necessarily imply that exceptions to the rules on immunities apply to all judicial bodies which may be categorized as 'international criminal courts'. Had that been the ICJ's intention, the Court would presumably have clarified the criteria for acquiring such a label.

2 *Journal of International Criminal Justice* (2004) 1118, 1124, and Nouwen (n 146) 651. This question is, however, not of particular interest for present purposes and will not be explored further.

[152] *Charles Taylor Decision on Immunity* (n 149) para. 51.

[153] *Arrest Warrant of 11 April 2000 (Democratic Republic of the Congo v. Belgium)* (Judgment) [2002] ICJ Rep 3.

[154] Diane Orentlicher, 'Submission of the Amicus Curiae on Head of State Immunity', *The Prosecutor v. Charles Ghankay Taylor*, Case SCSL-2003-01-I, 23 October 2003, 13–14.

[155] Philippe Sands, 'Submission of the Amicus Curiae on Head of State Immunity', *The Prosecutor v. Charles Ghankay Taylor*, Case SCSL-2003-01-I, 23 October 2003, para. 56.

[156] See also William Schabas, 'The Special Tribunal for Lebanon: Is a "Tribunal of an International Character" Equivalent to an "International Criminal Court"?' 21 *LJIL* (2008) 513, 514.

More likely, paragraph 61 simply underlines that the importance of the customary rules on immunities is to be decided in accordance with the relevant sources of law pertaining to each individual court. The mentioned courts were merely examples of international courts before which the rules on immunities do not apply for various reasons, *in casu* the bindingness of the Statutes of the ICTY and ICTR adopted under Chapter VII of the UN Charter and the bindingness of the ICC Statute on its member states. In other words, the ICJ did not rule out the possibility of an 'international court' before which the rules on immunity would apply.[157]

It lies beyond the present purpose to determine whether or not the Appeals Chamber erred in denying Charles Taylor immunity *ratione personae*.[158] The aim here is only to underline that the Appeals Chamber's reliance on 'the will of the international community'—which can be traced back to the 'States-only' conception of international legal personality—in order to categorize the SCSL as an international criminal court was clearly insufficient.

The applicability of the doctrine of joint criminal enterprise (hereafter JCE) before the ECCC provides another interesting case study of a criminal court's reliance on 'the involvement of the international community'.

6.3.4 The ECCC

The ECCC was set up by the Law on the Establishment of the Extraordinary Chambers in the Courts of Cambodia for the Prosecution of Crimes Committed During the Period of Democratic Kampuchea passed by the Cambodian National Assembly in 2001.[159] Thus, in contrast to the SCSL, the ECCC is not set up under an international agreement, but under domestic Cambodian law. The 2003 Agreement between the United Nations and the Royal Government of Cambodia concerning the Prosecution under Cambodian Law of Crimes Committed during the Period of Democratic Kampuchea details how the UN assists and participates in the ECCC.[160]

In Case 002 involving the most senior officials of the Khmer Rouge regime, the question foreseeably arose whether imposing JCE liability on the accused would constitute a violation of the principle of *nullum crimen sine lege*. Of particular interest for present purposes is the argument raised by the defence team of one of the accused, Ieng Sary, that the ECCC should apply the test of legality following from

[157] There is little indication in para. 61 that the ICJ found Article 27(2) of ICC Statute to apply vis-à-vis third States. The ICC Statute cannot override the rules on immunity under customary international law unless it is binding on the State in question—either because that State has ratified the Statute, or because the relevant situation has been referred to the Court by the UN Security Council in accordance with Article 13(b). See further Dapo Akande, 'International Law Immunities and the International Criminal Court', 98 *AJIL* (2004) 407, 416ff.

[158] See, for example, Zsuzsanna Deen-Racsmány, 'Prosecutor v. Taylor: The Status of the Special Court of Sierra Leone and Its Implications for Immunity', 18 *LJIL* (2005) 299, 313–20.

[159] The law as amended on 27 October 2004 is available at http://www.eccc.gov.kh/en/documents/legal/law-establishment-extraordinary-chambers-amended (accessed 21 January 2018).

[160] 2329 *UNTS* 117.

domestic Cambodian Law (as opposed to Article 15 of the ICCPR), because it is a domestic court of Cambodia.[161]

Unfortunately, none of the rulings on the applicability of JCE liability in Case 002 issued by the Office of the Co-Investigating Judges (hereafter OCIJ),[162] the Pre-Trial Chamber,[163] or the Trial Chamber[164] considered the legal nature of the ECCC in any great detail.

In support of its application of JCE liability under customary international law, the OCIJ relied exclusively on the fact that the ECCC 'holds indicia of an international court applying international law': 'Considering the international aspects of the ECCC, and considering that the jurisprudence relied upon in articulating JCE pre-existed the events under investigation at the ECCC, the Co-Investigating Judges find that there is a basis under international law for applying JCE'.[165]

The OCIJ did not elaborate on what it meant by 'indicia of an international court', but simply referred to a ruling regarding Case 001 in which the Pre-Trial Chamber concluded that the ECCC is a 'special internationalized tribunal'. In that ruling the Pre-Trial Chamber had stated:

> In reaching its conclusion, the Pre-Trial Chamber also refers to the decision of the Appeals Chamber of the Special Court for Sierra Leone in the case of *Taylor*, where it considered the indicia of an international court included the facts that the court is established by treaty, that it was 'an expression of the will of the international community', that it is considered 'part of the machinery of international justice' and that its jurisdiction involves trying the most serious international crimes.[166]

In its *20 May 2010 Decision*, the Pre-Trial Chamber overruled the OCIJ on this point by noting that it is 'immaterial whether the ECCC is a domestic or an international court because this does not impact on a finding that JCE is applicable, due to the clear terms of Articles 1 and 2 of the Establishment Law'.[167] According to the Pre-Trial Chamber, it follows from Article 2 that the ECCC has jurisdiction to apply forms of liability recognized under customary international law during the Khmer Rouge regime.[168] The Pre-Trial Chamber then stated: 'For the same reason, even if the OCIJ finding on an autonomous legal regime was in error, it would be superfluous and would not invalidate the finding on the applicability of the JCE

[161] Case No. 002/19-09-2007-ECCC-OCIJ, Ieng Sary's Supplementary Observations on the Application of the Theory of Joint Criminal Enterprise at the ECCC, 24 November 2008, para. 63. See further Case No. 002/19-09-2007-ECCC/OCIJ(PTC 75), Ieng Sary's appeal against the closing order, 25 October 2010, paras 103–114.

[162] Case No. 002/19-09-2007-ECCC-OCIJ, Order on the Application at the ECCC of the Form of Liability Known as Joint Criminal Enterprise, 8 December 2009 (hereafter *8 December 2009 Order*).

[163] Case No. 002/19-09-2007-ECCC/OCIJ (PTC38), Public Decision on the Appeals Against the Co-Investigative Judges Order on Joint Criminal Enterprise, 20 May 2010 (hereafter *20 May 2010 Decision*).

[164] Case No. 002/19-09-2007-ECCC/TC, Decision on the Applicability of Joint Criminal Enterprise, 12 September 2011 (hereafter *12 September 2011 Decision*).

[165] *8 December 2009 Order* (n 162) para. 21.

[166] Case No. 001/18-07-2007-ECCC-OCIJ (PTC01), Decision on Appeal against Provisional Detention Order of Kaing Guek Eav alias 'Duch', 3 December 2007, para. 20.

[167] *20 May 2010 Decision* (n 163) para. 47.

[168] Ibid, para. 48.

before the ECCC.'[169] Although perhaps not in unequivocal terms, the Pre-Trial Chamber thereby seems to confirm that the ECCC belongs to the national legal system of Cambodia. However, in a subsequent ruling, the Pre-Trial Chamber has stated: 'The extraordinary and specific nature of the ECCC as an internationalised court established by mutual agreement between the United Nations and the Cambodian authorities directs the Pre-Trial Chamber to examine the standard for the principle of legality to be applied before it by looking explicitly at its establishing instruments, the ECCC Law and Agreement.'[170]

From the point of view of international law the result is unproblematic since the standard set by Article 15 of the ICCPR does not depend on the nature of the criminal tribunal.[171] But the question remains whether it would have been relevant—from the perspective of domestic law—to consider in more detail if retroactive incorporation of JCE as a form of liability under customary international law was in compliance with Cambodian constitutional law.[172] This is of course strictly an issue of domestic Cambodian law, which will not be explored further in the present context. The point to be made here is simply that a lack of a clear distinction between international and domestic criminal courts is not just a formal matter. In particular, the terminological confusion pertaining to so-called hybrid or internationalized tribunals raises material legal questions that call for answers.

6.4 Conclusion: The Legal Personality of Individuals in International Criminal Law

Alongside international human rights law, which is the subject of Chapter 7, international criminal law is commonly put forward as evidence that the international

[169] Ibid.

[170] Case No. 002/19-09-2007-ECCC/OCIJ (PTC75), Public Decision on Ieng Sary's Appeal Against the Closing Order, 11 April 2011, para. 222 (hereafter *11 April 2011 Decision)*. The Trial Chamber affirmed this ruling in *12 September 2011 Decision* (n 164). See also Case No. 002/19-09-2007-ECCC/TC, Case 002/01 Judgment, 7 August 2014, para. 691. In the Appeal Judgment, the Supreme Court Chamber merely 'noted with approval' the PTC's findings regarding JCE III liability. Case No. 002/19-09-2007-ECCC/SC, Appeal Judgment, 23 November 2016, para. 791. See further paras 1122–1143.

[171] See, for example, Valentina Spiga, 'Non-retroactivity of Criminal Law', 9 *Journal of International Criminal Justice* (2011) 5–23, and Manfred Nowak, *UN Covenant on Civil and Political Rights: CCPR Commentary* (2nd edn, Engel, 2005) 360.

[172] A parallel objection can be made to the ECCC's findings on the application of the *ne bis in idem* principle:

> The Pre-Trial Chamber finds that no international *ne bis in idem* protection exists under the ICCPR. Taking into account its finding below that the ECCC is an internationalised court functioning separately from the Cambodian court structure, the Pre-Trial Chamber finds that the 'internal *ne bis in idem* principle' as enshrined in Article 14(7) of the ICCPR does not apply to the proceedings before the ECCC. In these circumstances, the Pre-Trial Chamber will seek guidance in the procedural rules established at the international level to determine if Ieng Sary's previous conviction by a national Cambodian court shall prevent the ECCC from exercising jurisdiction against him for the offences charged in the Closing Order.

11 April 2011 Decision (n 170) para. 131. See also Williams (n 128) 385–7.

legal system has evolved from a 'States-only' framework to encompassing non-State entities, including individuals. As the core objective of international criminal law is to impose international legal obligations directly on individuals, it might appear redundant to examine the international legal personality of individuals in this particular field. Two distinct points, however, warrant scrutiny in the context of the present study. First of all, it is not straightforward whether the practice of international criminal law supports the 'individualistic' or the 'a posteriori' conception of international legal personality. Second, the definitional distinction between 'international', 'internationalized', and 'domestic' criminal courts continues to give rise to considerable confusion, which seemingly originates from ingrained hesitance among post-Second World War international legal scholars to treat individuals as subjects of international law.

As apparent from Section 6.2, how one views the nature and source of individual responsibility in international criminal law is contingent upon one's approach to custom as a source of international law in general, and to the available case law in particular. While there is arguably significant support for the 'individualistic' conception of international legal personality in the practice of international criminal courts, these judgments may also be read as consistent with the 'a posteriori' conception and the notion that international legal personality must be determined on a case-by-case basis. The answer turns on whether one finds the relevant case law to sufficiently document a customary norm providing for individual responsibility for the international crime in question.

Pertaining to the definition of an 'international criminal court', the circumstances of the establishment of the IMT are of key importance. It is submitted that in the special situation of unconditional surrender, the Allied Powers had the choice between conferring obligations on German war criminals through domestic legislation or a treaty. Substantial elements of the London Agreement, including the IMT Charter, indicate that it is indeed a treaty. For that reason alone, the IMT is to be categorized as an international criminal court, regardless of the degree of 'involvement of the international community'.

Nevertheless, Woetzel's emphasis on the 'involvement of the international community' in the definition of an 'international' criminal court still dominates among both international legal scholars and practitioners. As mentioned in Section 6.3.2, Williams has recently advocated that we place criminal courts on a sliding scale according to the involvement of the international community. She acknowledges, however, that this exercise does not help to resolve the legal issues that such courts face. In accordance with the analysis of the practice of the SCSL and the ECCC in Sections 6.3.3 and 6.3.4, Williams concludes that questions concerning the applicability of the rules on immunities and the principle of legality require 'a proper analysis of the legal and jurisdictional basis and the constituent instruments of the particular tribunal.'[173] Against this background, it seems reasonable to inquire about the added value of categorizing criminal courts according to the degree of involvement

[173] Williams (n 128) 252.

of the international community. If anything, the above-mentioned examples indicate that this criterion in fact confuses the analysis that Williams calls for.

In accordance with the argument put forward in the present book,[174] the distinction between national and international criminal courts should revolve solely around the nature of the founding document: a court set up under international law is international, whereas a court set up under domestic law is domestic. The terms 'internationalized', 'hybrid', or 'mixed' courts have no independent legal meaning and should be abandoned. The proposed terminology would not only emphasize the decisiveness of each court's founding document relating to, for example, jurisdiction and applicable law. It would also be a consistent reflection of the overall distinction between the international legal system and national legal system(s), and would underline that the norms of the one legal system ultimately decide the effect given to the norms of the other.

[174] See Section 1.2.

7

The Legal Personality of Individuals in International Human Rights Law

International human rights law and, in particular, the right of individuals to enforce human rights law before an international judicial body are commonly presented as the principal evidence that the structure of the international system has changed since the end of the Second World War so as to include individuals as its subjects. Against this background, one might presume international human rights law to be a field in which the theory on international legal personality has played a particularly significant role. This chapter examines whether or not this assumption finds support in practice.

A detailed analysis of each of the numerous international and regional human rights instruments adopted during the past seven decades would greatly exceed the confines of the present work. Consequently, the following study concentrates on one prominent example, namely the European Convention on Human Rights (ECHR), which was the first proper 'human rights convention' to confer direct rights on individuals and to provide them with independent means of enforcement.

Section 7.1 opens with a brief presentation of key events in the (pre)history of international human rights law before the Second World War. Section 7.2's study of the ECHR comes in three parts. It examines the influence of the concept of international legal personality on the following: first, the evolution of the means of enforcement available to individuals under the Convention (Section 7.2.1); second, the European Court of Human Rights' (ECtHR's) interpretation of the Convention's material provisions (Section 7.2.2); and third, the Court's practice relating to the ECHR vis-à-vis other international legal instruments (Section 7.2.3). Section 7.3 concludes the chapter with a discussion of the widespread notion that post-Second World War developments in international human rights law (in conjunction with the developments in international criminal law discussed in Chapter 6) have fundamentally changed the international legal personality of individuals.

7.1 International Human Rights Law before the Second World War

It is common ground that a high demand for human rights protection at the international level arose in response to the atrocities of the Second World War. Before embarking on the post-Second World War period in international human rights law, however, it is pertinent to look briefly at some prior examples of international protection extended to individuals and groups of individuals.

7.1.1 The abolition of slavery

The abolition of slavery is frequently cited as the earliest forerunner of contemporary international human rights law. Yet, while the initial domestic legislation abolishing slavery was commonly construed as a right of freedom for every individual slave,[1] the first international legal rules on slavery did not consistently vest rights directly in individuals.

Notably, Article LXIV of the 1890 Brussels Slavery Convention[2] provided that '[a]ny fugitive slave arriving at the frontier of any of the powers mentioned in Article LXII shall be considered free, and shall have the right to claim letters of release from the competent authorities', which seems to indicate an individual right.[3] In 1926, however, the Brussels Slavery Convention was succeeded by the Slavery Convention[4] drawn up within the realm of the League of Nations. As apparent from Article 2, the Slavery Convention did not include individual rights, but rather laid down inter-State obligations:

> The High Contracting Parties undertake, each in respect of the territories placed under its sovereignty, jurisdiction, protection, suzerainty or tutelage, so far as they have not already taken the necessary steps:
>
> (a) To prevent and suppress the slave trade;
> (b) To bring about, progressively and as soon as possible, the complete abolition of slavery in all its forms.[5]

Contemporary international human rights instruments generally articulate the prohibition of slavery as an individual right.[6] The abolition of slavery thus appears to be a straightforward example of an issue relating to the conditions of individual human beings, which had traditionally been perceived as falling within the domestic sphere of each State, but gradually, as States came to see the benefit of collaboration, became the subject of international regulation.

[1] See for example Article III of the British Slavery Abolition Act, 3 & 4 Will. IV c. 73, 28 August 1833: 'all Slaves . . . shall from and after the passing of this Act be absolutely and entirely free to all Intents and Purposes whatsoever'.

[2] Slave Trade and Importation into Africa of Firearms, Ammunition, and Spirituous Liquors (General Act of Brussels), 2 July 1890 (available at https://www.loc.gov/law/help/us-treaties/bevans/m-ust000001-0134.pdf, accessed 21 January 2018).

[3] In contrast, the Brussels Slavery Convention did not confer direct obligations on individuals who participated in slave trading. Rather, the Member States undertook, according to Article V, to enact pertinent provisions in their respective penal laws. See also Section 6.1.1.

[4] Slavery, Servitude, Forced Labour and Similar Institutions and Practices Convention, 25 September 1926, 60 *LNTS* 253.

[5] See also Supplementary Convention on the Abolition of Slavery, 7 September 1956, 255 *UNTS* 3.

[6] See, for example, ECHR, Article 4 and ICCPR, Article 8.

7.1.2 Minorities protection

A number of League of Nations measures extending international protection to certain groups of individuals gave rise to debate on the international legal personality of individuals.[7] Such measures include for example the mandate system[8] established under Article 22 of the Covenant of the League of Nations[9] and the 1933 Convention Relating to the Status of Refugees.[10] But the most remarkable League of Nations initiative in the present context is the scheme set up for the protection of minorities, which is the subject of the rest of the present section.[11]

While proposals to confer rights of protection on all minorities in the Covenant of the League of Nations were suppressed,[12] the Peace Treaties ending the First World War required that treaties with the Allied Powers were signed in order to secure the protection of minorities. For example, Article 93 of the Treaty of Versailles stated: 'Poland accepts and agrees to embody in a Treaty with the Principal Allied and Associated Powers such provisions as may be deemed necessary by the said Powers to protect the interests of inhabitants of Poland who differ from the majority of the population in race, language, or religion.'[13]

The Polish Minorities Treaty[14] was the first to be adopted and served as a model for subsequent minorities treaties.[15] Its articles provided a number of

[7] See further Kate Parlett, *The Individual in the International Legal System—Continuity and Change in International Law* (CUP, 2011) 289.

[8] The mandate system placed 'the well-being and development' of inhabitants of the mandated territories under 'a sacred trust of civilisation'. It is not entirely clear whether inhabitants of mandated territories held direct rights vis-à-vis the mandatory state. Some provisions of the mandates were clearly construed as obligations of the mandatory states. See for example Article 8 of the Syria and Lebanon Mandate, reprinted in Quincy Wright, *Mandates under the League of Nations* (University of Chicago Press, 1930) 609, which provided inter alia that 'the Mandatory shall ensure to all complete freedom of conscience'. Other provisions, such as Article 15 of the Palestine (and Transjordan) Mandate, reprinted in ibid, 603, referred to the 'rights' of the inhabitants of the mandates. The Permanent Mandates Commission, which advised the Council on matters relating to the mandates, was authorized to receive petitions from individuals, but these petitions were merely regarded as a source of information. See further ibid, 171.

[9] Covenant of the League of Nations, 28 April 1919, 108 *LNTS* 188.

[10] Convention Relating to the Status of Refugees, 28 October 1933, 159 *LNTS* 3663. See also Convention Concerning to the Status of Refugees Coming from Germany, 10 February 1938, 4461 *LNTS* 61. See further James C. Hathaway, *The Rights of Refugees under International Law* (CUP, 2005) 87–91.

[11] Also during the interwar years, a number of conventions governing the conditions of individuals were drawn up by the International Labour Organization. While the Convention concerning Forced or Compulsory Labour, 28 June 1930, 39 *UNTS* 55, for example, laid down obligations for states, other conventions seemingly conferred direct rights on certain individuals. See for example Article 3(b) of the Convention concerning the Employment of Women before and after Childbirth, 28 November 1919, 38 *UNTS* 53.

[12] James Headlam-Morley, *A Memoir of the Paris Peace Conference 1919* (Methuen & Co. Ltd, 1972) 112–13.

[13] Treaty of St Germain-en-Laye (Austria), 10 September 1919, Article 51, pertaining to Yugoslavia; Treaty of Neuilly (Bulgaria), 27 November 1919, Article 46, pertaining to Greece; Treaty of Trianon (Hungary), 4 June 1920, Article 44, in relation to Yugoslavia. In the case of Turkey, a chapter on the protection of minorities was included in the general peace treaty. See Treaty of Lausanne (Turkey), 24 July 1923, Section III. See further Ed Bates, 'History', in Daniel Moeckli et al. (eds) *International Human Rights Law* (OUP, 2010) 30.

[14] On the practice of the PCIJ concerning the Polish Minorities Treaty, see Section 3.1.2.2.

[15] Inis Lothar Claude, *National Minorities—An International Problem* (Harvard University Press, 1955) 17.

guarantees to minorities in Poland concerning inter alia life and liberty,[16] freedom of religion,[17] acquisition of nationality,[18] recognition of languages, and various freedoms related to education.[19] Generally, these articles were formulated as individual rights accruing directly to members of the minorities. For example, Article 2(2) read: 'All inhabitants of Poland shall be entitled to the free exercise, whether public or private, of any creed, religion or belief, whose practices are not inconsistent with public order or public morals.' Similarly, Article 8 provided: 'Polish nationals who belong to racial, religious or linguistic minorities . . . shall have an equal right to establish, manage and control . . . schools and other educational establishments, with the right to use their own language and to exercise their religion freely therein.'[20]

According to Article 12, the obligations undertaken by Poland, which affected 'persons belonging to racial, religious or linguistic minorities' were 'of international concern' and were to be 'placed under the guarantee of the League of Nations.'[21] This guarantee was collective in the sense that it could be exercised by any State regardless of its relationship with the minority in question. Article 12 expressly provided that 'any member of the Council of the League of Nations shall have the right to bring to the attention of the Council any infraction, or any danger of infraction' of the rights included in the treaty. Notably, the idea of allowing individuals or groups of individuals to bring a case directly before the League of Nations had been rejected. Sir James Headlam-Morley, who was a member of the British delegation to Versailles and contributed significantly to the drafting of the minorities treaties, had initially favoured granting such a right to individuals under extraordinary circumstances:

> As a general principle it is, I believe, now accepted that it is most undesirable and would be most dangerous to allow the inhabitants or citizens of any state direct approach to the League except through their own government. If we once allow this principle, the French in Canada, the Jews in America, the Roman Catholics in England or in France, the Welsh, the Irish, the Scottish Highlanders, the Basques, Bretons or Catalonians, might approach the League . . . . [I]f the right is to be given to individual inhabitants, citizens or communities to approach the League, this can only be recognized as quite exceptional . . . .[22]

But Headlam-Morley was subsequently convinced that allowing individuals to appeal directly to the Council of the League of Nations 'would be difficult under any circumstances', because States would not accept such a system: 'This could be represented as a serious infraction of sovereignty, which would undoubtedly draw

[16] See Treaty of Peace between the United States, the British Empire, France, Italy, Japan and Poland, 28 June 1919, 13 *AJIL* Supp. (1919) 423–40, Article 2(1).

[17] Ibid, Article 2(2). [18] Ibid, Articles 3–6. [19] Ibid, Articles 7 and 9–10.

[20] See also Articles 3, 5, and 7.

[21] Moreover, Article 12 included Poland's consent to the jurisdiction of the PCIJ over disputes concerning the minorities treaties. See for example *Settlers of German Origin in Poland* (Advisory Opinion) [1923], PCIJ Ser. B, No. 6, 25, and *Acquisition of Polish Nationality* (Advisory Opinion) [1923] PCIJ Ser. B, No. 7, 16. See further Section 3.1.2.2.

[22] See Headlam-Morley (n 12) 109.

forth most energetic protests. These protests would be dangerous because they could point out that the Great Powers themselves do not allow such an appeal to their own nationals.'[23]

Evidently, the decision not to include in the minorities treaties a right of individuals to file complaints was based on considerations of political and pragmatic nature rather than conceptual misgivings related to the (lack of) international legal personality of individuals.[24]

The procedure to be followed when a State wished to complain to the Council of the League of Nations over another State's non-compliance was left open by the minorities treaties. A procedural system was subsequently adopted by the Council on 22 October 1920 on the basis of the Tittoni Report written by former Italian Prime Minister, Tommaso Tittoni.[25] According to the report, the treaties did not exclude the possibility that, for example, individuals belonging to a minority could call potential violations to the attention of the Council. However, 'this act must retain the nature of a petition, or a report pure and simple; it cannot have the legal effect of putting the matter before the Council and calling upon it to intervene.'[26] Since petitions submitted to the Council by individuals would thus have no consequences, unless the matter was put on the Council's agenda by a member,[27] no legal means of enforcement were conferred on individuals. Rather, individuals served as mere informers of the Council. To implement the Tittoni report, the Council established a Minorities Section which essentially screened petitions by individuals. If a petition was declared acceptable, a Minorities Committee would be set up to examine the merits.[28] There is little available information about the work of the Minorities Section and the Minorities Committees, which were not given publicity. The individual petitioner seems to have played a very inferior role, and he was not regarded as having a special legal interest in the case: '[T]he informative character of the petition remains unaffected, whether the petition comes from persons belonging to the minority itself or not.'[29]

A more elaborate minorities protection scheme was set up under the 1922 Geneva Convention Relating to Upper Silesia. It not only included a principle of reciprocity and more extensive material provisions, but also encompassed an independent right of petition and full procedural capacity of individuals before the Upper Silesia Mixed Commission.[30]

[23] Ibid, 139.

[24] See also Jacob Robinson et al., *Were the Minorities Treaties a Failure?* (Antin Press Inc., 1943) 85.

[25] 1 *LNOJ* (1920) 8–9. [26] Ibid, 9.

[27] See further A. W. Brian Simpson, *Human Rights and the End of Empire—Britain and the Genesis of the European Convention* (OUP, 2001) 130–1.

[28] The procedure is described in detail in *Report of the Work of the League of Nations in Relation to Protection of Minorities Prepared by a Committee Constituted by the Council of the League in Its Resolution of March 7, 1929*, reprinted in P. de Azcárate, *League of Nations and National Minorities—An Experiment* (Carnegie, 1945) 163. See also Helmer Rosting, 'Protection of Minorities by the League of Nations' 17 *AJIL* (1923) 641, 653ff.

[29] de Azcárate (n 28) 199–200. See also ibid, 119, and see further Robinson et al. (n 24) 247–65.

[30] See further Section 4.2.2.3.

With the exception perhaps of the latter dispute settlement body, the enforcement system set up in the interwar period to secure the protection of minorities has generally been regarded as unsuccessful.[31] Even so, it is hardly disputable that the minorities treaties entailed remarkable examples of direct individual rights at the time.[32] What is also remarkable is that the scholarly debate on the concept of international legal personality, which was flourishing in the interwar period,[33] seemingly had little bearing on the formation of the material provisions of the minorities treaties and the means of their enforcement.

7.2 International Human Rights Law after the Second World War: The Example of the ECHR

The UN Charter makes several references to human rights. For example, the Preamble reaffirms 'faith in fundamental human rights', while Article 1(3) states 'promoting and encouraging respect for human rights and for fundamental freedoms' as one of the purposes of the UN. Yet the Charter does not include any legally binding provisions conferring human rights on individuals. Likewise, the provisions of the Universal Declaration of Human Rights (hereafter UDHR) adopted by the UN General Assembly on 10 December 1948 did not impose any legal obligations on the UN Member States, although they were worded as to confer direct rights on individuals. It was explicitly envisioned by the vast majority of delegations that the UDHR would be followed by a legally binding instrument.[34] The adoption of such instruments—as it turned out—would take almost two decades to achieve. The 1966 ICCPR and the International Covenant on Economic, Social and Cultural Rights, however, will not be discussed in detail at this juncture.[35] Instead, the following sections are devoted to the ECHR, which was adopted shortly after the UDHR.

Although the ECHR was the first actual human rights treaty to confer direct rights on individuals, this is not a feature of the Convention that has given rise to much controversy. Indeed, it is a common notion that 'the novelty of the [ECHR] does not reside in the principles of the substantive law it embodies but in the means it supplies for their enforcement.'[36]

[31] See for example Robinson et al. (n 24) 107–8.

[32] Some scholars question whether the minorities treaties provided for rights of individual human beings or the minority as a group. See for example Parlett (n 7) 284–5 and 295. As stated in Section 1.3.1, this distinction is not attributed particular weight in the present work.

[33] See Chapter 2.

[34] See further Hersch Lauterpacht, 'The Universal Declaration on Human Rights', 25 *BYBIL* (1948) 354, 359.

[35] There is little dispute that both Covenants include direct individual rights which correspond to obligations of states. The UN human rights conventions related to particular issues, such as the Convention on the Elimination of All Forms of Racial Discrimination, 21 December 1965, 660 *UNTS* 195, are also left out of the analysis. For discussion of human rights and state obligations in the UN system, including the various means of enforcement, see Parlett (n 7) 312ff.

[36] 'Written communication by Karl Doehring for the second International Conference about the European Convention on Human Rights held in Vienna from 18–20 October 1965', reprinted in A.

A substantial portion of the present chapter is therefore devoted to a thorough examination of the evolution of the right of individuals to seize the ECtHR. Based on an examination of reports and meeting minutes from a number of organs set up under the auspices of the Council of Europe,[37] the following section discusses the influence of the theoretical debate about the international legal personality of individuals on the drafting processes leading up to the adoption of the ECHR in 1950 and Protocol 9 in 1990.

7.2.1 The procedural status of individuals before the ECtHR[38]

The very first draft of the ECHR was presented on 12 July 1949 by the International Juridical Section of the European Movement.[39] It was initially reviewed by the Consultative Assembly and submitted to the Committee on Legal and Administrative Questions, which prepared the famous Teitgen Report. Then, the revised draft was presented to the Committee of Experts on Human Rights and a Conference of Senior Officials set up by the Committee of Ministers. Ultimately, the draft was referred back to the Consultative Assembly and the Legal Committee before the final adoption by the Committee of Ministers. The analysis in what follows will focus mainly on the work of the Consultative Assembly, the Committee of Ministers, and the Conference of Senior Officials.[40]

Notably, Article 7 of the European Movement's draft drew no distinction between Member States and individuals with regard to the right to submit petitions:

(a) Any State a party to this Convention and any natural or corporate person in the territory of any such State shall have the right to petition the Council of Europe in respect of any infringement of Part I[41] of this Convention.
(b) The petitions shall be dealt with by a European Human Rights Commission ... and in proper cases by a European Court of Human Rights ....[42]

H. Robertson (ed.), *Human Rights in National and International Law* (Manchester University Press, 1968) 31.

[37] The Statute of the Council of Europe was signed on 5 May 1949 by ten European states wishing to achieve greater unity 'for the purpose of safeguarding and realising the ideals and principles which are their common heritage and facilitating their economic and social progress' (cf. Article 1). According to Article 10, the Council was to consist of two primary organs: the Committee of Ministers and the Consultative Assembly.

[38] This section is based on Astrid Kjeldgaard-Pedersen, 'The Evolution of the Right of Individuals to Seise the European Court of Human Rights', 12 *JHIL* (2010) 267.

[39] The European Movement was formally created on 25 October 1948 and served as a forum for the coordination of organizations set up in the aftermath of the Second World War. The Movement's first major accomplishment was the creation of the Council of Europe. According to the International Juridical Section, its draft ECHR had 'no other aim than to aid the Committee in its task.' The draft was not included in the original confidential version of the *travaux préparatoires*, but it is reproduced as an appendix to the *Collected Edition of the Travaux Préparatoires of the Convention*, Vols I–VII, (1975–85) (hereafter *Travaux Préparatoires*). See Vol. I, 48 and 296–302.

[40] For a detailed account see Kjeldgaard-Pedersen (n 38).

[41] Part I accounted for the protected rights.

[42] *Travaux Préparatoires* (n 39), Vol. I, 298.

This original idea, however, was abandoned early on in the drafting process and replaced by the proposal of a system that gave individuals the right to file an application with the Commission, but only allowed the Commission and Member States to seize the Court. The Commission would undertake a contestation of individuals' applications and, if necessary, an enquiry.[43] If it decided not to reject the application, it was to 'try to effect a reconciliation of the opposing parties',[44] and if this process failed, the Commission could 'on a majority vote, decide to transmit the documents in the case to the Court to obtain a legal ruling.'[45]

Several members of the Consultative Assembly had substantial objections to the outlined enforcement mechanisms of the ECHR. For example, British member Ungoed-Thomas stated: 'We are not a federation here. We are not at the moment a small League of Nations. We have not a federal constitution. We have not therefore any need for a federal Court.'[46] Yet, the majority seemingly concurred with this eloquent statement by Teitgen:[47]

> That the international machinery should be at the disposal of the victims is . . . the only means we have of persuading the men and women of Europe that something new has been done and that an advance has been achieved. We must say to them that even if the States take no further interest in them, and even if no one takes action on their behalf, they may, by virtue of their dignity as men, avail themselves on their own behalf of an international organ of protection.[48]

Subsequently, the Committee of Ministers decided to refer the revised draft Convention to a Conference of Senior Officials instructed by the governments to prepare the ground for the final political decisions.[49] Charged with the task of presenting to the Committee of Ministers a single text to consider, the Senior Officials had their work cut out for them. With regard to the possible establishment of the ECtHR, the Conference decided on the compromise solution proposed by the Swedish delegate: an optional court.[50]

On the matter of the individual's right to petition the Commission, the vast majority of officials voted in favour. The possibility of the individual safeguarding his or her rights by autonomous means was considered an essential element of the

[43] Ibid, 210. [44] Ibid. [45] Ibid. [46] Ibid, 168.

[47] *Travaux Préparatoires* (n 39), Vol. III, 22ff. Teitgen is often referred to as the 'father of the Convention'. See, for example Carlo Russo, 'The Drafting History of the European Convention on Human Rights and Fundamental Freedoms', in Salvino Busuttil (ed.), *Mainly Human Rights—Studies in Honour of J. J. Cremona* (Foundation Internationale Malte, 1999) 234, and Luzius Wildhaber, 'A Constitutional Future for the European Court of Human Rights', 23 *Human Rights Law Journal* (2002) 161, 162. He was a famous member of the French Resistance, and after the war he became an important figure in French law and politics. He served as minister in several French governments and was appointed judge at the ECtHR in 1976.

[48] *Travaux Préparatoires* (n 39), Vol. II, 178.

[49] *Travaux Préparatoires* (n 39), Vol. IV, 84.

[50] Ibid, 250. Only the United Kingdom and the Netherlands voted against, while the Danish and Norwegian delegates were in favour only if the compromise could obtain the support of a majority of the governments. For the final provisions on the jurisdiction of the Court see Articles 45–48 of the original ECHR.

Convention's purpose.[51] Only the British, Greek, and Dutch delegates reserved the position of their governments in fear that the right of petition would be abused in the interests of subversive propaganda. The British delegate stated inter alia that 'difficulties would arise due to the ideological struggle by which the world was at the moment divided.'[52]

The position of individuals was among the most controversial issues to be settled at the fifth session of the Committee of Ministers in August 1950. The Committee was to agree on a final draft Convention to be transmitted to the Consultative Assembly. Seven out of twelve delegations were in agreement on the wording of Article 23 of the Senior Officials' draft,[53] whereas five delegations proposed to suppress the right of petition of individuals.[54] To get out of the deadlock, the British delegate proposed a compromise: Just as the settlement reached with regard to the establishment of the Court, it should be optional for Member States to grant individuals the right to petition the Commission.[55] The new Article 25 read:

1. The Commission may receive petitions addressed to the Secretary General of the Council of Europe from any person, non-governmental organisation or group of individuals claiming to be the victim of a violation by one of the High Contracting Parties of the rights secured by this Convention, provided that the High Contracting Party complained against has declared that it recognises the competence of the Commission to receive such petitions. Those of the High Contracting Parties who have made such a declaration undertake not to hinder in any way the effective exercise of this right.
2. Such declarations may be made for a specific period.
3. The declarations shall be notified to the Secretary General of the Council of Europe who shall transmit copies thereof to the High Contracting Parties and publish them.

[51] Ibid, 132–4 and 252. The Conference agreed, however, that it would be useful to fix a time limit for filing a petition with the Commission. Ibid, 264. Accordingly, Articles 23 and 24 of the report of the Conference read as follows (ibid, 284):

> 23. Any person, any non-governmental organisation or any group of individuals, which claims to be the victim of a violation by one of the High Contracting Parties of the rights secured by this Convention may petition the Commission in an application addressed to the Secretary-General of the Council of Europe. The High Contracting Parties undertake not to hinder in any way the effective exercise of this right.
>
> 24. The Commission may only deal with the matter after all domestic remedies have been exhausted according to the generally recognised rules of international law and within a period of six months from the date on which the final decision was taken.

[52] Ibid, 134. See also the statement by the British representative at the fifth session of the Committee of Ministers: 'He thought it was essential to take into consideration the current political situation in which their political enemies, the Communists, would take every opportunity to abuse the right of access to the Commission of Human Rights.' *Travaux Préparatoires* (n 39), Vol. V, 114. The policy of the British government on this matter is dealt with at length in Simpson (n 27) 707ff.

[53] See note 51.

[54] *Travaux Préparatoires* (n 39), Vol. V, 98. The British, Greek, and Dutch delegates maintained the observations presented by their representatives during the Conference of Senior Officials, whereas Belgium and one other State (it is not shown in the meeting minutes which) had apparently changed position.

[55] Ibid, 68. The Chairman of the Committee speaking as the representative of Ireland was the only member who refuted this idea. In his opinion '[a] Convention on Human Rights which did not grant any right of redress to individuals was not worth the paper it was written on.' In the end, he reluctantly agreed that his vote be regarded as an abstention in order to achieve a unanimous decision. Ibid, 112.

4. The Commission shall only exercise the powers provided for in this Article when at least six High Contracting Parties are bound by declarations made in accordance with the preceding paragraphs.[56]

When the Consultative Assembly reconvened in August 1949 to discuss the draft submitted by the Committee of Ministers, many of its members, including the co-authors of the very first draft, Maxwell-Fyfe and Teitgen, expressed sincere disappointment that not only the jurisdiction of the Court but also the right of petition of individuals ended up being optional for Member States.[57]

While there seemed to be consensus among the majority of the Assembly that it was better to 'accept the Convention in this form rather than to have no Convention at all', they agreed to 'seek to make improvements.'[58] Their efforts were, however, of no avail. By a letter of 5 November 1950, Count Sforza, the Chairman of the Committee of Ministers, informed the president of the Consultative Assembly of the signing of the Convention and the referral of most of the Assembly's proposed amendments to the Committee of Experts for further study.[59]

The Committee of Experts convened in Paris in February 1951. Its work focused on drafting Protocol 1 to the ECHR. The rest of the Assembly's suggestions for amendments were left out of the discussion. The matter of the position of the individual in the Convention's control machinery was not to be dealt with substantially by the organs of the Council of Europe for the next twenty years.[60]

Given that the Convention's control machinery is consistently put forward as a key example of the reformation of the status of individuals in the international legal system since the Second World War,[61] it is noteworthy that there was hardly any mention of the concept of international legal personality during the preparation of the original ECHR. The content of the Convention's provisions seems to have been exclusively determined by political will and pragmatic considerations. Apparently, the main reason for the inferior status of the applicant was that most members of the Committee of Ministers were reluctant to subject their State to the interference by an international court with jurisdiction to hear individual complaints regarding human rights. Those who were opposed to setting up an extensive protection mechanism argued that the Member States of the Council of Europe were not ready for such a system. They feared that it would be abused, mainly by Communists, for subversive propaganda. During the entire drafting process of the original ECHR and Protocol 9, the concept of international legal personality was seemingly referred to only once. That was when Maxwell-Fyfe expressed his regret to the Consultative Assembly in August 1950 that the right of individual petition had become optional.

[56] Article 26 was identical to Article 24 of the previous draft. Ibid, 132.

[57] See for example ibid, 210 (Lord Layton), 226 (Maxwell-Fyfe), 236–7 (Lannung), 294 (Teitgen), 316 (Foster).

[58] Ibid, 228 (Maxwell-Fyfe). See also, for example, 282 (Teitgen).

[59] Ibid, 42 and 44.

[60] The role of the applicant within the existing framework was somewhat clarified and developed through the early practice of the Commission and the Court.

[61] See further Section 7.3.

Referring to the writings of Hersch Lauterpacht,[62] he stated that 'this is a retrogressive step in that the general modern tendency of international law has been to emphasise the rights and duties of an individual as a subject of international law.'[63]

The first twenty years of the ECHR's life are frequently referred to as its 'trial period', and the original Convention was hardly predestined for success.[64] It was described as 'a convention à la carte' with reference to its optional clauses, and major powers such as the UK, France, and Italy initially accepted neither the right of individual petition to the Commission nor the compulsory jurisdiction of the Court.[65] Only the smaller countries made the necessary declarations in order to be fully subjected to the Convention's enforcement mechanisms.[66]

The silence on the status of individuals in international law continued throughout the reform process which led to the adoption of Protocol 9 in 1990. Above all, the evolution of the position of the individual in the ECHR enforcement system between 1959 and 1990 was driven by the Commission and the Court. The recurring, and presumably decisive, argument throughout the process was that the Commission and the Court requested the reform.[67]

In the first cases before the Court, the involvement of the applicant in the proceedings was improved to the extent possible within the framework of the original Convention.[68] Towards the end of the initial 'trial period', the Commission and the Court expressed their frustration with the existing control machinery and argued in favour of furthering the participation of the applicant.

The Commission clearly stated that it considered the system at hand to be unsatisfactory, mainly because of the ambiguity of its role regarding applications introduced under Article 25 of the Convention. In the Commission's view, '[t]his difficulty could be eliminated if the applicant himself, in certain circumstances, could refer his case to the Court, and, duly represented and assisted, be a party in the proceedings.'[69]

The ECtHR, on the other hand, was discouraged by the 'heaviness and complexity'[70] of the existing framework, which did not allow the Court to live up to

62 Lauterpacht had been involved in the work of the International Juridical Section of the European Movement. See further Section 7.2.1. See A. W. Brian Simpson, 'Hersch Lauterpacht and the Genesis of the Age of Human Rights', 120 *Law Quarterly Review* (2004) 49, 75.

63 *Travaux Préparatoires* (n 39) Vol. V, 226.

64 See for example Mikael Rask Madsen, '"Legal Diplomacy"—Law, Politics and the Genesis of Postwar European Human Rights', in Stefan Ludwig Hoffmann (ed.), *Human Rights in the Twentieth Century: A Critical History* (CUP, 2010) 62, and Simpson (n 27) 1086.

65 A chart of the declarations made pursuant to the former Articles 25 and 46 of the ECHR is available at https://rm.coe.int/168048d4e8 (accessed 21 January 2018). Remarkably, Italy and France had voted in favour of a court with compulsory jurisdiction and a mandatory right of individual petition, but did not make the required declarations until 1971 and 1974 respectively. The United Kingdom became subjected to the Convention's control machinery in 1966.

66 A number of these declarations were to be renewed every three or five years under Article 25(2).

67 See Kjeldgaard-Pedersen (n 38) 297–302.

68 See further ibid, 283ff.

69 Short and Medium-Term Programme of the Council of Europe in the General Field of Human Rights, (Recommendation 683), CM(74)180, Appendix IV, Opinion of the Commission, 19 July 1974, 4.

70 Short and Medium-Term Programme of the Council of Europe in the General Field of Human Rights, (Recommendation 683), CM(74)180, Appendix IV, Opinion of the Court, 5.

the standards of fair trial prescribed by Article 6 of the Convention.[71] Moreover, the Court regretted that it had only issued eight judgments during the first fifteen years, and it emphasized the threatening competition from the ECJ in the field of human rights. The problem was, according to the ECtHR judges, that the Luxembourg Court was 'impinging on the domain of human rights'[72] by more and more frequent references to 'general principles of law' in its case law.[73] In the ECtHR's opinion, these new tendencies from the Luxembourg Court gave rise to serious concern, and could become far more decisive for the destiny of the ECHR than possible conflicting jurisdiction with the UN machinery: 'The effectiveness of the system of the Convention has therefore to be reinforced appreciably if it is wished to settle in auspicious circumstances the numerous questions which its co-existence with the Communities raises—for the present in theory but sooner or later in practice.'[74]

The effectuation of the reform of the ECHR enforcement mechanism was significantly helped by geopolitical tendencies founded in the post-decolonization atmosphere of the 1970s. Still, it took a considerable amount of time to establish sufficient political will for the adoption of the reform prescribed by Protocol 9 in 1990.

Summing up, the image that appears is that the authors of neither the ECHR nor Protocol 9 were particularly preoccupied with the concept of international legal personality. It seems safe to say that theoretical quandaries did not guide the Court's findings on matters regarding the applicant's involvement in the proceedings. To the contrary, the Court consistently proposed improving the procedural position of the applicant without considering possible implications of the scholarly debate concerning the subjectivity of individuals in international law.

Against this background, the following sections will ask whether the concept of international legal personality played a role with regard to a fundamentally different aspect, namely in the Court's application of the material provisions of the Convention. It will be argued in Section 7.2.2 that the 'States-only' conception of international legal personality has unduly prompted the ECtHR to draw a distinction between the ECHR and 'normal treaties'. Accordingly, the Court's reasons for requiring special means of interpretation for the ECHR and exercising judicial self-restraint vis-à-vis the Member States are drawn into question. Section 7.2.3 will then discuss the Court's practice concerning the place of the ECHR in the international legal system.

[71] Ibid, 2. [72] Ibid, 17.

[73] Ibid. Four months earlier, the ECJ had issued its Judgment in the *Nold* case, stating for the first time that the 'international treaties for the protection of human rights ... can supply guidelines which should be followed within the framework of community law.' See *Nold v. the Commission of the Communities*, C-4/73, 14 May 1974, para. 13.

[74] Short and Medium-Term Programme of the Council of Europe in the General Field of Human Rights, (Recommendation 683), CM(74)180, Appendix IV, Opinion of the Court, 17.

7.2.2 Special rules of interpretation for human rights treaties?

Given that the rights and freedoms of the ECHR were drawn up in very vague terms,[75] it is striking that the Convention contains no rules on interpretation. According to the *travaux préparatoires*, the matter of how the provisions were to be interpreted was not of special concern to the ECHR drafters. One might assume that they presupposed the application of the customary rules of treaty interpretation, which at the time had not yet been codified as the negotiations took place twenty years prior to the adoption of the VCLT. Another possibility is that the drafters—simply by establishing the Court—implicitly conferred sole discretion in the matter of interpretation on the judges.[76] Or perhaps the time frame of the drafting process lead to the conclusion that it would be most sensible to leave aside this inherently complex issue. The fact remains, as described in the following, that the matter of interpretation was only discussed very briefly.

7.2.2.1 The ECHR drafting process

The Teitgen Report of 5 September 1949, which was prepared by the Committee on Legal and Administrative Questions, proposed interpretation in light of '"the general principles of law as recognised by civilised nations" and referred to in Article 38(1)(c) of the Statute of the International Court of Justice.'[77] In his oral presentation of the Report, Teitgen elaborated on the meaning of 'general principles of law': 'These are the principles and legal rules which, since they are formulated and sanctioned by the internal law of all civilised nations at any given moment, can be regarded as constituting a principle of general common law, applicable throughout the whole of international society.'[78] The reference to one of the traditional sources of international law listed in Article 38 of the ICJ Statute indicated that the Committee on Legal and Administrative Questions regarded the ECHR as a 'normal' treaty. The Committee of Experts on Human Rights, however, subsequently deleted the reference to 'Article 38c'. They felt it 'might give rise to a certain ambiguity, since the Convention on Human Rights is concerned with general principles of law applied by the States within the sphere of the internal activities, and not the international field.'[79] In their final report to the Committee of Ministers the Experts reiterated:

> From the legal point of view, the Strasbourg system is based on the idea that the protected rights should be applied in the light of the general principles of law recognised by civilised

[75] As Christoffersen puts it: 'The drafting process . . . ultimately left the development of international human rights to subsequent practice.' Jonas Christoffersen, *Fair Balance—Proportionality, Subsidiarity and Primarity in the European Convention on Human Rights* (Martinus Nijhoff, 2009a) 14. See also Simpson (n 27) 737.

[76] See further Ole Kristian Fauchald and André Nollkaemper, 'Conclusions', in Ole Kristian Fauchald and André Nollkaemper (eds), *The Practice of International and National Courts and the (De-)Fragmentation of International Law* (Hart, 2012) 343, 345.

[77] *Travaux Préparatoires* (n 39) Vol. I, 230.

[78] Ibid, 280.

[79] *Travaux Préparatoires* (n 39) Vol. IV, 30.

nations. The European Court, if it were created, should base its findings in the Convention itself and on the general principles of law.[80]

The Experts seemingly implied that the ECHR could not by definition be perceived as a part of international law, because the Convention operated 'within the sphere of internal activities', that is, governed individuals directly in matters traditionally regulated by domestic law. However, the possible difference between the 'general principles of law' referred to in the report and in Article 38(1)(c) of the ICJ Statute was left unexplained. Notably, a parallel distinction—with equally uncertain implications—has been introduced in relation to the question of the law applicable to State contracts.[81] One might speculate that the Experts, like, for example, the arbitrators in *ARAMCO*, went out of their way to avoid potential controversy over a direct reference to the sources of international law in matters involving individuals.

As will become apparent in the following sections, the separation of the ECHR from other international agreements when it comes to interpretation has gained support in a number of ECtHR judgments and in the writings of international human rights scholars. It is not an uncommon view that the ECHR 'is a treaty in form rather than a treaty in substance'.[82] The subsequent analysis, however, by no means purports to give a comprehensive account of the interpretative framework developed through the practice of the ECtHR, or of its relationship with the general principles of treaty interpretation codified in the VCLT.[83] The aim is simply to illustrate that the 'States-only' conception of international legal personality has seemingly functioned as an underlying presumption in both ECtHR judgments and in scholarly writings concerning the interpretation and application of the ECHR.

7.2.2.2 The practice of the Court

In one of its very first cases, *Wemhoff v. Germany*, the Court defined the ECHR as 'a law-making treaty'[84] and suggested that it is to be interpreted in a different way than 'treaties of the classic kind':[85] 'Given that it is a law-making treaty, it is also necessary

[80] Ibid, 14.

[81] See for example *Saudi Arabia v. Arabian American Oil Company* (hereafter *ARAMCO*), Award, 23 August 1958, 27 *ILR* (1963) 117, 169. See further Section 8.1.2.

[82] Andrew Drzemczewski, 'The Sui Generis Nature of the European Convention on Human Rights', 29 *ICLQ* (1980) 62.

[83] See, for example, Christoffersen (n 75) and Jonas Christoffersen, 'Impact on General Principles of Treaty Interpretation', in Menno T. Kamminga and Martin Scheinin (eds), *The Impact of Human Rights Law on General International Law* (OUP, 2009b) 37–62, Magdalena Forowicz, *The Reception of International Law in the European Court of Human Rights* (OUP, 2010) 23–71, and Ragnar Nordeide, 'The ECHR and its Normative Environment: Difficulties Arising from a Regional Human Rights Court's Approach to Systemic Integration', in Ole Kristian Fauchald and André Nollkaemper (eds), *The Practice of International and National Courts and the (De-)Fragmentation of International Law* (Hart, 2012) 117–38, Andrew Legg, *The Margin of Appreciation in International Human Rights Law* (OUP, 2012) 106–13, and Shai Dothan, 'In Defence of Expansive Interpretation in the European Court of Human Rights', 3 *CJICL* (2014a) 508.

[84] See also Chapter 5, note 106.

[85] *Ireland v. United Kingdom*, App no 5310/71, 18 January 1978 (hereafter *Ireland v. United Kingdom*) para. 239.

to seek the interpretation that is most appropriate in order to realise the aim and achieve the object of the treaty, not that which would restrict to the greatest possible degree the obligations undertaken by the Parties.'[86]

Evidently, the Court implied that 'treaties of the classic kind' are as a starting point to be interpreted restrictively. In contrast, the ECHR, which is 'law-making', must be 'interpreted and applied so as to make its safeguards practical and effective', due to its 'object and purpose ... as an instrument for the protection of individual human beings'.[87] In *Soering v. United Kingdom* the Court further asserted that interpretation of the Convention must be carried out in consideration of 'its special character as a treaty for the collective enforcement of human rights and fundamental freedoms.'[88]

Several ECtHR judges have advocated outside the Court that human rights treaties require separate rules of interpretation. For example, Franz Matscher has defined the ECHR as a 'law-making treaty' and stated that 'interpretation ... must depart from the theory of classic international law.'[89] Similarly, Rudolf Bernhardt has claimed that 'the general rules of treaty interpretation are in principle also applicable to human-rights treaties, but the object and purpose of these treaties are different and, therefore, the traditional rules need some adjustment.'[90] According to Bernhardt 'most other international agreements' are 'concerned with the mutual relations and the exchange of benefits between sovereign States.' On the contrary, '[i]t is the internal order of these States and their behaviour towards their own citizens which are the subject of human-rights treaties.'[91]

These observations by the Court and judges are open to question. Not only do they reflect an understanding of international law, which even at the time found little support in practice as several treaties predating the ECHR governed individuals directly and provided them with independent means of enforcement.[92] The argument also misrepresents the general rules of treaty interpretation set forth in the VCLT. Pursuant to Article 31(1), any treaty is as a starting point to be interpreted in the way stipulated by the Court in the *Wemhoff v. Germany* quote above. Applying

[86] *Wemhoff v. Germany*, App no 2122/64, 27 June 1968 (hereafter *Wemhoff v. Germany*) para. 8.

[87] *Soering v. United Kingdom*, App no 14038/8, 7 July 1989, para. 87.

[88] Ibid. The 'special character of a human rights treaty' is also underlined in the practice of the UN Human Rights Committee. See e.g. CCPR/C/21/Rev.1/Add.6, *General Comment No. 24*, 4 November 1994.

[89] Franz Matscher, 'Methods of Interpretation of the Convention', in R. S. J. Macdonald, Franz Matscher, and Herbert Petzold (eds), *The European System for the Protection of Human Rights* (Martinus Nijhoff, 1993) 63, 66. See also Matscher's separate opinion to *König v. Germany*, App no 6232/73, 28 June 1978.

[90] Rudolf Bernhardt, 'Thoughts on the Interpretation of Human Rights Treaties', in Franz Matscher and Herbert Petzold (eds), *Protecting Human Rights: The European Dimension—Studies in Honour of Gerard Wiarda* (Carl Heymanns Verlag, 1988) 65, 70–1.

[91] Ibid, 66. Notably, Gerald Fitzmaurice, who subsequently became a judge of the ECtHR, proposed differentiating between treaties on the basis of their content when he was acting as Special Rapporteur during the ILC's preparation of the VCLT. See II *YILC* (1957) 31. As his separate opinion in *Golder v. United Kingdom* illustrates, Fitzmaurice was a strong proponent of restrictive interpretation of the ECHR. *Golder v. United Kingdom*, App no 4451/70, paras 38–39. See also Forowicz (n 83) 34–5.

[92] See, for example, Sections 4.1.1 and 7.1.2.

'the interpretation that is most appropriate in order to realise the aim and achieve the object of the treaty' is not reserved for treaties with 'law-making' attributes, whatever the term implies.[93] Even so, the ECtHR case law does not stand alone in requiring special rules of interpretation for human rights treaties. For example, the IACtHR explicitly applied the rules set out in the VCLT in its Opinion on *Restrictions to the Death Penalty*, but then stated:

> In the case of human rights treaties, moreover, objective criteria of interpretation that look to the texts themselves are more appropriate than subjective criteria that seek to ascertain only the intent of the Parties. This is so because human rights treaties, as the Court has already noted,[94] 'are not multilateral treaties of the traditional type concluded to accomplish the reciprocal exchange of rights for the mutual benefit of the contracting States'; rather 'their object and purpose is the protection of the basic rights of individual human beings, irrespective of their nationality, both against the State of their nationality and all other contracting States'.[95]

Today, it seems to be a common view in international human rights literature that the general principles of treaty interpretation are insufficient when it comes to this particular field.[96] For example, Jacobs, White, and Ovey make the following observation in their classic textbook on the ECHR:

> While the relevant provisions of the Vienna Convention are sufficiently general to give some guidance, they must be applied with caution in view of the special features of the Convention. Although it is an international treaty, the Convention has a special character which goes beyond merely setting out the rights and obligations of the Contracting Parties.[97]

In his extensive study of the ECtHR's practice, published in 2009, Jonas Christoffersen refrains from concluding on the necessity of special rules of interpretation for human rights treaties.[98] He does, however, find that the Court, regardless of its various indications of the opposite, has adopted a method of interpretation which is 'firmly rooted within the traditional canons of interpretation of general

[93] In neither *Ireland v. United Kingdom* (n 85) nor *Wemhoff v. Germany* (n 86) did the Court clarify what it meant by, respectively, 'a treaty of the classic kind' or 'a law-making treaty'. See further Section 3.4.2.

[94] See *The Effect of Reservations on the Entry Into Force of the American Convention on Human Rights (Arts. 74 and 75)*, Advisory Opinion OC-2/82, September 24, 1982, Inter-Am. Ct. HR (Ser. A) No. 2 (1982).

[95] *Restrictions to the Death Penalty (Arts. 4(2) and 4(4) of the American Convention on Human Rights)*, Advisory Opinion OC-3/83, 8 September 1983, Inter-Am. Ct. HR (Ser. A) No. 3 (1983), para. 50. See also *Ivcher Bronstein v. Peru (Competence)*, Judgment, 24 September 1999, Inter-Am. Ct. HR (Ser. C) No. 54 (1999), paras 42ff.

[96] Notably, the ICJ has not advocated that special methods of interpretation apply to treaties regarding the rights of individuals. See further Section 3.1.2.

[97] Francis G. Jacobs, Robin C. A. White, and Clare Ovey, *The European Convention on Human Rights*, 7th edn edited by Bernadette Rainey, Elizabeth Wicks, and Clare Ovey (OUP, 2017) 66. In the earlier editions, the quote went on: 'The European Convention penetrates the national legal orders by requiring Contracting States to behave in a particular way towards their own citizens. What was previously treated by international law as a matter within the domestic jurisdiction of States is brought within an international system of protection and supervision.' See ibid (2nd edn, OUP, 1996) 28 and ibid (4th edn, OUP, 2006) 40.

[98] Christoffersen (n 75) 67.

international law.'[99] By drawing a parallel with the CJEU's conception of European Union Law as a separate legal order,[100] Christoffersen ventures the following explanation for the ECtHR's development of 'a new line of reasoning to supplement the "traditional" arguments based on a very narrow perception of the VCLT': 'A "special" doctrine of interpretation might have been considered helpful to avoid criticism for judicial legislation, since a novel discourse might be free of prejudged conceptions about the scope of legitimate treaty interpretation.'[101] Christoffersen goes on to say that regardless of the Court's underlying rationale, it has significantly contributed to the changing structure of international law 'by taking ordinary means of interpretation seriously, although in disguise of the special nature of the ECHR'.[102] Christoffersen's analysis of the Court's underlying rationale no doubt has significant merit. Yuval Shany, for one, concurs that 'international human rights courts ... such as the ECtHR ... seem to focus their energies on promoting State compliance with specific treaty norms.'[103] Nevertheless, it is important to accentuate that the reasoning employed by the Court as well as scholars in support of the necessity of special means of interpretation at least partly rests on a misconception of the position of individuals in international law.

Arguably, the idea that the ECHR requires special principles of interpretation has in some cases prompted the Court to give Member States a more favourable treatment in the Convention's inherent conflict between human rights protection and national sovereignty than mere application of Articles 31–33 of the VCLT would have warranted. Indeed, contrary to its above-cited statement on interpretation in *Wemhoff v. Germany*, the ECtHR's application of the ECHR may in some respects be described as restrictive.[104] The primary example of restraint is the widespread use of the 'principle of subsidiarity' and the 'margin of appreciation doctrine', for which the Court is famous.[105] The Court first talked about 'the subsidiary nature of the international machinery of collective enforcement established by the Convention'

[99] Ibid, 37. For an explicit statement by the Court to that effect, see, for example, *Al-Adsani v. United Kingdom*, App no 35763/97, 21 November 2001, para. 55.

[100] See further Section 8.3.2.

[101] Christoffersen (n 75) 68. On the concept of 'law-making treaties', Christoffersen finds (ibid, 51):

> The Court may have misunderstood the general principles of treaty interpretation, but it is more likely that the 'law-making' argument reflects the Court's desire to defend itself against accusations of its taking the ECHR beyond the confines of a narrow—but not necessarily adequate—construction of ordinary doctrines of interpretation of international treaties.

[102] Ibid, 68.

[103] Yuval Shany, 'One Law to Rule Them All', in Ole Kristian Fauchald and André Nollkaemper (eds), *The Practice of International and National Courts and the (De-)Fragmentation of International Law* (Hart, 2012) 15, 20. See further Shai Dothan, *Reputation and Judicial Tactics—A Theory of National and International Courts* (CUP, 2014b) Chapter 6.

[104] See also Paul Mahoney, 'Judicial Activism and Judicial Self-Restraint in the European Court of Human Rights: Two Sides of the Same Coin', 11 *Human Rights Law Journal* (1990) 57.

[105] The IACtHR applied a margin of appreciation in one of its first Advisory Opinions. See *Proposed Amendments to the Naturalization Provision of the Constitution of Costa Rica*, Inter-AmCtHR, Series A, No. 4 (1984) para. 58. See further Yuval Shany, 'Toward a General Margin of Appreciation Doctrine in International Law?', 19 *EJIL* (2006) 907, 929.

in the *Belgian Linguistic Case* of 1968.[106] About one month earlier, the Court had in effect limited itself to subsidiary review, since Germany only needed to provide 'relevant and sufficient' reasons for why the detention of Mr Wemhoff was not a violation of Article 5(3) of the ECHR.[107] In the leading precedent, *Handyside* of 1976, the Court explicitly used the term 'margin of appreciation'[108] and provided 'the prototype of "margin" analysis'.[109] The point here is not to go into the details of the principle of subsidiarity and the margin of appreciation doctrine as they have subsequently been developed in the Court's jurisprudence.[110] No doubt these legal instruments form a key part of the response to the problem of the Court's exorbitant caseload as well as the scepticism towards the Court, which currently seems to be on the rise in many Member States.[111] If and when Protocol 15 enters into force, the principle of subsidiarity and the margin of appreciation doctrine will become inscribed into the Preamble of the ECHR as follows:

> Affirming that the High Contracting Parties, in accordance with the principle of subsidiarity, have the primary responsibility to secure the rights and freedoms defined in this Convention and the Protocols thereto, and that in doing so they enjoy a margin of appreciation, subject to the supervisory jurisdiction of the European Court of Human Rights established by this Convention.[112]

Indeed, it has for some time been a common notion among commentators that the principle of subsidiarity and the margin of appreciation doctrine are inherent elements of an international judicial system, which serve the purpose of balancing the Member States' sovereignty with the aim of the relevant Convention, *in casu*

[106] *Case relating to Certain Aspects of the Laws on the Use of Languages in Education in Belgium,* 23 July 1968, Series A, No. 6, 34, para. 10 (hereafter *Belgian Linguistic Case*).

[107] *Wemhoff v. Germany* (n 86) para. 12.

[108] *Handyside v. United Kingdom,* App no 5493/72, 7 December 1976, para. 48 (hereafter *Handyside*). See also para. 50.

[109] Yutaka Arai-Takahashi, 'The margin of appreciation doctrine: a theoretical analysis of Strasbourg's variable geometry', in Andreas Føllesdal, Birgit Peters, and Geir Ulfstein, *Constituting Europe—The European Court of Human Rights in a National, European and Global Context* (CUP, 2013) 68. See also Christoffersen (n 75) 251ff.

[110] Abundant literature has been written on the subject of the ECtHR's margin of appreciation doctrine. See, for example, Yutaka Arai-Takahashi, *The Margin of Appreciation Doctrine and the Principle of Proportionality in the Jurisprudence of the ECHR* (Intersentia, 2002), Arai-Takahashi (n 109), Christoffersen (n 75), Chapter 3, Legg (n 83), Chapter 3, Petr Agha (ed.), *Human Rights Between Law and Politics: The Margin of Appreciation in Post-National Contexts* (Hart, 2016), Oddný Mjöll Arnardóttir, 'Rethinking the Two Margins of Appreciation', 12 *European Constitutional Law Review* (2016) 27.

[111] See, for example, Robert Spano, 'Universality or Diversity of Human Rights?: Strasbourg in the Age of Subsidiarity', 14 *Human Rights Law Review* (2014) 487, and Mikael Rask Madsen, 'The Challenging Authority of the European Court of Human Rights: From Cold War Legal Diplomacy to the Brighton Declaration and Backlash', 79 *Law and Contemporary Problems* (2016) 141, 174.

[112] On the extent to which the Brighton Declaration (2012) and its associated Protocols 15 and 16 have already taken effect, see Mikael Rask Madsen, 'Rebalancing European Human Rights: Has the Brighton Declaration Engendered a New Deal on Human Rights in Europe?', *Journal of International Dispute Settlement*, published online 27 June 2017, iCourts Working Paper Series No. 100 (available at https://ssrn.com/abstract=2993222, accessed 21 January 2018).

the protection of human rights in the ECHR.[113] The aim of this section is certainly not to criticize this development from a normative perspective. The point is simply to challenge the rationale offered by the Court and numerous scholars when these norms were originally introduced. Following the argument of this book, nothing prevents States from entering into treaties with a content reaching far into areas that have traditionally been reserved to national law. If the contracting States wish to include particular principles of interpretation in such a treaty, they are free to do so. But in the case of the ECHR, they did not. Nothing in the ECHR itself—or in any other pertinent source of law, including the *travaux préparatoires*—requires the Court to exercise judicial restraint.[114] The straightforward answer (without presumptions concerning the international legal personality of individuals) would therefore seem to be that the ECHR should be interpreted according to the customary rules of international law now codified in the VCLT. As mentioned earlier, it is also arguable that States, merely by setting up a judicial body to oversee an instrument with an imprecise content like the ECHR, accept that the Court is free to invent its own interpretation framework. The implications of these diverging positions, including the fundamental questions relating to the legitimacy of the relevant dispute settlement body and the possible fragmentation of the international legal system, shall not be explored further at this juncture.[115] It is noteworthy, however, that the ILC's 2006 report on the Fragmentation of International Law provides as follows: 'A minimal conclusion that one can draw from practice and literature is that articles 31 and 32 of the VCLT are always applicable unless specifically set aside by other principles of interpretation. This has been affirmed by practically all existing international law-applying bodies.' [116]

On the basis of the study in Section 7.2.1, the ECtHR may be said to have favoured a horizontal relationship between the individual applicant and the responding State with regard to procedural issues. In terms of the material application of the ECHR, however, the Court at times has viewed the relationship between the parties as vertical in kind:[117] the Court has consistently promoted the procedural status of the individual applicant, while to some extent limiting itself to review of the national authorities' reasoning instead of independently subsuming the facts of the case under the relevant provisions. In this way, the procedure before the Court has become increasingly similar to hearings regarding violations of citizens'

[113] See, for example, L. R. Hefner and A. M. Slaughter, 'Toward a Theory of Effective Supranational Adjudication', 107 *Yale Law Journal* (1997) 273, 317. See also George Letsas, 'Two Concepts of the Margin of Appreciation', 26 *Oxford Journal of Legal Studies* (2006) 705, 720.

[114] H.C. Yourow, *The Margin of Appreciation Doctrine in the Dynamics of the European Human Rights Jurisprudence* (Martinus Nijhoff, 1996) 196.

[115] See generally Ole Kristian Fauchald and André Nollkaemper (eds), *The Practice of International and National Courts and the (De-)Fragmentation of International Law* (Hart, 2012).

[116] Fragmentation of International Law: Difficulties Arising from the Diversification and Expansion of International Law, Report of the Study Group of the International Law Commission, Finalized by Martti Koskenniemi, UN Doc. A/CN.4/L.682, 13 April 2006 (available at http://legal.un.org/docs/?symbol=A/CN.4/L.682, accessed 21 January 2018), 92. See ibid, note 231 for references to case law. See also *Kasikili/Sedudu Island (Botswana/Namibia)* (Judgment) [1999] ICJ Rep 1045, para. 93.

[117] Ole Spiermann, 'Twentieth Century Internationalism in Law' 18 *EJIL* (2007) 785, 803.

constitutional rights in a domestic setting. Procedurally, the parties are equal, but with regard to the substance of the case the Court shows a certain degree of judicial restraint vis-à-vis the national authorities. One might wonder whether the ECtHR judges were consciously mimicking domestic constitutional review. In the same vein, it seems reasonable to wonder whether presumptions concerning the role of the individual in the international legal system are what have directed the Court and numerous authors towards talk of federalism[118] and especially constitutionalism[119] with respect to the ECHR. The Court explicitly spoke of the Convention 'as a constitutional instrument of European public order' for the first time in 1995 in *Loizidou v. Turkey*.[120] This idea is still very much alive and it assumes particular practical importance in the determination of the hierarchical relationship between the Convention and other international legal norms. In a number of recent judgments concerning potential norm conflicts between the ECHR and UN Security Council resolutions, the characterization of the ECHR as a 'constitutional instrument' was explicitly reiterated by the Court. A key issue in these cases was whether acts of the Security Council may overrule the ECHR by virtue of Article 103 of the UN Charter, which provides: 'In the event of a conflict between the obligations of the Members of the United Nations under the present Charter and their obligations under any other international agreement, their obligations under the present Charter shall prevail.'

7.2.3 The ECHR in the international legal system

In *Behrami* from 2007, the ECtHR put forward the argument that the Security Council exercised 'ultimate authority and control' over the territory by authorizing a military mission in Kosovo.[121] Against this background, the Court concluded that conduct of UNMIK and KFOR[122] troops in Kosovo was attributable to the UN rather than the contributing States. The question relating to Article 103 thus never

[118] Colin Warbrick, '"Federal" Aspects of the European Convention on Human Rights', 10 *Michigan Journal of International Law* (1989) 698.

[119] See J. G. Merrills, *The Development of International Law by the European Court of Human Rights* (2nd edn, Manchester University Press, 1993) 10, and Andrew Drzemczewski, 'The Sui Generis Nature of the European Convention on Human Rights', 29 *ICLQ* (1980) 62. See also Iain Cameron, '*Protocol 11* to the European Convention on Human Rights: the European Court of Human Rights as a Constitutional Court?' 15 *Yearbook of European Law* (1995) 219. See further Section 2.4 on the role of human rights in international constitutionalist scholarship.

[120] *Loizidou v. Turkey*, App no 15318/89 (preliminary objections), 23 March 1995, para. 75. It went on to describe the role of the Convention institutions as '... exclusively limited to direct supervisory functions in respect of a law-making treaty such as the Convention.' Ibid, para. 84. In this way the Court explicitly claimed to have a different role than the International Court of Justice. See also *Bosphorus Hava Yollari Turizm ve Ticaret Anonim Sirketi v. Ireland*, App no 45036/98, 30 June 2005 (hereafter *Bosphorus*) para. 156.

[121] *Behrami and Behrami v. France, Saramati v. France, Germany and Norway*, App nos 71412/01 and 78166/01, 2 May 2007 (hereafter *Behrami*) paras 133ff.

[122] UNMIK is the acronym of United Nations Interim Administration Mission in Kosovo, while KFOR is the acronym of the NATO Kosovo Force.

became pertinent. The Court did, however, reiterate its findings in *Bosphorus*, in which it had stated as follows:

> [W]here . . . State action was taken in compliance with international legal obligations flowing from its membership of an international organisation and where the relevant organisation protected fundamental rights in a manner which could be considered at least equivalent to that which the Convention provides, a presumption arose that the State had not departed from the requirements of the Convention. Such presumption could be rebutted, if in the circumstances of a particular case, it was considered that the protection of Convention rights was manifestly deficient: in such a case, the interest of international cooperation would be outweighed by the Convention's role as a 'constitutional instrument of European public order' in the field of human rights . . . .[123]

Especially on the point of attribution, *Behrami* has been (rightfully) criticized.[124] The Court's Judgment in *Al-Jedda* was therefore eagerly awaited. Instead of applying or overruling *Behrami* in *Al-Jedda*, however, the ECtHR distinguished between the facts of the two cases, and concluded that the detention of Mr Al-Jedda by British forces in Iraq was attributable to the UK, even though the US and the UK had been authorized to preventively detain individuals for security reasons by UN Security Council in Resolution 1546 (2004). The Court was then faced with the possible norm conflict between Resolution 1546 (2004) and Article 5 of the ECHR, including the question concerning Article 103 of the UN Charter. The Court found that:

> [I]n interpreting its resolutions, there must be a presumption that the Security Council does not intend to impose any obligation on Member States to breach fundamental principles of human rights. In the event of any ambiguity in the terms of a Security Council Resolution, the Court must therefore choose the interpretation which is most in harmony with the requirements of the Convention and which avoids any conflict of obligations. In the light of the United Nations' important role in promoting and encouraging respect for human rights, it is to be expected that clear and explicit language would be used were the Security Council to intend States to take particular measures which would conflict with their obligations under international human rights law.[125]

Rather than saying that the ECHR is separate from international law and the UN Charter,[126] the ECtHR indicated that the Convention is a 'normal treaty' in the sense that it forms part of the hierarchical structure of the international legal system. At the same time, however, the Court created a—strong—interpretative presumption that the UN Security Council does not intend to overrule international human rights law. The Court did not spell out whether a UN Security Council resolution could displace the ECHR if the language of a measure to that effect was sufficiently

[123] *Behrami* (n 121) para. 145.

[124] As Milanović points out, 'practically everyone who has ever read Behrami thought it to be wrongly decided'. Marko Milanović, '*Al-Skieni* and *Al-Jedda* in Strasbourg', 23 *EJIL* (2012) 121, 135. See also Kjetil Mujezinović Larsen, 'Attribution of Conduct in Peace Operations: The "Ultimate Authority and Control" Test', 19 *EJIL* (2008) 509, and ILC, *Seventh Report on Responsibility of International Organizations*, Special Rapporteur Giorgio Gaja, 27 March 2009, para. 26.

[125] *Al-Jedda v. United Kingdom*, App no 27021/08, 7 July 2011 (hereafter *Al-Jedda*) para. 102.

[126] See further Section 8.3.2 for a discussion of the ECJ's 2008 *Kadi I* Judgment, *Yassin Abdullah Kadi & Al Barakaat International Foundation v. Council & Commission* [2008] ECLI:EU:C:2008:461.

'clear and explicit'. It may be inferred that the Court's acceptance of this argument is understood in its line of reasoning. However, the Court's silence on the matter may also be read as reluctance to accept the possible prevalence of UN Security Council measures.[127] In sum, the Court's stance on the relationship between the ECHR and Article 103 of the UN Charter was left unresolved by Al-Jedda.

The *Nada* case decided in 2012 presented a new opportunity for clarification. The applicant, Mr Nada, had been listed by the UN Sanctions Committee, and—according to the Taliban Ordinance, which Switzerland had adopted in order to implement its obligations under Security Council Resolutions 1267 (1999), 1333 (2000), and 1390 (2000)—he was, therefore, prevented from leaving Campione d'Italia, a small Italian enclave within Switzerland. The Court found that Switzerland had violated Mr Nada's rights under Articles 8 and 13 of the ECHR. Pertaining to the right to respect for private and family life enshrined in Article 8, the Court first reiterated its findings in *Al-Jedda* and held that the interpretative presumption had indeed been rebutted in *Nada*, 'having regard to the clear and explicit language, imposing an obligation to take measures capable of breaching human rights, that was used' in the relevant Resolutions.[128] Yet, the Court concluded that 'the respondent State could not validly confine itself to relying on the binding nature of Security Council resolutions, but should have persuaded the Court that it had taken, or at least had attempted to take, all possible measures to adapt the sanctions regime to the applicant's individual situation.'[129] The Court underlined, however, that this did not involve a determination of hierarchy between the obligations arising from the ECHR and the obligations under the UN Charter. Rather, '[i]n the Court's view, the important point is that the respondent Government have failed to show that they attempted, as far as possible, to harmonise the obligations that they regarded as divergent.'[130]

The Court's statements concerning the right to effective remedy under Article 13 are even more remarkable. The Swiss government argued that Mr Nada's request to be deleted from the list annexed to the Taliban Ordinance had been heard—and dismissed with reference to the prevalence of obligations under the UN Charter over other international instruments—by the Federal Court.[131] As the ECtHR noted, 'the Federal Court took the view that whilst it could verify whether Switzerland was bound by the Security Council resolutions, it could not lift the sanctions imposed on the applicant on the ground that they did not respect human rights'.[132] With reference to the ECJ's Judgment in *Kadi I*, however, the ECtHR found this conclusion to be too restrictive. The ECtHR argued that the ECJ's finding concerning the competence of the Community judicature to review the legality of a Community act, even if the purpose of the act is to give effect to a Security Council resolution, applies *mutatis mutandis* to the Swiss authorities.[133] In other words, the ECtHR

[127] See further Milanović (n 124) 138. See also Ragnar Nordeide, 'Fragmentation and the Leeway of the VCLT', 20 *Finnish Yearbook of International Law* (2009) 189, 204–6.

[128] *Nada v. Switzerland*, App no. 10593/08, 12 September 2012 (hereafter *Nada*) para. 172.

[129] Ibid, para. 196.

[130] Ibid, para. 197.

[131] The Federal Court's Judgment of 14 November 2007 is described in detail in ibid, paras 41–52.

[132] Ibid, para. 210.

[133] Ibid, para. 212. As to *Kadi I* (n 126), see further Section 8.3.2.

reasoned that the Swiss authorities should have assumed the competence to review the conformity of the Taliban Ordinance with the ECHR. This part of the ECtHR's *Nada* Judgment is particularly interesting for present purposes as it specifically relates to the question of the relationship between legal orders. What the ECtHR seemingly implies is that the hierarchy between obligations arising from the UN Charter and from the ECHR at the international level has no bearing on the competence of domestic courts to test the legality of domestic law, because domestic courts operate within a different legal order. The problem with this rationale, however, is that the ECtHR does not explain how Switzerland can incur responsibility for violating Article 13 of the ECHR at the international level, without at the same time challenging the prevalence of the Security Council resolutions under Article 103 of the UN Charter. Each of a State's international legal obligations does not exist in a vacuum. If international law stipulates that norm A prevails over norm B, States are exempted from responsibility for a violation of norm B if the violation is a precondition for compliance with norm A. It is, therefore, difficult to understand how the ECtHR could hold Switzerland responsible for a violation of Article 13 without contesting that binding Security Council resolutions take precedence over the ECHR at the international level. This is not to say, of course, that a domestic court might consider itself competent to overrule domestic legislation, which has been adopted to implement a Security Council resolution, because it violates fundamental domestic legal norms in that particular State. Such fundamental norms may very well follow from the ECHR (or perhaps the legal instrument incorporating the Convention into domestic law), but that does not change the fact that the domestic court's decision would be based on domestic law rather than the ECHR as an international legal obligation incumbent upon the State. As discussed in Section 1.3.2, domestic law ultimately decides the impact attributed to international law in a domestic legal system. That does not mean, however, that a State is exempted from international legal responsibility if it invokes the lower-ranking of two conflicting norms of international law.

Again without overtly deciding whether, in the event of a genuine norm conflict, Article 103 of the UN Charter may displace the ECHR, the Grand Chamber held in the *Al-Dulimi* Judgment of 2016 that Switzerland had violated Article 6(1) of the Convention. The Court stated that when a Security Council resolution such as Resolution 1483 (2003) 'does not contain any clear or explicit wording excluding the possibility of judicial supervision of the measures taken for its implementation, it must always be understood as authorising the courts of the respondent State to exercise sufficient scrutiny so that any arbitrariness can be avoided.'[134] The majority of the Grand Chamber judges thereby confirmed that they are willing to go to great lengths in terms of harmonious interpretation in order to avoid an actual norm conflict.[135]

[134] *Al-Dulimi and Montana Management Inc. v. Switzerland*, App no. 5809/08, 21 June 2016 (hereafter *Al-Dulimi*) para. 146.

[135] See ibid, para. 149. See further Marko Milanović, 'Grand Chamber Judgment in Al-Dulimi', https://www.ejiltalk.org/grand-chamber-judgment-in-al-dulimi-v-switzerland/, 23 June 2016

Some ECtHR judges, however, favoured a more radical approach. In a striking concurring opinion, Judge Pinto de Albuquerque, joined by three other judges, argued that '[t]he Council of Europe is an autonomous legal order' and that the ECtHR should, therefore, have reasoned like the ECJ in the *Kadi I* case.[136] Seemingly influenced by international legal constitutionalism, including the idea invoked by some constitutionalist scholars that the notion of dualism is inherently tied to the 'States-only' conception of international legal personality,[137] Judge Pinto de Albuquerque contended as follows:

> Being more than just a multilateral agreement on reciprocal obligations of States Parties, the Convention creates obligations for States Parties towards all individuals and private entities within their jurisdiction. [T]he Convention is subordinated neither to domestic constitutional rules, nor to allegedly higher rules of international law, since it is the supreme law of the European continent. In the Council of Europe's own internal hierarchy of norms, United Nations law is equal to any other international agreement and subordinated to the primacy of the Convention as a constitutional instrument of European public order.[138]

7.3 Conclusion: The Legal Personality of Individuals in International Human Rights Law

Before the end of the Second World War, no actual human rights conventions conferring rights directly on individuals were adopted. The early antecedents of contemporary international human rights law, such as the rules on slavery, did not consistently confer rights directly on individuals. During the interwar period, a number of groups of individuals were granted protection against their home State under international law, some in the form of individual rights. In particular, the system set up within the realm of the League of Nations for the protection of minorities conferred direct rights on groups of individuals. Apart from the Upper Silesia Mixed Commission, however, the individual generally played an inferior role in the system set up to oversee State compliance with the minorities treaties. As apparent from the memoirs of Sir James Headlam-Morley, the limited capacity of individuals was not the result of theoretical quandaries. Rather, the drafters of the minorities treaties were driven by political and pragmatic concerns, primarily the assumption that the relevant States would be unwilling to adopt such an enforcement system. In the case of the Upper Silesia Mixed Commission, the rationale seems to have

(accessed 21 January 2018), and Alexander Orakhelashvili, 'Al-Dulimi v. Switzerland', 110 *AJIL* (2016) 767.

[136] See Section 8.3.2. [137] See Section 2.4.

[138] *Al-Dulimi* (n 134), Concurring opinion of Judge Pinto de Albuquerque, joined by Judges Hajiyev, Pejchal, and Dedov, para. 59. See also the argument in ibid, para. 71, that 'the Council of Europe prefers a multicentre and cosmopolitan view of international law, which envisages the relationship between international law and Convention law beyond the orthodox, yet outdated, monist/dualist dichotomy.' See further Paulo Pinto de Albuquerque, 'Is the ECHR facing an existential crisis?', Speech delivered at the Mansfield College, Oxford, 28 April 2017 (available at https://www.law.ox.ac.uk/sites/files/oxlaw/pinto_opening_presentation_2017.pdf, accessed 21 January 2018).

been that granting individuals independent means of enforcement was necessary in order to realize the purpose of the 1922 Geneva Convention Relating to Upper Silesia.[139] In these examples from the interwar period, the concept of international legal personality thus appears to have been equally unimportant in the creation of the dispute settlement bodies that did provide for individual petitions and in the creation of those that did not.[140]

The ECHR control machinery is frequently presented as a primary example of the changed position of individuals in international law since the Second World War. For example, Ludger Kühnhardt refers to Article 25 of the original ECHR as a revolutionary innovation, which 'elevates the individual to the status of a subject of international law.'[141] Nevertheless, the study of the development of the ECHR and its enforcement mechanism provides further support for the impression that practical concerns rather than theoretical issues are decisive, at least when it comes to the procedural role of individuals in international law. On one hand, the proponents of granting individuals independent means of enforcement under the original ECHR argued that such a system would best serve the purpose of the Convention. Those opposed to setting up an extensive protection mechanism, on the other hand, argued that the Member States of the Council of Europe were not prepared to accept a system, and that it might be abused, for example for communist propaganda. The development between 1959 and 1990 towards further procedural capacity of individuals was advanced by the Commission and the Court, because they were frustrated with the way the system functioned in practice.

In sum, it speaks strongly to the limited practical relevance of the concept of international legal personality, that the theoretical debate on the role of individuals in international law is almost entirely missing from the drafting processes leading up to both the ECHR of 1950 and Protocol 9 in 1990. By contrast, however, presumptions about the international legal personality of individuals appear to some extent to have influenced the ECtHR's development of a framework for interpreting and applying the material provisions of the Convention. From the viewpoint of general international law, there were no legal reasons why the Court would require special means of interpretation for the ECHR or exercise judicial restraint vis-à-vis the Member States. Nevertheless, examples from the Court's practice arguably reflect the idea that the ECHR—because it governs individuals directly—cannot be perceived as a 'normal treaty'. As mentioned earlier, it is not the aim here to criticize the Court's normative development of the principle of subsidiarity and the margin of appreciation doctrine, which with the entry into force of Protocol 15 will become a part of the ECHR's preamble. The purpose is simply to underline that the ECtHR's original explanation for introducing these principles involved a deficient description of the role of the individual as a matter of positive international law, which echoes the 'States-only' conception of international legal personality. As will become apparent in Section 8.3.2, the same line of reasoning—that 'normal' treaties cannot by

[139] See further Section 4.2.2.3. [140] See also Section 4.4.

[141] Ludger Kühnhardt, 'European Court and Human Rights', in Douglas Greenberg et al. (eds), *Constitutionalism and Democracy: Transitions in the Contemporary World* (OUP, 1993) 126, 129.

definition govern individuals directly—underlies the common notion established in the ECJ's early case law that EU Law forms a separate legal order.

Comparing the practice of the ECJ (and the CJEU) with the ECtHR's case law is especially interesting as regards the relationship between the respective conventions and the UN Charter. While a few ECtHR judges, who seem to be inspired by international constitutionalist scholarship,[142] have advocated that the ECtHR should adopt a similar approach to that of the ECJ and the CJEU, the majority of the ECtHR judges have maintained that the ECHR does not set up an autonomous legal system separate from international law. Instead, the ECtHR has so far—through harmonious interpretation—avoided having to decide whether a State's obligations under the ECHR may be displaced by a UN Security Council resolution in accordance with Article 103 of the UN Charter. In the *Nada* case from 2012, the Court did, however, reach the remarkable conclusion that, since domestic courts operate within a different legal order, the norm hierarchy at the international level does not influence the competence of domestic courts to test the legality of domestic law. Remarkably, the ECtHR did not clarify how it could hold Switzerland responsible for violating Article 13 of the ECHR without rejecting the prevalence of the UN Security Council resolution in question.

As mentioned, it is commonly suggested that international human rights law—together with international criminal law—has played a pivotal role in transforming international law from exclusively applying between States before the Second World War to governing individuals today. Paola Gaeta, for example, has argued as follows:

> The development of the international law of human rights, and the parallel recognition that individuals are entitled to be protected in their own right against abusive state conduct, has had enormous influence on the corpus of international rules and their proper interpretation. Under contemporary international law, individuals are no longer considered the 'objects' of rights accruing only to states, but are also considered to enjoy rights themselves vis-à-vis states under international law.[143]

While this analysis seems to underrate the numerous prior examples of individuals asserting rights and incurring responsibility directly under international law, it cannot be denied that the human rights movement has had a significant impact on the number and extent of international legal rules pertaining to the conditions of individuals.[144] In this respect it is nevertheless important to accentuate the distinction between the formal status of the individual in the international legal system and her material rights and obligations under current international law. The argument put forward here is that where international law has developed significantly towards further involvement of individuals as a matter of substance, it is a mistake to imply that

[142] See Section 2.4.

[143] Paola Gaeta, 'Are Victims of War Crimes Entitled to Compensation?', in Orna Ben-Naftali (ed.), *International Humanitarian Law and International Human Rights Law* (OUP, 2011) 305, 319. See also, for example, Manfred Nowak and Karolina Miriam Januszewski, 'Non-State Actors and Human Rights', in Math Noortmann, August Reinisch, and Cedric Ryngaert (eds), *Non-State Actors in International Law* (Hart, 2015) 113.

[144] See further Section 3.4.1.

this development has had any influence on their overall international legal personality. Rather, in line with the a posteriori conception, the capacity of an individual to possess international legal rights and duties has always been an empirical question which depends solely on interpretation of concrete norms of international law.

Arguably, the seemingly prevalent view—which corresponds to the modified 'States-only' conception—that individuals have only been endowed with international legal personality in the post-Second World War era not only misrepresents positive international law, but also creates significant confusion about the interpretation and application of existing international legal norms, including human rights. It is, for example, the subject of ongoing scholarly debate whether international law may confer human rights *obligations* directly on individuals and other non-State actors.[145] Employing the 'a posteriori' conception of international legal personality in conjunction with the principle of legislative jurisdiction (which in this book is discussed in relation to international humanitarian law[146] and international criminal law[147]), it is submitted that there are no conceptual obstacles to such international regulation from the point of view of international law.[148] In the words of Milanović: 'States have generally refrained from binding individuals by treaties not because of abstract, doctrinal attitudes towards the position of the individual in international law, but because it would be wholly impracticable to do so.'[149]

[145] See, for example, Katharine Fortin, *The Accountability of Armed Groups under Human Rights Law* (OUP, 2017), Daragh Murray, *Human Rights Obligations of Non-State Armed Groups* (Hart, 2016), Philip Alston (ed.), *Non-State Actors and Human Rights* (OUP, 2005), Andrew Clapham, 'Accountability/Liability for Violations of the Law: Focusing on Non-State Actors', in Andrew Clapham and Paola Gaeta (eds), *The Oxford Handbook of International Law in Armed Conflict* (OUP, 2014) 755, Cedric Ryngaert, 'Imposing International Duties on Non-State Actors and the Legitimacy of International Law', in Math Noortmann and Cedric Ryngaert (eds), *Non-State Actor Dynamics in International Law* (Ashgate, 2010) 69, Cedric Ryngaert, 'Non-State Actors: Carving out a Space in a State-Centred International Legal System', 63 *Netherlands International Law Review* (2016) 183, 191–2, Eric de Brabandere, 'Non-State Actors and Human Rights: Corporate Responsibility and the Attempts to Formalize the Role of Corporations as Participants in the International Legal System', in Jean d'Aspremont (ed.), *Participants in the International Legal System* (Routledge, 2011) 268–83, and Yaël Ronen, 'Human Rights Obligations of Territorial Non-State Actors' 46 *Cornell International Law Journal* (2013a) 21.

[146] See Section 5.4.3.4. [147] See Sections 6.2.4 and 6.3.1.

[148] For a different view see Chapter 2, note 172. The question of investors' human rights obligations was recently addressed in a remarkable ICSID award. The tribunal clearly rejected the investor's argument that as a corporation it was incapable of bearing international legal obligations. See *Urbaser et al. v. The Argentine Republic*, Award, ICSID Case No. ARB/07/26, 8 December 2016, para. 1194. Notably, Article 18(2) of the Nigeria–Morocco BIT, signed in late 2016 (available at http://investmentpolicyhub.unctad.org/Download/TreatyFile/5409, accessed 21 January 2018) provides that '[i]nvestors and investments shall uphold human rights in the host state.'

[149] Marko Milanović, 'Is the Rome Statute Binding on Individuals? (And Why We Should Care)', 9 *JICJ* (2011) 25, 46. See also Nehal Bhuta, 'The Role International Actors Other Than States can Play in the New World Order', in Antonio Cassese (ed.), *Realizing Utopia* (OUP, 2012) 61, 75. Imposing direct international legal obligations on individuals may of course be problematic from a domestic law perspective, but this is not an issue of immediate relevance to the present work.

8

The Legal Personality of Individuals in International Economic Law

The subjects of Chapter 4 and the present chapter overlap to the extent that they both examine claims of individuals for pecuniary damages brought against foreign States. Whereas Chapter 4 primarily studies the role of injured individuals in international claims practice arising out of a number of specific historic events, however, this chapter pertains to the substantive rights and obligations, as well as the procedural capacity, of individuals within the field of the international economic law.

International economic law is not a very precise term.[1] It comprises a wide range of topics relating to economic relations at the international level. In 1987, the American Law Institute included a distinct part entitled 'International Economic Relations' in its third *Restatement of the Law* and described the field as follows: 'The law of international economic relations in its broadest sense includes all the international law and international agreements governing economic transactions that cross state boundaries or that otherwise have implications for more than one state'.[2]

International economic law is frequently divided into two principal sub-fields: international trade law (chiefly WTO law), and international investment law. While a number of international agreements include both trade chapters and investment chapters,[3] international trade law and international investment law currently differ in fundamental ways, not least as regards the role attributed to individuals. As is argued in Section 8.2, the conditions of foreign investors are governed directly by a vast number of bilateral and plurilateral investment treaties, and investors are given

[1] See for example Gerhard Loibl, 'International Economic Law', in Malcolm D. Evans (ed.), *International Law* (3rd edn, OUP, 2010) 722.

[2] *Restatement of the Law Third: The Foreign Relations Law of the United States* (American Law Institute, 1987) vol. 2, 261.

[3] Recent examples include the Comprehensive and Progressive Agreement for Trans-Pacific Partnership (CPTPP, also known as TPP11) concluded on 23 January 2018, and the Comprehensive Economic and Trade Agreement (CETA) between the EU and Canada, which entered into force provisionally on 21 September 2017. Notably, CETA includes a multilateral investment court as part of an EU vision of reshaping investment disputes. This policy has also materialized in the EU–Vietnam Free Trade Agreement concluded on 2 December 2015. As this institution is not yet functioning, it will not be discussed in the present chapter. See further the negotiating directives for a multilateral investment court adopted and published by the Council on 20 March 2018 (http://data.consilium.europa.eu/doc/document/ST-12981-2017-ADD-1-DCL-1/en/pdf, accessed 29 March 2018).

the capacity to submit disputes, for example to international arbitration, without the interposition of their home State. To the contrary, the objective of the constituent document of the WTO is to provide for 'the common institutional framework for the conduct of trade relations among its Members'.[4] The Marrakesh Agreement makes no mention of its relationship to the individual trader, and to the extent that the interrelated trade agreements attached to the Agreement confer material rights on individuals, they only do so indirectly.[5] Moreover, and of particular importance in the present context, the WTO dispute settlement system exclusively hears disputes between States, while individuals have no independent standing before the Dispute Settlement Body or the Appellate Body.[6]

The explanation for the contrasts between international investment law and international trade law is likely to be found in the essential difference between making a long-term investment in a foreign State and engaging in a single trade transaction. The commercial risk undertaken by an investor is innately greater than that taken by the trader.[7] International trade law is therefore of lesser interest to a study of the international legal personality of individuals—except as an example of a field where States have seemingly had little cause to confer rights and obligations directly on individuals, and therefore have not done so. Consequently, the (limited) role of individuals in WTO law will not be examined further at this juncture. Instead, Section 8.2 focuses on the position of the individual in international investment law, following a brief introduction of State contracts in Section 8.1.

Subsequently, Section 8.3 examines some interesting aspects of EU law in relation to the international legal personality of individuals. A section on EU law in the present chapter may seem curious, since it is not commonly regarded as a part of international (economic) law, but indeed as a 'new legal order' of its own. However, as will become apparent, a major point of Section 8.3 is to challenge the popular conception of EU law as separate from the international legal system, and to illustrate that this notion is—at least in part—based on the 'States-only' conception of international legal personality. While contemporary EU law regulates a large number of issues which cannot reasonably be said to fall within the category of 'international economic law', the economic integration of Europe was the original purpose of the Union and remains an underlying rationale for the cooperation between the EU Member States.

[4] Agreement Establishing the World Trade Organization (hereafter Marrakesh Agreement), 15 April 1994, Article 1.

[5] See, for example, Steve Charnovitz, 'The WTO and the Rights of the Individual' 36 *Intereconomics* (2001) 98–108, and Sarah Joseph, *Blame it on the WTO?: A Human Rights Critique* (OUP, 2011) 36. See also Joost Pauwelyn, 'The Role of Public International Law in the WTO: How Far Can We Go?' 95 *AJIL* (2001) 535, 552.

[6] See Annex 2 to the Marrakesh Agreement: Understanding on Rules and Procedures Governing the Settlement of Disputes.

[7] See further Rudolf Dolzer and Christoph Schreuer, *Principles of International Investment Law* (2nd edn, OUP, 2012) 19.

8.1 State Contracts

Before embarking on the treaty regulation of foreign investments, it is pertinent to make some general remarks on so-called State contracts, that is, contracts to which at least one party is a State and at least one other party is an individual. In the *Serbian Loans* Judgment of 1929, the PCIJ made two fundamental assertions about State contracts. First, it stated plainly that only contracts between States are a part of international law, whereas a contract between a State and a private person or entity would always be governed by the domestic law of a given State. Second, the PCIJ declared that the answer to the question of *which* State's domestic law was to be found in private international law, a body of norms that according to the PCIJ itself belonged to national law:

> Any contract which is not a contract between states in their capacity as subjects of international law is based on the municipal law of some country. The question as to which this law is forms the subject of that branch of law which is at the present day usually described as private international law or the doctrine of the conflict of laws. The rules thereof may be common to several states and may even be established by international conventions or customs, and in the latter case may possess the character of true international law governing the relations between states. But apart from this, it has to be considered that these rules form part of municipal law.[8]

The PCIJ's findings concerning, first, the nature of State contracts and, second, the question of applicable law are discussed in turn in Sections 8.1.1 and 8.1.2.

8.1.1 The nature of State contracts

The PCIJ's contention that a contract between a State and an individual does not in itself form part of international law is generally accepted.[9] This is hardly surprising as the opposite view would clearly conflict with the prevalent theory on the sources of international law. A contract between a State and an individual is undoubtedly not a treaty. Nevertheless, examples from practice do exist where State contracts have, explicitly or by implication, been conceived as treaties. Although they remain exceptional and have been profoundly criticized, it is meaningful for present purposes to dwell upon a few of these instances, because they show how different conceptions of international legal personality have muddled the debate about the nature of State contracts. In both *TOPCO/CALASIATIC* and *Sandline International*, the private party was lifted conceptually to the international level, but there were substantial differences between the ways in which this manoeuvre was carried out.

[8] *Case Concerning the Payment of Various Serbian Loans Issued in France* (Judgment) [1929] PCIJ Ser. A, No. 20, 41.

[9] See for example ICJ, *Anglo-Iranian Oil Co. (United Kingdom v. Iran)(Jurisdiction)* (Judgment) [1952] ICJ Rep 93, 112.

In the *TOPCO/CALASIATIC*[10] award from 1977, the sole arbitrator, René-Jean Dupuy, expressly stated that the companies TOPCO and CALASIATIC were not States and that their concession agreement with Libya was not a treaty.[11] Nevertheless, he essentially treated the contract as if it were a treaty, and concluded that 'the legal order from which the binding nature of the contract derives … is international law'.[12] Moreover, Dupuy found that the choice of law clause in the contract pointed to international law.[13] In his opinion, it necessarily followed that the private parties to the dispute were to be perceived as international legal persons, because Libya had recognized them as such in the particular context of the contract.[14] In this sense, *TOPCO/CALASIATIC* reflects the modified 'States-only' conception of the individual as a derivative international legal person.[15] Dupuy referred explicitly to the ICJ's 1949 Advisory Opinion in *Reparations for Injuries* and asserted:

> [S]tating that a contract between a State and a private person falls within the international legal order means that for the purposes of interpretation and performance of the contract, it should be recognized that a private contracting party has specific international capacities. But, unlike a State, the private person has only a limited capacity and his quality as a subject of international law does enable him only to invoke, in the field of international law, the rights which he derives from the contract.[16]

In addition, Dupuy reiterated the statements of Special Rapporteur F. V. García Amador in his *Fourth report on State Responsibility* from 1958, which in turn referred to the writings of Schwarzenberger.[17] The report inter alia concludes that 'it cannot be argued on the basis of the traditional position that because individuals are not subjects of international law rights and obligations resulting from a contract between a State and an individual cannot be regarded as "international" in character.'[18]

Dupuy's award has subsequently been criticized for neglecting what by proponents of the modified 'States-only' conception of international legal personality is perceived as a precondition for attributing international legal personality to the

[10] *Texaco Overseas Petroleum Company and California Asiatic Oil Company v. The Government of the Libyan Arab Republic*, Award on the Merits, Sole Arbitrator Dupuy, 19 January 1977, 53 *ILR* 389 (hereafter *TOPCO/CALASIATIC*).

[11] Ibid, para. 46.

[12] Ibid, para. 26. See further Ole Spiermann, 'Applicable Law', in Peter Muchlinski, Federico Ortino, and Christoph Schreuer (eds), *The Oxford Handbook of International Investment Law* (OUP, 2008) 89, 99. The majority of arbitrators in *Revere Copper & Brass, Inc. v. Overseas Private Investment Corporation*, Award, 24 August 1978, 56 *ILR* (1980) 261, 271 largely followed Dupuy's argument, when they stated that 'long term economic development agreements … while not made between governments and therefore wholly international, are basically international in that they are entered into as a part of a contemporary international process of economic development'. See also A. V. M. Struycken, 'Arbitration and State Contracts', 374 *Recueil des Cours* (2014) 9, 37–9.

[13] *TOPCO/CALASIATIC* (n 10) paras 40–45.

[14] Ibid, para. 48.

[15] See Section 2.2.1.

[16] *TOPCO/CALASIATIC* (n 10) para. 47.

[17] See Section 2.2.1.

[18] ILC, *Fourth report on State Responsibility*, Special Rapporteur F.V. García-Amador (1959) para. 129.

private party to a State contract,[19] namely that this was clearly the intention of the State in question.[20]

The arbitral award in *Sandline International* from 1998 implies the perception of the private party as a participant in the international legal system.[21] It makes no mention of the concept of international legal personality, but merely finds that '[a]n agreement between a private party and a State is an international, not a domestic, contract. This tribunal is an international, not a domestic, arbitral tribunal and is bound to apply the rules of international law.'[22]

The tribunal thus applied international law to the contract, although the choice of law clause unmistakably pointed to English law.[23] Apparently, the tribunal did not consider its findings on the applicable law to be at odds with the contract, because the rules of international law 'are not excluded from, but form part of, English law which is the law chosen by the parties to govern their contract.'[24] Against this background, the tribunal invoked the principle codified in Article 27 of the VCLT and stated that 'a state cannot rely on its own internal laws as the basis for a plea that a contract concluded by it is illegal.'[25] It was, evidently, not considered necessary to present a doctrinal explanation for the application of this international legal principle to the contract in question. The tribunal simply relied on the international features of both the contract and the arbitration[26] in order to internationalize the legal personality of *Sandline International*.[27]

Additional examples of arbitral awards, which have conceptually lifted State contracts to the international level, include *Sapphire International Petroleums Ltd v. National Iranian Oil Company* from 1963,[28] and *AGIP SpA v. The Government of the People's Republic of the Congo* from 1979.[29]

8.1.2 The law applicable to State contracts

The second implication of *Serbian Loans* regarding the law applicable to State contracts is less simple than the PCIJ's categorization of State contracts as national law. The PCIJ clearly infers that State contracts cannot be governed by international law, because one of the parties to such contracts by definition lacks international legal

[19] See further Section 2.2.1. See also Roland Portmann, *Legal Personality in International Law* (CUP, 2010) 124.

[20] See for example Christopher Greenwood, 'State Contracts in International Law—The Libyan Oil Arbitrations', 53 *BYBIL* (1982) 27, 50ff, and A. A. Fatouros, 'International Law and the Internationalized Contract', 74 *AJIL* (1980) 134, 135–6. The award is, however, praised for confirming the possibility of applying international law to a state contract. See, for example, Portmann (n 19) 125 and Julien Cantegreil, 'The Audacity of the *Texaco/Calasiatic Award*: René-Jean Dupuy and the Internationalization of Foreign Investment Law', 22 *EJIL* (2011) 441.

[21] Section 2.5.

[22] *Sandline International Inc. v. Papua New Guinea*, Interim Award, 9 October 1998, 117 *ILR* (2000) 552, para. 10.1. (hereafter *Sandline International*).

[23] Ibid, para. 6.3. [24] Ibid. [25] Ibid, para. 10.2.

[26] See ibid, para. 10.1 (cited above n 22). [27] See further Portmann (n 19) 239–42.

[28] *Sapphire International Petroleums Ltd v. National Iranian Oil Company*, Award, 15 March 1963, 35 *ILR* (1967) 136, 175–6. See further Ivar Alvik, *Contracting with Sovereignty* (Hart, 2011) 35.

[29] *AGIP SpA v. The Government of the People's Republic of the Congo*, Award, 30 November 1979, 1 *ICSID Reports* (1993) 306, 324. Notably, René-Jean Dupuy was one of three arbitrators.

personality. In that respect, *Serbian Loans* is a reflection of the 'States-only' conception.[30] However, as will be exemplified in the following, subsequent international arbitration of commercial disputes has significantly challenged the PCIJ's reasoning.

Notably, even the *Serbian Loans* case itself, and the *Brazilian Loans*[31] case decided by the PCIJ on the same day, suggested that the application of national law is subject to certain international norms, including the principle of *pacta sunt servanda*. Against the background of the paragraph 41 cited above, one might have expected the PCIJ to conduct a thorough examination of Serbian law, which it had found to be the primary applicable law.[32] But instead the PCIJ relied heavily on the international legal principles of good faith as an integral part of the principle of *pacta sunt servanda*.[33] In the words of Thomas W. Wälde: 'The Serbian Loans case therefore stands primarily for the primacy of the contract text itself rather than for any recognition of state powers to modify such obligations with reference to domestic law.'[34] Similarly, a number of subsequent awards purporting to apply domestic law in fact let international legal principles in through the back door.[35]

A more direct approach was taken by the tribunal in the *Lena Goldfields Arbitration*[36] of 1930 concerning a dispute between a British company and the Soviet Union. The tribunal openly followed the argument of Lena Goldfields' counsel, Vladimir R. Idelson, that it should apply 'general principles of law such as those recognized by Article 38 of the Statute of the Permanent Court of International Justice'.[37] The award is frequently cited as an early, possibly the first, commercial arbitration tribunal to explicitly apply international law rather than domestic law as 'the proper law of the contract'.[38] V. V. Veeder has famously stated that 'Idelson's

30 See Section 2.2. See also Portmann (n 19) 74–5.

31 *Case Concerning the Payment in Gold of Brazilian Federal Loans contracted in France* (Judgment) [1929] PCIJ Ser. A, No. 21 (hereafter *Brazilian Loans*).

32 *Serbian Loans* (n 8) 42. The PCIJ found French law to govern issues concerning the currency in which payment was to be made. Ibid, 43.

33 See ibid, 33, 36, and 41. See also *Brazilian Loans* (n 31), for example 116, 111–12, and 114–15. See further Ole Spiermann, 'Twentieth Century Internationalism in Law' 18 *EJIL* (2007) 785, 808, and Thomas W. Wälde, 'The Serbian Loans Case: A Precedent for Investment Treaty Protection of Foreign Debt?', in Todd J. Weiler (ed.), *International Investment Law and Arbitration: Leading Cases from the ICSID, NAFTA, Bilateral Treaties and Customary International Law* (Cameron May, 2005) 383, 396–8. In the sense that the PCIJ made a doctrinal proclamation, which it went on to effectively contradict, the *Serbian Loans* Judgment resembles the Permanent Court's contemporary Advisory Opinion in *Jurisdiction of the Courts of Danzig*. See further Section 3.1.2.2.1.

34 Wälde (n 33), 398.

35 See for example *Administration of Posts and Telegraphs of Czechoslovakia v. Radio Corporation of America*, 1 April 1932, reprinted in 30 *AJIL* (1936) 523, 530–1, and *AGIP*, 30 November 1979, 323. More outspoken awards from the early period simply found national law to be inadequate. See for example *Petroleum Development Ltd. v. Sheikh of Abu Dhabi*, September 1951,18 *ILR* (1951) 144, 149, which states: 'If any municipal system of law were applicable, it would *prima facie* be that of Abu Dhabi. But no such law can reasonably be said to exist.' See similarly *Ruler of Qatar v. International Marine Oil Company Ltd.*, June 1953, 20 *ILR* (1953) 534, 544–5. See further Spiermann (n 33) 808–9.

36 Reprinted in Arthur Nussbaum, 'Arbitration Between the Lena Goldfields Ltd and the Soviet Government', 36 *Cornell Law Quarterly* (1950–1) 31, 42–53.

37 Ibid, 50 (para. 22).

38 Ibid. See also V. V. Veeder, 'The Lena Goldfields Arbitration: The Historical Roots of Three Ideas' 47 *ICLQ* (1998) 747, 751.

internationalisation of a transnational contract was a gigantic first step for international commercial arbitration, almost equivalent to the caveman's discovery of fire.'[39]

In the seminal *ARAMCO* award of 1958, the arbitral tribunal did not rely exclusively on Saudi Arabian law, but regarded general principles of law as a part of the proper law of the contract:

> Matters pertaining to private law are, in principle, governed by the law of Saudi Arabia but with one important reservation. That law must, in case of need, be interpreted or supplemented by the general principles of law, by the custom and practice in the oil business and by notions of pure jurisprudence, in particular whenever certain private rights—which must inevitably be recognized to the concessionaire if the Concession is not to be deprived of its substance—would not be secure in an unquestionable manner by the law in force in Saudi Arabia.[40]

With the State contract as 'the fundamental law of the Parties',[41] the tribunal found that 'general principles of law' and systems of national law were equally possible choices as applicable law. The label 'general principles of law' as opposed to 'international law' is most likely to be explained as a corollary to the overall distinction between private and public international law.[42] By referring to 'general principles of law', the arbitrators perhaps tried to steer clear of scholarly uproar, which might at the time have been the result of direct application of international law to individuals.[43] For example, McNair claimed as follows in 1957: '[T]he legal system appropriate to the type of contract under consideration is not public international law but shares with public international law a common source of recruitment and inspiration, namely, "the general principles of law recognized by civilized nations"'.[44] In McNair's opinion, 'economic development agreements' thus make up a special category of contracts, which is governed neither by international law nor national law, but belongs to a separate legal order comprising 'the general principles of law recognized by civilized nations'.[45] As for the suggestion of 'a separate legal order', McNair's statement might be read as a premonition of the ECJ's 1963 *Van Gend en Loos* Judgment.[46]

39 Ibid, 772. See also Spiermann (n 33) 808–9, and Alvik (n 28) 31–3.

40 *Saudi Arabia v. Arabian American Oil Company*, Award, 23 August 1958, 27 *ILR* (1963) 117, 169.

41 Ibid, 168.

42 See also Section 2.5.

43 See further Spiermann (n 33) 210. See also Section 7.2.2.1.

44 Arnold McNair, 'General Principles of Law Recognized by Civilized Nations' 33 *BYBIL* (1957) 1, 6. See also ibid, 10 and 19. For a contemporary example of this line of thought, see Alexander Orakhelashvili, 'The Position of the Individual in International Law', 31 *California Western International Law Journal* (2001) 241, 260–1.

45 Similarly, Verdross has argued that a contract not governed by domestic law by itself made up a new legal order with the sole function of regulating the relationship between the parties. Alfred Verdross, 'Quasi-International Agreements and International Economic Transactions', *Yearbook of World Affairs* (1964) 230, 246. See also Alvik (n 28) 48–50.

46 *Van Gend en Loos v. Nederlandse Administratie der Belastingen* [1963] ECLI:EU:C:1963:1. See further Section 8.3.2.

There is substantial variation in the ways in which the 'internationalization of State contracts'[47] has been executed by various arbitral tribunals. Further examination of this issue, however, lies outside the scope of the present work. Suffice it to note that the applicable law has indeed been internationalized as legal standards beyond national law have come to play a significant role in the resolution of disputes over State contracts.[48]

Some contemporary investment law scholars nevertheless remain highly critical of the idea of applying international law to State contracts. Sornarajah, for example, claims that '[t]he theory of internationalization, though it continues to be advanced in modern writings, can be dismissed as having no merit.'[49] Sornarajah evidently bases his claim in part on the 'States-only' conception of international legal personality:

> There are obvious defects with the theory that international law could apply to foreign investment transactions. The foreign party to the transaction, at least in the eyes of positivist international lawyers, does not have sufficient personality in international law to enter into relations with a state or to be a possessor of rights in international law.[50]

Along similar lines, A. F. M. Maniruzzaman ties the idea of internationalization of State contracts—via the view that individuals are the subjects of all law—to the monistic construction of the relationship between international law and domestic law.[51] Maniruzzaman begins his argument by quoting the following statement from Hersch Lauterpacht's Separate Opinion to the ICJ's Judgment in the *Certain Norwegian Loans* case in 1957:

> It may be admitted, in order to simplify a problem which is not at all simple, that an 'international' contract must be subject to some national law; this was the view of the Permanent Court of International Justice in the case of the Serbian and Brazilian Loans. However, this does not mean that national law is a matter which is wholly outside the orbit of international law. National legislation—including currency legislation—may be contrary, in its intention or effects, to the international obligations of the State. The question of conformity of national legislation with international law, is a matter of international law. The notion that if a matter is governed by national law it is for that reason at the same time outside the sphere

[47] This widely used term is somewhat misleading as it is, of course, not the state contract itself that is internationalized, but the law applicable to it.

[48] See further Spiermann (n 12) 94–9 and 102–7. See also Nagal Nassar, 'Internationalization of State Contracts: ICSID, The Last Citadel', 14 *Journal of International Arbitration* (1997) 185.

[49] M. Sornarajah, *The International Law of Foreign Investment* (4th edn, CUP, 2017) 341. See further ibid, 339–49.

[50] Ibid, 342. Notably, Sornarajah concedes that the application of the principle of *pacta sunt servanda* to State contracts is not founded on the assimilation of State contracts to treaties, but rather on the idea that this norm is a general principle of law, that is, a source of international law. Ibid, 346. In contrast to the dominant view, however, he does not believe that a body of international law governing state contracts exists. Rather, he argues (ibid, 342),

> [t]he extraction of law on the basis of such a weak source of law in such a controversial area is unsatisfactory. The principles which have been extracted have been challenged as being based on subjective choices of individual arbitrators and scholars predisposed to building up a system of investment protection.

[51] A. F. M. Maniruzzaman, 'State Contracts in Contemporary International Law: Monist versus Dualist Controversies', 12 *EJIL* (2001) 309.

of international law is both novel and, if accepted, subversive of international law. It is not enough for a State to bring a matter under the protective umbrella of its legislation, possibly of a predatory character, in order to shelter it effectively from any control by international law.[52]

According to Maniruzzaman, Lauterpacht's statement must be dismissed because it rests on his 'monist-naturalist' ideas, including the notion that 'the individual is the centre of all law'.[53] Arguably, Maniruzzaman thereby (mis)reads Lauterpacht's work on international legal theory into his statement as an ICJ judge. Taken at face value, the quoted paragraph from Lauterpacht's Separate Opinion neither implies a presumption for the subjectivity of individuals in international law nor a monistic construction of the relationship between international law and domestic law.[54] Instead, it merely reiterates the rather uncontroversial notion that—from the point of view of international law—national law cannot be invoked as an excuse for violating international law. The crux of the matter is thus whether international legal norms governing State contracts can be shown to exist. In that sense, the quote is neatly in tune with the 'a posteriori' conception of international legal personality and the point put forward in this book, which specifically pertaining to State contracts may be summed up as follows: international law applies to State contracts either if the parties to the contract have made this choice of law or if a relevant international norm, such as 'general principles of law' or Article 42(1) of the Convention on the Settlement of Investment Disputes between States and Nationals of Other States,[55] so provides.

Turning to treaty regulation of foreign investments, the following section will commence with a brief outline of the historical development. Section 8.2.1 will present the International Centre for Settlement of Investment Disputes (hereafter ICSID), while Sections 8.2.2 and 8.2.3 will discuss the role of individuals under primary and secondary rules of international investment treaties.

8.2 International Investment Law

Traditionally, claims against a host State concerning foreign investments were asserted through diplomatic protection. Today, diplomatic protection is generally not an option open to the home State in the settlement of a dispute between an investor and the host State, when the dispute is governed by an investment treaty.[56]

As a special field of study, international investment law mainly developed over two principal periods. From 1870 to the First World War there was a significant increase in foreign investments. This early development was predominantly met

[52] *Certain Norwegian Loans (France v. Norway)*(Judgment) [1957] ICJ Rep 9, Separate Opinion of Judge Sir Hersch Lauterpacht, 37. Maniruzzaman (n 51) 311–12.

[53] Maniruzzaman (n 51) 312.

[54] Lauterpacht's 'individualistic' conception of international legal personality is outlined in Section 2.4.

[55] Convention on the Settlement of Investment Disputes between States and Nationals of Other States (hereafter ICSID Convention), 18 March 1985, 4 *ILM* (1965) 524.

[56] Zachary Douglas, *The International Law of Investment Claims* (CUP, 2009) 1.

by national legal responses, with only a few examples of international regulation. During the two world wars and in the interwar period, there was little activity in terms of foreign investments. After 1945 the field progressed very slowly until the 1990s, whereupon the number of foreign investments grew drastically.[57]

The analysis in what follows distinguishes between the primary and secondary international legal rules, which have been adopted in response to the outlined expansion of international investments. The distinction is a pertinent analytical tool in this context, because it has a direct bearing on important issues, such as the host State's ability to invoke countermeasures as a circumstance precluding wrongfulness and the investor's competence to waive its right to submit a dispute to arbitration. To be clear, the term 'primary rules' refers to the material rules concerning standards of treatment in international investment law, while the term 'secondary rules' covers the means of enforcing the material rules. Section 8.2.2 will study the role attributed to private investors under the primary rules of bilateral and regional investment treaties, while Section 8.2.3 will discuss the procedural position of individuals pursuant to the secondary rules on investment treaty arbitration. At the outset, however, it is appropriate to comment briefly on the constituent document of the favoured forum for arbitration under investment treaties, namely ICSID.[58]

8.2.1 The International Centre for Settlement of Investment Disputes

The ICSID is an independent international institution set up under the ICSID Convention with the principal purpose of facilitating reconciliation and arbitration of international investment disputes. The ICSID Convention was adopted in 1965 but remained virtually ineffective until the beginning of the 1990s, with only a couple of registered cases per year on average. Since the mid 1990s the caseload has grown remarkably. Today, the ICSID has more than 150 Member States, and by mid 2017 the total number of registered cases had reached 619.[59]

One of the principal objectives behind the adoption of the ICSID Convention was to make sure that agreements between foreign investors and host States were binding under international law not only on the parties to the relevant agreement, but also in the relationship between the host State and the investor's home State.[60] Under Article 25(1) of the ICSID Convention, ICSID has jurisdiction only upon the consent of both the host State and the investor:

> The jurisdiction of the Centre shall extend to any legal dispute arising directly out of an investment, between a Contracting State (or any constituent subdivision or agency of a Contracting

[57] See further Dolzer and Schreuer (n 7) 4–8.

[58] Some treaties alternatively refer disputes to the International Chamber of Commerce, the Court of Arbitration, or ad hoc arbitration in accordance with the Arbitration Rules of the United Nations Commission on International Trade Law (hereafter UNCITRAL Rules). See note 3 regarding the EU initiative of multilateral investment court.

[59] A chart with the total number of ICSID cases registered by calendar year is available at https://icsid.worldbank.org/en/.

[60] Spiermann (n 33) 810.

State designated to the Centre by that State) and a national of another Contracting State, which the parties to the dispute consent in writing to submit to the Centre.

According to the summary record of discussions of the drafters, the ICSID Convention was considered to be a step on the road towards further recognition of the international legal personality of individuals:

[A] far more important feature of the Convention was that in traditional international law a wrong done to a national of one State for which another State was internationally responsible was actionable not by the injured national but by his State. In practice that principle had been superseded by a number of instances in which the provision had been made for settlement of investment disputes by direct conciliation or arbitration between the host State and the foreign investor. The internationally binding character of such arrangements had not, however, been recognised hitherto, and the Convention was designed to fill that gap. Thus the Convention would be in harmony with the growing recognition of the individual as a subject of international law.[61]

Correspondingly, Aron Broches, who as General Counsel of the International Bank of Development and Reconstruction played a pivotal role in the drafting of the ICSID Convention, stated in retrospect:

From a legal point of view the most striking feature of the Convention is that it firmly establishes the capacity of a private individual or a corporation to proceed directly against a State in an international forum, thus contributing to the growing recognition of the individual as a subject of international law.[62]

Some participants in the drafting process objected to the proposed detachment of the home State and the corollary independence of the foreign investor.[63] But Broches' argument concerning the practical benefits from the perspective of both host States and investors prevailed:

As to the suggestion that disputes between an investor and a host State should be lifted to the level of inter-State disputes, it would, of course, be possible to work out such a system, which would be consistent with traditional concepts of international law. The present draft, however, sought to do just the opposite in the belief that not only investors but States would prefer to deal with each other directly . . . and that to translate a dispute between the investor and a State into the realm of inter-State relations might be undesirable.[64]

A pertinent question arising out of Article 25(1) in conjunction with an investment treaty, which confers a right on investors to submit disputes to ICSID arbitration, is

[61] *Convention on the Settlement of Investment Disputes between States and Nationals of Other States*, Vol. II (ICSID 1968) 303. See also ibid, 464.

[62] Aron Broches, 'The Convention of the Settlement of Investment Disputes Between States and Nationals of Other States', 136 *Recueil des Cours* (1972-II) 331, 349.

[63] *Convention on the Settlement of Investment Disputes between States and Nationals of Other States*, Vol. II (ICSID 1968), 493–4 and 501.

[64] Ibid, 495. See also ibid, 496, 499, and 502. See also *Convention on the Settlement of Investment Disputes between States and Nationals of Other States*, Vol. I, (ICSID 1970) 110–18, See further Christoph H. Schreuer et al., *The ICSID Convention—A Commentary* (2nd edn, CUP, 2009) 160–1.

whether an investor may waive his right to consent to the ICSID's jurisdiction. This issue will be discussed in Section 8.2.3.1.

8.2.2 Primary rules of international investment law

Parallel to the vast increase in foreign investments, the number of bilateral investment treaties (BITs) grew from 500 in 1990 to 2,000 at the end of the decade. Today, the number of signed BITs worldwide is approximately 3,000. The following section will focus on the role of the private investor under a number of model BITs and the two most prominent plurilateral investment protection instruments currently in force, namely Chapter 11 of the North American Free Trade Agreement (hereafter NAFTA), which entered into force in 1994, and Chapter 3 of the Energy Charter Treaty (hereafter ECT), which entered into force in 1998.[65]

Generally, investment treaties confer obligations on host States in order to promote investments. For example, they commonly prohibit uncompensated expropriation and prescribe standards of fair and equitable treatment and non-discrimination. What is significant in the present context, however, is not the extent of the protection afforded by these substantive rules, but whether they confer corresponding rights directly on the foreign investor or merely comprise inter-State obligations. This issue has been the subject of heated scholarly debate for some time.[66]

A key element in the analysis of the relevant treaty provisions, which some authors seem to neglect, is the distinction between primary and secondary rules.[67] Zachary Douglas, for example, takes the doctrine of diplomatic protection as his point of departure in the evaluation of the nature of primary rules contained in investment treaties. He finds that the doctrine of diplomatic protection 'is inappropriate as a foundation for the rationalisation of the legal relationship between the private investor and the host State'. Instead, he opines, their relationship can only be characterized as *sui generis*.[68] Douglas assumes that a State exercising diplomatic protection

[65] North American Free Trade Agreement, 17 December 1992, 32 *ILM* 612, and Energy Charter Treaty, 17 December 1994, 2080 *UNTS* 100.

[66] In the words of Tillmann Rudolf Braun: 'Given the current remarkable state of development of international investment law, it is surprising that to date neither the *actual nature* of the investor's rights resulting from investment treaties nor the possible *consequences* which arise for the investor, the states and international law, have been sufficiently defined' (emphasis in original). See Tillmann Rudolf Braun, 'Globalization-driven Innovation: The Investor as a Partial Subject in Public International Law—An Inquiry into the Nature and Limits of Investor Rights', Jean Monnet Working Paper 04/13 (2013), New York University School of Law (available https://ssrn.com/abstract=2286607, accessed 21 January 2018).

[67] On the importance of the distinction, see further Eric de Brabandere, *Investment Treaty Arbitration as Public International Law* (CUP, 2014) 55ff.

[68] Douglas (n 56) 6. See further ibid, 94–5. Overall, Douglas finds that even a 'superficial appraisal of the different legal relationships and categories arising out of the investment treaty regime is sufficient to disclose its hybrid or *sui generis* character'. See Zachary Douglas, 'The Hybrid Foundations of Investment Treaty Arbitration', 74 *Arbitration International* (2003) 151, 152–3. See also Anthea Roberts, 'Clash of Paradigms: Actors and Analogies Shaping the Investment Treaty System', 107 *AJIL* (2013) 45, 94. For critique of this view, see Martin Paparinskis, 'Analogies and Other Regimes of International Law', in Zachary Douglas, Joost Pauwelyn, and Jorge E. Viñuales (eds), *The Foundations of International Investment Law* (OUP, 2014) 73–4.

'is ... seeking redress for the breach of an obligation owed to itself' rather than to its national.[69] Based on this presumption, he conducts a comparative analysis of the principal features of diplomatic protection and investment treaty arbitration and finds them to diverge on essential points.[70] On this foundation, Douglas then concludes that '[t]he fundamental assumption underlying the investment treaty regime is clearly that the investor is bringing a cause of action based upon the vindication of its own rights rather than those of its national State.'[71]

While Douglas's conclusion as to the secondary rules is fully viable,[72] it does not follow that the primary rules of investment treaties are necessarily direct individual rights.[73] This question cannot be resolved by examining how the primary rules are enforced. Rather, the nature of the primary rules must—in accordance with the argument put forward in this book—be discerned by application of the general principles of treaty interpretation without prejudice as to the international legal personality of non-State entities.[74]

Pursuant to Article 31 of the VCLT, an examination of whether the standards of treatment prescribed by an investment treaty amount to rights of investors must take the text of the treaty as its point of departure. The wording of the relevant provisions varies significantly. Some provisions clearly suggest that direct rights accrue to the investor. For example, Article 7(3) of the Austria Model BIT reads: 'An investor of a Contracting Party which claims to be affected by expropriation by the other Contracting Party shall have the right to prompt review of its case'.[75] Likewise, Article 13(2) of the ECT provides that the investor 'shall have the right to' judicial review in case of expropriation.[76] But most provisions in investment treaties concerning standards of protection are more ambiguous. For instance, Article 3(1) of the China Model BIT from 1997 reads: 'Investments and investors of each Contracting

[69] Douglas (n 56) 14. As explained in Section 3.3, diplomatic protection is a set of secondary rules applied in situations where the primary rule concerns the interests of individuals, regardless of whether the provision in question is construed as an individual right.

[70] Douglas (n 56) 10–32.

[71] Ibid, 32. See also Douglas, 'The Hybrid Foundations of Investment Treaty Arbitration' (n 68) 182.

[72] See further Section 8.2.3.

[73] As regards Douglas's position on the relationship between the rights of the investor and the home State, see Douglas (n 56) 94–5 and Douglas, 'The Hybrid Foundations of Investment Treaty Arbitration' (n 68) 190–1. For critique, see Martins Paparinskis, 'Investment Treaty Arbitration and the (New) Law of State Responsibility', 24 *EJIL* (2013) 617, 640–1.

[74] See further Section 3.4. A number of arbitral tribunals have promoted the idea that investment treaties must be interpreted in favour of the investor. See for example *SGS Société Générale de Surveillance SA v. Republic of the Philippines*, Decision of the Tribunal on Objections to Jurisdiction, 29 January 2004, 8 *ICSID Reports* (2005) 515, para. 116. Pertaining to a dispute over the proper meaning of a BIT provision, the tribunal said: 'It is legitimate to resolve uncertainties in its interpretation so as to favour the protection of covered investments.' For pertinent critique of this notion, see Zachary Douglas, 'Nothing if not Critical for Investment Treaty Arbitration: Occidental, Eureko and Methanex', 22 *Arbitration International* (2006) 27, 51, and Kate Parlett, *The Individual in the International Legal System—Continuity and Change in International Law* (CUP, 2011) 113–14. See further Tarcisio Gazzini, *Interpretation of International Investment Treaties* (Hart, 2016) 51–3.

[75] Austria Model BIT, 2008 (available at http://investmentpolicyhub.unctad.org/Download/TreatyFile/4770, accessed 21 January 2018).

[76] To be clear, the right to review of expropriation claims laid down by these articles must be perceived as a primary rule, since it has to do with the substantial conditions to be provided by the host state.

Party shall all the time be accorded fair and equitable treatment in the territory of the other Contracting Party.'[77] Similarly, Article 1105 of NAFTA provides that '[e]ach Party shall accord to investments of investors of another Party . . . fair and equitable treatment'. Alternatively, Article 13(1) of the ECT prescribes that investors 'shall not be . . . subjected to' expropriation, while Article 3 of the Netherlands Model BIT from 2004 obliges each contracting party to 'ensure fair and equitable treatment' of investors.[78] As it is not evident whether these provisions indicate individual rights, it is hardly surprising that they have been construed differently by different observers.

In the example of NAFTA, it further adds to the confusion that key actors such as the Member States have advocated divergent interpretations in various contexts. In its Statement on Administrative Action from November 1993, which accompanied the implementing bill for NAFTA, the US Government seemingly argued that the primary rules set forth in Section A of the Chapter 11 confer rights directly on investors: 'The NAFTA provides US investors with the right to . . . receive the same treatment as domestic businesses. . . . In addition, the NAFTA gives US industries in Canada and Mexico . . . the right to international law protection against expropriation . . .'.[79] Later in the same document, however, it is contended that the primary rules contain inter-State obligations, while only the secondary rules included in Section B apply directly to individuals: 'Chapter Eleven comprises two parts. Part A sets out each government's obligations with respect to investors from other NAFTA countries and their investments in its territory. Part B affords investors the right to seek compensation through international arbitration for a violation of the provisions of Part A . . . .'[80]

Concurring with the latter conclusion, Canada has stated as follows before the Federal Court of Canada while seeking review of the ICSID award of 2000 in *S. D. Myers, Inv. v. the Government of Canada*:[81]

The obligations listed in Section A of NAFTA Chapter Eleven are not owed directly to individual investors. Rather, the disputing investor must prove that the NAFTA Party claimed

[77] China Model BIT (1997), reprinted in Zachary Douglas, *The International Law of Investment Claims* (CUP, 2009) 525–31. Similarly, Articles 3 and 4 of the US Model BIT provide that '[e]ach party shall accord to investors of the other party' certain treatment. See US Model BIT (2012), reprinted in Dolzer and Schreuer (n 7). See also Turkey Model BIT (2009), Article 3 (available at http://investmentpolicyhub.unctad.org/Download/TreatyFile/2852, accessed 21 January 2018), and UK Model BIT (2005), Articles 2, 3, and 4, reprinted in Dolzer and Schreuer (n 7) 371–2. See also Article III(2) of Agreement for the Promotion and Protection of Investments between the members of the Association of Southeast Asian Nations, 15 December 1987, available at http://asean.org/?static_post=the-1987-asean-agreement-for-the-promotion-and-protection-of-investments.

[78] Netherlands Model BIT (2004) (available at http://investmentpolicyhub.unctad.org/Download/TreatyFile/2859, accessed 21 January 2018). See also France Model BIT (2006), Article 4, reprinted in Douglas (n 56) 532–8.

[79] The North American Free Trade Agreement Implementation Act, Statement of Administrative Action, 4 November 1993, 8.

[80] Ibid, 140.

[81] *S. D. Myers, Inv. v. the Government of Canada*, Award (Merits), 13 November 2000, 8 *ICSID Reports* (2005) 18.

against has breached an obligation owed to another NAFTA Party under Section A and that the investor has incurred loss or damage by reason of or arising out of that breach.[82]

The debate on whether investment treaties merely lay down inter-State obligations or whether they confer rights directly on investors is ongoing in international legal scholarship. A number of contemporary observers support the 'derivative rights model' contending that individuals only indirectly benefit from the rights of their home State under international investment treaties.[83] Other scholars are sceptical of this analysis. Favouring the 'direct rights model', Martins Paparinskis has noted that 'the nature of investors' rights is far from settled',[84] but that 'in the absence of contrary practice it is more natural to interpret the rights as direct'.[85] This perspective is not exceptional. Subsequent to his comparative analysis of investment treaty arbitration and diplomatic protection, Douglas, for example, finds that '[a] textual analysis of investment treaties ... appears to be consistent with the conclusion that the substantive investment protection obligations proclaimed by the State parties are owed to investors directly'.[86] Referring to both primary and secondary rules, Spiermann concurs that '[i]t would take an excessively narrow standard of interpretation to find that modern bilateral investment treaties do not vest rights in private investors as subjects of international law.'[87]

Remarkably, however, Crawford reaches the opposite conclusion, although he—like Spiermann—explicitly finds it to be solely a matter of interpretation of the relevant investment treaty provisions whether the obligations set forth are owed directly to investors or only to the other contracting party.[88] Without particular effort to substantiate this argument, Crawford finds that, as far as primary rules are concerned, 'a standard bilateral or regional investment treaty is an interstate agreement, to which individual investors are not privy'.[89]

In line with the arguments of Paparinskis, Douglas, and Spiermann, the present author submits that interpretation in accordance with Articles 31–33 of the VCLT of provisions worded like the above-cited reasonably leads to the conclusion that

[82] Statutory Review in the Federal Court of Canada, *Amended Memorandum of Fact and Law of the Applicant, Attorney General of Canada v. S. D. Myers*, Inc., Court File No. T-225-01, 2001, para. 67.

[83] See, for example, Anastasios Gourgourinis, 'Investors' Rights Qua Human Rights? Revisiting the "Direct"/"Derivative" Rights Debate', in Malgosia Fitzmaurice and Panos Merkouris (eds), *The Interpretation and Application of the European Convention of Human Rights: Legal and Practical Implications* (Brill, 2012) 147. Notably, the distinction between primary or secondary rules is not always taken into account in the debate on the 'derivative model' vs the 'direct model'. The scholarly interest seems primarily to revolve around the nature of the secondary rules. See further Section 8.2.3.

[84] See also Martins Paparinskis, 'Investment Arbitration and the Law of Countermeasures', 79 *British Year Book of International Law* (2008) 264, 268.

[85] Ibid, 335. See also Martins Paparinskis, *The International Minimum Standard and Fair and Equitable Treatment* (OUP, 2013) 148: 'The weight of authority supports the view that investor–State arbitration is an invocation of State responsibility regarding obligations owed to the investor.'

[86] Douglas (n 56) 35. See also Douglas, 'The Hybrid Foundations of Investment Treaty Arbitration' (n 68) 183–4.

[87] Spiermann (n 33) 811.

[88] James Crawford, 'The ILC's Articles of Responsibility of States for Internationally Wrongful Acts: A Retrospect', 96 *AJIL* (2002a) 874, 887.

[89] Ibid, 888.

they do provide for individual rights of the investors. In the case of the ECT, this viewpoint is reflected in *The Energy Charter Treaty—A Reader's Guide*, issued by the Energy Charter Secretariat, which, for example, states that 'the Treaty grants a number of fundamental rights to foreign investors'.[90] Moreover, the idea of substantive individual rights under investment treaties finds—albeit perhaps hesitant—support in the English Court of Appeal's Judgment from 2005 in *Republic of Ecuador v. Occidental Exploration and Production Company*. Pertaining to a BIT between the US and Ecuador, the Court of Appeal inter alia held:

> Under the present treaty, a dispute may ... arise out of or relate to (a) a commercial agreement, (b) an executive authorization or (c) an alleged breach of a treaty right.... The treaty would have to be regarded as conferring or creating direct rights in international law in favour of investors either from the outset, or at least (and in this event retrospectively) as and when they pursue claims in one of the ways provided.... The former analysis is in our view natural and preferable, but it does not matter which applies.[91]

A more forthright endorsement of the notion of direct primary rights may be found in the 2016 *Urbaser* award concerning the Spain–Argentina BIT from 1991. The tribunal stated:

> A principle may be invoked in this regard according to which corporations are by nature not able to be subjects of international law and therefore not capable of holding obligations as if they would be participants in the State-to-State relations governed by international law. While such principle had its importance in the past, it has lost its impact and relevance in similar terms and conditions as this applies to individuals. A simple look at the MFN Clause of Article VII of the BIT shows that the Contracting States accepted at least one hypothesis where investors are entitled to invoke rights resulting from international law (in addition to the rights resulting from Article X).

As indicated by the Court of Appeal in the above-cited statement from the *Occidental* case, the question of whether primary rules in investment treaties prescribe individual or State rights is of limited practical relevance when a claim concerning infringement of such rights has been submitted to arbitration. In these situations, the arbitral tribunal is simply called upon to evaluate whether the host State has violated its obligations under the investment treaty to afford the investor particular standards of treatment. The nature of the primary rules has no bearing on the evaluation of the possible breach of the treaty and the potential assessment of damages.[92] Nonetheless, the question of the proper right holder assumes importance when the

[90] Energy Charter Secretariat, *The Energy Charter Treaty—A Reader's Guide* (2002) 19. See also 24 and 27 (available at https://is.muni.cz/el/1422/jaro2016/MVV2368K/um/ECT_Guide_ENG.pdf, accessed 21 January 2018). See also Jan Paulsson, 'Arbitration Without Privity', in T. W. Wälde (ed.), *The Energy Charter Treaty: An East–West Gateway for Investment and Trade* (Kluwer, 1996b) 422, 429.

[91] *Republic of Ecuador v. Occidental Exploration and Production Company (No. 1)*, 9 September 2005, 138 *ILR* (2010) 92, 133–4 (hereafter *Occidental*). See further Douglas (n 74) 37–8.

[92] See also James Crawford, 'Treaty and Contract in Investment Arbitration' 24 *Arbitration International* (2008) 351, 355. See further August Reinisch, 'Investors', in Math Noortmann, August Reinisch, and Cedric Ryngaert (eds), *Non-State Actors in International Law* (Hart, 2015) 253, 262, and de Brabandere (n 67) 58.

investor purports to waive its rights under the treaty, or when the host State invokes countermeasures as a circumstance precluding wrongfulness.

Given that the ability of the investor to waive rights under investment treaties primarily arises in practice in the context of secondary rules, this issue will be deferred to Section 8.2.3.1. The following analysis will focus on the possibility of the host State evading responsibility by claiming that violations of an investment treaty were countermeasures precluding wrongfulness.

8.2.2.1 Countermeasures as a circumstance precluding wrongfulness

Article 22 of ARSIWA concerning 'countermeasures in respect of an internationally wrongful act' reads: 'The wrongfulness of an act of a State not in conformity with an international obligation towards another State is precluded if and to the extent that the act constitutes a countermeasure taken against the latter State in accordance with chapter II of Part Three.' The wording clearly indicates that countermeasures may only be taken against a State; an interpretation which is corroborated by Article 49 laying down the 'objects and limits of countermeasures':

1. An injured State may only take countermeasures against a State which is responsible for an internationally wrongful act in order to induce that State to comply with its obligations under Part Two.
2. Countermeasures are limited to the non-performance for the time being of international obligations of the State taking the measures towards the responsible State.

The ILC's Commentary on Article 49 confirms that 'countermeasures may only be adopted against a State which is the author of the internationally wrongful act.' However, it is explained that '[t]his does not mean that countermeasures may not incidentally affect the position of third States or indeed other third parties.'[93] As countermeasures may thus exclusively be invoked as a circumstance precluding wrongfulness against States, it follows that a defence on this basis is unavailable to the host State in situations where the rights under an investment treaty accrue directly to the investor. The categorization of the primary rules in an investment treaty as either 'State rights' or 'individual rights' therefore becomes important.[94]

Three different NAFTA tribunals were confronted with this issue, in 2007, 2008, and 2009. They all concluded that Mexican taxes were in breach of Article 1102 of NAFTA concerning national treatment, and subsequently had to decide on Mexico's argument that the wrongfulness of the breach was precluded according to rules on countermeasures.

In the first case, *Archer Daniels Midland Company and Tate & Lyle Ingredients Americas, Inc. v. United Mexican States* (hereafter *ADM*), two of the three arbitrators agreed with the claimants 'that international law may under specific circumstances

[93] II *YILC* (2001) 130.

[94] See further Paparinskis (n 73) 632, and Sergio Puig, 'No Right Without a Remedy: Foundations of Investor–State Arbitration', in Zachary Douglas, Joost Pauwelyn, and Jorge E. Viñuales (eds), *The Foundations of International Investment Law* (OUP, 2014) 235, 249.

confer direct rights on individuals.'[95] As for the primary rules of Chapter 11, however, the majority found that 'the proper interpretation of the NAFTA does not substantiate that investors have individual rights'.[96] In their opinion, the 'substantive protection obligations' established under Section A of Chapter 11 remain inter-State, while the investor's procedural right to instigate arbitration under Section B is 'an exceptional right of action ... that would not otherwise exist under international law.'[97]

The third arbitrator, Arthur W. Rovine, appended a concurring opinion in which he argued 'that the substantive investment protections conferred by treaty upon NAFTA investors include the substantive right of legal redress for breaches of Section A of Chapter Eleven.'[98] In essence, Rovine construed the secondary rights of investors under NAFTA as primary rights and thereby eliminated the possibility for the host State to invoke countermeasures as a circumstance precluding wrongfulness. This manoeuvre is somewhat unfortunate, because the turning point in the context of countermeasures would seem to be the nature of the material provisions setting forth certain standards of protection, rather than the means of their enforcement.[99]

In *Corn Products International, Inc. v. United Mexican States* (hereafter *Corn Products*), the majority of arbitrators found that NAFTA does confer direct primary rights on investors: 'In the case of Chapter XI of the NAFTA, the Tribunal considers that the intention of the Parties was to confer substantive rights directly upon investors. That follows from the language used and is confirmed by the fact that Chapter XI confers procedural rights upon them.'[100] Moreover, they affirmed that the nature of the relevant provision is to be determined by application of the general principles of treaty interpretation:

> It is now clear that States are not the only entities which can hold rights under international law; individuals and corporations may also possess rights under international law, the question will be whether the text of the treaty reveals an intention to confer rights not only upon the Parties thereto but also upon individuals and/or corporations.[101]

The third tribunal, which gave its award in *Cargill, Incorporated v. United Mexican States* (hereafter *Cargill*) on 18 September 2009, also rejected Mexico's argument regarding countermeasures. The tribunal unambiguously stated that investors hold rights under Chapter 11, but it did not find it necessary to determine whether these were primary or secondary rights:

[95] *Archer Daniels Midland Company and Tate & Lyle Ingredients Americas, Inc. v. United Mexican States*, Award, 21 November 2007, ICSID Case No. ARB(AF)/04/05) para. 170.

[96] Ibid, para. 171. [97] Ibid, paras 172–173.

[98] Ibid, *Concurring Opinion of Arthur W. Rovine: Issues of Independent Investor Rights, Diplomatic Protection and Countermeasures*, para. 46.

[99] See similarly, however, *Cargill, Incorporated v. United Mexican States*, 18 September 2009, ICSID No. ARB(AF)/05/2, para. 426 (cited in what follows, see note 102).

[100] *Corn Products International, Inc. v. United Mexican States*, Decision on Responsibility, 15 January 2008, ICSID Case No. ARB(AF)/04/01) para. 169.

[101] Ibid, para. 168. While stressing that he found their analysis within the framework of 'traditional international law' to be unnecessary, the third arbitrator seemingly agreed with the majority's findings on this point. See ibid, *Separate Opinion of Andreas F. Lowenfeld*, paras 4–5.

That the origin of individual rights may be found in the act of a sovereign, or in the joint act of sovereigns, does not negate the existence of the rights conferred. It is the view of this Tribunal that Chapter 11 creates a framework within which it is the investor that acts upon and benefits from the obligations which are set forth in Chapter 11. It is not fruitful, in the Tribunal's view, to characterize the issue as whether the rights conferred upon the investor are substantive or merely procedural. The fact is that it is the investor that institutes the claim, that calls a tribunal into existence, and is the named party in all respects to the resulting proceedings and award.[102]

In light of the above conclusions on the nature of the primary rights in investment treaties, it will be of no surprise that the present author finds the arguments put forward in *Corn Products* to be the most persuasive. In this award, the tribunal simply applied general principles of treaty interpretation to reach the conclusion that Chapter 11 confers direct primary rights on investors. In contrast, the majority in *ADM* reached the opposite conclusion that Chapter 11 of NAFTA confers only secondary rights on the investors, and that countermeasures could, therefore, in principle be invoked.[103] These arbitrators seem to have applied a presumption against direct rights of individuals, given their statement that the investor's procedural right to instigate arbitration under Section B is 'an exceptional right of action ... that would not otherwise exist under international law.' Finally, *Cargill*'s deliberate disregard for the distinction between primary and secondary rights is somewhat confusing, since the tribunal does not explain why countermeasures should be ruled out if the primary rights are State rights, while the investor only holds secondary rights.

8.2.3 Secondary rules of international investment law

A key feature of international investment treaties is that they commonly include provisions which allow the private investor to refer disputes to international arbitration and to retain exclusive control over the claim during the proceedings.[104] Following an examination of whether the secondary rules set forth in model BITs and regional investment treaties govern investors directly, Section 8.2.3.1 will assess investors' capacity to waive, for example, ICSID jurisdiction.

Typically, BITs include both a provision conferring on the private investor the ability to commence commercial arbitration, and a provision which provides for arbitration between the Member States. In this context, disputes between investors and host States are naturally of primary interest.

Although the text of the relevant provisions varies between investment treaties, they seem to point consistently towards individual procedural rights of the investor. Article 8(2) of the UK Model BIT, for example, provides that the investor 'may agree

[102] *Cargill, Incorporated v. United Mexican States*, 18 September 2009, ICSID No. ARB(AF)/05/2, para. 426.

[103] The majority in *ADM* found, however, that the tax enacted by Mexico 'was not a valid countermeasure because it was not adopted to induce US's compliance with the NAFTA; nor does the Tax meet the proportionality requirements under customary international law.' See *ADM* (n 95) para. 180, and also Paparinskis (n 84) 336.

[104] See further David Collins, *An Introduction to International Investment Law* (CUP, 2017) 214.

to refer the dispute' to arbitration, whereas Article 10(2) of the Germany Model BIT prescribes that disputes 'shall, at the request of the investor . . . be submitted to arbitration.'[105] Moreover, Article 9(2) of the China Model BIT provides that disputes 'shall be submitted by the choice of the investor' to arbitration.[106] Article 1120 of NAFTA provides that 'a disputing investor may submit the claim to arbitration', while Article 26(2) of the ECT reads: 'the Investor party to the dispute may choose to submit it for resolution'.[107]

As is the case concerning primary rules (see Section 8.2.2), opinions are divided on whether or not the rights under secondary rules of investment treaties accrue directly to investors.[108] Remarkably, NAFTA Member States have expressed that investors merely enjoy derivative secondary rights under the Agreement.[109] Instead of regarding the investor as a holder of a direct right to submit disputes under investment treaties to arbitration, the argument is that the State has delegated its right to exercise diplomatic protection to the investor.[110] An oft-cited authority for the 'derivative' perception of claims submitted to arbitration by foreign investors is the *Loewen* award from 2003: 'There is no warrant for transferring rules derived from private law into a field of international law where claimants are permitted for convenience to enforce what are in origin the rights of Party states.'[111] On this basis, the *Loewen* tribunal applied the rule of continuous nationality under the doctrine of diplomatic protection. Similar to the US Government's argument in the *Loewen* case, [112] Mexico stated in a challenge to a NAFTA award before the Supreme Court of British Columbia in 2001 that investors making Chapter 11 claims are merely allowed to 'step into the shoes of' and 'assert the rights of' their home State.[113]

[105] See also the France Model BIT, Article 8.

[106] See similarly the Turkey Model BIT, Article 9(2).

[107] According to Articles 1116 and 1117 of NAFTA and Article 26(1) of the ECT investors may only bring claims based on the material provisions of respectively Chapter 11 of NAFTA and Part III of the ECT.

[108] See further Gourgourinis (n 83), de Brabandere (n 67) 60–7, and Paparinskis (n 73).

[109] See further Douglas (n 56) 16–17, and Jacomijn van Haersolte-van Hof and Anne K. Hoffmann, 'The Relationship between International Tribunals and Domestic Courts', in Peter Muchlinski, Federico Ortino, and Christoph Schreuer (eds), *The Oxford Handbook of International Investment Law* (OUP, 2008) 964, 992. See, however, The North American Free Trade Agreement Implementation Act, Statement of Administrative Action, November 1993, 8. See further Section 8.2.2.

[110] See for example Orakhelashvili (n 44) 262: 'The arbitration mechanism under the [ICSID] seems to reflect the traditional diplomatic protection system.'

[111] *The Loewen Group Inc. and Raymond L. Loewen v. United States of America*, Award, 26 June 2003, 7 *ICSID Reports* (2005) 421, para. 233. See further Douglas (n 56) 16, and Parlett (n 74) 109–10. Curiously, the derivative model advocated in para. 233 of the *Loewen* award seems to be inconsistent with the tribunal's prior statement in para. 223: 'Chapter Eleven of NAFTA represents a progressive development in international law whereby the individual investor may make a claim on its own behalf and submit the claim to international arbitration . . .'.

[112] See for example the statements of the US Government in connection with the *Loewen* case: *Reply of the United States of America to the Counter-Memorial of the Loewen Group Inc. on Matters of Jurisdiction and Competence*, 26 April 2002, ICSID Case No. ARB(AF)/98/3, 33ff.

[113] *United Mexican States v. Metalclad*, Transcript of Proceedings, 19 February 2001, 61 (available at https://nsarchive2.gwu.edu/NSAEBB/NSAEBB65/cjrt02192001.pdf, accessed 21 January 2018). See also Charles H. Brower II, 'Investor–State Disputes under NAFTA: The Empire Strikes Back', 40 *Columbia Journal of Transnational Law* (2001–2) 43, 70. A number of arbitral tribunals have required investors to resort to domestic courts without dismissing the direct procedural rights of the investor

In contrast to the 'derivative model' advocated by the *Loewen* award, there is substantial support in both practice and academic writings of the notion that investors hold direct procedural rights under investment treaties. However, there is some disagreement as to whether the investor is to be perceived as a direct right holder under the investment treaty from the outset, or only subsequently assumes this status.[114]

Crawford, who as mentioned in Section 8.2.2 does not find investment treaties to include primary rights of the investor, seems to favour the notion that the investor becomes the holder of secondary rights only at the point in time when a dispute is actually submitted to arbitration:

> [T]he secondary obligations arising from a breach may be owed directly to the beneficiary of the obligation, in this case the investor, who effectively opts in to the situation as a secondary right holder by commencing arbitral proceedings under the treaty. A new legal relation, directly between the investor and the responsible state, is thereby formed, if it did not already exist.[115]

Amazu A. Asouzu is equally hesitant to recognize the investor as the holder of procedural rights directly under investment treaties, but argues that the secondary rights of investors are 'activated' upon the signing of an investment contract providing the investor with the possibility of referring disputes to international arbitration: 'Conferring benefits or rights on private parties in treaties would appear possible if ... the private party agrees with any of [the contracting] states to use the facilities provided and actually incorporated a corresponding clause in the investment contract with that state.'[116] Similarly, Sornarajah found in 1994 that '[t]he right is created not in the contracting State but its national. For the right to be utilised, there must also be an arbitration clause in the contract which is concluded by the national.'[117]

under the investment treaty in question. Instead, they have perceived the exhaustion of local remedies as a precondition for establishing a violation of the relevant primary international norm. As explained by the tribunal in *Waste Management, Inc. v. United Mexican States* in 2004: 'in this context the notion of exhaustion of local remedies is incorporated into the substantive standard and is not only a procedural prerequisite to an international claim.' *Waste Management, Inc. v. United Mexican States*, Award, 30 April 2004, 43 *ILM* 967, para. 97. See further Dolzer and Schreuer (n 7) 265–7. See also Christoph Schreuer, 'Calvo's Grandchildren: The Return of the Local Remedies in Investment Arbitration', 4 *The Law and Practice of International Courts and Tribunals* (2005a) 1, and Ole Spiermann, 'Premature Treaty Claims', in Christina Binder et al. (eds), *International Investment Law for the 21st Century—Essays in Honour of Christoph Schreuer* (OUP, 2009) 463.

[114] See further Douglas (n 56) 35.

[115] Crawford, 'The ILC's Articles of Responsibility of States for Internationally Wrongful Acts: A Retrospect' (n 88) 888. See also James Crawford, *International Law as an Open System* (Cameron May, 2002b) 36 (emphasis in original):

> But under many ... BITs ..., the better view may be that provided there is standing at the time the investor commences the arbitration, a public obligation under a treaty is converted into a private right of action of the investor, even if the *content* of that right is determined by the treaty.

[116] Amazu A. Asouzu, *International Commercial Arbitration and African States: Practice, Participation and Institutional Development* (CUP, 2001) 343. See further ibid, 342–6 and 359–60.

[117] M. Sornarajah, *The International Law of Foreign Investment* (1994), 267. Curiously, Sornarajah appears to have changed his opinion several times. In M. Sornarajah, 'State Responsibility and Bilateral Investment Treaties', 20 *Journal of World Trade Law* (1986) 79, 93, he stated that 'no benefits or rights

In the eyes of the present author, interpretation of the cited provisions according to the general principles reflected in Articles 31–33 of the VCLT reasonably leads to the conclusion that investors hold rights to submit claims to international arbitration directly under the investment treaty in question. This view finds considerable support in international legal scholarship[118] and in a number of investment treaty awards. For example, the tribunal in *CMS Gas Transmission Company v. The Republic of Argentina* argued as follows in 2003:

> To some extent, diplomatic protection is intervening as a residual mechanism to be resorted to in the absence of other arrangements recognizing the direct right of action by individuals. It is precisely this kind of arrangement that has come to prevail under international law, particularly in respect of foreign investments, the paramount example being that of the 1965 Convention.[119]

The matter of when the investor becomes holder of the secondary right to submit a dispute to arbitration assumes practical importance when an investment contract includes a forum or arbitration clause derogating from an investment treaty to which the investor's home State and the host State are parties. In fact, investment contracts do not uncommonly include a provision selecting the domestic courts of the host State as the forum for dispute resolution.[120] The question is: At which point may the investor waive the right conferred upon it by an investment treaty to submit disputes to arbitration?

8.2.3.1 *The power of investors to waive international arbitration*

The question of the ability of investors to waive their secondary rights under investment treaties has been the subject of dispute in both practice and scholarship. It goes without saying that an investor cannot waive a right which is not vested in itself but in its home State.[121] The answer thus clearly depends on whether—and, if so, when—the secondary rules under investment treaties may be construed as

flow directly to the affected individual. Hence, it will be difficult to see how such a person could have a standing under the treaty'. *The International Law of Foreign Investment* (2nd edn, CUP, 2004) is silent on the issue of the secondary right holder, while the 3rd and 4th editions from 2010 and 2017 favour the derivative model: 'The enforcement of the right is outsourced to the foreign investor but it remains the right of the host [sic] state.' In Sornarajah (n 49) 254 (217 in the 3rd edition).

[118] See for example Thomas W. Wälde, 'Investment Arbitration under the Energy Charter Treaty—From Dispute Settlement to Treaty Implementation', 12 *Arbitration International* (1996) 429, 436, Jan Paulsson, 'Dispute Resolution', in Robert Pritchard (ed.), *Economic Development, Foreign Investment and the Law: Issues of Private Sector Involvement, Foreign Investment and the Rule of Law in a New Era* (Kluwer, 1996a) 209, 238, Rex J. Zedalis, 'Claims by Individuals in International Economic Law', 7 *American Review of International Arbitration* (1996) 115, 116–17, Ole Spiermann, 'Individual Rights, State Interests and the Power to Waive ICSID Jurisdiction under Bilateral Investment Treaties', 20 *Arbitration International* (2004) 179, 185, Douglas (n 56) 35, Parlett (n 74) 118, and de Brabandere (n 67) 63.

[119] *CMS Gas Transmission Company v. The Republic of Argentina*, Decision of the Tribunal on Objections to Jurisdiction, 17 July 2003, 42 *ILM* 788, para. 45.

[120] See further Spiermann (n 118) 180.

[121] See further Section 4.2.3 concerning Calvo clauses.

individual rights. But while the existence of individual rights under investment treaties is an obligatory precondition for the investor's ability to waive international arbitration, it is not necessarily adequate.

First, the present section will briefly examine examples from arbitral practice concerning the concept of individual rights under investment treaties in the context of the investor's waiver. Subsequently, the question of whether the interests of the home State might in any case supersede such waivers will be discussed, and finally, some remarks will be made about the relevance of the relationship between international and national law to the issue at hand.

In the first arbitral decision to give effect to a forum clause in respect of the ICSID's jurisdiction, *SGS v. Philippines* from 2004, the arbitral tribunal held that 'the general provisions of BITs should not, unless clearly expressed to do so, override specific and exclusive dispute settlement agreements made in the investment contract itself.'[122] However, the tribunal expressly distinguished between contract claims and treaty claims, and since the dispute did not entail claims based on the BIT independently of contract claims, the question of waiver of treaty rights was left open.[123]

In *Eureko v. Poland* from 2005, the arbitral tribunal supported the view that secondary rights in investment treaties only accrue directly to investors as of the referral of the dispute to arbitration:

> International law thus recognizes that an investor may, after a claim against a State has arisen, enter into a settlement agreement with that State and commit to a final waiver of those claims. The State can subsequently rely on that waiver and assert it as a defense against the investor, should such investor attempt to raise those claims again.[124]

To the contrary, the arbitral tribunal in *TSA Spectrum v. Argentina* indicated (with reference to possible breaches of both the relevant investment contract and BIT) that the investor was capable of waiving its right to resort to international arbitration by agreeing to terms to that effect in the investment contract. But it had to be clearly established that this had actually been done: '[I]f Argentina had intended that the Concession Contract should have the far-reaching effect of excluding application of the remedies under the BIT, it must have been incumbent on Argentina to indicate this in a clear manner in the Contract or in connection with the conclusion of the Contract....'[125]

As argued earlier, investment treaty provisions such as Article 10(2) of the Germany Model BIT, Article 1120 of NAFTA and Article 26(2) of the ECT must be interpreted so as to confer direct rights on the investor to submit claims to international arbitration. Consistently, it is submitted that an investor as a starting point

[122] *SGS Société Générale de Surveillance SA v. Philippines*, Decision on Objections to Jurisdiction, 29 January 2004, 8 *ICSID Reports* (2005) 515, para. 134.

[123] See, however, ibid, para. 154, which will be discussed in what follows.

[124] *Eureko v. Poland*, Partial Award, 19 August 2005, 12 *ICSID Reports* (2007) 335, para. 175.

[125] *TSA Spectrum de Argentina SA v. Argentina*, Award, 19 December 2008, para. 62. See also Spiermann (n 118) 191, concerning *Lanco International Inc. v. Argentina*, Preliminary Decision, 8 December 1998, 5 *ICSID Reports* (2002) 367.

has the ability to waive its rights as of the point in time when it qualifies as an investor under the terms of an investment treaty.[126] There is little in the above-cited provisions to indicate otherwise. But it is of course open to the States parties to explicitly rule out the possibility of waiver in an investment treaty. In situations where the investment treaty is silent, the question of whether investors can waive their access to investment treaty arbitration can only be settled by interpretation of the applicable sources of law in each case.[127]

Arbitral practice indicates a tendency towards narrow interpretation of waivers.[128] It must be clearly established that the investor purported to renounce his rights under the relevant investment treaty, before a deviating forum or arbitration clause in an investment contract is given effect. In addition, there is a presumption that forum or arbitration clauses in investment contracts apply exclusively to contract claims, while treaty claims are unaffected. For example, the Decision on Jurisdiction from 2005 in *Aguas del Tunari v. Bolivia* reads:

> [A]n explicit waiver by an investor of its rights to invoke the jurisdiction of ICSID pursuant to a BIT could affect the jurisdiction of an ICSID tribunal. However, the Tribunal will not imply a waiver or modification of ICSID jurisdiction without specific indications of the common intentions of the Parties.[129]

Even though it is accepted that the investor holds direct rights under investment treaties, it is pertinent to ask whether the interest of the home State might yet have a bearing on the investor's possibility of waiving these rights. As mentioned above, the tribunal in *SGS v. Philippines* did not draw any conclusions as to an investor's waiver of treaty rights, but it did indicate that the interests of the home State might have an influence:

> It is, to say the least, doubtful that a private party can by contract waive rights or dispense with the performance of obligations imposed on the States parties to those treaties under international law. Although under modern international law, treaties may confer rights, substantive and procedural, on individuals, they will normally do so in order to achieve some public interest.[130]

126 See also van Haersolte-van Hof and Hoffmann (n 109) 1002–3 and 1006.

127 As discussed further in what follows, this interpretative act might take into consideration the broader purpose of the parties to the investment treaty. See further de Brabandere (n 67) 69–70, Bart L. Smit Duijzentkunst, 'Of Rights and Powers: Waiving Investment Treaty Protection', blog post on EJILTalk!, 9 December 2013 (available at https://www.ejiltalk.org/of-rights-and-powers-waiving-investment-treaty-protection/, accessed 21 January 2018), and Anne Peters, *Beyond Human Rights—The Legal Status of the Individual in International Law* (CUP, 2016) 327.

128 Besides *SGS v. Philippines*, para. 154, and *TSA Spectrum v. Argentina*, para. 62, which are cited above, additional examples include *CAA and Vivendi Universal (CGE) v. Argentina*, Decision on Annulment, 3 July 2002, 6 *ICSID Reports* (2004) 340, para. 76, and *Azurix Corp. v. Argentina*, Decision on Jurisdiction, 8 December 2003, 43 *ILM* (2004) 262, paras 75ff.

129 *Aguas del Tunari v. Bolivia*, Decision on the Respondent's Objection to Jurisdiction, 21 October 2005, paras 118–119 (available at http://www.iisd.org/pdf/2005/AdT_Decision-en.pdf, accessed 21 January 2018).

130 *SGS v. Philippines* (n 122), para. 154. See also Spiermann (n 118) 199–200.

According to Jeswald W. Salacuse, the aim of promoting economic relations between the two contracting parties rules out the possibility of investors waiving their rights to institute arbitration: 'Investors should not be allowed to permanently waive those rights and thus risk undermining the international legal structure between the contracting states.'[131]

What is at stake is thus the consideration of the 'public interest' of the home State vis-à-vis the party autonomy of the investor in question—a balance between interests similar to the case of Calvo clauses discussed in Section 4.2.3. There is a fundamental difference, however, between a clause in an investment contract amounting to the investor's waiver of international arbitration and a clause whereby a foreign national waives the protection of his home State in all matters concerning the contract. In the former instance, the investor is waiving its own rights under international law, while the national in the latter instance is waiving the rights of his home State. The right of the home State to exercise diplomatic protection on behalf of its national is not impaired by an investment contract clause referring disputes to, for example, national courts.[132]

Finally, it is noteworthy that the question of the capability of the investor to waive, for example, ICSID jurisdiction in a number of cases has been perceived as a matter of the relationship between international and national law. For example, the tribunal stated in *CAA and Vivendi Universal (CGE) v. Argentina* that '[a] state cannot rely on an exclusive jurisdiction clause in a contract to avoid the characterisation of its conduct as internationally unlawful under a treaty.'[133]

It should be underlined that the deciding factor as to the jurisdiction of, for example, the ICSID is consent of the parties to the dispute. It is neither the relationship between international law and national law nor the distinction between treaty claims and contract claims. A waiver of a right under international law, which otherwise meets the requirements, may perfectly well take the form of a provision in a document belonging to domestic law, such as forum selection clause in an investment contract.[134] What matters is not the nature of the document, but rather the content of the relevant provision. The following categorical statement by Christoph Schreuer is thus open to question:

> [A] forum selection clause contained in a contract between the investor and the host State does not affect the competence of a tribunal, based on a BIT. The two proceedings are based on different causes of action even though they may arise from the same set of facts. Dispute settlement clauses in contracts are designed to deal with contract claims. ICSID tribunals based on BITs are competent to hear claims arising from the terms of the BIT.[135]

[131] Jeswald W. Salacuse, *The Law of Investment Treaties* (2nd edn, OUP, 2015) 433–4. Salacuse dismisses the above-cited paragraph of *Aguas del Tunari v Bolivia*, cf. note 129, not only because it is an *obiter dictum*, but also because 'the tribunal did not fully analyse the role of the investor–state arbitration in the preservation of the investment regime created by investment treaties.' Ibid, 434.

[132] See further Spiermann (n 118) 205–8.

[133] *CAA and Vivendi Universal (CGE) v. Argentina*, Decision on Annulment, 3 July 2002, 6 *ICSID Reports* (2004) 340, para. 103.

[134] Spiermann (n 118) 205.

[135] Christoph Schreuer, 'Investment Treaty Arbitration and Jurisdiction over Contract Claims—the *Vivendi I* case Considered', in Todd Weiler (ed.), *International Investment Law and Arbitration: Leading*

8.3 European Union Law

It is scarcely disputable that individuals have substantive rights and obligations under EU law, including both the founding treaties and legal instruments based on the founding treaties, while they only have limited access to the Court of Justice of the European Union (hereafter CJEU). For present purposes, however, it is not so much the content of the primary and secondary rules of EU law that attracts attention. The controversy over the concept of international legal personality in relation to this field revolves first and foremost around the following question: Has the fact that EU law substantially governs individuals directly led to a separation of this treaty regime from general international law and the creation of a 'new legal order'? Before discussing this matter in Section 8.3.2, however, some introductory remarks about the procedural position of individuals before the CJEU are called for.

8.3.1 The right of individuals to petition the CJEU

The legal standing of individuals before the CJEU is, as mentioned, relatively limited. Article 263(4) of the Treaty on the Functioning of the European Union (hereafter TFEU)[136] gives individuals the right to challenge various institutions, bodies, offices, or agencies of the EU, while Article 340 TFEU allows individuals to claim damages for injury suffered as a result of EU action. In addition, individuals have indirect access to the Court under Article 267 concerning requests by national courts of preliminary rulings on 'the interpretation of the Treaties' or 'the validity and interpretation of acts of the institutions, bodies, offices or agencies of the Union'. The following cursory inquiry will focus on the example of actions brought by individuals for the annulment of EU acts under Article 263(4) TFEU and its predecessors. Article 173(4) of the EEC Treaty read: 'Any natural or legal person may ... institute proceedings against a decision addressed to that person or against a decision which, although in the form of a regulation or a decision addressed to another person, is of direct and individual concern to the former.'

The meaning of 'direct and individual concern' to non-addressees was construed very narrowly in the practice of the ECJ. In the leading *Plaumann* case of 1963, the Court found that a decision would only be of individual concern to non-addressees if 'that decision affects them by reason of certain attributes which are peculiar to them or by reason of circumstances in which they are differentiated from all other persons and by virtue of these factors distinguishes them individually just as in the case of the person addressed.'[137]

Cases from the ICSID, NAFTA, Bilateral Treaties and Customary International Law (Cameron May, 2005b) 281, 293.

[136] Treaty on the Functioning of the European Union (latest consolidated version), 2010 OJ (C83) 47.

[137] *Plaumann v. Commission* [1963] ECLI:EU:C:1963:17, 107. As for the identification of 'direct concern', see *Paraiki-Patraiki v. Commission* [1985] ECLI:EU:C:1985:18, paras 6–10.

Evidently, the ECJ created a very high threshold, which few applicants would be able to pass.[138] The content of Article 173(4) remained the same through the subsequent treaty amendments until the adoption of the Lisbon Treaty.[139] A material change brought about by the Lisbon Treaty is that individuals no longer have to prove that 'a regulatory act which . . . does not entail implementing measures' is of 'individual concern', but only of 'direct concern' to them. The definitions of 'a regulatory act' and 'implementing measures' in Article 263(4) TFEU are of course of key importance, and since the Lisbon Treaty itself is silent on this matter, clarification by the CJEU was much awaited.[140]

In its Order in the *Inuit* case of 6 September 2011, the General Court distinguished between regulatory and legislative acts, and upheld the criterion of 'individual concern' as regards legislative acts.[141] The General Court thus took a cautious and somewhat formalistic approach to Article 263(4), given its emphasis of the way in which an act is adopted.[142] The CJEU affirmed this interpretation in its 2013 Judgment in the case, underlining that

> the purpose of the alteration to the right of natural and legal persons to institute legal proceedings, laid down in the fourth paragraph of Article 230 EC, was to enable those persons to bring, under less stringent conditions, actions for annulment of acts of general application other than legislative acts.[143]

Likewise, the term 'implementing measures' has been construed narrowly by the CJEU. It follows from *Telefónica SA v. European Commission* from 2013[144] and *T & L Sugars* from 2015[145] that even 'implementing measures'

[138] Attempts to limit the demands were shut down by the ECJ. For example the Court found in *Unión de Pequeños Agricultores v. Council* [2002] ECLI:EU:C:2002:462, para. 41, that any reform of the legal standing of individuals would require treaty reform. It thereby overruled the Opinion of Advocate General Jacobs in the case and the Judgment of the General Court in *Jégo Quéré v. Commission* [2002] ECLI:EU:T:2002:112. See also *Commission v. Jégo Quéré* [2004] ECLI:EU:C:2004:210, para. 36. See further Albertina Albors-Llorens, 'Sealing the Fate of Private Parties in Annulment Proceedings? The General Court and the New Standing Test in Article 263(4) TFEU', 71 *Cambridge Law Journal* (2012) 52, 52.

[139] Treaty of Lisbon, 13 December 2007, 2007 OJ (C 306) 1.

[140] See, for example, Francis Jacobs, 'Access by individuals to judicial review in EU law', in Henning Koch et al. (eds), *Europe—The New Legal Realism* (Djøf Publishing, 2010) 263, 273, and Christoph Werkmeister, Stephan Pötters, and Johannes Traut, 'Regulatory Acts within Article 263(4) TFEU—A Dissonant Extension of *Locus Standi* for Private Applicants', 13 *Cambridge Yearbook of European Legal Studies* (2010–11) 311.

[141] *Inuit Tapiriit Kanatami and Others v. European Parliament, Council of the European Union, Kingdom of the Netherlands, European Commission* [2011] ECLI:EU:T:2011:419, paras 41ff.

[142] See further Albors-Llorens (n 138) 54–5. See also the General Court's Judgment of 25 October 2011 in the *Microban* case confirming that the notion of 'direct concern' in Article 263(4) TFEU is to be interpreted is the same way as the predecessor Article 230(4) TEC. *Microban International and Microban (Europe) v. Commission* [2011] ECLI:EU:T:2011:623, para. 30.

[143] *Inuit Tapiriit Kanatami and Others v. European Parliament and Council of the European Union* [2013] ECLI:EU:C:2013:625, para. 59.

[144] *Telefónica SA v. European Commission* [2013] ECLI:EU:C:2013:852.

[145] *T & L Sugars Ltd and Sidul Açúcares, Unipessoal Lda v. European Commission* [2015] ECLI:EU:C:2015:284. Remarkably, Advocate General Cruz Villalón had argued that the action should be found admissible, due to the lack of discretion of the implementing authority. He found that the contested measures were 'management measures' rather than 'implementing measures'. *Opinion of*

leaving no discretion to the implementing authority are covered by Article 263(4).[146]

The fact that individuals have so clearly been perceived as subjects of EU law in spite of their limited ability to directly petition the CJEU and the ECJ might be seen as confirmation that international legal subjectivity does not presuppose the existence of independent international means of enforcement.[147] However, as will become apparent in Section 8.3.2, the ECJ has strongly questioned whether EU law forms part of the international legal system to begin with. It therefore goes without saying that the development of the legal standing of individuals within the judicial system of the EU has had little to do with the theoretical concept of personality in international law. Like the evolution of the right of individuals to seize the ECtHR,[148] the interpretation of Article 173 of the EEC Treaty by the ECJ and of Article 263(4) TFEU has most likely been influenced by practical concerns; in this case the fear of being flooded by challenges to EU law and of unduly impeding the institutions' ability to adopt legislation.[149] The practice of the CJEU reinforces the overall idea that national courts are the proper fora for individual complaints concerning the legality or EU measures, and that natural and legal persons only in exceptional cases should have direct access to the EU courts in Luxembourg.[150]

8.3.2 A new legal order?

As mentioned in Chapter 1, the ECJ famously declared in its landmark *Van Gend en Loos* Judgment of 1963 that 'the Community constitutes a new legal order of international law'. The reason that the international legal system was deemed insufficient to encompass Community law was that the subjects of Community law 'comprise not only Member States but also their nationals.'[151] The Court thus clearly inferred

Mr Advocate General Cruz Villalón, T & L Sugars Ltd and Sidul Açúcares Unipessoal Lda v. European Commission [2014] ECLI:EU:C:2014:2283, paras 30 and 47.

[146] See further Camilla Buchanan and Luca Bolzonello, 'Towards a Definition of "Implementing Measures" under Article 263, Paragraph 4, TFEU', 6 *European Journal of Risk Regulation* (2015) 671–6.

[147] See further Section 3.1.2.2.2.

[148] See further Section 7.2.1.

[149] See further Adam Cygan, 'Recent Developments in Judicial Review and Article 230 EC', 4 *ERA Forum* (2003) 67, 73–4.

[150] See further Carl Fredrik Bergström, 'Defending Restricted Standing for Individuals to Bring Direct Actions against "Legislative" Measures', 10 *European Constitutional Law Review* (2014) 481, 495–6, and Carla Ferstman, *International Organizations and the Fight for Accountability* (OUP, 2017) 179–81. In a recent case concerning EU trade relations with Morocco, the General Court appeared to slightly broaden the scope of 'direct and individual concern' by declaring admissible an annulment action brought by Front Polisario, the liberation movement for Western Sahara. See *Front populaire pour la libération de la saguia-el-hamra et du rio de oro (Front Polisario) v. Council of the European Union* [2015] ECLI:EU:T:2015:953, paras 104–114. See further Sandra Hummelbrunner and Anne-Carlijn Prickartz, 'It's not the Fish that Stinks! EU Trade Relations with Morocco under Scrutiny of the General Court of the European Union', 32 *Utrecht Journal of International and European Law* (2016) 19, 26–7. In December 2016, however, the CJEU dismissed the case with the argument that the relevant agreement did not apply to the territory of Western Sahara. *Council of the European Union v. Front populaire pour la libération de la saguia-el-hamra et du rio de oro (Front Polisario)* [2016] ECLI:EU:C:2016:973. See further Jed Odermatt, 'Council of the European Union v Front populaire pour la libération de la saguia-el-hamra et du rio de oro (Front Polisario)—Case C-104/16 P', 111 *AJIL* (2017) 731–8.

[151] *Van Gend en Loos* (n 46) 12.

that only States may be the subjects of international law. Since Community law applied to individuals directly,[152] it could not by definition be regarded as a part of the international legal system. EU lawyers have generally embraced the ECJ's approach, and it continues to be conventional wisdom in these circles that international law—contrary to EU law—does not count individuals among its subjects.[153]

The year after *Van Gend en Loos*, in 1964, the ECJ indicated that 'the new legal order' was national rather than international in kind: 'By contrast with ordinary international treaties, the EEC Treaty has created its own legal system which, on the entry into force of the Treaty, became an integral part of the legal systems of the Member States and which their courts are bound to apply.'[154] Subsequently, the 'new legal order' phraseology was supplemented by constitutional rhetoric.[155] In 1993, the ECJ clearly affirmed the constitutional nature of the EEC Treaty and the separateness of Community law from the international legal system:

> [T]he EEC Treaty, albeit concluded in the form of an international agreement, none the less constitutes the constitutional charter of a Community based on the rule of law. As the Court of Justice has consistently held, the Community treaties established a new legal order for the benefit of which the States have limited their sovereign rights, in ever wider fields, and the subjects of which comprise not only Member States but also their nationals (see, in particular, the judgment in Case 26/62 Van Gend en Loos [1963] ECR 1). The essential characteristics of the Community legal order which has thus been established are in particular its primacy over the law of the Member States and the direct effect of a whole series of provisions which are applicable to their nationals and to the Member States themselves.[156]

Joseph H. H. Weiler, a prominent proponent of the notion of a separate legal order of the EU,[157] acknowledges 'that *Ven Gend en Loos* and its progeny are not the result of a new hermeneutics and that the decision would, or at least could be the same

[152] In the case at hand, the ECJ concluded that Article 12 of the EEC Treaty 'must be interpreted as producing direct effects and creating individual rights which national courts must protect.' Ibid, 13.

[153] Textbook examples include Damian Chalmers et al., *European Union Law—Cases and Materials* (3rd edn, CUP, 2014) 15, Koen Lenaerts and Piet van Nuffel, *European Union Law* (3rd edn, Sweet & Maxwell, 2011) 18ff, Paul Craig and Gráinne de Búrca, *EU Law—Text, Cases, and Materials* (6th edn, OUP, 2015) 188–90. See also ILC, *Fragmentation of International Law: Difficulties Arising from the Diversification and Expansion of International Law—Report of the Study Group of the International Law Commission*, finalized by Martti Koskenniemi, 13 April 2006, 112.

[154] *Flaminio Costa v. ENEL* [1964] ECLI:EU:C:1964:51, 593.

[155] See for example *Les Verts v. European Parliament* [1986] ECLI:EU:C:1986:166, para. 23. See also Eric Stein's seminal article 'Lawyers, Judges and the Making of a Transnational Constitution', 75 *AJIL* (1981) 1. Stein argues that the ECJ initiated a process of constitutionalization by creating inter alia the doctrine of direct effect.

[156] *Opinion 1/91 (EEA Agreement I)* [1993] ECLI:EU:C:1991:490, para. 21. See further Barbara Brandtner, 'The Drama of the EEA Comments on Opinions 1/91 and 1/92', 3 *EJIL* (1992) 300, 305–6. *Opinion 1/91 (EEA Agreement I)* was echoed in 2011 in the CJEU's *Opinion 1/09 (Unified Patent Litigation System)* when the Court found the establishment of a European and Community Patents Court to be incompatible with the EU legal order. *Opinion 1/09 (Unified Patent Litigation System)* [2011] ECLI:EU:C:2011:123, paras 64–67, 80, and 89. See further Matthew Parish, 'International Courts and the European Legal Order', 23 *EJIL* (2012) 141.

[157] See for example Joseph H. H. Weiler, 'The Transformation of Europe', 100 *Yale Law Journal* (1990–1) 2403, 2422, and Joseph H. H. Weiler and Ulrich R. Haltern, 'The Autonomy of the Community Legal Order—Through the Looking Glass' 37 *HILJ* (1996) 411.

under the traditional rules of interpretation of public international law.'[158] He nevertheless implies a presumption against individual rights in international law: 'The obligation contained in Article 12 is part of an international Treaty and is not part of domestic law. With nothing more, this would create a generic presumption against interpreting Article 12 as allowing an individual from relying on the provision in making a claim for violation of rights.'[159]

In this respect, Weiler's argument bears resemblance to the distinction between 'law-making treaties' and 'treaties of the classic kind' advocated, for example, by the ECtHR.[160] By introducing 'a new legal discourse', the ECJ, similar to the ECtHR, became conveniently free from what both courts perceived to be the restraints of general principles of treaty interpretation.[161] However, as argued in this book, there is no legal basis for applying a presumption against direct individual rights in international law.[162]

Weiler and Ulrich Haltern asked in 1996: 'In light of the overwhelming practice of the last three or four decades, if the Community order is treated as constitutional who cares what it "really" is?'[163] One answer is that international lawyers (ought to) care, at least as long as key arguments supporting the notion of a separate legal order of the EU rest on a misconception of international law. Indeed, the detachment of EU law from the international legal system has been consistently questioned by a number of international legal scholars.[164] These critics would seem to find practical support in Betlem and Nollkaemper's 2003 study, which shows that in practice EU law and international law are generally applied in domestic law in the same manner. Against this background, Betlem and Nollkaemper conclude that '[t]he difference

158 Joseph H. H. Weiler, 'Rewriting Van Gend & Loos: Towards a Normative Theory of ECJ Hermeneutics'. in Ola Wiklund (ed.), *Judicial Discretion in European Perspective* (Kluwer Law International, 2003) 150, 151.

159 Weiler (n 158) 157. See also Weiler, 'The Transformation of Europe' (n 157) 2413 addressing the doctrine of direct effect: 'The European Court reversed the normal presumption of public international law whereby international legal obligations are result-oriented and addressed to states.'

160 See further Section 7.2.2.2.

161 See further Jonas Christoffersen, *Fair Balance—Proportionality, Subsidiarity and Primarity in the European Convention on Human Rights* (Martinus Nijhoff, 2009a) 67–8, relying on Weiler's analysis of the practice of the ECJ.

162 See, for example, Sections 3.1.2.2.1 and 3.4.3.1.

163 Weiler and Haltern (n 157) 416.

164 See for example Derrick Wyatt, 'New Legal Order, or Old?', 7 *European Law Review* (1982) 147, Bruno de Witte, 'Retour à "Costa"—La primauté du droit communautaire à la lumière du droit International' 20 *Revue trimestrielle de droit européen* (1984) 425, Bruno de Witte, 'Treaty Revision in the European Union: Constitutional Change through International Law', 35 *Netherlands Yearbook of International Law* (2004) 51, Bruno de Witte, 'Sources and the Subjects of International Law: The European Union's Semi-Autonomous System of Sources', in Samantha Besson and Jean d'Aspremont (eds), *The Oxford Handbook on the Sources of International Law* (OUP, 2017) 769, 770, Theodor Schilling, 'The Autonomy of the Community Legal Order: An Analysis of Possible Foundations', 37 *HILJ* (1996) 389, Ole Spiermann, 'The Other Side of the Story: An Unpopular Essay on the Making of the European Community Legal Order', 10 *EJIL* (1999) 763, 770, Spiermann (n 33) 804–8, Marko Milanović, 'Norm Conflict in International Law: Whither Human Rights?', 20 *Duke Journal of Comparative & International Law* (2009) 69, 107, Ole Spiermann, 'On Law and Policy in the European Court of Justice', in Henning Koch et al. (eds), *Europe—The New Legal Realism* (Djøf Publishing, 2010) 715, 717ff, Portmann (n 19) 77–9, and Bruno Simma and Dirk Pulkowski, 'Of Planets and the Universe: Self-contained Regimes in International Law', 17 *EJIL* (2006) 482, 516.

between the legal orders of EC law and public international law is one of degree rather than of principle.'[165]

Similar to the example of the ECtHR discussed in Section 7.2.2.2, it is arguable that the ECJ has applied a number of provisions in a way which, from the perspective of international law, is in fact restrictive. For example, the doctrine of direct effect has influenced the Court's application of secondary legislation listed in Article 288 TFEU. Article 288 distinguishes between a 'regulation', which 'shall be binding in its entirety and directly applicable in all Member States' and a 'directive', which 'shall be binding, as to the result to be achieved, upon each Member State to which it is addressed, but shall leave to the national authorities the choice of form and methods.' From the viewpoint of an international lawyer, the distinction between regulations and directives has to do with the implementation of international law into national law. Whether or not a provision in either kind of instrument confers rights or duties directly on individuals, however, is solely a matter of interpretation of its content. In the *Marshall* Judgment from 1986, the ECJ nevertheless held that by definition only regulations can have direct effect between private parties:

> [T]he binding nature of a directive, which constitutes the basis for the possibility of relying on the directive before a national court, exists only in relation to 'each Member State to which it is addressed'. It follows that a directive may not of itself impose obligations on an individual and that a provision of a directive may not be relied upon as such against such a person.[166]

By conflating the question of the entities governed by EU legal norms with the question of their effect in domestic law, the Court thus ends up limiting the effect of directives in the relationship between individuals.

Another parallel to the practice of the ECtHR[167] is the question of the relationship between EU law and international law, which was the core issue in the ECJ's famous *Kadi I* Judgment of 2008. The ECJ stated that notwithstanding the UN Charter's primacy in international law under Article 103 (which the Court did not question),[168] the Community judicature is always competent to review the lawfulness of a Community act, even if the purpose of the act is to give effect to a Security Council resolution:

> [O]bligations imposed by an international agreement cannot have the effect of prejudicing the constitutional principles of the EC Treaty, which include the principle that all Community acts must respect fundamental rights, that respect constituting a condition of their lawfulness which it is for the Court to review in the framework of the complete system of legal remedies established by the Treaty.[169]

[165] Gerrit Betlem and André Nollkaemper, 'Giving Effect to Public International Law and European Community Law before Domestic Courts—A Comparative Analysis of the Practice of Consistent Interpretation', 14 *EJIL* (2003) 569, 588.

[166] *Marshall v. Southampton and South-West Hampshire Area Health Authority* [1986] ECLI:EU:C:1986:84, para. 48. See further Spiermann (n 33) 807–8.

[167] See Section 7.2.3.

[168] *Yassin Abdullah Kadi & Al Barakaat International Foundation v. Council & Commission* [2008] ECLI:EU:C:2008:461, para. 288 (cited in what follows).

[169] Ibid, para. 285. The General Court reaffirmed this position in *Yassin Abdullah Kadi v. European Commission* [2010] ECLI:EU:T:2010:418, paras 115–129. The CJEU dismissed the appeal by the

The Court thus seized the opportunity to underline that EU law as an autonomous legal order determines the terms on which it gives effect to international law[170]—just like a national legal order.[171] According to Katja S. Ziegler, the *Kadi I* Judgment 'marks a leap in the constitutionalism of the legal order of the European Community'.[172] It is noteworthy, however, that the ECJ did not draw any conclusions as to whether the material obligations of Member States towards the EU would be limited in a situation, where it would be impossible for the Member State to comply with a UN Security Council resolution and an EU measure at the same time. The Court simply stated that 'any judgment given by the Community judicature deciding that a Community measure intended to give effect to such a resolution is contrary to a higher rule of law in the Community legal order would not entail any challenge to the primacy of that resolution in international law.'[173]

European Commission, Council, and United Kingdom in *European Commission and Others v. Yassin Abdullah Kadi* [2013] ECLI:EU:C:2013:518, paras 65–69.

170 Article 216(2) TFEU provides: 'Agreements concluded by the Union are binding upon the institutions of the Union and on its Member States.' See further, for example, de Witte, 'Sources and the Subjects of International Law: The European Union's Semi-Autonomous System of Sources' (n 164) 777–8, and Jed Odermatt, 'The Court of Justice of the European Union: International or Domestic Court', 3 *CJILC* (2014) 696.

171 See further Jean d'Aspremont and Frédéric Dopagne, 'Kadi: The ECJ's Reminder of the Elementary Divide between Legal Orders', 5 *International Organizations Law Review* (2008a) 317, Veronica Fikfak, 'Kadi and the Role of the Court of Justice of the European Union in the International Legal Order', 15 *Cambridge Yearbook of European Legal Studies* (2013) 587, Gráinne de Búrca, 'The European Court of Justice and the International Legal Order After *Kadi*', 51 *HILJ* (2010) 1, 2–4. Notably, de Búrca compares the ECJ's *Kadi* judgment to the US Supreme Court's decision in *Medellin v. Texas*, 552 US 491 (2008). See further Daniel Halberstam, 'Constitutional Heterarchy: The Centrality of Conflict in the European Union and the United States', in Jeffrey Dunoff and Joel P. Trachtmann (eds), *Ruling the World—Constitutionalism, International Law, and Global Governance* (CUP, 2009) 326.

172 Katja S. Ziegler: 'Strengthening the Rule of Law, but Fragmenting International Law: The *Kadi* Decision of the ECJ from the Perspective of Human Rights', 9 *Human Rights Law Review* (2009) 288. See further, for example, Jean d'Aspremont and Frédéric Dopagne, 'Two Constitutionalisms in Europe: Pursuing an Articulation of the European and International Legal Orders', 36 *ZaöRV* (2008b) 939, Gráinne de Búrca, 'The ECJ and the international legal order: a re-evaluation', in Gráinne de Búrca and Joseph H. H. Weiler, *The Worlds of European Constitutionalism* (CUP, 2012) 105, and Juliane Kokott and Christoph Sobotta, 'The Kadi Case—Constitutional Core Values and International Law—Finding the Balance?' 23 *EJIL* (2012) 1015.

173 *Kadi I* (n 168) para. 288. As discussed in Section 7.2.3, this line of reasoning has subsequently served as inspiration for the ECtHR in the *Nada* case. It also appears to have inspired the Danish Supreme Court in its 2016 ruling in the *Ajos* case (U.2017.824H). Contrary to the guidelines set forth by the CJEU in a preliminary ruling (ECLI:EU:C:2016:278), a majority of eight out of nine Danish Supreme Court judges held that Court-made principles of EU law developed after the latest amendments of the Danish Accession Act, for example the general principle of non-discrimination on grounds of age, were inapplicable to the case. With a rationale not unlike *Kadi I*, para. 288, the majority stated:

> It is therefore for the EU Court of Justice to rule on whether a rule of EU law has direct effect and takes precedence over a conflicting national provision .... The question whether a rule of EU law can be given direct effect in Danish law, as required under EU law, turns first and foremost on the Law on accession by which Denmark acceded to the European Union.

(Cited from unofficial English translation of U.2017.824H, available at http://www.supremecourt.dk/supremecourt/nyheder/pressemeddelelser/Documents/Judgment%2015-2014.pdf, accessed 21 January 2018). See further Mikael Rask Madsen, Henrik Palmer Olsen, and Urška Šadl, 'Competing Supremacies and Clashing Institutional Rationalities: The Danish Supreme Court's Decision in the Ajos Case and the National Limits of Judicial Cooperation', *European Law Journal*, Vol. 23, 140–50.

A recent—and controversial—reiteration of the CJEU's position that the EU forms an autonomous constitutional order may be found in *Opinion 2/13 (on EU accession to the ECHR)* of 16 December 2014. Concluding that the Draft Agreement on Accession of the EU to the ECHR was incompatible with the EU Treaties, the Court inter alia emphasized that 'the accession of the EU to the ECHR as envisaged by the draft agreement is liable adversely to affect the specific characteristics of EU law and its autonomy.'[174]

As a final point of this section, it is illustrative to briefly compare the case law of the ECJ and the CJEU with that of a court of another regional integration organization, namely the Caribbean Court of Justice (hereafter CCJ) set up under the Caribbean Community (CARICOM). Notably, the CCJ exercises both appellate jurisdiction over civil and criminal cases decided by the domestic courts of the Member States[175] and original jurisdiction with regard to the Revised Treaty of Chaguaramas (hereafter RTC).[176] In the latter function, the CCJ has in key respects chosen a different path to its European counterpart.[177] In its 2013 Judgment in *Myrie v. Barbados and Jamaica*, the Court echoed *Van Gend en Loos* in declaring that the Caribbean Community Law constitutes 'a new legal order', but went on to state that 'Community law and the limits it imposes on the Member States must take precedence over national legislation, in any event at the Community level.'[178] This statement must be read in conjunction with the CCJ's previous finding in the same Judgment:

> Although it is evident that a State with a dualist approach to international law sometimes may need to incorporate decisions taken under a treaty and thus enact them into municipal law in order to make them enforceable at the domestic level, it is inconceivable that such a transformation would be necessary in order to create binding rights and obligations *at the Community level*.[179]

[174] *Opinion 2/13 (on EU accession to the ECHR)* [2014] ECLI:EU:C:2014:2454, para. 200. See further, for example, Daniel Halberstam, 'It's the Autonomy, Stupid: A Modest Defence of Opinion 2/13 on EU Accession to the ECHR, and the Way Forward', 16 *German Law Journal* (2015) 105, and Louise Halleskov Storgaard, 'EU Law Autonomy versus European Fundamental Rights Protection—On *Opinion 2/13* on EU Accession to the ECHR', 15 *Human Rights Law Review* (2015) 485–521.

[175] As of 2017, only Barbados, Belize, Dominica, and Guyana have accepted the CCJ's appellate jurisdiction.

[176] The Revised Treaty of Chaguaramas, 2259 *UNTS* 293, was adopted in 2001 to replace the 1973 Treaty of Chaguaramas which established the Caribbean Community and the CARICOM Single Market and Economy.

[177] As to the *locus standi* of individuals before the CCJ (when it exercises original jurisdiction and solves disputes concerning the interpretation and application of the RTC), the CCJ appears to take a less restrictive approach compared to the ECJ. See *Trinidad Cement Ltd. v. Guyana*, CCJ Application No. AR 1 of 2008, Judgment, 15 January 2009 (available at http://www.caribbeancourtofjustice.org/wp-content/uploads/2012/02/ar12008_judgement.pdf, accessed 21 January 2018), and *Trinidad Cement Ltd. v. Caribbean Community*, CCJ Application No. AR 3 of 2008, Judgment, 5 February 2009 (available at http://www.caribbeancourtofjustice.org/judgments/ar3_2008/ar32008.pdf, accessed 21 January 2018). See further David S. Berry, 'Trinidad Cement Ltd. v. Caribbean Community. Judgment (Jurisdiction). [2009] CCJ 2 (OJ): Doreen Johnson v. Caricad. Judgment (Jurisdiction). [2009] CCJ 3 (OJ).' 103 *AJIL* (2009) 561–7.

[178] *Myrie v. Barbados and Jamaica*, CCJ Application No. OA 002 of 2012, Judgment, 4 October 2013, para. 69.

[179] Ibid, para. 50 (emphasis added). By comparison, the CACJ of the Central American Integration System (SICA) explicitly copied the 'new and autonomous legal order' approach devised by *Van Gend*

In the eyes of the present author, the CCJ's reasoning is far more appealing than that of the ECJ in *Van Gend en Loos*. Contrary to the ECJ, the CCJ does not imply that international law cannot bind individuals directly. Instead, the CCJ explicitly separates the question of direct applicability of the provisions of the RTC to individuals from the question of the effect of the RTC in domestic law. While the Court unequivocally confirms that individuals hold direct rights under the RTC,[180] which are enforceable before the CCJ, it acknowledges that the effect of these rights domestically is ultimately a matter of domestic law.[181]

8.4 Conclusion: The Legal Personality of Individuals in International Economic Law

The 'internationalization' of State contracts through practice, which has been discussed in Section 8.1.2, corresponds well with the idea of international legal personality as an a posteriori concept: the parties to a State contract acquire rights and duties under international law and thereby international legal personality, when a pertinent source of law—such as the contract itself, 'general principles of law', or Article 42(1) of the ICSID Convention—prescribes the application of international law to the contract.[182] In this way, practice has contradicted the second conclusion in paragraph 41 of the *Serbian Loans* Judgment, whereby the PCIJ invoked the 'States-only' conception of international legal personality.[183] That is not to say, however, that practice has been consistent. *Serbian Loans* is far from the only case where the concept of international legal personality has seemingly confused the analysis pertaining to State contracts. Contrary to the *Sandline International* award, which embodied the 'participant' conception, international law cannot be applied automatically in the absence of a relevant source of law referring to it. Neither is

en Loos in a 1996 ruling. See CACJ 09-04-08-1996 (available at http://cendoc.ccj.org.ni/Documentos/9-04-08-1996/02442/Res-09-04-08-1996.pdf, accessed 21 January 2018). See further Salvatore Caserta, 'Regional Integration through Law and International Courts—the Interplay between De Jure and De Facto Supranationality in Central America and the Caribbean', 30 *LJIL* (2017) 579, 590. The Andean Tribunal of the Andean Community of States also adopted a *Van Gend en Loos*-like approach, claiming that Andean law had supremacy over national law and direct effect within the legal orders of Member States. See 1-IP-87 (available at intranet.comunidadandina.org/Documentos/Procesos/1-ip-87.doc, accessed 21 January 2018) and 2-IP-88 (available at intranet.comunidadandina.org/Documentos/Procesos/2-ip-88.doc, accessed 21 January 2018). In subsequent cases, however, the Andean Tribunal has been far more reluctant to follow in the ECJ's footsteps and it has not promoted a 'constitutionalization' of the Andean Subregional Integration Agreement (Cartagena Agreement), 26 May 1969, 8 *ILM* 910. See further Karen J. Alter and Laurance R. Helfer, 'Legal Integration in the Andes: Law-Making by the Andean Tribunal of Justice' 17 *European Law Journal* (2011) 701, 706–11, Karen J. Alter and Laurance R. Helfer, 'Nature or Nurture? Judicial Lawmaking in the European Court of Justice and the Andean Tribunal of Justice' 64 *International Organization* (2010) 563, 570–3, and André Nollkaemper, 'The Duality of Direct Effect of International Law', 25 *EJIL* (2014) 105–25, 123.

180 See also *Tomlinson v. Belize and Tomlinson v. Trinidad and Tobago*, CCJ Applications No. OA 1 and OA 2 of 2013, Judgment, 10 June 2016, para. 20.

181 See further Caserta (n 179) 591, and Salvatore Caserta and Mikael Rask Madsen, 'Tomlinson v. Belize; Tomlinson v. Trinidad and Tobago' 110 *AJIL* (2016) 533, 538.

182 See further Portmann (n 19) 281.

183 See note 8.

it—as indicated in the *TOPCO/CALASIATIC* award, which reflected the modified 'States-only' conception—a prerequisite for or a consequence of applying international law to the contract that the non-State party is recognized as an international legal person.

Examples from the practice of international investment tribunals also promote the modified 'States-only' conception of international legal personality by applying a presumption against individual rights under treaties. In *ADM* from 2007, for one, the majority of arbitrators argued that international law only exceptionally applies directly to individuals and that in casu the rules of Chapter 11 of NAFTA did not amount to individual rights. The *Loewen* award of 2003 was even more restrictive as it implied—in line with the orthodox 'States-only' conception—that individuals cannot by definition hold direct procedural rights in international law. On the whole, the argument that international legal personality is an a posteriori concept nonetheless appears to find convincing support in the study of international investment law. First of all, it is noteworthy that the theoretical debate on the international legal personality of individuals does not seem to have been particularly influential in the adoption of key provisions such as Article 25(1) of the ICSID Convention. The practical benefits of bringing investors onto the same level as States in matters concerning the investment apparently prevailed over some delegates' doubts about detaching the home State. Second, the notion—which follows the 'a posteriori' conception of international legal personality—that the rights of investors must be determined through interpretation of investment treaties according to the general principles of treaty interpretation has received considerable endorsement in arbitral awards as well as in academic writings. In that respect, however, it is important to uphold the distinction between the primary and secondary rights of investors. Whether or not the obligations set forth in an investment treaty are owed directly to investors from a substantive perspective says little about the existence of the investor's procedural right to submit claims concerning breaches of such obligations to international arbitration—and vice versa.[184] It is submitted that presumption-free interpretation of provisions such as those cited in Section 8.2.3 reasonably leads to the conclusion that investors indeed do hold secondary rights under investment treaties. In addition, a number of primary rules quoted in Section 8.2.1 are indicative of individual rights, although some more clearly so than others. As discussed in Sections 8.2.3.1 and 8.2.2.1 respectively, these findings have implications for significant questions, including the investor's capacity to waive its right to submit a dispute to arbitration and the host State's ability to invoke countermeasures as a circumstance precluding wrongfulness. It is, however, pertinent to underline that determining the nature of, for example, the secondary rights of the investor under an investment treaty is not in itself sufficient as other applicable sources of law may well rule out the investor's power to waive arbitration.

[184] See also van Haersolte-van Hof and Hoffmann (n 109) 1002–3.

The study of the role of the concept of international legal personality in EU law has primarily focused on the assessing the influence of the 'States-only' conception on the application of the EU law by the CJEU.

The development of the (relatively limited) legal standing of individuals before the courts of the EU appears to have been guided by pragmatic considerations concerning primarily the caseload of the Court and the risk of impeding the EU institutions' ability to adopt legislation.

By failing to distinguish the question of the entities governed by an EU legal norm from the question of that norm's effect in domestic law, however, the Court has limited the impact of directives in the relationship between individuals.

The *Van Gend en Loos* Judgment is arguably the most important manifestation in practice of the 'States-only' conception of international legal personality.[185] Although EU law to an unprecedented extent governs matters which have traditionally belonged to the domestic sphere of each Member State, the fact remains that the founding treaties are treaties and as such form part of international law. The Court's detachment of EU law from the international legal system is explicitly based on the idea that international law—in contrast to EU law—by definition cannot govern individuals directly.

[185] See further Portmann (n 19) 77–9.

9

Conclusion

Jochen von Bernstorff's recent remark that 'international law is what happens to the world while scholars are busy making plans for its reform and development'[1] seems particularly pertinent when it comes to the concept of the international legal personality of the individual. While it is frequently argued that the involvement of individuals has brought about a change in the structure of the international legal system, scholars have failed to explain what exactly this change consists of.[2] The lack of clarity will come as no surprise against the background of the preceding study. For the image that appears is that, contrary to common belief, the 'States-only' conception of international legal personality has in fact never reflected the realities of practice—at least not for as long as there has been substantial practice to consider. Insofar as it suited their concrete purpose, States have consistently entered into treaties governing the conditions of individuals without regard to the concept of international legal personality, and—notwithstanding a number of notable exceptions—international judicial organs have generally given such provisions full effect. As early as 1928, in its Advisory Opinion in *Jurisdiction of the Courts of Danzig*, the PCIJ applied the *Beamtenabkommen* directly to the employees of the Polish Railway Administration. Although the Court famously paid lip service to the orthodox 'States-only' conception of international legal personality, it thereby effectively rebutted the notion that individuals are not subjects of international law.

While individual rights and obligations under treaties might have been few and far between in the early days, they are by no means exclusively post-Second World War phenomena. Neither are they reserved for certain subfields such as international human rights law and international criminal law. In the *LaGrand* Judgment of 2001, the ICJ not only unequivocally confirmed the existence of individual rights under treaties, but also that the category of 'individual rights' comprises more than 'human rights'. In addition, the Court made clear that no independent means of enforcement are required before a provision may be said to amount to an 'individual right'. Consistently, neither the ICJ's Advisory Opinion in *Wall* of 2004 nor *Kosovo*

[1] Jochen von Bernstorff, 'The Relationship between Theory and Practice in International Law', in Jean d'Aspremont, Tarcisio Gazzini, André Nollkaemper, and Wouter Werner, *International Law as a Profession* (CUP, 2017) 222, 242.

[2] Jean d'Aspremont, 'International Law-Making by Non-State Actors: Changing the Model or Putting the Phenomenon into Perspective?', in Math Noortmann and Cedric Ryngaert (eds), *Non-State Actor Dynamics in International Law—From Law-Takers to Law-Makers* (Ashgate, 2010) 171.

of 2010 indicate that the Court takes issue with the idea that non-State actors bear international legal obligations.

As the examination of *lex lata* pertaining to the historical and current position of individuals in five special fields of international law confirms, the important change since 1945 lies not in the number and nature of international legal persons, but rather in the material issues perceived as affecting the interests of several States and therefore demanding international legal regulation.

Chapter 4, which discusses the establishment and practice of various international arbitral tribunals and commissions since the end of the eighteenth century, shows that it is hardly reasonable to speak of a progressive development in the role attributed to individuals in international claims. It is neither possible to argue that individuals' claims against foreign States could only be enforced through diplomatic protection before the Second World War, nor that diplomatic protection has outplayed its role and been replaced by individual claims after 1945. To the contrary, individual claims and diplomatic protection have coexisted throughout the twentieth century and will most likely continue to do so. This further accentuates the importance of assessing the primary and secondary rules governing individuals separately, since—as also underscored by the study of the doctrine of diplomatic protection in Chapter 3—the means of enforcement say nothing about the nature of the underlying primary right and vice versa.

Chapter 5 illustrates that while international humanitarian law is a body of rules inherently concerned with the protection of individuals, the norms governing international armed conflicts primarily consist of inter-State obligations. The international norms adopted between the middle of the nineteenth and the beginning of the twentieth centuries to regulate the means and methods of warfare are consistent with the inter-State approach. So are the first Geneva Conventions from 1864, 1906, and 1929, which did not contain individual rights or duties, but laid down obligations of States to provide a certain standard of treatment. The four Geneva Conventions adopted in 1949, however, are more ambiguous. The wording of the major part of the substantive provisions indicates inter-State obligations to secure a minimum level of protection of various groups. But all four Conventions include a number of provisions, inter alia a saving clause and a non-renunciation clause, which imply 'rights' of various protected persons. Although the correct answer is hardly straightforward, interpretation of these provisions according to the principles codified in Articles 31–33 of the VCLT may reasonably lead to the conclusion that they contain individual rights. This analysis is equally applicable to Additional Protocol I and customary international humanitarian law.

As to non-international armed conflict, it is a given that international legal norms will govern at least one non-State actor. During the eighteenth century, internal armed conflicts began to affect the interests of several States to a degree that called for international regulation. The answer was at first the doctrine of 'recognition of belligerency', and no treaty-based regulation of internal armed conflict was adopted before common Article 3 of the 1949 Geneva Conventions. There is little doubt that armed opposition groups are governed directly by common Article 3 and Additional Protocol II of 1977. The controversy rather centres on the jurisprudential underpinnings of this conclusion. Chapter 5 analyses this debate and endorses the argument that a State has legislative jurisdiction to govern the whole of its population, including groups that rebel against it. It should be stressed, however, that the 'legislative jurisdiction' argument rests on the assumption that there are no inherent boundaries to the kind of entities that may possess international legal personality.

Similar to the discussion on non-international armed conflict, Chapter 6 explains that the key disagreement in the field of international criminal law is not whether individuals are bound by international legal obligations, but when and how their responsibility for international crimes arises. The question is whether the responsibility of individuals is an inherent part of categorizing an act as an international crime (i.e. individuals are a priori legal persons in international criminal law), or if the liability of individuals must be established on a case-by-case basis (i.e. individuals are a posteriori international legal persons). Against the background of case law from the IMT, the ICTY, and the ICTR, it is concluded that both positions are defendable, but that the analysis essentially turns on the observer's approach to the sources of international law, particularly customary international law.

As Chapter 7 describes, no actual human rights conventions conferring rights directly on individuals were adopted until after the Second World War. But the interwar period witnessed a number of treaties adopted within the realm of the League of Nations, which granted groups of individuals protection against their home State, in part in the form of individual rights. Except for the Upper Silesia Mixed Commission, however, the individual petitioner was not given independent means of enforcing his rights under the minorities treaties. As is well known, the aftermath of the Second World War brought about a number of 'proper' human rights treaties, which not only conferred primary rights on individuals but also provided independent means of enforcement. The principal case study of Chapter 7, the ECHR, illustrates how the procedural capacities of the individual claimant were gradually expanded; at first through the practice of the ECtHR and eventually by the adoption of Protocol 9 in 1990.

Chapter 8 deals with practice relating to State contracts, international investment law, and EU law under the joint heading of 'international economic law'. As regards State contracts, the study concludes that international law is applicable insofar as this follows from the parties' choice of law or from a relevant international norm, for example 'general principles of law' or Article 42(1) of the ICSID Convention. Consequently, practice has overruled the conclusion of the PCIJ in the *Serbian Loans* Judgment of 1929 that a contract between a State and a private person or entity is invariably governed by the domestic law of some State. Although the outcome is not exactly clear-cut, interpretation—without presumptions about the role of individuals in international law—of a number of investment treaty provisions leads to the conclusion that individuals do hold both primary and secondary rights in international investment law. Finally, when it comes to EU law, it is beyond dispute that provisions of both the founding treaties and secondary legislation apply directly to individuals.

Overall, the study of international *lex lata* in Chapters 3–8 shows that rights, duties, and capacities were conferred directly on individuals in a number of international legal fields throughout the twentieth century. No doubt the number and extent of such provisions grew massively after the Second World War, but it would be a mistake to imply that these events have changed international law from a 'States-only' system into a system which includes individuals as its subjects. What has undergone a groundbreaking transformation is rather the perception of what constitutes 'an international problem' and the corresponding political will to govern the conditions of individuals through international law.

This conclusion may be said to find support in the fact that the notion of international legal personality has generally been overlooked in the drafting processes leading up to the adoption of treaties governing the conditions of individuals. The key example in that regard is the evolution of the procedural position of individuals before the ECtHR. Although the right of individuals to petition first the Commission and subsequently the ECtHR is frequently presented as the foremost evidence that individuals have acquired international legal personality, the concept seems to have been inconsequential to the drafters of the original Convention and Protocol 9, as well as to the Commission and Court. The limited practical importance of the concept of international legal personality is further exemplified by the minorities treaties of the interwar period. It appears that the subjectivity of individuals in international law was equally irrelevant in the adoption of the treaties that did not provide for independent means of enforcement and the Geneva Convention Relating to Upper Silesia of 1922 that did. Similarly, practical considerations—in casu the benefits of bringing investors onto the same level as the host States—were decisive to the adoption of Article 25(1) of the ICSID Convention. That authors of textbooks on international law have largely avoided elaborate explanations for the definition of international legal personality corroborates its lack of significance in practice. So does the fact that no definite conclusions were drawn, even when the concept of international legal personality was indeed discussed by treaty drafters, for example in connection with the formulation of common Article 3 of the 1949 Geneva Conventions. What is more, the ILC has on several occasions, for example relating to the VCLT and the Nürnberg Principles, been confronted with the question of the subjectivity of individuals in international law. But each time the ILC has refrained from drawing any general conclusions on the matter—on occasion by explicitly underlining its purely academic relevance.

As a prominent exception to this trend, the international legal personality of individuals was debated extensively by the Advisory Committee of Jurists drafting the PCIJ Statute in 1920. But it is noteworthy that only one member of the Committee consistently based his arguments against, on one hand, granting legal standing before the PCIJ to individuals and, on the other, creating a High Court of International Justice on the theoretical position that individuals are not subjects of international law. Meanwhile, it was apparently unproblematic for other members to express one position on international legal personality in the matter of individuals' standing before the Court, and another as regards individual criminal obligations under international law. The arguments of most members seem to have been motivated by whether they considered the particular problem involving the interests of individuals to affect States to such a degree that an international solution was called for.

In sum, it is submitted that the analysis in the preceding chapters supports Kelsen's 'a posteriori' conception of international legal personality in the sense that no certain preconditions have to be met before individuals can be governed directly by international law. Neither do particular consequences arise from individuals' attainment of international legal personality. The rights, duties, and capacities of individuals arise a posteriori and must be established on a case-by-case basis through (unprejudiced) interpretation in accordance with Articles 31–33 of the VCLT of the relevant international norm.

Importantly, the adoption of Kelsen's 'a posteriori' conception of international legal personality does presuppose a necessary unity between international law and national law. Only the orthodox 'States-only' conception connects the question of international legal personality with the question of how to identify international law vis-à-vis national law.

Although it has been abandoned as a general position in international legal theory since the Second World War, the notion that only States are subjects of international law is seemingly so ingrained in the minds of many contemporary international lawyers that they inadvertently rely on it when faced with the international legal regulation of non-State entities. Still today, international legal scholars and judges of international courts raise arguments building on the idea that international legal personality is reserved exclusively for States. There are remarkable examples of this tendency in international legal theory as well as practice across the board in international law. In some instances, such as EU law and transnational law scholarship, the orthodox 'States-only' conception of international legal personality is made explicit. These fields are overtly separated from international law with the argument that the latter by definition cannot govern individuals directly. In other cases—for example among international investment lawyers supporting the 'derivative' model, international criminal lawyers distinguishing between criminal courts on the basis of 'the involvement of the international community', and international human rights lawyers advocating for special means of interpretation for so-called law-making treaties such as the ECHR—the idea that only States are subjects of international law mostly operates as an underlying premise. Furthermore, the 'States-only' conception of international legal personality may be said to be invoked indirectly each time international lawyers conflate the question of the possible entities that international law may govern and the effect of an international norm in domestic law. As is apparent, for example, in the debates concerning the constitutionalization of international law, the theoretical foundation for binding armed opposition groups, the 'internationalization' of State contracts, and the direct effect of directives between private parties in EU law, it is a frequent cause of confusion that the idea of the direct application of international law to non-State actors is viewed as inseparable from the question of the relationship between international law and national law.

In practice, adopting Kelsen's approach to international legal personality means, first, that the international legal personality of any entity is solely a matter of presumption-free interpretation of international norms, and, second, that the concept of international legal personality is unhelpful in the delineation of international law vis-à-vis national law. Since the international legal personality of an entity is solely dependent on the existence of an international norm directed at it, this concept cannot assist in identifying *which* norms belong to the international legal system. Instead, the line between the international legal order and the national legal order(s) is defined solely by the criteria for what constitutes a source of international and national law respectively.

Against this background, it seems sensible to wonder about the general value of the concept of personality in international law. Above all, the notion of international legal personality as a theoretical construct appears to have muddled the analysis of fundamental issues, namely the international legal rights, duties, and capacities of individuals and other non-State entities as well as the relationship between international law and national law.

Bibliography

Abbott, Kenneth W. (1999): 'International Relations Theory, International Law, and the Regime Governing Atrocities in Internal Conflicts', *American Journal of International Law*, vol. 93, 361–79.

Agha, Petr (ed.) (2016): *Human Rights Between Law and Politics: The Margin of Appreciation in Post-National Contexts* (London: Hart).

Akande, Dapo (2004): 'International Law Immunities and the International Criminal Court', *American Journal of International Law*, vol. 98, 407–33.

Akande, Dapo (2009): 'Sources of International Criminal Law', in Antonio Cassese et al. (eds), *Oxford Companion to International Criminal Justice* (Oxford: Oxford University Press), 41–53.

Akande, Dapo (2014): 'International Organizations', in Malcolm D. Evans (ed.), *International Law*, 4th edn (Oxford: Oxford University Press) 248–79.

Albors-Llorens, Albertina (2012): 'Sealing the Fate of Private Parties in Annulment Proceedings? The General Court and the New Standing Test in Article 263(4) TFEU', *Cambridge Law Journal*, vol. 71, 52–5.

Aldrich, George H. (1996): 'Individuals as Subjects of International Humanitarian Law', in Jerzy Makarczyk (ed.), *Theory of International Law at the Threshold of the 21st Century: Essays in Honour of Krzysztof Skubiszewski* (The Hague: Kluwer) 851–8.

Aldrich, George H. (2003): 'The Work of the Eritrea–Ethiopia Claims Commission', *Yearbook of International Humanitarian Law*, vol. 6, 435–42.

Alston, Philip (ed.) (2005): *Non-State Actors and Human Rights* (Oxford: Oxford University Press).

Alter, Karen J., and Helfer, Laurance R. (2010): 'Nature or Nurture? Judicial Lawmaking in the European Court of Justice and the Andean Tribunal of Justice', *International Organization*, vol. 64, 563–92.

Alter, Karen J., and Helfer, Laurance R. (2011): 'Legal Integration in the Andes: Law-Making by the Andean Tribunal of Justice', *European Law Journal*, vol. 17, 701–15.

Alvik, Ivar (2011): *Contracting with Sovereignty* (Oxford: Hart).

Alzamora, Carlos (1993): 'Reflections on the UN Compensation Commission', *Arbitration International*, vol. 9, 349–58.

Ambos, Kai (1999): 'Article 25', in Otto Triffterer and Kai Ambos (eds), *Commentary on the Rome Statute of the International Criminal Court* (Munich: C. H. Beck) 979–1029.

Amerasinghe, Chittharanjan F. (2008): *Diplomatic Protection* (Oxford: Oxford University Press).

Anzilotti, Dionisio (1902): *Teoria generale della responsabilità dello Stato nel diritto intemazionale* (Florence: F. Lumachi Libraio-Editore).

Anzilotti, Dionisio (1905): *Il diritto internazionale nei giudizi interni* (Bologna: N. Zanichelli).

Anzilotti, Dionisio (1928): *Corso di diritto intemazionale*, 3rd edn (Rome: Atheneum).

Anzilotti, Dionisio (1929): *Cours de droit international* (Paris: Recueil Sirey).

Arai-Takahashi, Yutaka (2002): *The Margin of Appreciation Doctrine and the Principle of Proportionality in the Jurisprudence of the ECHR* (Antwerp: Intersentia).

Arai-Takahashi, Yutaka (2013): 'The Margin of Appreciation Doctrine: A Theoretical Analysis of Strasbourg's Variable Geometry', in Andreas Føllesdal, Birgit Peters, and Geir

Ulfstein (eds) *Constituting Europe—The European Court of Human Rights in a National, European and Global Context* (Cambridge: Cambridge University Press).

Arangio-Ruiz, Gaetano (1975–6): 'L'État dans le sens du Droit des Gens et la Notion du Droit international', *Österreichische Zeitschrift für öffentliches Recht*, vol. 26, 3–63 and 265–406.

Arangio-Ruiz, Gaetano (1990-VI): 'Le Domaine Réservé. L'Organisation Internationale et le Rapport entre Droit International et Droit Interne', *Recueil des cours de l'Académie de droit international de La Haye*, vol. 225, 9–484.

Arangio-Ruiz, Gaetano (2007): 'International Law and Interindividual Law', in Janne Nijman and André Nollkaemper (eds), *New Perspectives on the Divide Between National and International Law* (Oxford: Oxford University Press) 15–51.

Arnardóttir, Oddný Mjöll (2016): 'Rethinking the Two Margins of Appreciation', *European Constitutional Law Review*, vol. 12, 27–53.

Asouzu, Amazu A. (2001): *International Commercial Arbitration and African States: Practice, Participation and Institutional Development* (Cambridge: Cambridge University Press).

Aufricht, Hans (1943): 'Personality in International Law', *The American Political Science Review*, vol. 37, 217–43.

Bantekas, Ilias, and Nash, Susan (2007): *International Criminal Law*, 3rd edn (London: Routledge).

Barberis, Julio A. (1983): 'Nouvelles Questions Concernant la Personnalité Juridique Internationale', *Recueil des Cours*, vol. 179, 145–304.

Bassiouni, M. Cherif (2005): *The Legislative History of the International Criminal Court*, vol. 2 (Ardsley, NY: Transnational Publishers Inc.).

Bassiouni, M. Cherif (2008): 'The Nuremberg Legacy', in Guénaël Mettraux (ed.), *Perspectives on the Nuremberg Trial* (Oxford: Oxford University Press) 577–98.

Bassiouni, M. Cherif (2011): *Crimes Against Humanity—Historical Evolution and Contemporary Application* (Cambridge: Cambridge University Press).

Bates, Ed (2010): 'History', in Daniel Moeckli, Sangeeta Shah, and Sandesh Sivakumaran (eds), *International Human Rights Law* (Oxford: Oxford University Press) 30–8.

Bathurst, M. E. (1945): 'The United Nations War Crimes Commission', *American Journal of International Law*, vol. 39, 565–70.

Baxter, Richard (1974): 'Jus in Bello Interno: The Present and Future Law', in John Norton Moore, *Law and Civil War in the Modern World* (Baltimore, MD: Johns Hopkins University Press) 518–36.

Beckett, W. E. (1930): 'Decisions of the Permanent Court of International Justice on Points of Law and Procedure of General Application', *British Yearbook of International Law*, vol. 11, 1–54.

Ben-Naftali, Orna (ed.) (2011): *International Humanitarian Law and International Human Rights Law—Pas de Deux* (Oxford: Oxford University Press).

Bentham, Jeremy (1879, first published 1789): *An Introduction to the Principles of Morals and Legislation* (Oxford: Clarendon Press).

Bergström, Carl Fredrik (2014): 'Defending Restricted Standing for Individuals to Bring Direct Actions Against "Legislative" Measures', *European Constitutional Law Review*, vol. 10, 481–99.

Bernhardt, Rudolf (1988): 'Thoughts on the Interpretation of Human Rights Treaties', in Franz Matscher and Herbert Petzold (eds), *Protecting Human Rights: The European Dimension—Studies in Honour of Gerard Wiarda* (Cologne: Carl Heymanns) 65–71.

von Bernstorff, Jochen (2010): *The Public International Law Theory of Hans Kelsen* (Cambridge: Cambridge University Press).

von Bernstorff, Jochen (2017): 'The Relationship Between Theory and Practice in International Law', in Jean d'Aspremont, Tarcisio Gazzini, André Nollkaemper, and Wouter Werner (eds) *International Law as a Profession* (Cambridge: Cambridge University Press) 222–43.

Berry, David S. (2009): 'Trinidad Cement Ltd. v. Caribbean Community. Judgment (Jurisdiction). [2009] CCJ 2 (OJ): Doreen Johnson v. Caricad. Judgment (Jurisdiction). [2009] CCJ 3 (OJ)', *American Journal of International Law*, vol. 103, 561–7.

Betlem, Gerrit, and Nollkaemper, André (2003): 'Giving Effect to Public International Law and European Community Law before Domestic Courts—A Comparative Analysis of the Practice of Consistent Interpretation', *European Journal of International Law*, vol. 14, 569–89.

Bhuta, Nehal (2012): 'The Role International Actors Other Than States Can Play in the New World Order', in Antonio Cassese (ed.), *Realizing Utopia* (Oxford: Oxford University Press) 61–75.

Blackburn, Glen A. (1930): 'International Control of the River Danube', *Current History*, vol. 42, 1154–9.

Bogdandy, Armin von (2006): 'Constitutionalism in International Law: Comment on a Proposal from Germany', *Harvard International Law Journal*, vol. 47, 223–42.

Bogdandy, Armin von (2008): 'Pluralism, Direct Effect, and the Ultimate Say: On the Relationship Between International and Domestic Constitutional Law', *International Journal of Constitutional Law*, vol. 6, 397–413.

Borchard, Edwin M. (1916): *The Diplomatic Protection of Citizens Abroad* (New York: The Banks Law Publishing Co.).

Borchard, Edwin M. (1930): 'The Access of Individuals to International Courts', *American Journal of International Law*, vol. 24, 359–65.

Bos, Maarten (1952): 'The Franco-Italian Conciliation Commission', *Acta Scandinavica Juris Gentium*, vol. 22, 133–59.

Bothe, Michael, Partsch, Karl Josef, and Solf, Waldemar A. (1982): *New Rules for Victims of Armed Conflicts* (The Hague: Martinus Nijhoff).

Bourquin, Maurice (1931-I): 'Règles Générales du Droit de la Paix', *Recueil des Cours*, vol. 35, 5–232.

Brabandere, Eric de (2011): 'Non-State Actors and Human Rights: Corporate Responsibility and the Attempts to Formalize the Role of Corporations as Participants in the International Legal System', in Jean d'Aspremont (ed.), *Participants in the International Legal System* (London: Routledge) 268–83.

Brandtner, Barbara (1992): 'The Drama of the EEA Comments on Opinions 1/91 and 1/92', *European Journal of International Law*, vol. 3, 300–27.

Braun, Tillmann Rudolf (2013): 'Globalization-driven Innovation: The Investor as a Partial Subject in Public International Law—An Inquiry into the Nature and Limits of Investor Rights', Jean Monnet Working Paper 04/13, New York University School of Law (available https://ssrn.com/abstract=2286607, accessed 21 January 2018).

Brierly, James Leslie (1936-IV): 'Règles Générales du Droit de la Paix', *Recueil des Cours*, vol. 58, 5–242.

Brierly, James Leslie (1958, English translation of a lecture delivered in 1928): 'The Basis of Obligation in International Law', in Hersch Lauterpacht and C. H. M. Waldock (eds), *The Basis of Obligation in International Law and Other Papers by the Late James Leslie Brierly* (Oxford: Clarendon Press) 1–67.

Broches, Aron (1972): 'The Convention on the Settlement of Investment Disputes Between States and Nationals of Other States', *Recueil des Cours*, vol. 136, 331–410.

Brower, Charles N., and Brueschke, Jason D. (1998): *The Iran–United States Claims Tribunal* (The Hague: Martinus Nijhoff).

Brower II, Charles H. (2001–2): 'Investor–State Disputes under NAFTA: The Empire Strikes Back', *Columbia Journal of Transnational Law*, vol. 40, 43–88.

Brown, Henry B. (1908): 'The Proposed International Prize Court', *American Journal of International Law*, vol. 2, 476–89.

Brownlie, Ian (1964): 'The Place of the Individual in International Law', *Virginia Law Review*, vol. 50, 435–62.

Brownlie, Ian (1966): *Principles of Public International Law*, 1st edn (Oxford: Clarendon Press).

Brölmann, Catherine (2005): 'Law-Making Treaties: Form and Function in International Law', *Nordic Journal of International Law*, vol. 74, 383–404.

Buchanan, Camilla, and Bolzonello, Luca (2015): 'Towards a Definition of "Implementing Measures" under Article 263, Paragraph 4, TFEU', *European Journal of Risk Regulation*, vol. 6, 671–6.

Buchanan, William I. (1908): *The Central American Peace Conference—Report of Mr. William I. Buchanan representing the United States of America* (Washington, DC: Government Printing Offices).

Bugnion, François (2001): 'Droit de Genève et droit de La Haye', *Revue internationale de la Croix-Rouge*, No. 844, 901–22.

de Búrca, Gráinne (2010): 'The European Court of Justice and the International Legal Order After *Kadi*', *Harvard International Law Journal*, vol. 51, 1–49.

Butte, George C. (1912): 'The "Protocole Additionnel" To the International Prize Court Convention', *American Journal of International Law*, vol. 6, 799–929.

Cameron, Iain (1996): 'Protocol 11 to the European Convention on Human Rights: the European Court of Human Rights as a Constitutional Court?', *Yearbook of European Law 1995*, vol. 15, 219–60.

Cançado Trindade, Antônio Augusto (2005): 'International Law for Humankind: Towards a New Jus Gentium—Part I', *Recueil des Cours*, vol. 316, 9–439.

Cançado Trindade, Antônio Augusto (2011): *The Access of Individuals to International Justice* (Oxford: Oxford University Press).

Cantegreil, Julien (2011): 'The Audacity of the *Texaco/Calasiatic Award*: René-Jean Dupuy and the Internationalization of Foreign Investment Law', *European Journal of International Law*, vol. 22, 441–58.

Caron, David D. (1990): 'The Nature of the Iran–United States Claims Tribunal and the Evolving Structure of International Dispute Resolution', *American Journal of International Law*, vol. 84, 104–56.

Caron, David D. (2000): 'War and International Adjudication: Reflections on the 1899 Peace Conference', *American Journal of International Law*, vol. 94, 4–30.

Caron, David D., and Morris, Brian (2002): 'The UN Compensation Commission: Practical Justice, not Retribution', *European Journal of International Law*, vol. 13, 183–99.

Caserta, Salvatore (2017): 'Regional Integration through Law and International Courts—the Interplay Between De Jure and De Facto Supranationality in Central America and the Caribbean', *Leiden Journal of International Law*, vol. 30, 579–601.

Caserta, Salvatore, and Madsen, Mikael Rask (2016): 'Tomlinson v. Belize; Tomlinson v. Trinidad and Tobago', *American Journal of International Law*, vol. 110, 533–40.

Cassese, Antonio (1981): 'The Status of Rebels under the 1977 Geneva Protocol on Non-International Armed Conflicts', *International & Comparative Law Quarterly*, vol. 30, 416–39.

Cassese, Antonio (2000): 'The Martens Clause: Half a Loaf or Simply Pie in the Sky?', *European Journal of International Law*, vol. 11, 187–216.

Cassese, Antonio (2005): *International Law*, 2nd edn (Oxford: Oxford University Press).

Cassese, Antonio (2008): *International Criminal Law*, 2nd edn (Oxford: Oxford University Press).

Cassese, Antonio (2009) (ed.) *The Oxford Companion to International Criminal Justice* (Oxford: Oxford University Press).

Castberg, Frede (1952): *Studier i Folkerett* (Oslo: Akademisk Forlag).

Castrén, Erik (1965): 'Recognition of Insurgency', *Indian Journal of International Law*, vol. 4, 443–54.

Castrén, Erik (1966): *Civil War* (Helsinki: Suomalaisen Kirjallisuuden Kirjapaino Oy).

Cavaglieri, Arrigo (1925): 'I soggetti del diritto internazionale', 20 *Rivista di diritto internazionale*, 18–32 and 169–87.

Cavaglieri, Arrigo (1929-I): 'Régles Genérales du Droit de la Paix', *Recueil des Cours*, vol. 26, 310–585.

Chalmers, Damian, Davies, Gareth, and Monti, Giorgio (2010): *European Union Law—Cases and Materials*, 2nd edn (Cambridge: Cambridge University Press).

Chen, Lung-chu (2015): *An Introduction to Contemporary International Law—A Policy-Oriented Perspective*, 3rd edn (Oxford: Oxford University Press).

Cheng, Tai-Heng (2011): 'Positivism, New Haven Jurisprudence and the Fragmentation of International Law', in Todd Weiler and Freya Baetens (eds), *New Directions in International Economic Law: In Memoriam Thomas Wälde* (Dordrecht: Martinus Nijhoff) 411–38.

Chinkin, Christine (1993): *Third Parties in International Law* (Oxford: Clarendon Press).

Choate, Joseph H. (1913): *The Two Hague Conferences* (Princeton, NJ: Princeton University Press).

Christoffersen, Jonas (2009a): *Fair Balance—Proportionality, Subsidiarity and Primarity in the European Convention on Human Rights* (Leiden: Martinus Nijhoff).

Christoffersen, Jonas (2009b): 'Impact on General Principles of Treaty Interpretation', in Menno T. Kamminga and Martin Scheinin (eds), *The Impact of Human Rights Law on General International Law* (Oxford: Oxford University Press) 37–62.

Clapham, Andrew (2006): *Human Rights Obligations of Non-State Actors* (Oxford: Oxford University Press).

Clapham, Andrew (2008): 'Extending International Criminal Law beyond the Individual to Corporations and Armed Opposition Groups', *Journal of International Criminal Justice*, vol. 6, 899–926.

Clapham, Andrew (2010): 'The Role of the Individual in International Law', *European Journal of International Law*, vol. 21, 25–30.

Clapham, Andrew (2014): 'Accountability/Liability for Violations of the Law: Focusing on Non-State Actors', in Andrew Clapham and Paola Gaeta (eds), *The Oxford Handbook of International Law in Armed Conflict* (Oxford: Oxford University Press).

Claude, Inis Lothar (1955): *National Minorities—An International Problem* (Cambridge, MA: Harvard University Press).

Coing, Helmut (1992): 'Bank for International Settlements', in Rudolf Bernhardt (ed.), *Encyclopedia of Public International Law*, vol. 1, 342–3.

Collins, David (2017): *An Introduction to International Investment Law* (Cambridge: Cambridge University Press).

Collins, Richard (2009): 'Constitutionalism as Liberal-Juridical Consciousness: Echoes from International Law's Past', *Leiden Journal of International Law*, vol. 22, 251–87.

Combacau, Jean, and Alland, Denis (1985): 'Primary and Secondary Rules in the Law of State Responsibility: Categorizing International Obligations', *Netherlands Yearbook of International Law*, vol. 16, 81–109.

Cotterell, Roger (2012): 'What Is Transnational Law?', *Law & Social Inquiry*, vol. 37, 500–24.

Craig, Paul, and de Búrca, Gráinne (2015): *EU Law—Text, Cases, and Materials*, 6th edn (Oxford: Oxford University Press).

Crawford, Emily (2007): 'Unequal before the Law: The Case for the Elimination of the Distinction Between International and Non-international Armed Conflicts', *Leiden Journal of International Law*, vol. 20, 441–65.

Crawford, Emily (2010): *The Treatment of Combatants and Insurgents under the Law of Armed Conflict* (Oxford: Oxford University Press).

Crawford, James (2002a): 'The ILC's Articles of Responsibility of States for Internationally Wrongful Acts: A Retrospect', *American Journal of International Law*, vol. 96, 874–90.

Crawford, James (2002b): *International Law as an Open System* (London: Cameron May).

Crawford, James (2006): *The Creation of States in International Law*, 2nd edn (Oxford: Oxford University Press).

Crawford, James (2008): 'Treaty and Contract in Investment Arbitration', *Arbitration International*, vol. 24, 351–74.

Crawford, James (2012): *Brownlie's Principles of Public International Law*, 8th edn (Oxford: Oxford University Press).

Crawford, James (2013): 'Chance, Order, Change: The Course of International Law', *Recueil des Cours*, vol. 365, 9–390.

Cryer, Robert (2009): 'Nuremberg International Military Tribunal', in Cassese, Antonio (ed.), *The Oxford Companion to International Criminal Justice* (Oxford: Oxford University Press) 441–3.

Cryer, Robert, Friman, Håkan, Robinson, Darryl, and Wilmshurst, Elizabeth (2010): *An Introduction to International Criminal Law and Procedure*, 2nd edn (Cambridge: Cambridge University Press).

Cullen, Anthony (2010): *The Concept of Non-International Armed Conflict in International Humanitarian Law* (Cambridge: Cambridge University Press).

Cygan, Adam (2003): 'Recent Developments in Judicial Review and Article 230 EC', *ERA Forum*, vol. 4, 67–78.

D'Amato, Anthony (2011): 'Non-State Actors from the Perspective of the Policy Oriented School: Power, Law, Actors and the View from New Haven', in d'Aspremont, Jean (ed.), *Participants in the International Legal System: Multiple Perspectives on Non-State Actors in International Law* (London: Routledge) 64–75.

d'Aspremont, Jean (2007): 'The Foundations of the International Legal Order', *Finnish Yearbook of International Law*, vol. 18, 219–55.

d'Aspremont, Jean (2010): 'International Law-Making by Non-State Actors: Changing the Model or Putting the Phenomenon into Perspective?', in Math Noortman and Cedric Ryngaert, *Non-State Actor Dynamics in International Law* (Farnham: Ashgate) 171–94.

d'Aspremont, Jean (2011a): 'Non-State Actors from the Perspective of Legal Positivism', in d'Aspremont, Jean (ed.), *Participants in the International Legal System: Multiple Perspectives on Non-State Actors in International Law* (London: Routledge) 23–40.

d'Aspremont, Jean (2011b): *Formalism and the Sources of International Law* (Oxford: Oxford University Press).

d'Aspremont, Jean (2013): 'The Idea of "Rules" in the Sources of International Law', *British Yearbook of International Law*, vol. 84, 103–30.

d'Aspremont, Jean (2016): 'Subjects and Actors in International Lawmaking: The Paradigmatic Divides in the Cognition of International Norm-Generating Processes', in Catherine Brölmann and Yannick Radi (eds) *Research Handbook on the Theory and Practice of International Lawmaking* (Cheltenham: Edward Elgar) 32–55.

d'Aspremont, Jean (2018): 'Non-State Actors and the Formation of International Customary Law: Unlearning Some Common Tropes', in Iain Scobbie and Sufyan Droubi (eds), *Non-State Actors and the Formation of Customary International Law* (Manchester: Manchester University Press, forthcoming 2018).

d'Aspremont, Jean, and Dopagne, Frédéric (2008a): 'Kadi: The ECJ's Reminder of the Elementary Divide Between Legal Orders', *International Organizations Law Review*, vol. 5, 317–79.

d'Aspremont, Jean, and Dopagne, Frédéric (2008b): 'Two Constitutionalisms in Europe: Pursuing an Articulation of the European and International Legal Orders', *ZaöRV*, vol. 36, 939–77.

de Azcárate, P. (1945): *League of Nations and National Minorities—An Experiment* (Washington, DC: Carnegie Endowment for International Peace).

de Brabandere, Eric (2014): *Investment Treaty Arbitration as Public International Law* (Cambridge: Cambridge University Press).

de Búrca, Gráinne (2012): 'The ECJ and the International Legal Order: A Re-Evaluation', in Gráinne de Búrca and Joseph H. H. Weiler, *The Worlds of European Constitutionalism* (Cambridge: Cambridge University Press) 105–49.

Deen-Racsmány, Zsuzsanna (2002): 'Diplomatic Protection and the LaGrand Case', *Leiden Journal of International Law*, vol. 15, 87–103.

De Wet, Erika (2006): 'The International Constitutional Order', *International & Comparative Law Quarterly*, vol. 55, 51–76.

De Wet, Erika (2012): 'The Constitutionalization of Public International Law', in Michel Rosenfeld and András Sajó (eds), *The Oxford Handbook of Comparative Constitutional Law* (Oxford: Oxford University Press) 1209–29.

Dinstein, Yoram (2010): *The Conduct of Hostilities under the Law of International Armed Conflict*, 2nd edn (Cambridge: Cambridge University Press).

Dinstein, Yoram (2014): Yoram Dinstein, *Non-International Armed Conflicts in International Law* (Cambridge: Cambridge University Press).

Dixon, Martin (2013): *Textbook on International Law*, 7th edn (Oxford: Oxford University Press).

Doehring, Karl (1968): Written communication by Karl Doehring for the second International Conference about the European Convention on Human Rights held in Vienna from 18–20 October 1965, in A. H. Robertson (ed.), *Human Rights in National and International Law* (Manchester: Manchester University Press) 31–4.

Dolzer, Rudolf, and Schreuer, Christoph (2012): *Principles of International Investment Law*, 2nd edn (Oxford: Oxford University Press).

Domingo, Rafael (2011): 'Gaius, Vattel and the New Global Law Paradigm', *European Journal of International Law*, vol. 22, 627–47.

Donlon, Fidelma (2011): 'Hybrid Tribunals', in William Schabas and Nadia Bernaz (eds), *Routledge Handbook on International Criminal Law* (London: Routledge) 85–105.

Dothan, Shai (2014a): 'In Defence of Expansive Interpretation in the European Court of Human Rights', *Cambridge Journal of International and Comparative Law*, vol. 3, 508–31.

Dothan, Shai (2014b): *Reputation and Judicial Tactics—A Theory of National and International Courts* (Cambridge: Cambridge University Press).

Douglas, Zachary (2003): 'The Hybrid Foundations of Investment Treaty Arbitration', *British Yearbook of International Law*, vol. 74, 151–289.

Douglas, Zachary (2006): 'Nothing if not Critical for Investment Treaty Arbitration: Occidental, Eureko and Methanex', *Arbitration International*, vol. 22, 27–51.

Douglas, Zachary (2009): *The International Law of Investment Claims* (Cambridge: Cambridge University Press).

Doyle, Michael W. (2009): 'The UN Charter—A Global Constitution?', in Jeffrey L. Dunoff and Joel P. Trachtman (eds), *Ruling the World? Constitutionalism, International Law and Global Governance* (Cambridge: Cambridge University Press) 113–32.

Draper, G. I. A. D. (1958): *The Red Cross Conventions* (New York: Frederick A. Praeger).

Draper, G. I. A. D. (1965-I): 'The Geneva Conventions of 1949', *Recueil des Cours*, vol. 114, 60–163.

Dreier, Horst (1990): *Rechtslehre, Staatssoziologie und Demokratietheorie bei Hans Kelsen*, 2nd edn (Baden-Baden: Nomos).

Drzemczewski, Andrew (1980): 'The Sui Generis Nature of the European Convention on Human Rights', *International & Comparative Law Quarterly*, vol. 29, 54–63.

Duchesne, Matthew S. (2004): 'The Continuous-Nationality-of-Claims Principle: Its Historical Development and Current Relevance to Investor–State Investment Disputes', *George Washington International Law Review*, vol. 36, 783–815.

Dunoff, Jeffrey L., and Trachtman, Joel P. (eds) (2009): *Ruling the World? Constitutionalism, International Law and Global Governance* (Cambridge: Cambridge University Press).

Ehard, Hans (1949): 'The Nuremberg Trials Against the Major War Criminals and International Law', *American Journal of International Law*, vol. 43, 223–45.

Elder, David A. (1979): 'The Historical Background of Common Article 3 of The Geneva Convention of 1949', *Case Western Reserve Journal of International Law*, vol. 11, 37–69.

Eser, Albin (2002), 'Individual Criminal Responsibility', in Cassese et al (eds), *The Rome Statute of the International Criminal Court: A Commentary* (Oxford: Oxford University Press) 767–822.

Falk, Richard A. (1964): 'Janus Tormented: The International Law of Internal War', in James N. Rosenau (ed.), *International Aspects of Civil Strife* (Princeton, NJ: Princeton University Press) 185–248.

Fassbender, Bardo (2009a): *The United Nations Charter as the Constitution of the International Community* (Leiden: Brill).

Fassbender, Bardo (2009b): 'Rediscovering a Forgotten Constitution: Notes on the Place of the UN Charter in the International Legal Order', in Jeffrey L. Dunoff and Joel P. Trachtman (eds), *Ruling the World? Constitutionalism, International Law and Global Governance* (Cambridge: Cambridge University Press).

Fatouros, A. A. (1980): 'International Law and the Internationalized Contract', *American Journal of International Law*, vol. 74, 134–41.

Fauchald, Ole Kristian, and Nollkaemper, André (2012): 'Conclusions', in Ole Kristian Fauchald and André Nollkaemper (eds), *The Practice of International and National Courts and the (De-)Fragmentation of International Law* (Oxford: Hart).

Feller, A. H. (1933): 'The German–Mexican Claims Commission', *American Journal of International Law*, vol. 27, 62–79.

Feller, A. H. (1935): *The Mexican Claims Commissions* (New York: Macmillan).

Fertman, Carla (2017): *International Organizations and the Fight for Accountability* (Oxford: Oxford University Press).

Ferstman, Carla, and Rosenberg, Sheri P. (2009): 'Reparations in Dayton's Bosnia and Herzegovina', in Ferstman et al. (eds), *Reparations for Victims of Genocide, War Crimes and Crimes Against Humanity* (Leiden: Brill) 482–514.

Fikfak, Veronica (2013): 'Kadi and the Role of the Court of Justice of the European Union in the International Legal Order', *Cambridge Yearbook of European Legal Studies*, vol. 15, 587–617.

Fleiner-Gerster, Thomas, and Meyer, Michael A. (1985): 'New Developments in Humanitarian Law: A Challenge to the Concept of Sovereignty', *International & Comparative Law Quarterly*, vol. 34, 267–83.

Forowicz, Magdalena (2010): *The Reception of International Law in the European Court of Human Rights* (Oxford: Oxford University Press).

Fortin, Katharine (2017): *The Accountability of Armed Groups under Human Rights Law* (Oxford: Oxford University Press).

Franck, Thomas M. (1990): *The Power of Legitimacy Among Nations* (Oxford: Oxford University Press).

Friedmann, Wolfgang (1964): *The Changing Structure of International Law* (London: Stevens & Sons).

Friedmann, Wolfgang (1969-II): 'General Course in Public International Law', *Recueil des Cours*, vol. 127, 39–246.

Frigessi di Rattalma, Marco, and Treves, Tullio (eds) (1999): *The United Nations Compensation Commission: A Handbook* (The Hague: Kluwer Law International).

Gaeta, Paola (2011): 'Are Victims of War Crimes Entitled to Compensation?', in Orna Ben-Naftali (ed.), *International Humanitarian Law and International Human Rights Law*, 305–27.

Gaja, Giorgio (1992): 'Positivism and Dualism in Dionisio Anzilotti', *European Journal of International Law*, vol. 3, 123–38.

Gaja, Giorgio (2007): 'Dualism—a Review', in Janne Nijman and André Nollkaemper (eds), *New Perspectives on the Divide Between National and International Law* (Oxford: Oxford University Press) 52–62.

Gaja, Giorgio (2010): 'The Position of Individuals in International Law: An ILC Perspective', *European Journal of International Law*, vol. 21, 11–14.

Gardiner, Richard K. (2008): *Treaty Interpretation* (Oxford: Oxford University Press).

Gattini, Andrea (2002): 'The UN Compensation Commission: Old Rules, New Procedures on War Reparations', *European Journal of International Law*, vol. 13, 161–81.

Gazzini, Tarcisio (2016): *Interpretation of International Investment Treaties* (Oxford: Hart).

Gormley, W. Paul (1966): *The Procedural Status of the Individual before International and Supranational Tribunals* (The Hague: Martinus Nijhoff).

Gourgourinis, Anastasios (2012): 'Investors' Rights Qua Human Rights? Revisiting the "Direct"/"Derivative" Rights Debate', in Malgosia Fitzmaurice and Panos Merkouris (eds), *The Interpretation and Application of the European Convention of Human Rights: Legal and Practical Implications* (Leiden: Brill) 147–82.

Gray, Christine (2006): 'The Eritrea/Ethiopia Claims Commission Oversteps Its Boundaries: A Partial Award?', *European Journal of International Law*, vol. 17, 699–721.

Green, Leslie C. (2008): *The Contemporary Law of Armed Conflict*, 3rd edn (Manchester: Manchester University Press).

Greenwood, Christopher (1982): 'State Contracts in International Law—The Libyan Oil Arbitrations', *British Yearbook of International Law*, vol. 53, 27–81.

Gregory, Charles Noble (1908): 'The Proposed International Prize Court and Some of Its Difficulties', 2 *American Journal of International Law*, vol. 2, 458–75.

Grotius, Hugo (1625): *De Jure Bellis ac Pacis Libri Tres*. English translation by Francis W. Kelsey (1925, Oxford: Clarendon Press).

Hafner, Gerhard (2011): 'The Emancipation of the Individual from the State under International Law', *Recueil des Cours*, vol. 358, 262–453.

Halberstam, Daniel (2009): 'Constitutional Heterarchy: The Centrality of Conflict in the European Union and the United States', in Jeffrey Dunoff and Joel P. Trachtman (eds), *Ruling the World? Constitutionalism, International Law, and Global Governance* (Cambridge: Cambridge University Press) 326–55.

Halberstam, Daniel (2015): 'It's the Autonomy, Stupid: A Modest Defence of Opinion 2/13 on EU Accession to the ECHR, and the Way Forward', *German Law Journal*, vol. 16, 105–46.

Hall, William Edward (1924): *Treatise of International Law*, 8th edn (Oxford: Clarendon Press).

Halleskov Storgaard, Louise (2015): 'EU Law Autonomy versus European Fundamental Rights Protection—On *Opinion 2/13* on EU Accession to the ECHR', *Human Rights Law Review*, vol. 15, 485–521.

van Haersolte-van Hof, Jacomijn J., and Hoffmann, Anne K. (2008): 'The Relationship Between International Tribunals and Domestic Courts', in Peter Muchlinski, Federico Ortino, and Christoph Schreuer (eds), *The Oxford Handbook of International Investment Law* (Oxford: Oxford University Press) 962–1007.

Hampson, Françoise J. (1991): 'Human Rights Law and International Humanitarian Law: Two Coins or Two Sides of the Same Coin?', *Bulletin of Human Rights*, vol. 1, 46–54.

Harbom, Lotta and Wallensteen, Peter (2010): 'Armed Conflict 1946–2009', *Journal of Peace Research*, vol. 47, 501–9.

Hart, H. L. A. (1994): *The Concept of Law*, 2nd edn (Oxford: Oxford University Press).

Hart, H. L. A. (1998, first published 1968): 'Kelsen's Doctrine of the Unity of Law', reprinted in Stanley L. Paulson and Bonnie L. Paulson (eds), *Normativity and Norms. Critical Perspectives on Kelsenian Themes* (Oxford: Clarendon Press) 553–81.

Hartmann, Jacques (2010): 'Kosovos uafhængighedserklæring', *Juristen*, No. 6/7, 176–82.

Hathaway, James C. (2005): *The Rights of Refugees under International Law* (Cambridge: Cambridge University Press).

Headlam-Morley, James (1972): *A Memoir of the Paris Peace Conference 1919* (London: Methuen).

Hefner, L. R. and Slaughter, A. M. (1997): 'Toward a Theory of Effective Supranational Adjudication', *Yale Law Journal*, vol. 107, 273–91.

Heller, Kevin Jon (2011): *The Nuremberg Military Tribunals and the Origins of International Criminal Law* (Oxford: Oxford University Press).

Henckaerts, Jean-Marie and Doswald-Beck, Louise (2005): *Customary International Humanitarian Law*, vols I–II (Cambridge: Cambridge University Press).

Herik, L. J. van den (2005): *The Contribution of the Rwanda Tribunal to the Development of International Law* (Leiden: Martinus Nijhoff).

Hernández, Gleider I. (2011): 'Non-State Actors from the Perspective of the International Court of Justice', in Jean d'Aspremont (ed.), *Participants in the International Legal System: Multiple Perspectives on Non-State Actors in International Law* (London: Routledge) 140–64.

Higgins, Rosalyn (1985): 'Conceptual Thinking About the Individual in International Law', in Richard Falk, Friedrich Kratochwil, and Saul H. Mendlovitz (eds), *International Law—A Contemporary Perspective* (Boulder, CO: Westview Press) 476–94.

Higgins, Rosalyn (1991-V): 'International Law and the Avoidance, Containment and Resolution of Disputes—General Course on Public International Law', *Recueil des Cours*, vol. 230, 9–341.

Higgins, Rosalyn (1994): *Problems & Process—International Law and How We Use it* (Oxford: Clarendon Press).

Hoof, G. J. H. van (1983): *Rethinking the Sources of International Law* (Deventer: Kluwer Publishing).

Hummelbrunner, Sandra, and Prickartz, Anne-Carlijn (2016): 'It's not the Fish that Stinks! EU Trade Relations with Morocco under Scrutiny of the General Court of the European Union', *Utrecht Journal of International and European Law*, vol. 32, 19–40.

Hudson, Manley O. (1932): 'The Central American Court of Justice', *American Journal of International Law*, vol. 26, 759–86.

Hull, William I. (1908): *The Two Hague Conferences* (Boston, MA: Ginn & Company).

Igarashi, Masahiro (2000): 'Post-War Compensation Cases, Japanese Courts and International Law', *Japanese Annual of International Law*, vol. 45, 45–82.

Jackson, John H. (2006): *Sovereignty, the WTO, and Changing Fundamentals of International Law* (Cambridge: Cambridge University Press).

Jacobs, Francis (2010): 'Access by Individuals to Judicial Review in EU Law', in Henning Koch, Karsten Hagel-Sørensen, Ulrich Haltern, and Joseph H. H. Weiler (eds), *Europe—The New Legal Realism* (Copenhagen: Djøf Publishing) 263–76.

Jacobs, Francis G., White, Robin C. A., and Ovey, Clare (2017): *The European Convention on Human Rights*, 7th edn edited by Bernadette Rainey, Elizabeth Wicks, and Clare Ovey (Oxford: Oxford University Press).

Jenks, C. Wilfred (1958): *The Common Law of Mankind* (London: Stevens and Sons).

Jenks, C. Wilfred (1960): 'Hersch Lauterpacht—The Scholar as Prophet', *British Yearbook of International Law*, vol. 36, 1–103.

Jennings, Sir Robert (2001): 'The LaGrand Case', *The Law and Practice of International Courts and Tribunals*, vol. 1, 13–54.

Jennings, Robert and Watts, Arthur (1992): *Oppenheim's International Law*, 9th edn (London: Longman).

Jessup, Philip C. (1947): 'The Subjects of a Modern Law of Nations', *Michigan Law Review*, vol. 45, 383–408.

Jessup, Philip C. (1948): *A Modern Law of Nations* (New York: Macmillan).

Jessup, Philip C. (1956): *Transnational Law* (New Haven, CT: Yale University Press).

Jones, David Lloyd (1983–4): 'The Iran–United States Claims Tribunal: Private Rights and State Responsibility', *Virginia Journal of International Law*, vol. 24, 259–85.

Jordison, Sasha Maldonado (2009): 'The Central American Court of Justice: Yesterday, Today and Tomorrow?' *Connecticut Journal of International Law*, vol. 25, 183–243.

Joseph, Sarah (2011): *Blame It on the WTO?: A Human Rights Critique* (Oxford: Oxford University Press).

Jouannet, Emmanuelle (1998): *Emer de Vattel et l'Émergence doctrinale du Droit International Classique* (Paris: Editions A. Pédone).

Kaeckenbeeck, Georges (1935): 'The Character and Work of the Arbitral Tribunal of Upper Silesia', *Transactions of the Grotius Society*, vol. 21, 27–44.

Kaeckenbeeck, Georges (1936): 'The Protection of Vested Rights in International Law', *British Yearbook of International Law*, vol. 17, 1–18.

Kaeckenbeeck, Georges (1942): *The International Experiment of Upper Silesia* (Oxford: Oxford University Press).

Kaeckenbeeck, Georges (1946): 'Upper Silesia under the League of Nations', *Annals of the American Academy of Political and Social Science*, vol. 243, 129–33.

Kammerhofer, Jörg (2010a): 'Gaps, the Nuclear Weapons Advisory Opinion and the Structure of International Legal Argument Between Theory and Practice', *British Yearbook of International Law*, vol. 80, 333–60.

Kammerhofer, Jörg (2010b): 'Constitutionalism and the Myth of Practical Reason: Kelsenian Responses to Methodological Problems', *Leiden Journal of International Law*, 723–40.

Kammerhofer, Jörg (2011): 'Hans Kelsen's Place in International Legal Theory', in Alexander Orakhelashvili (ed.), *Research Handbook on the Theory and History of International Law* (Cheltenham: Edward Elgar) 143–67.

Kammerhofer, Jörg, and d'Aspremont, Jean (2014): 'Introduction: The Future of International Legal Positivism', in Kammerhofer, Jörg, and d'Aspremont, Jean (eds), *International Legal Positivism in a Post-Modern World* (Cambridge: Cambridge University Press).

Kelsen, Hans (1920a): *Das Problem der Souveränität und die Theorie des Völkerrechts* (Tübingen: J. C. B. Mohr).

Kelsen, Hans (1920b): 'Der völkerrechtliche Strafanspruch wegen völkerrechtswidriger Kriegshandlungen', *Neue Freie Presse Wien*, 8 September 1920, available at http://anno.onb.ac.at/.

Kelsen, Hans (1926-IV): 'Les Rapports de Système entre le Droit Interne et le Droit International Public', *Recueil des Cours*, vol. 14, 227–331.

Kelsen, Hans (1928a): *Die philosophischen Grundlagen der Naturrechtslehre und des Rechtspositivismus* (Berlin: Pan-Verlag Rolf Heise).

Kelsen, Hans (1928b—reprinted in 1962), *Der soziologische und der juristische Staatsbegriff. Kritische Untersuchung des Verhältnisses von Staat und Recht*, 2nd edn (Aalen: Scientia).

Kelsen, Hans (1932-IV): 'Theorie Générale du Droit International Public—Problèmes Choisis', *Recueil des Cours*, vol. 42, 119–351.

Kelsen, Hans (1934): 'Die Technik des Völkerrechts und die Organisation des Friedens', *Zeitschrift für öffentliches Recht*, vol. 14, 240–55.

Kelsen, Hans (1944): *Peace through Law* (Chapel Hill, NC: The University of North Carolina Press).

Kelsen, Hans (1945): *General Theory of Law and State* (Cambridge, MA: Harvard University Press).

Kelsen, Hans (1947): 'Will the Judgment in the Nuremberg Trial Constitute a Precedent in International Law?', *International Law Quarterly*, vol. 1, 153–71.

Kelsen, Hans (1953-III): 'Theorie du Droit International Public', *Recueil des Cours*, vol. 84, 5–203.

Kelsen, Hans (1960, first published 1923): *Hauptprobleme der Staatsrechtslehre*, 2nd edn (Aalen: Scientia).

Kelsen, Hans (1966): *Principles of International Law*, 2nd edn revised and edited by Robert W. Tucker (New York: Holt, Rinehart and Winston).

Kelsen, Hans (1968, first published 1953): 'Was ist die Reine Rechtslehre?', reprinted in Hans Klecatsky et al. (eds) *Die Wiener rechtstheoretische Schule. Schriften von Hans Kelsen, Adolf Merkl, Alfred Verdross* (Wien: Europa) 611–29.

Kelsen, Hans (1970): *Pure Theory of Law* (translation by Max Knight) (Clark, NJ: The Lawbook Exchange).

Kelsen, Hans (1979): (edited by Kurt Ringhofer and Robert Walter) *Allgemeine Theorie der Normen* (Vienna: Manzche Verlags- und Universitätsbuchhandlung).

Kelsen, Hans (1991): (translated by Michael Hartney) *General Theory of Norms* (Oxford: Oxford University Press).

Kelsen, Hans (1998, first published in 1962): 'Sovereignty', reprinted in translation in Stanley L. Paulson and Bonnie L. Paulson (eds), *Normativity and Norms. Critical Perspectives on Kelsenian Themes* (Oxford: Clarendon Press) 525–36.

Kennedy, David (1986): 'Primitive Legal Scholarship', *Harvard International Law Journal*, vol. 27, 1–98.

Kittichaisaree, Kriangsak (2001): *International Criminal Law* (Oxford: Oxford University Press).

Kjeldgaard-Pedersen, Astrid (2005): *Statsrepræsentanters immunitet* (Copenhagen: Thomson).

Kjeldgaard-Pedersen, Astrid (2010): 'The Evolution of the Right of Individuals to Seise the European Court of Human Rights', *Journal of the History of International Law*, vol. 12, 267–306.

Kjeldgaard-Pedersen, Astrid (2011): 'Individuals as Subjects of International Law: The Example of the European Convention on Human Rights', in Sten Schaumburg-Müller and Jens Vedsted-Hansen (eds), *Ret, individ og kollektiv* (Copenhagen: Djøf Publishing) 105–30.

Kjeldgaard-Pedersen, Astrid (2014): 'The Influence of the Concept of International Legal Personality in the Drafting on the Statute of the Permanent Court of International Justice', *Journal of the History of International Law*, vol. 16, 9–25.

Kjeldgaard-Pedersen, Astrid (2015): 'What Defines an International Criminal Court?: A Critical Assessment of "the Involvement of the International Community" as a Deciding Factor', *Leiden Journal of International Law*, vol. 28, 113–31.

Kjeldgaard-Pedersen, Astrid (2016): 'A Ghost in the Ivory Tower: Positivism and International Legal Regulation of Armed Opposition Groups', *Journal of International Humanitarian Legal Studies*, vol. 7, 32–62.

Klabbers, Jan (2013): *International Law* (Cambridge: Cambridge University Press).

Klabbers, Jan, Peters, Anne, and Ulfstein, Geir (2009): *The Constitutionalization of International Law* (Oxford: Oxford University Press).

Kleinlein, Thomas (2011): 'Non-State Actors from an International Constitutionalist Perspective: Participation Matters!', in Jean d'Aspremont (ed.), *Participants in the International Legal System* (London: Routledge) 41–53.

Koh, Harold Hongju (1996): 'Transnational Legal Process', 75 *Nebraska Law Review*, 181–207.

Koh, Harold Hongju (2007): 'Is There a "New" New Haven School of International Law?', 32 *Yale Journal of International Law*, 559–73.

Kokott, Juliane, and Sobotta, Christoph (2012): 'The Kadi Case—Constitutional Core Values and International Law—Finding the Balance?', *European Journal of International Law*, vol. 23, 1015–24.

Kolb, Robert (2001): 'The Jurisprudence of the Yugoslav and Rwandan Criminal Tribunals on Their Jurisdiction and on International Crimes', *British Yearbook of International Law*, vol. 71, 259–315.

Korowicz, Marek St. (1956): 'The Problem of the International Legal Personality of Individuals', *American Journal of International Law*, vol. 50, 533–62.

Koskenniemi, Martti (2001): *The Gentle Civilizer of Nations. The Rise and Fall of International Law 1870–1960* (Cambridge: Cambridge University Press).

Koskenniemi, Martti (2005): *From Apology to Utopia—The Structure of International Legal Argument* (reissue with new Epilogue) (Cambridge: Cambridge University Press).

Koskenniemi, Martti, and Leino, Päivi (2002): 'Fragmentation of International Law? Postmodern Anxieties', *Leiden Journal of International Law*, vol. 15, 553–79.

Krehbiel, Edward (1918): 'The European Commission of the Danube: An Experiment in International Administration', *Political Science Quarterly*, vol. 33, no. 1, 38–55.

Kreß, Claus (last updated March 2009): 'International Criminal Law' in *Max Planck Encyclopaedia of International Law* (available at http://opil.ouplaw.com/home/EPIL, accessed 21 January 2018).

Kühnhardt, Ludger (1993): 'European Court and Human Rights', in Douglas Greenberg et al. (eds), *Constitutionalism and Democracy: Transitions in the Contemporary World* (Oxford: Oxford University Press) 126–38.

Kunz, Josef L. (1923): *Völkerrechtswissenschaft und reine Rechtslehre* (Leipzig/Vienna: F. Deuticke).

Kunz, Josef L. (1925): 'La Primauté de droit des gens', *Revue de droit international et de législation comparée*, vol. VI, 3rd Series (1925) 556–98.

Künzli, Annemarieke (2005): 'Case Concerning Mexican Nationals', *Leiden Journal of International Law*, vol. 18, 49–64.

Larsen, Kjetil Mujezinovic (2009): 'Attribution of Conduct in Peace Operations: The "Ultimate Authority and Control" Test', *European Journal of International Law*, vol. 19, 509–31.

Lasswell, Harold D. and McDougal, Myres S. (1992): *Jurisprudence for a Free Society: Studies in Law, Science and Policy* (Dordrecht: Martinus Nijhoff).

Lauterpacht, Elihu (2010): *The Life of Sir Hersch Lauterpacht* (Cambridge: Cambridge University Press).

Lauterpacht, Hersch (1933): 'Kelsen's Pure Science of Law', reprinted in Elihu Lauterpacht (ed.) (1975): *International Law—Being the Collected Papers of Hersch Lauterpacht*, vol. II (Cambridge: Cambridge University Press) 404–30.

Lauterpacht, Hersch (1934): *The Development of International Law by the Permanent Court of International Justice* (London: Stevens & Sons).

Lauterpacht, Hersch (1947): *Recognition in International Law* (Cambridge: Cambridge University Press).

Lauterpacht, Hersch (1948): 'The Universal Declaration of Human Rights', *British Yearbook of International Law*, vol. 25, 354–81.

Lauterpacht, Hersch (1950): *International Law and Human Rights* (London: Stevens & Sons).

Lauterpacht, Hersch (1958): *The Development of International Law by the International Court* (London: Stevens & Sons).

Lauterpacht, Sir Hersch (1970a, previously unpublished): 'International Law—The General Part', printed in Elihu Lauterpacht (ed.), *International Law—Being the Collected Papers of Hersch Lauterpacht*, vol. I (Cambridge: Cambridge University Press) 5–178.

Lauterpacht, Sir Hersch (1970b, previously unpublished): 'General Rules of the Law of Peace', printed in Elihu Lauterpacht (ed.), *International Law—Being the Collected Papers of Hersch Lauterpacht*, vol. I (1970) 179–444.

Lauterpacht, Sir Hersch (1975, previously published in two parts in 1947 and 1948): 'The Subjects of the Law of Nations', reprinted in Elihu Lauterpacht (ed.), *International Law—Being the Collected Papers of Hersch Lauterpacht*, vol. II (Cambridge: Cambridge University Press) 487–533.

Lauterpacht, Sir Hersch (2012, previously unpublished): 'Draft Nuremberg Speeches', *Cambridge Journal of International and Comparative Law*, vol. 1, 45–111.

Leben, Charles (2010): *The Advancement of International Law* (Oxford: Hart).

Legg, Andrew (2012): *The Margin of Appreciation in International Human Rights Law: Deference and Proportionality* (Oxford: Oxford University Press).

Leibniz, Gottfried Wilhelm (1693): *Codex juris gentium diplomaticus* (Hannover) in the translation of Riley, Patrick (ed.), *Leibniz Political Writings*, 2nd edn (Cambridge: Cambridge University Press, 1988).

Lenaerts, Koen, and van Nuffel, Piet (2011): *European Union Law*, 3rd edn (London: Sweet & Maxwell).

Letsas, George (2006): 'Two Concepts of the Margin of Appreciation', *Oxford Journal of Legal Studies*, vol. 26, 705–32.

Lillich, Richard B. and Brower, Charles N. (1997–1998): 'Opinion Regarding the Jurisdiction and Powers of the United Nations Compensation Commission', *Virginia Journal of International Law*, vol. 38, 25–50.

Lillich, Richard B. and Weston, Burns H. (1988): 'Lump Sum Agreements: Their Continuing Contribution to the Law of International Claims', *American Journal of International Law*, vol. 82, 69–80.

Lippman, Matthew (1992–3): 'The Other Nuremberg: American Prosecutions of Nazi War Criminals in Occupied Germany', *Indiana International & Comparative Law Review*, vol. 3, 1–100.

Loibl, Gerhard (2010): 'International Economic Law', in Evans, Malcolm D. (ed.), *International Law*, 3rd edn (Oxford: Oxford University Press) 722–51.

Lootsteen, Yair M. (2000): 'The Concept of Belligerency in International Law', *Military Law Review*, vol. 166, 109–41.

McCorquodale, Robert (2004): 'An Inclusive International Legal System', *Leiden Journal of International Law*, vol. 17, 477–504.

McCorquodale, Robert (2014): 'The Individual and the International Legal System', in Malcolm D. Evans (ed.) *International Law*, 4th edn (Oxford: Oxford University Press) 280–308.

McCorquodale, Robert (2017): 'Sources and the Subjects of International Law—A Plurality of Law-Making Participants', in Samantha Besson and Jean d'Aspremont (eds), *The Oxford Handbook on the Sources of International Law* (Oxford: Oxford University Press) 749–68.

McCoubrey, Hilaire (1998): *International Humanitarian Law*, 2nd edn (Aldershot: Ashgate Publishing Limited).

McDougal, Myres S. (1959): 'The Impact of International Law upon National Law: A Policy-Oriented Perspective', *South Dakota Law Review*, vol. 1, 25–92.

McKernan, Louis W. (1938): 'Special Mexican Claims', *American Journal of International Law*, vol. 32, 457–66.

McNair, Arnold (1928) (ed.): *Oppenheim's International Law*, vol. 1, 4th edn (London: Longmans, Green and Co.).

McNair, Arnold (1956): (selected and annotated) *International Law Opinions*, vol. I (Cambridge: Cambridge University Press).

McNair, Arnold (1957): 'The General Principles of Law Recognized by Civilized Nations', *British Yearbook of International Law*, vol. 33, 1–19.

McNair, Arnold (1961): *The Law of Treaties* (Oxford: Clarendon Press).

Madsen, Mikael Rask (2010): 'Legal Diplomacy. Law, Politics and the Genesis of Postwar European Human Rights', in Stefan Ludwig Hoffmann (ed.) *Human Rights in the Twentieth Century: A Critical History* (Cambridge: Cambridge University Press) 62–81.

Madsen, Mikael Rask (2016): 'The Challenging Authority of the European Court of Human Rights: From Cold War Legal Diplomacy to the Brighton Declaration and Backlash', *Law and Contemporary Problems*, vol. 79, 141–78.

Madsen, Mikael Rask (2017): 'Rebalancing European Human Rights: Has the Brighton Declaration Engendered a New Deal on Human Rights in Europe?', *Journal of International Dispute Settlement*, published online 27 June 2017, iCourts Working Paper Series No. 100 (available at https://ssrn.com/abstract=2993222, accessed 21 January 2018).

Madsen, Mikael Rask, Olsen, Henrik Palmer, and Šadl, Urška (2017): 'Competing Supremacies and Clashing Institutional Rationalities: The Danish Supreme Court's

Decision in the Ajos Case and the National Limits of Judicial Cooperation', *European Law Journal*, vol. 23, 140–50.

Mahoney, Paul (1990): 'Judicial Activism and Judicial Self-Restraint in the European Court of Human Rights: Two Sides of the Same Coin', *Human Rights Law Journal*, vol. 11, 57–88.

Malanczuk, Peter (1997): *Akehurst's Modern Introduction to International Law*, 7th edn (London: Routledge).

Maniruzzaman, A. F. M. (2001): 'State Contracts in Contemporary International Law: Monist versus Dualist Controversies', *European Journal of International Law*, 309–28.

Manner, George (1952): 'The Object Theory of the Individual in International Law', *American Journal of International Law*, vol. 46, 428–49.

Matheson, Michael J. (2010): 'The Damage Awards of Eritrea–Ethiopia Claims Commission', *The Law and Practice of International Courts and Tribunals*, vol. 9, 1–15.

Matscher, Franz (1993): 'Methods of Interpretation of the Convention', in R. S. J. Macdonald, F. Matscher, and H. Petzold (eds), *The European System for the Protection of Human Rights* (Dordrecht: Martinus Nijhoff) 63–81.

Mégret, Frédéric (2012): 'International Law as Law', in James Crawford and Martti Koskenniemi (eds), *The Cambridge Companion to International Law* (Cambridge: Cambridge University Press) 64–92.

Mennecke, Martin and Tams, Christian J. (2002): 'LaGrand Case (Germany v. United States of America)' *International & Comparative Law Quarterly*, vol. 51, 449–55.

Menon, P. K. (1990): 'The Subjects of Modern International Law', *Hague Yearbook of International Law*, vol. 3, 30–86.

Meron, Theodor (2000a): 'The Martens Clause, Principles of Humanity, and Dictates of Public Conscience', *American Journal of International Law*, vol. 94, 78–89.

Meron, Theodor (2000b): 'The Humanization of Humanitarian Law', *American Journal of International Law*, vol. 94, 239–78.

Merrills, J. G. (1993): *The Development of International Law by the European Court of Human Rights*, 2nd edn (Manchester: Manchester University Press).

Mettraux, Guénaël (2008): 'Judicial Inheritance: The Value and Significance of the Nuremberg Trial to Contemporary War Crimes Tribunals', in Guénaël Mettraux, *Perspectives on the Nuremberg Trial* (Oxford: Oxford University Press) 599–614.

Milano, Enrico (2004): 'Diplomatic Protection and Human Rights before the International Court of Justice: Re-Fashioning Tradition', *Netherlands Yearbook of International Law*, vol. 35, 85–142.

Milanović, Marko (2009): 'Norm Conflict in International Law: Whither Human Rights?', *Duke Journal of Comparative & International Law*, vol. 20, 69–131.

Milanović, Marko (2011): 'Is the Rome Statute Binding on Individuals? (And Why We Should Care)', *Journal of International Criminal Justice*, vol. 9, 25–52.

Milanović, Marko (2012): '*Al-Skieni* and *Al-Jedda* in Strasbourg', *European Journal of International Law*, vol. 23, 121–39.

Minear, Richard H. (1971): *Victor's Justice—The Tokyo War Crimes Trial* (Princeton, NJ: Princeton University Press).

Moir, Lindsay (2002): *The Law of Internal Armed Conflict* (Cambridge: Cambridge University Press).

Moore, John Bassett (1898): *History and Digest of the International Arbitrations to Which the United States Has Been a Party* (Washington, DC: Government Printing Office) vols. I–VI.

Moore, John Bassett (1906): *A Digest of International Law* (Washington, DC: Government Printing Office) vols I–VIII.

Morris, Virginia (1998): 'Prosecutor v. Kanyabashi, Decision on Jurisdiction. Case No. ICTR-96-15-T', *American Journal of International Law*, vol. 92, 66–70.

Müller, Andreas Th. (2012): 'Kate Parlett. The Individual in the International Legal System. Continuity and Change in International Law', *European Journal of International Law*, vol. 23, 294–9 (book review).

Murray, Daragh (2016): *Human Rights Obligations of Non-State Armed Groups* (Oxford: Hart).

Nassar, Nagal (1997): 'Internationalization of State Contracts: ICSID, The Last Citadel', 14 *Journal of International Arbitration*, 185–207.

Neff, Stephen C. (2005): *War and the Law of Nations—A General History* (Cambridge: Cambridge University Press).

Nijman, Janne Elisabeth (2004): *The Concept of International Legal Personality—An Inquiry into the History and Theory of International Law* (The Hague: TMC Asser Press).

Nijman, Janne Elisabeth (2010): 'Non-State Actors and the International Rule of Law: Revisiting the "Realist Theory" of International Legal Personality', in Math Noortmann and Cedric Ryngaert (eds), *Non-State Actor Dynamics in International Law* (Farnham: Ashgate) 91–124.

Nijman, Janne and Nollkaemper, André (2007): 'Beyond the Divide', in Janne Nijman and André Nollkaemper (eds), *New Perspectives on the Divide Between National and International Law* (Oxford: Oxford University Press) 341–60.

Nollkaemper, André (2009): *The Power of Secondary Rules of International Law to Connect the International and National Legal Orders*, Amsterdam Center for International Law Working Papers, (available at http://ssrn.com/abstract=1515771, accessed 31 January 2018).

Nollkaemper, André (2011): *National Courts and the International Rule of Law* (Oxford: Oxford University Press).

Nollkaemper, André (2014): 'The Duality of Direct Effect of International Law', *European Journal of International Law*, vol. 25, 105–25.

Nollkaemper, André and Jacobs, Dov (2013): 'Shared Responsibility in International Law: A Conceptual Framework', 34 *Michigan Journal of International Law*, 359–438.

Noortmann, Math (2010): 'Understanding Non-State Actors in the Contemporary World Society: Transcending the International, Mainstreaming the Transnational, or Bringing the Participants Back In?', in Math Noortmann and Cedric Ryngaert (eds), *Non-State Actor Dynamics in International Law* (Farnham: Ashgate) 153–70.

Noortmann, Math and Ryngaert, Cedric (eds) (2010): *Non-State Actor Dynamics in International Law* (Farnham: Ashgate).

Nordeide, Ragnar (2009): 'Fragmentation and the Leeway of the VCLT', *Finnish Yearbook of International Law*, vol. 20, 189–207.

Nordeide, Ragnar (2012): 'The ECHR and its Normative Environment: Difficulties Arising from a Regional Human Rights Court's Approach to Systemic Integration', in Ole Kristian Fauchald and André Nollkaemper (eds) (Oxford: Hart) 117–38.

Nowak, Manfred, and Januszewski, Karolina Miriam (2015): 'Non-State Actors and Human Rights', in Math Noortmann, August Reinisch, and Cedric Ryngaert (eds), *Non-State Actors in International Law* (Oxford: Hart) 113–61.

Nussbaum, Arthur (1950–1): 'Arbitration Between the Lena Goldfields Ltd. and the Soviet Government', *Cornell Law Quarterly*, vol. 36, 31–53.

Nystuen, Gro, and Tronvoll, Kjetil (2008): 'The Eritrean–Ethiopian Peace Agreement: Exploring the Limits of Law', *Nordisk Tidsskrift for Menneskerettigheder*, vol. 26, 16–37.

Nørgaard, Carl Aage (1962): *The Position of the Individual in International Law* (Copenhagen: Munksgaard).

O'Connell, D. P. (1970): *International Law*, 2nd edn (London: Stevens & Sons) vol. I.

Odermatt, Jed (2014): 'The Court of Justice of the European Union: International or Domestic Court', 3 *Cambridge Journal of International and Comparative Law*, 696–718.

Odermatt, Jed (2017): 'Council of the European Union v Front populaire pour la libération de la saguia-el-hamra et du rio de oro (Front Polisario)—Case C-104/16 P', *American Journal of International Law*, vol. 111, 731–8.

Oellers-Frahm, Karin, and Wühler, Norbert (1984): *Dispute Settlement in Public International Law* (Berlin: Springer).

Oglesby, Roscoe R. (1971): 'The Decline of Belligerent Recognition: Desuetude in International Law', in Roscoe R. Oglesby (ed.), *Internal War and the Search for Normative Order* (The Hague: Martinus Nijhoff).

O'Keefe, Roger (2015): *International Criminal Law* (Oxford: Oxford University Press).

Okowa, Phoebe (2014): 'Issues of Admissibility and the Law on International Responsibility', in Malcolm D. Evans (ed.), *International Law*, 4th edn (Oxford: Oxford University Press) 477–508.

Oppenheim, Lassa (1905): *International Law—A Treatise: Peace*, vol. I (London: Longmans, Green, and Co.).

Oppenheim, Lassa (1906): *International Law—A Treatise: War and Neutrality*, vol. II (London: Longmans, Green, and Co.).

Oppenheim, Lassa (1920): *International Law—A Treatise*, 3rd edn (London: Longmans, Green, and Co.).

Orakhelashvili, Alexander (2001): 'The Position of the Individual in International Law', *California Western International Law Journal*, vol. 31, 241–76.

Orakhelashvili, Alexander (2016): 'Al-Dulimi v. Switzerland', *American Journal of International Law*, vol. 110, 767–74.

Paparinskis, Martins (2008): 'Investment Arbitration and the Law of Countermeasures', *British Yearbook of International Law*, vol. 79, 264–352.

Paparinskis, Martins (2013): 'Investment Treaty Arbitration and the (New) Law of State Responsibility', 24 *European Journal of International Law*, vol. 24, 617–47.

Paparinskis, Martins (2014): 'Analogies and Other Regimes of International Law', in Zachary Douglas, Joost Pauwelyn, and Jorge E. Viñuales (eds), *The Foundations of International Investment Law* (Oxford: Oxford University Press) 73–107.

Parish, Matthew (2012): 'International Courts and the European Legal Order', *European Journal of International Law*, vol. 23, 141–53.

Parlett, Kate (2008): 'The PCIJ's Opinion in Jurisdiction of the Courts of Danzig. Individual Rights under Treaties', *Journal of the History of International Law*, vol. 10, 119–45.

Parlett, Kate (2011): *The Individual in the International Legal System—Continuity and Change in International Law* (Cambridge: Cambridge University Press).

Parry, Clive (ed.) (1969–81): *The Consolidated Treaty Series, 1648–1919* (Dobbs Ferry, NY: Oceana).

Paulsson, Jan (1996a): 'Dispute Resolution', in Robert Pritchard (ed.), *Economic Development, Foreign Investment and the Law: Issues of Private Sector Involvement, Foreign Investment and the Rule of Law in a New Era* (London: Kluwer Law International) 209–46.

Paulsson, Jan (1996b): 'Arbitration Without Privity', in T. W. Wälde (ed.), *The Energy Charter Treaty: An East–West Gateway for Investment and Trade* (London: Kluwer Law International) 422–42.

Paulus, Andreas (2009): 'The International Legal System as a Constitution', in Jeffrey L. Dunoff and Joel P. Trachtman (eds), *Ruling the World? Constitutionalism, International Law and Global Governance* (Cambridge: Cambridge University Press) 69–109.

Paust, Jordan J. (2003–4): 'The Reality of Private Rights, Duties and Participation in the International Legal Process', *Michigan Journal of International Law*, vol. 25, 1229–49.

Pauwelyn, Joost (2001): 'The Role of Public International Law in the WTO: How Far Can We Go?', *American Journal of International Law*, vol. 95, 535–78.

Pellet, Alain (2010): 'The Palestinian Declaration and the Jurisdiction of the International Criminal Court', *Journal of International Criminal Justice*, vol. 8, 981–99.

Percival, John H. (1938): 'International Arbitral Tribunals and the Mexican Claims Commissions', *Journal of Comparative Legislation and International Law*, vol. 19, 98–104.

Pergantis, Vasileios (2006): 'Towards a "Humanization" of Diplomatic Protection', *Zeitschrift für ausländisches öffentliches Recht und Völkerrecht*, vol. 66, 351–97.

Peters, Anne (2007): 'The Globalization of State Constitutions', in Janne E. Nijman and André Nollkaemper (eds), *New Perspectives on the Divide Between National and International Law* (Oxford: Oxford University Press) 251–308.

Peters, Anne (2009): 'Supremacy Lost: International Law Meets Domestic Constitutional Law', *Vienna Journal on International Constitutional Law*, vol. 3, 170–98.

Peters, Anne (2012): 'Are we Moving towards Constitutionalization of the World Community?', in Antonio Cassese (ed.), *Realizing Utopia* (Oxford: Oxford University Press) 118–35.

Peters, Anne (2014): *Jenseits der Menschenrechte—Die Rechtsstellung des Individuums im Völkerrecht* (Tübingen: Mohr Siebeck).

Peters, Anne (2016): *Beyond Human Rights—The Legal Status of the Individual in International Law* (Cambridge: Cambridge University Press).

Pictet, Jean (ed.) (1952): *Commentary on the Geneva Conventions of 12 August 1949* (Geneva: International Committee of the Red Cross) vol. I.

Pictet, Jean (ed.) (1958): *Commentary on the Geneva Conventions of 12 August 1949* (Geneva: International Committee of the Red Cross) vol. IV.

Pictet, Jean (ed.) (1960a): *Commentary on the Geneva Conventions of 12 August 1949* (Geneva: International Committee of the Red Cross) vol. III.

Pictet, Jean (ed.) (1960b): *Commentary on the Geneva Conventions of 12 August 1949* (Geneva: International Committee of the Red Cross) vol. II.

Politis, Nicolas (1925–6): 'How the World Court Has Functioned', *Foreign Affairs*, vol. 4, 443–53.

Politis, Nicolas (1927): *Les Nouvelles Tendances du Droit International* (Paris: Librairie Hachette).

Portmann, Roland (2010): *Legal Personality in International Law* (Cambridge: Cambridge University Press).

Provost, René (2002): *International Human Rights and Humanitarian Law* (Cambridge: Cambridge University Press).

Puig, Sergio (2014): 'No Right Without a Remedy: Foundations of Investor-State Arbitration', in Zachary Douglas, Joost Pauwelyn, and Jorge E. Viñuales (eds), *The Foundations of International Investment Law* (Oxford: Oxford University Press) 235–56.

Quadri, Rolando (1964-III): 'Cours Générale de Droit International Public', *Recueil des Cours*, vol. 113, 245–483.

Raitz von Frentz, Christian (1999): *A Lesson Forgotten: Minority Protection under the League of Nations: The Case of the German Minority in Poland, 1920–1934* (Münster: LIT).

Rama-Montaldo, Manuel (1970): 'International Legal Personality and Implied Powers of International Organizations', *British Year Book International Law*, vol. 44, 111–56.

Reinisch, August (2015): 'Investors', in Math Noortmann, August Reinisch, and Cedric Ryngaert (eds), *Non-State Actors in International Law* (Oxford: Hart) 253–71.

Reisman, W. Michael, Wiessner, Siegfried, and Willard, Andrew R. (2007): 'The New Haven School: A Brief Introduction', *Yale Journal of International Law*, vol. 32, 575–82.

Riley, Patrick (ed.) (1988): *Leibniz: Political Writings*, 2nd edn (Cambridge: Cambridge University Press).

Roberts, Anthea (2013): 'Clash of Paradigms: Actors and Analogies Shaping the Investment Treaty System', *American Journal of International Law*, vol. 107, 45–94.

Roberts, Lawrence D. (1992–3): 'United Nations Security Council Resolution 687 and Its Aftermath: The Implications for Domestic Authority and the Need for Legitimacy', *New York University Journal of International Law and Politics*, vol. 25, 593–626.

Robinson, Jacob, Karbach, Oscar, Laserson, Max M., Robinson, Nehemiah, and Vichniak, Marc (1943): *Were the Minorities Treaties a Failure?* (New York: Antin Press).

Rogers, A. P. V. (1990): 'War Crimes Trials under the Royal Warrant: British Practice 1945–1949', *International & Comparative Law Quarterly*, vol. 90, 780–800.

Röling, B. V. A. (edited by Antonio Cassese) (1993): *The Tokyo Trial and Beyond—Reflections of a Peacemonger* (Oxford: Polity Press).

Ronen, Yaël (2010): 'ICC Jurisdiction over Acts Committed in the Gaza Strip', *Journal of International Criminal Justice*, vol. 8, 3–27.

Ronen, Yaël (2013a): 'Human Rights Obligations of Territorial Non-State Actors', *Cornell International Law Journal*, vol. 46, 21–50.

Ronen, Yaël (2013b): 'Blind in their Own Cause: The Military Courts in the West Bank', *Cambridge Journal of International and Comparative Law*, vol. 2, 738–63.

Ross, Alf (1947): *A Textbook of International Law* (London: Longmans, Green and Co.).

Rosting, Helmer (1923): 'Protection of Minorities by the League of Nations', *American Journal of International Law*, vol. 17, 641–60.

Rub, Alfred (1995): *Hans Kelsens Völkerrechtslehre—Versuch einer Würdigung* (Zürich: Schulthess Polygraphischer).

Russo, Carlo (1999): 'The Drafting History of the European Convention on Human Rights and Fundamental Freedoms', in Salvino Busuttil (ed.), *Mainly Human Rights—Studies in Honour of J. J. Cremona* (Malta: Foundation Internationale Malte) 234–44.

Ryngaert, Cedric (2010): 'Imposing International Duties on Non-State Actors and the Legitimacy of International Law', in Math Noortmann and Cedric Ryngaert (eds), *Non-State Actor Dynamics in International Law* (Farnham: Ashgate) 69–89.

Ryngaert, Cedric (2011): 'Non-State Actors in International Humanitarian Law', in Jean d'Aspremont (ed.), *Participants in the International Legal System* (London: Routledge) 284–94.

Ryngaert, Cedric (2016): 'Non-State Actors: Carving out a Space in a State-Centric International Legal System', *Netherlands International Law Review*, vol. 63, 183–95.

Salacuse, Jeswald W. (2015): *The Law of Investment Treaties*, 2nd edn (Oxford: Oxford University Press).

Sandoz, Yves, Swinarski, Christophe, and Zimmerman, Bruno (eds) (1987): *Commentary on the Additional Protocols of 8 June 1977 to the Geneva Conventions of 12 August 1949* (Geneva: International Committee of the Red Cross/Martinus Nijhoff).

Sands, Philippe (2012): 'Twin Peaks: The Hersch Lauterpacht Draft Nuremberg Speeches', *Cambridge Journal of International and Comparative Law*, vol. 1, 37–44.

Scelle, Georges (1932a): *Précis de Droit des Gens, Principes et Systématique* (Paris: Librairie du Recueil Sirey).

Scelle, Georges (1932b): 'La Doctrine de Duguit et les Fondements du Droit des Gens' 1–2 *Archives de Philosophie du Droit et de Sociologie Juridique* (Paris: Librairie du Recueil Sirey) 83–119.

Scelle, Georges (1933-IV): 'Règles générales du Droit de la paix', *Recueil des Cours*, vol. 46, 327–703.

Scelle, Georges (1953): 'Some Reflections on Juridical Personality in International Law', in George A. Lipsky (ed.), *Law and Politics in the World Community. Essays on Hans Kelsen's Pure Theory and Related Problems in International Law* (Berkeley and Los Angeles, CA: University of California Press) 49–58.

Schabas, William (2003): 'Interpreting the Statutes of the Ad Hoc Tribunals' in L. C. Vohrah et al. (eds), *Man's Inhumanity to Man: Essays on International Law in Honour of Antonio Cassese* (The Hague: Kluwer Law International) 847–88.

Schachter, Oscar (1982-V): 'International Law in Theory and Practice: General Course in Public International Law', *Recueil des Cours*, vol. 178, 9–396.

Schilling, Theodor (1996): 'The Autonomy of the Community Legal Order: An Analysis of Possible Foundations', *Harvard International Law Journal*, vol. 37, 389–409.

Schindler, Dietrich (1979): 'The Different Types of Armed Conflicts According to the Geneva Conventions and Protocols', *Recueil des Cours*, vol. 163, 117–163.

Schindler, Dietrich, and Toman, Jiří (eds) (2004): *Laws of Armed Conflicts: A Collection of Conventions, Resolutions, and Other Documents*, 4th edn (Dordrecht: Martinus Nijhoff).

Schlögel Anton (1971): 'La guerre civile', *International Review of the Red Cross*, vol. 52, 137–48.

Schreuer, Christoph (1993): 'The Waning of the Sovereign State: Towards a New Paradigm for International Law?', *European Journal of International Law*, vol. 4, 447–71.

Schreuer, Christoph (2005a): 'Calvo's Grandchildren: The Return of the Local Remedies in Investment Arbitration', *The Law and Practice of International Courts and Tribunals*, vol. 4, 1–17.

Schreuer, Christoph (2005b): 'Investment Treaty Arbitration and Jurisdiction over Contract Claims—the *Vivendi I* case Considered', in Todd Weiler (ed.), *International Investment Law and Arbitration: Leading Cases from the ICSID, NAFTA, Bilateral Treaties and Customary International Law* (London: Cameron May) 281–324.

Schreuer, Christoph H., with Malintoppi, Loretta, Reinisch, August, and Sinclair, Anthony (2009): *The ICSID Convention—A Commentary*, 2nd edn (Cambridge: Cambridge University Press).

Schwarzenberger, Georg (1947): 'The Judgment of Nuremberg', *Tulane Law Review*, vol. 21, 329–61.

Schwarzenberger, Georg (1950a): *A Manual of International Law*, 2nd edn (London: Stevens & Sons).

Schwarzenberger, Georg (1950b): 'The Problem of an International Criminal Law', *Current Legal Problems*, vol. 3, 263–96.

Schwarzenberger, Georg (1955-I): 'The Fundamental Principles of International Law', *Recueil des Cours*, vol. 87, 191–385.

Schwarzenberger, Georg (1967): *A Manual of International Law*, 5th edn (New York: Frederick A. Praeger).

Schwarzenberger, Georg (1976): *A Manual of International Law*, 6th edn (Milton, UK: Professional Book Ltd.).

Schwebel, Stephen M. (1996), 'May Preparatory Work Be Used to Correct Rather Than Confirm the Clear Meaning of a Treaty Provision?', in Jerzy Makarczyk, *Theory of International Law at the Threshold of the 21st Century: Essays in Honour of Krzysztof Skubiszewski* (The Hague: Kluwer Law International) 541–47.

Scobbie, Iain G. M. (1997): 'The Theorist as Judge: Hersch Lauterpacht's Concept of the International Judicial Function', *European Journal of International Law*, vol. 8, 264–98.

Scobbie, Iain G. M. (2017): 'Legal Theory as a Source of International Law: Institutional Facts and the Identification of International Law', in Samantha Besson and Jean d'Aspremont (eds) *The Oxford Handbook on the Sources of International Law* (Oxford: Oxford University Press) 493–512.

Scobbie, Iain, and Droubi, Sufyan (eds), *Non-State Actors and the Formation of Customary International Law* (Manchester University Press, forthcoming 2018).

Scott, James Brown (1908): 'The Central American Peace Conference of 1907', *American Journal of International Law*, vol. 2, 121–43.

Scott, James Brown (1909): *The Hague Peace Conferences*, vol. I (Baltimore, MD: Johns Hopkins Press).

Scott, James Brown (1914): 'The Declaration of London of February 26, 1909', *American Journal of International Law*, vol. 8, 274–329.

Scott, James Brown (ed.) (1916): *Resolutions of the Institute of International Law*, (reprinted in 2003, Buffalo, NY: William Hein & Co.).

Scott, James Brown (1920a): *The Proceedings of the Hague Peace Conferences, The Conference of 1899* (New York: Oxford University Press).

Scott, James Brown (1920b): *The Proceedings of the Hague Peace Conferences, The Conference of 1907*, vol. I (New York: Oxford University Press).

Scott, James Brown (1921): *The Proceedings of the Hague Peace Conferences, The Conference of 1907*, vol. III (New York: Oxford University Press).

Seyersted, Finn (1963): *Objective International Personality of Intergovernmental Organizations* (Copenhagen: Krohns Bogtrykkeri).

Shany, Yuval (2006): 'Toward a General Margin of Appreciation Doctrine in International Law?', *European Journal of International Law*, vol. 19, 907–40.

Shany, Yuval (2012): 'One Law to Rule Them All', in Ole Kristian Fauchald and André Nollkaemper (eds), *The Practice of International and National Courts and the (De-)Fragmentation of International Law* (Oxford: Hart) 15–34.

Shaw, Malcolm N. (2003): *International Law*, 5th edn (Cambridge: Cambridge University Press).

Shaw, Malcolm N. (2014): *International Law*, 7th edn (Cambridge: Cambridge University Press).

Simma, Bruno (1994): 'From Bilateralism to Community Interest in International Law', *Recueil des Cours*, vol. 250, 217–384.

Simma, Bruno (1995): 'The Contribution of Alfred Verdross to the Theory of International Law', *European Journal of International Law*, vol. 6, 33–54.

Simma, Bruno, and Paulus, Andreas (1999): 'The Responsibility of Individuals for Human Rights Abuses in Internal Conflicts: A Positivist View', *American Journal of International Law*, vol. 93, 302–16.

Simma, Bruno, and Pulkowski, Dirk (2004): 'Of Planets and the Universe: Self-contained Regimes in International Law', *European Journal of International Law*, vol. 17, 482–529.

Simpson, A. W. Brian (2001): *Human Rights and the End of Empire—Britain and the Genesis of the European Convention* (Oxford: Oxford University Press).

Simpson, A. W. Brian (2004): 'Hersch Lauterpacht and the Genesis of the Age of Human Rights', *Law Quarterly Review*, vol. 120, 49–80.

Sivakumaran, Sandesh (2006): 'Binding Armed Opposition Groups', *International & Comparative Law Quarterly*, vol. 55, 369–94.

Sivakumaran, Sandesh (2017): 'Who Makes International Law? The Case of the Law of Armed Conflict' (available at SSRN: https://ssrn.com/abstract=3084238, accessed 21 January 2018).

Slaughter, Anne-Marie (1995): 'International Law in a World of Liberal States', *European Journal of International Law*, vol. 6, 503–38.

Smith, Herbert Arthur (1932): *Great Britain and the Law of Nations* (London: P. S. King & Son).

Solis, Gary D. (2010): *The Law of Armed Conflict* (Cambridge: Cambridge University Press).

Somek, Alexander (2012): 'Monism: A Tale of the Undead', in Matej Avbelj and Jan Komárek (eds), *Constitutional Pluralism in the European Union and Beyond* (Oxford: Hart) 343–79.

Sornarajah, M. (1994): *The International Law on Foreign Investment*, 1st edn (Cambridge: Cambridge University Press).

Sornarajah, M. (2010): *The International Law on Foreign Investment*, 3rd edn (Cambridge: Cambridge University Press).

Sornarajah, M. (2017): *The International Law on Foreign Investment*, 4th edn (Cambridge: Cambridge University Press).

Spano, Robert (2014): 'Universality or Diversity of Human Rights?: Strasbourg in the Age of Subsidiarity', *Human Rights Law Review*, vol. 14, 487–502.

Spiermann, Ole (1999): 'The Other Side of the Story: An Unpopular Essay on the Making of the European Community Legal Order', *European Journal of International Law*, vol. 10, 763–89.

Spiermann, Ole (2002): '"Who Attempts Too Much Does Nothing Well": The 1920 Advisory Committee of Jurists and the Statute of the Permanent Court of International Justice', *British Yearbook of International Law*, vol. 73, 187–260.

Spiermann, Ole (2003a): 'A National Lawyer Takes Stock: Professor Ross' Textbook and Other Forays into International Law', *European Journal of International Law*, vol. 14, 675–702.

Spiermann, Ole (2003b): 'The LaGrand Case and the Individual as a Subject of International Law', *Zeitschrift für Öffentliches Recht*, vol. 58, 197–221.

Spiermann, Ole (2004): 'Individual Rights, State Interests and the Power to Waive ICSID Jurisdiction under Bilateral Investment Treaties', *Arbitration International*, vol. 20, 179–211.

Spiermann, Ole (2005): *International Legal Argument in the Permanent Court of International Justice—The Rise of the International Judiciary* (Cambridge: Cambridge University Press).

Spiermann, Ole (2006): *Moderne Folkeret*, 3rd edn (Copenhagen: Djøf Publishing).

Spiermann, Ole (2007): 'Twentieth Century Internationalism in Law', *European Journal of International Law*, vol. 18, 785–814.

Spiermann, Ole (2008): 'Applicable Law', in Peter Muchlinski, Federico Ortino, and Christoph Schreuer (eds), *The Oxford Handbook of International Investment Law* (Oxford: Oxford University Press) 89–118.

Spiermann, Ole (2009): 'Premature Treaty Claims', in Christina Binder et al. (eds), *International Investment Law for the 21st Century—Essays in Honour of Christoph Schreuer* (Oxford: Oxford University Press) 463–89.

Spiermann, Ole (2010): 'On Law and Policy in the European Court of Justice', in Henning Koch et al. (eds), *Europe—The New Legal Realism* (Copenhagen: Djøf Publishing) 715–27.

Spiropoulos, Jean (1929-V): 'l'Individu et le Droit International', *Recueil des Cours*, vol. 30, 195–267.

Starke, J. G. (1936): 'Monism and Dualism in the Theory of International Law', *British Yearbook of International Law*, vol. 17, 66–81.

Stein, Eric (1981): 'Lawyers, Judges and the Making of a Transnational Constitution', *American Journal of International Law*, 1–27.

Stone, Julius (1933): *Regional Guarantees of Minority Rights: A Study of Minorities Procedure in Upper Silesia* (New York: Macmillan).

Strebel, Helmut (1997): 'Martens' Clause', in Rudolf Bernhardt (ed.), *Encyclopedia of Public International Law*, vol. III, 326–27.

Strupp, Karl (1920): *Das völkerrechtliche Delikt* (Berlin: W. Kohlhammer).

Strupp, Karl (1932): *Grundzüge des positiven Völkerrechts*, 5th edn (Bonn and Cologne: Ludwig Röhrscheid).

Strupp, Karl (1934-I): 'Règles générales du Droit de la Paix', *Recueil des Cours*, vol. 47, 259–595.

Struycken, A. V. M. (2014): 'Arbitration and State Contracts', *Recueil des Cours*, vol. 374, 9–52.

Stuyt, A. M. (1972): *Survey of International Arbitration 1794–1970* (Leiden: A. W. Sijthoff).

Tams, Christian J. (2002): 'Consular Assistance: Rights, Remedies and Responsibility: Comments on the ICJ's Judgment in the LaGrand Case', *European Journal of International Law*, vol. 13, 1257–9.

Taylor, Linda A. (2009): 'The United Nations Claims Commission', in Ferstman et al. (eds), *Reparations for Victims of Genocide, War Crimes and Crimes Against Humanity* (Leiden: Brill) 197–214.

Taylor, Telford (1949): *Final Report to the Secretary of the Army on the Nuernberg War Crimes Trials under Control Council Law No. 10* (Washington, DC: US Government Printing Office).

Taylor, Telford (1993): *The Anatomy of the Nuremberg Trial—A Personal Memoir* (London: Bloomsbury).

Thomas, Ann Van Wynen, and A. J. Thomas, Jr. (1971): 'The Civil War in Spain', in Richard A. Falk (ed.), *The International Law of Civil War* (Baltimore, MD: Johns Hopkins Press) 111–78.

Tomuschat, Christian (1999): 'International Law: Ensuring the Survival of Mankind on the Eve of a New Century—General Course on Public International Law', *Recueil des Cours*, vol. 281, 9–438.

Totani, Yuma (2008): *The Tokyo War Crimes Trial—The Pursuit of Justice in the Wake of World War II* (Cambridge, MA: Harvard University Press).

Triepel, Heinrich (1899): *Völkerrecht und Landesrecht* (Tübingen: J. C. B. Mohr (Paul Siebeck)).

Triepel, Heinrich (1923): 'Les Rapports entre le Droit Interne et le Droit International', *Recueil des Cours*, vol. 1, 77–121.

Tuori, Kaarlo (2014): 'Transnational Law—On Legal Hybrids and Perspectivism', in Miguel Maduro, Kaarlo Tuori, and Suvi Sankari (eds), *Transnational law—Rethinking European Law and Legal Thinking* (Cambridge: Cambridge University Press).

Vattel, Emmerich de (1916): *Le Droit des Gens ou Principes de la Loi Naturelle*, vols I–II, (Washington, DC: Carnegie Institution of Washington).

Veeder, V. V. (1998): 'The Lena Goldfields Arbitration: The Historical Roots of Three Ideas', *International & Comparative Law Quarterly*, vol. 47, 747–92.

Verdross, Alfred (1923): *Die Einheit des rechtlichen Weltbildes* (Tübingen: J. C. B. Mohr).

Verdross, Alfred (1937): *Völkerrecht*, 1st edn (Berlin: Springer).

Vermeer-Künzli, Annemarieke (2007a): 'As If: The Legal Fiction in Diplomatic Protection', *European Journal of International Law*, vol. 18, 37–68.

Vermeer-Künzli, Annemarieke (2007b): 'Diallo and the Draft Articles: The Application of the Draft Articles on Diplomatic Protection in the Ahmadou Sadio Diallo Case', *Leiden Journal of International Law*, vol. 20, 941–54.

Verzijl, Jan Hendrik Willem (1969): *International Law in Historical Perspective, vol. II: International Persons* (Leiden: A. W. Sijthoff).

Virally, Michel (1983-V): 'Panorama du droit international contemporain; cours general de droit international public', *Recueil des Cours*, vol. 183, 9–382.

Visscher, Charles de (1925): 'La Codification du droit international', *Recueil des Cours*, vol. 6, 325–455.

Wälde, Thomas W. (1996): 'Investment Arbitration under the Energy Charter Treaty—From Dispute Settlement to Treaty Implementation', *Arbitration International*, vol. 12, 429–66.

Wälde, Thomas W. (2005): 'The Serbian Loans Case: A Precedent for Investment Treaty Protection of Foreign Debt?' in Weiler, Todd J. (ed.), *International Investment Law and Arbitration: Leading Cases from the ICSID, NAFTA, Bilateral Treaties and Customary International Law* (London: Cameron May) 383–423.

Waldock, Humphrey (1962-II): 'General Course on Public International Law', *Recueil des Cours*, vol. 106, 192–229.

Wallace, Rebecca M. M. (2002): *International Law*, 4th edn (London: Sweet & Maxwell).

Walter, Christian (2007): 'International Law in a Process of Constitutionalization', in Janne Nijman and André Nollkaemper (eds), *New Perspectives on the Divide Between National and International Law* (Oxford: Oxford University Press) 191–215.

Warbrick, Colin (1989): '"Federal" Aspects of the European Convention on Human Rights', *Michigan Journal of International Law*, vol. 10, 698–734.

Weil, Prosper (1983): 'Towards a Relative Normativity in International Law?', *American Journal of International Law*, vol. 77, 413–42.

Weil, Prosper (1992-VI): 'Cours Générale du Droit International Public: Le Droit International en Quête de son Identité', *Recueil des Cours*, vol. 237, 9–369.

Weiler, Joseph H. H. (1990–1): 'The Transformation of Europe', *Yale Law Journal*, vol. 100, 2403–83.

Weiler, Joseph H. H. (2003): 'Rewriting Van Gend & Loos: Towards a Normative Theory of ECJ Hermeneutics', in Ola Wiklund (ed.), *Judicial Discretion in European Perspective*, 150–63.

Weiler, Joseph H. H., and Haltern, Ulrich R. (1996): 'The Autonomy of the Community Legal Order—Through the Looking Glass', *Harvard International Law Journal*, vol. 37, 411–43.

Werkmeister, Christoph, Pötters, Stephan, and Traut, Johannes (2010–11): 'Regulatory Acts within Article 263(4) TFEU—A Dissonant Extension of *Locus Standi* for Private Applicants', *Cambridge Yearbook of European Legal Studies*, vol. 13, 311–32.

Werle, Gerhard (2005): *Principles of International Criminal Law* (The Hague: TMC Asser Press).

Werner, Wouter (2007): 'The Never-Ending Closure: Constitutionalism and International Law', in Nicholas Tsagourias (ed.), *Transnational Constitutionalism* (Cambridge: Cambridge University Press) 329–67.

Wheaton, Henry (1936): *Elements of International Law*, 1866 edn (Oxford: The Clarendon Press).

Wildhaber, Luzius (2002): 'A Constitutional Future for the European Court of Human Rights', *Human Rights Law Journal*, vol. 23, 161–5.

Witte, Bruno de (1984): 'Retour à "Costa"—La primauté du droit communautaire à la lumière du droit International' *Revue trimestrielle de droit européen*, vol. 20, 425–54.

Witte, Bruno de (2004): 'Treaty Revision in the European Union: Constitutional Change through International Law', 35 *Netherlands Yearbook of International Law*, vol. 35, 51–84.

Witte, Bruno de (2017): 'Sources and the Subjects of International Law: The European Union's Semi-Autonomous System of Sources', in Samantha Besson and Jean d'Aspremont (eds) *The Oxford Handbook on the Sources of International Law* (Oxford: Oxford University Press) 769–86.

Wolff, Martin (1933): *Internationales Privatrecht* (Berlin: Springer).

Wright, Quincy (1930): *Mandates under the League of Nations* (Chicago: University of Chicago Press).

Wright, Quincy (1947): 'The Law of the Nuremberg Trial', *American Journal of International Law*, vol. 41, 38–72.

Wright, Quincy (1971): 'The American Civil War (1861–65)', in Richard A. Falk (ed.), *The International Law of Civil War* (Baltimore, MD: Johns Hopkins Press) 30–109.

von Wright, Georg Henrik (1998): 'Is and Ought', in Stanley L. Paulson and Bonnie Litschewski Paulson (eds), *Normativity and Norms—Critical Perspectives on Kelsenian Themes* (Oxford: Oxford University Press) 365–82.

Wühler, Norbert (1997): 'Mixed Arbitral Tribunals', in Rudolf Bernhardt, *Encyclopedia of Public International Law* (Amsterdam: Elsevier Science BV) vol. III, 433–6.

Wyatt, Derrick (1982): 'New Legal Order, or Old?', *European Law Review*, vol. 7, 147–66.

Yourow, Howard Charles (1996): *The Margin of Appreciation Doctrine in the Dynamics of the European Human Rights Jurisprudence* (Dordrecht: Martinus Nijhoff).

Zahar, Alexander, and Sluiter, Göran (2008): *International Criminal Law—A Critical Introduction* (Oxford: Oxford University Press).

Zeck, William Allen (1947–8): 'Nuremberg: Proceedings Subsequent to Goering Et Al', *North Carolina Law Review*, vol. 26, 350–89.

Zegveld, Liesbeth (2002): *The Accountability of Armed Opposition Groups in International Law* (Cambridge: Cambridge University Press).

Ziegler, Katja S. (2009): 'Strengthening the Rule of Law, but Fragmenting International Law: The *Kadi* Decision of the ECJ from the Perspective of Human Rights', *Human Rights Law Review*, vol. 9, 288–305.

Zolo, Danilo (1998): 'Hans Kelsen: International Peace through International Law', *European Journal of International Law*, vol. 9, 306–24.

Zumbansen, Peer (2012–13): 'Defining the Space of Transnational Law: Legal Theory, Global Governance, and Legal Pluralism', *Transnational Law and Contemporary Problems*, vol. 21, 305–35.

Öberg, Marko Divac (2011): 'The Legal Effects of United Nations Resolutions in the Kosovo Advisory Opinion', *American Journal of International Law* (2011) vol. 105, 81–90.

Index

Advisory Committee of Jurists, 49–51, 60–2, 77, 136, 149, 233
Ago, Roberto, 9–10, 48, 69
aggression, 140, 149
Allied Powers's legislative jurisdiction over Germany after Second World War, 142, 150, 155, 157, 165
American Civil War, 117–8
Andean Tribunal of Justice, 227
Anzilotti, Dionisio, 17–9, 54–5, 98
'A posteriori' conception of international legal personality, 3, 6, 14, 15, 23–9, 43–5, 49, 77, 151, 165, 193, 202, 228, 234
armed opposition groups, 7, 20, 115–31, 133–4, 231, 234

Bank for International Settlements, 94
belligerency, recognition of, 116–9, 121, 128, 133, 231
Brierly, James Leslie, 30, 55, 142–43

Calvo clause, 93, 218
Cançado Trindade, Antônio Augusto, 34, 35, 42, 113
Caribbean Community, 226
Caribbean Court of Justice (CCJ), 226–7
Cassese, Antonio, 36–7, 128, 150
Cavaglieri, Arrigo, 20–2, 52
Central American Court of Justice (CACJ), 48, 81, 83–5, 102, 226–7
Churchill, Winston, 138–9
Commission for Real Property Claims of Displaced Persons and Refugees, 100–1
Common Article 3 of the Geneva Conventions, 116, 120–34, 231
Constitutionalization of international law. *see* international legal constitutionalism
Corporations, 7, 39, 40, 100, 127, 193, 209, 211
Council of Europe, 173, 176, 190–1
countermeasures, 210–2
Court of Justice of the European Union (CJEU) (for specific cases, *see* Table of Cases)
  legal standing of individuals, 219–21
crimes against humanity, 140, 141, 145, 147, 149

domestic law. *see* international law and domestic law
debellatio, 151, 155. *see also* Allied Powers's legislative jurisdiction of Germany after Second World War
'derivative model' vs 'direct model' in international investment law, 208–18
diplomatic protection, 11, 51, 57, 62–70, 77, 79–80, 86, 91–3, 95–103, 202, 205–6, 208, 213, 215, 218, 231
  classification of claims, 66–8
  exhaustion of local remedies, 68–9
  future of, 69–70
Draper, G.I.A.D, 123–4, 130
dualism, 7–9, 19, 25–7, 36, 39, 158, 190

erga omnes, 32, 65
Eritrea-Ethiopia Claims Commission (EECC), 101–2
European Convention for the Protection of Human Rights and Fundamental Freedoms (ECHR) (for specific provisions, *see* Table of Treaties)
  interpretation of, 179–86
  in the international legal system, 186–90
  travaux préparatoires, 173–80, 185
European Court of Human Rights (ECtHR) (for specific cases, *see* Table of Cases)
  legal standing of individuals, 173–8, 221
European Court of Justice (ECJ) (for specific cases, *see* Table of Cases)
  legal standing of individuals, 219–21
EU law, 4, 219–29, 234 (for specific provisions, *see* Table of Treaties)
  new legal order, 4, 221–7
Extraordinary Chambers in the Courts of Cambodia (ECCC) (for specific cases, *see* Table of Cases), 5, 159, 162–4

Fitzmaurice, Gerald, 48, 73, 143–4, 181
fragmentation of international law, 40–1, 185

genocide, 145, 147, 149
Germany
  cases concerning compensation for violations of international humanitarian law, 107–8
  status after the Second World War, 154–5
groups
  of individuals, 7
  of insurgents, 120, 121, 123, 124, 129

Hague Regulations, 106, 108, 132
Hall, William Edward, 118
Hart, HLA, 9–10, 27
Higgins, Rosalyn, 35, 38–9, 41, 58
High Court of International Justice, 47, 60–2, 77, 136, 149, 233

humanity, 33
laws of, 109, 118, 137
crimes against (*see* crimes against humanity)
human rights
obligations of individuals, 193
vs individual rights, 71–2
hybrid criminal courts. *see* internationalized criminal courts

Immunity of State representatives, 5, 137, 147, 160–2, 165
'individualistic' conception of international legal personality, 12, 14–5, 30–7, 43–6, 113, 135, 142, 151–2, 165, 202
individual, definition of, 7
individual obligations
for violations of human rights, 193
PCIJ and ICJ decisions pertaining to, 57–9
under customary international law, 60–3
individual rights
determination of, 70–5, 76–8
independent means of enforcement of, 47, 77, 167, 230–3
relationship with diplomatic protection, 63–70, 231
vs human rights, 71–2, 230
vs interests of individuals, 66, 106
individual responsibility for international crimes, 75–6, 135, 145–53
L'Institut de Droit International, 118
insurgents. *see* armed opposition groups
insurgency, recognition of, 118–9
Inter-American Court of Human Rights (IACtHR), 13 (for specific cases, *see* Table of Cases)
International Centre for the Settlement of Investment Disputes (ICSID), 203–5 (for specific cases, *see* Table of Cases)
International Committee of the Red Cross (ICRC), 112, 114, 115, 119, 120, 121, 129, 130, 132
International Court of Justice (ICJ) (for specific cases, *see* Table of Cases)
on concept of international legal personality, 2–3, 22–3
International Criminal Court (ICC), 149–51 (for specific cases, *see* Table of Cases)
international criminal court, definition of, 153–66
internationalized criminal courts, 135, 153–66
International Criminal Tribunal for the former Yugoslavia (ICTY), 121, 145–7 (for specific cases, *see* Table of Cases)
International Criminal Tribunal for Rwanda (ICTR), 147–8 (for specific cases, *see* Table of Cases)
international community, 5, 12, 20, 31, 33, 34, 65, 124, 126, 136, 156–64, 165–6
International law and domestic law
distinction between, 6, 18–9, 22, 26, 28, 44
incorporation of international law into domestic law, 8–9, 54, 74, 123, 128, 130
relationship between, 7–9, 22, 26–9, 31–2, 35–7, 38–9, 44–5, 98, 123, 130, 158
International Law Commission (ILC). *see* Table of Other Materials
international lawmaking capacities, 39, 41, 42, 43
of individuals, 7, 34, 41
international legal constitutionalism, 15, 32–7, 42, 46, 190, 192
International Military Tribunal at Nuremberg (IMT), 140–1
Judgment of 1 October 1946 (*see* Table of Cases)
legal nature of, 21, 154–8
international organizations, 2, 19, 38, 74, 76, 127–8, 159
International Prize Court, 81–3, 85, 102, 105
Iran-United States Claims Tribunal (IUSCT), 96–9, 102–3 (for specific cases, *see* Table of Cases)

Jessup, Philip, 39–41
joint criminal enterprise (JCE), 162–4
jus cogens, 32, 34, 77, 108, 122, 128, 155

Kaeckenbeeck, Georges, 90, 103
Kaiser Wilhelm II, 137–8
Kelsen, Hans
conception of international legal personality (*see* 'a posteriori' conception of international legal personality)
conception of the State, 25
Grundnorm, 18, 24, 31
Pure Theory of Law, 23–6
unity of international law and national law, 26–8
Koh, Harold, 39–40

Laswell, Harold D., 37
Lauterpacht, Hersch, 30–5, 43–5, 54–5, 177, 201–2
League of Nations, 90, 169–72, 190, 232
legislative jurisdiction, 193
in international criminal law, 151, 155
in international humanitarian law, 124, 125, 129–31, 232
legitimacy, 7, 41, 42, 130, 185
Leibniz, Gottfried Wilhelm, 16
Lieber Code of 1863, 118

mandate system, 169
margin of appreciation, 13, 180–5, 191
Martens Clause, 108–9
Maxwell-Fyfe, David, 176
McDougal, Myres S., 37–9
McNair, Arnold, 19, 73, 200
Mexican Revolution Commissions, 91–4
mixed claims, 66–7, 79
mixed criminal courts. *see* internationalized criminal courts

monism, 8, 22, 26–9, 31–2, 35–7, 44–5, 131
municipal law. *see* international law and domestic law

national law. *see* international law and domestic law
natural law, 16, 24, 30–1, 33–5, 44, 152–3
ne bis in idem, 164
New Haven School, 37–9, 43
nullum crimen sine lege, 140–1, 146, 150, 162–4

Oppenheim, Lassa, 17–9, 52
Orakhelashvili, Alexander, 8, 42, 91, 151

pacta sunt servanda, 19, 48, 199, 201
'participant' conception of international legal personality, 14, 15, 37–43, 46, 227
Permanent Court of Arbitration, 85
Permanent Court of International Justice (PCIJ) (for specific cases, *see* Table of Cases)
  access of individuals, 49–51, 61–2
  decisions pertaining to individual rights, 52–6
Peters, Anne, 33–6, 42–4, 72, 152–3
pluralism, 8
piracy, 36, 136
policy-oriented jurisprudence. *see* New Haven School
Politis, Nicolas, 30
positivism, 6, 29
  positivist conceptions of international legal personality, 15, 43–6
primary rules vs secondary rules, 9–10, 66, 203
principle of legality. see *nullum crimen sine lege*
preparatory work. see *travaux préparatoires*

recognition of international legal personality, 21–2
Roosevelt, Franklin D., 138–9
Ross, Alf, 9, 19
rules-based approach to international law, 15

Scelle, Georges, 30–2, 40, 142–4
Schwarzenberger, Georg, 20–2, 154–5, 197
secondary rules vs primary rules. *see* primary rules vs secondary rules
self-determination, right of, 41, 51
slavery, 168, 190
Spanish Civil War, 119
Special Court for Sierra Leone (SCSL), 4–5, 126, 159–162 (for specific cases, *see* Table of Cases)
Special Tribunal for Lebanon, 159
Stalin, Joseph, 138–9
State contracts
  internationalization of, 198–201, 227, 234
  nature of, 196–8
Statehood, 11, 14, 17–8, 20, 25, 116–7, 129
'States-only' conception of international legal personality
  orthodox, 4–6, 12–3, 15, 17–20, 22, 29, 32, 33, 36–7, 39–42, 44–6, 52, 55–6, 77, 133–4, 228, 230, 234
  modified, 3, 5–6, 20–3, 43, 45, 108, 127, 155, 193, 197, 228
Strupp, Karl, 20–2
subsidiarity principle, 184–5, 191

Teitgen, Pierre-Henri, 173, 174, 176, 179
third parties, armed opposition groups as, 127–8, 134
transnational law, 39–42, 46, 234
travaux préparatoires, 11, 73, 78
  1907 Hague Conventions, 105–7
  Additional Protocol I to the Geneva Conventions, 115
  Additional Protocol II to the Geneva Conventions, 124–5, 128
  Convention Relative to the Creation of an International Prize Court, 81–3
  Convention for the Establishment of a Central American Court of Justice, 83–4
  ECHR, 173–80, 185
  Geneva Conventions of 1949, 111, 121
  ICSID Convention, 204
  Statute of the International Criminal Court, 149–50
  Statute of the Permanent Court of International Justice, 49–51, 60–2
Triepel, Heinrich, 17–8, 36

UN Charter, 2, 22, 33, 159, 172, 186–90, 224 (for specific provisions, *see* Table of Treaties)
United Nations Compensation Commission (UNCC), 99–100
United Nations War Crimes Commission (UNWCC), 138
UN Security Council resolutions (for specific resolutions, *see* Table of Other Materials)
  bindingness on individuals, 58–9
  prevalence over other international agreements, 186–90, 224–5
Upper Silesia Arbitral Tribunal, 48, 89–91, 103
Upper Silesia Mixed Commission, 89–90, 171–2, 232

Vattel, Emmerich de, 16, 63, 116
Verdross, Alfred, 32, 33, 52, 200
Vienna Convention on the Law of Treaties (VCLT) (for specific provisions, *see* Table of Treaties)
  draft Article 66 on the application of treaties to individuals, 48–49
  interpretation according to Articles 31–33, 72–8, 113, 125, 131, 133, 183–5, 208, 215, 231, 234
  third parties, 128

World Trade Organization (WTO), 194–5
waiver, 216–8
war crimes, 136, 138, 140, 145, 149, 151, 152

The manufacturer's authorised representative in the EU for product safety is Oxford University Press España S.A. of el Parque Empresarial San Fernando de Henares, Avenida de Castilla, 2 – 28830 Madrid (www.oup.es/en or product.safety@oup.com). OUP España S.A. also acts as importer into Spain of products made by the manufacturer.

www.ingramcontent.com/pod-product-compliance
Lightning Source LLC
LaVergne TN
LVHW011749200926
848484LV00003B/656
9780198820376